SEVE

SEVE
RYDER CUP HERO

LAUREN ST JOHN

Foreword by Paul Azinger

RUTLEDGE HILL PRESS
NASHVILLE, TENNESSEE

Published in Nashville, Tennessee, by Rutledge Hill Press, 211 Seventh Avenue North, Nashville, Tennessee 37219.

Originally published in Great Britain by Partridge Press, a division of Transworld Publishers Ltd.

Printing History:
Partridge Press edition published 1993.
Corgi edition published 1994.
Corgi edition reprinted 1996.
Rutledge Hill Press edition revised and published 1997.

Typography by E. T. Lowe Publishing Company, Nashville, Tennessee.
Cover photo by Phil Sheldon.

Library of Congress Cataloging-in-Publication Data

St John, Lauren, 1966–
    Seve / Lauren St John.
      p. cm.
    Original ed.: London :   Partridge Press, 1993.
    Includes index.
    ISBN 1-55853-489-X
    1. Ballesteros, Severiano.   2. Golfers—Spain—Biography.
I. Title.
GV964.B35S8   1997
796.352'092–dc21
  [B]   97-9974
                                                           CIP

Printed in the United States of America

1 2 3 4 5 6 7 8 9—99 98 97

For my sister, Lisa,

to whom I can only return

the best advice in the world:

Accept nothing less

than everything.

CONTENTS

FOREWORD

No golfer in the world stirs up emotional responses from his peers quite the way Seve Ballesteros does. That includes me. Mention his name to anyone who has competed against him in Ryder Cup play or been paired with him down the stretch of a major tournament, and you will get an earful ranging from praises to curses. Still, all things considered, I have the utmost admiration and respect for Seve, even when I was unintentionally stirring up a storm by dubbing him "the king of gamesmanship."

One of the defining points of my professional golf career has been my competitive rivalry with Seve. Circumstances, nationalistic passions, and a shared will to win have drawn us together, most noticeably in the intense biennial match-play event known as the Ryder Cup. I wouldn't put a Ballesteros-Azinger rivalry on the level of Hogan-Snead or Palmer-Nicklaus, but I believe it has added spice to the unprecedented interest in worldwide golf. Although Seve is only three years older than me, he has been winning majors and beating the best in golf since the late seventies. He was a teen-age golf prodigy when I was still a high school hacker struggling to break 80. By the time I had played on my first Ryder Cup team in 1989, Seve already had four Cup experiences under his belt. That says a lot about what he has accomplished.

No player has done more than Seve to raise the stakes of Ryder Cup competition. He is the consummate Ryder Cup team MVP whether it be as a player, a sideline cheerleader, or the captain of the European team for the 1997 matches in his home country of Spain. Moving the Ryder Cup to

Spain was a wonderful testament to the significant role Seve has played in making golf an international phenomenon.

It's one thing to have Seve rooting for you as a playing partner and quite another to be paired against him in Ryder Cup play. It's not easy. I found that out on the last day of the 1989 matches at the Belfry, when I took on Seve in the lead-off match of singles play. Our match ended with me holing a five-footer to beat Seve, 1-up. (Unfortunately, for the U.S. team, it wasn't enough to win back the Cup.) It was a much-talked-about match. There was controversy on both sides. Beginning on the second hole, when I questioned Seve about his taking a ball out of play, our competitive spirits clashed for the next four hours. Seve even accused me of taking a questionable drop on the eighteenth hole, when, in fact, he walked over to the water's edge at eighteen and told referee Andy McFee and me where to drop the ball. But this is all water under the bridge. Seve and I had a conversation about it several months later in Jamaica and we put it all to rest.

At the end of that match in 1989, Seve and I quickly shook hands at the eighteenth. We then went our separate ways. It wasn't until later, when a television commentator told me so, that I learned Seve had left the eighteenth with tears in his eyes. Nobody, *nobody*, takes the Ryder Cup more seriously than Seve, and I'm sure that will be the case when he captains the European team in the 1997 competition.

Lauren St John has written an interesting and exciting book about one of the most flamboyant and charismatic golfers who has ever played the game. I'm sure you'll enjoy it.

—Paul Azinger
February 1997

ACKNOWLEDGMENTS

I am eternally grateful to Dudley Doust, not only for being good enough to speak to me but also for the breadth of understanding and knowledge he brought to *Seve: The Young Champion*, which helped considerably in the research for this book. Also to everyone at Partridge Press, especially Debbie Beckerman, my publisher, who has seemingly infinite reserves of patience, energy and good humor; to Mike Towle and Larry Stone at Rutledge Hill Press, for believing in me; and to my agent, Sara Menguc, at David Higham, for always knowing what's best for me.

Thanks to all members of the Association of Golf Writers, particularly John Hopkins, Chris Plumridge, Renton Laidlaw, Michael Williams, and Liz Kahn, all of whom have helped me more than they know; to Joe Collet, Ballesteros's manager, for giving so generously of his time; to Robert Green for allowing me access to *Golf World*'s library; to the players and caddies of the European Tour, especially Tony Jacklin and Dave Musgrove; to Ben Crenshaw, whose love for the game is an inspiration to anyone who meets him; to Frances Simpson for a million things, but particularly for the garret with the carpet; to Lynne Warnick for the supply of Lion bars and Greek yogurt; and lastly, but most importantly, thanks to my mom and dad, to whom I owe everything.

INTRODUCTION

When the passage of time takes the luster off the game's brightest careers, only greatness endures, its acid test being that the player is respected as much by his peers as by the public, that, through artistry, skill, and passion, he adds a dimension to the sport that was never previously there, and that his last shot is as important as his first.

Few players have had an impact on golf at every stage of their career the way Severiano Ballesteros has: first as a prodigy, reinventing the game; then as an angry young man, black-eyed and emotional; later as a gracious major champion, handsome and brave; and finally, as an elder statesman, humbled by his flaws. In his early years, Ballesteros was world golf's hurricane. From the moment he executed that butterfly-light miracle chip on the last green at Royal Birkdale to finish runner-up to Johnny Miller as a teenager in the 1976 British Open, he has never stopped amazing us. In two decades of drama—of conflicts and glorious victories, of legal battles and theatrical escapes—his intelligence, honesty, kindness, and humor have shown him to be worthy of a place in our hearts, not just the record books.

At the age of forty, Ballesteros's five major championship victories (the 1979, 1984, and 1988 British Opens; and the 1980 and 1983 Masters) and five World Match Play titles stand out as his greatest achievements, but it is the Ryder Cup that might eventually come to define his career. There is scarcely a match that Ballesteros has participated in that has not been unforgettable, and there is no finer testimony to his bravery and heart than the inspiration he exhibited during his darkest hour, the singles match he lost to Tom Lehman in the 1995 Ryder Cup at Oak Hill. When agonizing back problems threatened to keep Ballesteros out of the matches in 1993, Payne Stewart voiced what everyone else thought: "It wouldn't be the Ryder Cup as I know it if Seve wasn't playing."

Ballesteros's latest manifestation, as captain of the European team at the 1997 Ryder Cup in Valderrama, Spain, may be his most awe-inspiring role yet.

Over the years Tour policies on both sides of the Atlantic, petty bureaucracies, and homesickness have prevented the Spaniard from playing in the United States as much as he would have liked, but the Ryder Cup has filled this void by bringing his gifts and his charisma to a wider audience. "Ballesteros has been the most influential non-American golfer since Harry Vardon," *Golf World* magazine reported in 1996. "His performances in America in the late 1970s and early 1980s convinced other international players that the U.S. was not an impregnable fortress. His magnetic presence persuaded officials to include continental golfers in the Ryder Cup matches, his dazzling skills inspired Europe to win it, and his heroic leadership helped transform the event into the most dazzling rivalry the game has ever known."

But Tom Callahan showed another side to the story in *Golf Digest*. "A great failure of the American sporting press is that it has not communicated Ballesteros adequately to the people of the United States," he said. "American golf fans know that he is great and that he won two U.S. Masters and three British Opens. But they think of him as "their Palmer" when he might have been our Seve, too. There's a quality to his effort that plays on spines [in Europe] and sends a ripple through a grandstand that is the sincere opposite of the American wave. The Spaniard cares and the people love him."

Nick Price, who dueled with Ballesteros in the 1988 British Open at Lytham, said that even now Ballesteros is the only player he would go out onto the course to watch: "Seve can shoot 64 a hundred different ways. Faldo can do it only one way: down the middle, on the green, one or two putts."

Nowadays, Ballesteros has more frailties than he perhaps had when he dominated the game throughout the 1980s. Family life has become more important to him and has made him a more rounded person, a more compassionate person. Once, golf was his whole world; now, he says that if he only had one hour to live, he would spend it talking to his sons. But he still has the capacity to astonish us with his gift on the course. He still has grace, power, and charisma. He still has presence, he still has genius. Most importantly, he still inspires love as well as admiration.

Years ago Ballesteros said that when his career was over, he only wanted to be remembered as "someone who did what he did with honor."

He'll be remembered for all of that and more.

"There are many good players but they are not champions in their hearts. To be a champion it has to be inside. Some people they have that naturally and other people they don't. That's why they don't become champions."

Severiano Ballesteros

THE SEEDS OF GREATNESS

"When I was small, I never think about winning. I never even was thinking about the majors. I was just thinking about being a champion. I was thinking, I'd like to be the best."

Severiano Ballesteros, March 1990

It was almost midnight when Severiano Ballesteros, aged nine, stirred, stretched, and cautiously pushed back the covers. For hours he had lain in the darkness, feigning sleep, until he heard his brother Vicente, with whom he shared a single bed and the windowless room they called "the dungeon," come quietly through the door, and his parents' muffled tread on the stairs. Now he listened. When there was no sound save Vicente's rhythmic breathing and the low roar of the distant sea, he dressed silently, felt for his precious golf club, and went out into the balmy night air. A cool and dusty track led the way from the farmhouse. Wraithlike, he slipped down the hill to the Real Club de Golf de Pedreña—built in 1929 at the behest of King Alfonso XIII of Spain, and strictly out of bounds to small peasant farmers' sons—and there, alone but for the swaying shadows of the pines, he hit a hundred or more balls at the benign silver moon. "I could not see them but I could tell how good and how straight I hit them by the feel in the hands and the sand."

Most nights he practiced on the second hole, a 198-yard par-three named La Rivera, measuring his progress over the seasons by the club he took to reach the green. "My ambition was to be able to use an iron. I would ask, 'When will I be big enough?' And my brothers would answer, 'Soon, soon.' "

He also played golf along the seashore, or stood in the backyard and hit balls over the high trees and onto the second green—a distance of 150 yards.

1

These stolen hours, ghostly and filled with dreams, remain with him still. "My *best* memories are of sneaking onto the golf course and playing when it was dark." At last, cold and exhausted, he would return to the sleeping house. But when dawn broke he would be out again, searching for the lost balls and occasionally playing. Day in and day out Ballesteros did this, in sunshine and in snow. Then he would walk along the dirt road to the golf club where he caddied, often arriving shivering, muddy, and bedraggled, to wait for the first amateurs to drive up.

Years later, long after he had become the best golfer in the world, he could still remember the jeers of the other boys and feel the sharp sting of injured pride. "All the other caddies, they laugh at me—and the more when it rained and I come in in the morning and they say I am the drowning rat." But their taunts goaded him, strengthened him, made the desire burn more fiercely in his heart; and in 1984, when he won the British Open Championship for the second time, he could say with quiet assurance:

"No, they have not laughed now for some years."

Severiano Ballesteros was born on April 9, 1957, in a stone farmhouse overlooking the Bay of Santander in the village of Pedreña in northern Spain. The youngest son of Baldomero Ballesteros Presmanes and Carmen Sota Ocejo, he grew up in the shadows of the Cantabrian Mountains, not far from the Bay of Biscay, running barefoot and free over the hills. He had three brothers: Baldomero Jr., nicknamed Merin (pronounced Marine), who was ten years older than he was, Manuel, and Vicente, who were, respectively, seven and five years older. A fourth brother, the firstborn, had died at the age of two from a wasp sting.

The house in which Ballesteros spent the first sixteen years of his life was a quaint white-washed double-story, with an uneven red-tiled roof, red-brick sides, jade-green doors and railings, and an adjoining half-painted extension of delightfully homemade appearance. Built by his great-grandparents in 1882, it once belonged to his mother's uncle. At the back of the house were some stables—where the family kept several dairy cows, a few chickens, a donkey, and some rabbits, all of which had names and were tended to by Severiano and his father. The basement of the house was lit by the cozy glow of an elderly wood stove. Here, Ballesteros used to practice on the harshest winter days, smashing balls interminably into a heavy canvas cloth hung from the rafters. From there, a shadowy staircase led to the living quarters. There were four bedrooms. The two older brothers each had their own, but Severiano shared a narrow bed with Vicente until he was ten and the dark cell-like room where they slept until he was fourteen. His earliest memory is of his mother coming in to wake him up for school and finding him on the floor, Vicente having pushed him there when he was sleeping. Outside was a well which provided water for the house.

The Ballesteros family lived simply and toiled hard, subsisting off the land where they could. They milked their cows, gathered eggs from their chickens, and grew vegetables. As a family friend observes, "They didn't just go down to the supermarket to buy the butter, they had to churn it." They appeared to be peasant farmers, but Dudley Doust, former sports correspondent for *The Sunday Times* and author of Ballesteros's early biography, *Seve: The Young Champion*, maintains that, although "the illusion is cast of a small-holding, struggling family, actually, the Ballesteroses, even before the youngest son achieved fame and fortune, had accumulated untold [acres] of land. If not wealthy, the family is near to it."

Later, he talks of the characteristics of the Montañcses, the people of the Cantabrian Mountains and coastline around Santander, among whom are the Ballesteros and Sota families. Doust describes them as brave, resourceful, suspicious, superstitious, and thrifty to the point of meanness. Ballesteros himself has been richly endowed with these qualities. The *Encyclopedia Britannica* has it that their forebears, the Cantabri, an Iberian tribe which occupied the region until the first century AD, "were regarded as the fiercest people in the peninsula." It was on the cliffs near Pedreña, so it is said, that bonfires were once lit and ships lured onto the rocks so that their cargoes could be pillaged and sold; it was men from the Cantabrian coast—navigators, cartographers, and traders carrying wool, flour, and eucalyptus wood—who took a shop for the New World, returning as wealthy men; and it was into this bleak and beautiful landscape, where legend and reality are intertwined, that one of the most gifted golfers the world has ever seen was born.

The picture Ballesteros paints of his boyhood is one of perfect contentment. He can only ever remember it as being idyllic. "We have always been

Young, gifted, and supremely confident, Seve Ballesteros, his precious golf clubs on his shoulder, heads out from his Pedreña farmhouse for a little practice. (© Chris Smith)

a happy family. It was tough, of course, as well, but that also helped me." Warm-hearted and sunny by nature, with dark hair, laughing brown eyes, and an impish grin, he was adored by his close-knit family. "My parents spoilt me but I had to do everything for my brothers," he told *The Times*. "I shopped for them. I was the one who, every Sunday, had to clean all their shoes. For that I got five pesetas, which was enough to go to the cinema."

Sundays were special days in the Ballesteros household. While Severiano helped his father in the cow shed, his mother would prepare a three-course lunch. "She would put it on the fire to cook and then we would walk to church, which was five minutes away. My father would go for an aperitif with his friends, come home for lunch, and then he would go and caddie. . . . He fished, too, for clams—for us to eat and also to sell. . . . It seemed he was always working and so was my mother. . . . One thing I still find hard to take is how hard my mother worked for all of us. She would go to the supermarket to buy food, cook, and clean the house, and then she would help my father with the cows. She never seemed to stop working. . . . This is one thing together that they transmit to me. I have never forgotten how tough life can be and how hard you must work to achieve all you want."

When he was seven years old Ballesteros was given his first golf club—the rusting head of an ancient three-iron. It became his pride and joy. He polished it till it shone, and afterward went out and searched for sticks for its shafts. These slender pieces of wood, carefully chosen for durability, he hid from his brothers. Whenever one broke, which they did almost daily, he would go through the slow process of cutting a new "shaft" to length, whittling it to a point, fitting it into the hosel, and then soaking it overnight in a bucket of water so that the wood swelled to fill the narrow neck of the club. With golf balls he had to be equally resourceful because his brothers wouldn't give him theirs. He roamed the beach hunting for pebbles of their approximate size and, when he found them, would spirit them away to his cache. His golf courses were the illicit fairways of Club de Golf de Pedreña by night, and those of his own invention on the beach and around the farm—with twigs for pins and paper for flags—by day.

His devotion to the game was absolute. He lived it, breathed it, and slept it; thoughts of it occupied his every waking hour. And while that in itself is not uncommon, obsessions of one kind or the other (usually fleeting and directionless) being an integral part of childhood, what is rare is to find a boy as young as Ballesteros pursuing his goal with such enduring fervor and single-mindedness.

"Seve had a love of golf you could almost touch," Manuel once observed. "Without a golf club in his hand, he was like a man with no legs. It was part of him. You never saw him without a golf club."

At the age of eight Ballesteros began caddying at Club de Golf de Pedreña, where Ramon Sota, his famous uncle, was the professional, for the equivalent of twenty-five pence a day. He earned forty pesetas for the first bag he ever carried and gave it all to his mother. Soon he was given his first golf club—another three-iron—by Manuel, and it was at that point that his competitive nature truly began to assert itself. In the summers Ballesteros spent most of his time down at the course, lounging about with an assortment of dark-eyed vagabond caddies. These boys occupied themselves with games of ferocious intensity. Every conceivable competition, within the limits of the resources available to them, was devised by them, a favorite being the egg and spoon races they had up and down the beach using golf balls and clubs. Ballesteros reached the state where he would wager virtually every peseta he made on his ability to triumph in any contest the other caddies could name. "I would bet more than I could afford to lose to make myself win."

BALLESTEROS REACHED THE STATE WHERE HE WOULD WAGER VIRTUALLY EVERY PESETA HE MADE ON HIS ABILITY TO TRIUMPH IN ANY CONTEST THE OTHER CADDIES COULD NAME.

The first trophy he ever won was for running rather than golf. He swept to victory in the regional fifteen-hundred-meter championship by some sixteen seconds. "My friend, Javier, couldn't keep up with me even on a bicycle," he recalled proudly. That tiny cup, shaped like a thimble, still has a special place in his trophy cabinet. Running, at that age, was his passion and the sport he feels he would have been most successful at if he had not chosen golf. "Like everybody, I played soccer, but I was bad. I remember I was quite fast but I had no real ability. It was not my game. I was a good runner—running fifteen hundred meters. I think if I had gone that way instead of playing golf, maybe I'd have been easily as good as Sebastian Coe or Steve Ovett."

Slowly, his incredible talent for golf began to manifest itself. When he was nine, he stole around the 6,315-yard Pedreña course in about an hour. A year later, playing in his first caddie tournament, he made 10 on the opening hole, and was inconsolable when he finished fifth with a nine-hole total of 51. At eleven, he was runner-up in the same event with a score of 42. But when he was twelve and it became an eighteen-hole tournament, he won with a nine-over-par 79, wearing his first pair of golf shoes—an oversized pair given to him by a club member. By the end of the year he was playing to the equivalent of a scratch handicap and, not long afterward, beat his tournament professional brother, Manuel, for the first time. There are no records to prove it, but it seems probable that Ballesteros was one of the most advanced players for his age in the history of the game.

The bane of young Severiano's life was the National Primary School in Pedreña. He played truant at every opportunity and paid no attention either to the teachers or his mother, who told him that he would not make a career out of golf. Already that streak of defiance, which he was to use to such great effect later on in life, was inherent in him, and rather than working harder at his algebra he simply thought more determinedly of winning tourna-ments—"Every one in the world and by twenty strokes."

When he was twelve years old he became drunk for the first time. "My father and mother had gone fishing," he recalls. "My lunch had been left and there was a bottle of wine, so I took a drink. I had four glasses. I was drunk when I got back to school. I slapped the woman teacher and I was sus-pended. It was revenge because she had smacked me across the hand with a ruler because I was talking in class." Two years later he gave up attending school altogether and vowed never to touch another glass of alcohol. "I used to have white wine at lunch. It never affected me. I smoked a little, too, but I saw that all the good players didn't drink or smoke. So I said to myself: 'Seve, if you want to be a good player, you stop.' So I stop."

On the afternoons when he wasn't playing sports Ballesteros's favorite form of amusement was television. At that time in Pedreña, which had a population of little more than three thousand, there was only one of these in existence and that was to be found in a village bar. He whiled away many enjoyable hours in the jovial and smoky atmosphere of that tavern, gazing with rapt attention at American programs like *Bonanza* and *The Fugitive* dubbed in Spanish. "There was no golf on TV in Spain in those days," he re-members. "I never saw golf on television until I was sixteen."

In this instance, at least, there can be little doubt that fortune smiled upon Ballesteros—as it did when it handed him one club instead of fourteen. Instead of spending his youth trying to learn from the example of tournament professionals of unexceptional talent, with staid and conservative golf games, and gradually becoming inured to the fact that golf should not be a great ad-venture but should be approached methodically, like chess, Ballesteros learned by imitation and thought of nothing else but getting the ball in the hole from the tee. With his three-iron he could play any shot that had ever been in-vented. And it was by playing with one ambition, to be the best golfer in the world, that he developed all the flair, strength, fire, individuality, and original-ity which eventually helped him realize his dream.

"Today the biggest mistake that a person could make with a youngster is to give him a full set of golf clubs," says Lee Trevino, who taught himself the game with only a five-iron. "Because," he says, " 'this nine-iron goes 120 yards, the eight goes 135,' and they hit the shot that is called for instead of standing there and imagining some type of a shot with a seven-iron that you only have to hit 50 yards, or you might have to duck-hook it and hit it 190 yards."

"I don't think there's any question about that," agrees Ben Crenshaw, the two-time Masters champion. "You can certainly see that with Seve, who played every shot with that three-iron. He played on the beach, around the greens, and everywhere. He learned to be more inventive, and inventiveness is a great part of the game because it cultivates imagination."

Ballesteros's desire to be the best did not stop at golf. He was a natural athlete and, like Nick Faldo, who had the same deep and abiding affection for sports when he was a boy, wanted to excel at everything. Thus, he spent his days running, swimming, cycling, playing football (soccer), and boxing. His love of competition was jointly inherited from the two men who were to influence him most: his father, Baldomero Ballesteros, and his mother's brother, Ramon Sota.

Baldomero Sr. was a tall, lean, soft-spoken man, with strong arms and huge hands. On the heel of his left hand was a scar which had been incurred during the Spanish Civil War. An ardent Franco supporter, he had been recruited into the Republican Army in 1937 and had shot himself through the hand in protest. He was court-martialed, convicted of self-mutilation, and sentenced to twenty years in prison. But a fate worse than death was spared him when Santander fell to Franco's troops not long after he had emerged from the hospital, and he fought alongside the Franquistas until the end of the war. On his return home, Baldomero married Carmen Sota Ocejo and took over the dairy farm bequeathed to him by his father. His wife was of agricultural stock. Her family had farmed the valley of the River Cubas in Pedreña for generations, and it was her father who, in 1928, sold the land that eventually became part of the first, fourth, and sixth holes of the Real Club de Golf de Pedreña. Baldomero was the great-grandson of an acclaimed bell-founder whose own son had learned the trade but had exchanged it for dairy farming upon his father's death. After the war, he threw himself wholeheartedly not only into the agricultural business but also into training for the Regata de Traineras, an annual three-mile race around Santander Bay which dates back to the early eighteenth century. Five times he helped row the Pedreña boat to victory, and in 1946 he and his thirteen fellow *remeros* (oarsmen) set a record that stands to this day. He was well respected in the local community and his courage as an oarsman was renowned throughout the region. A close associate of the Ballesteroses describes him as "beloved by all the family and a real father figure."

Certainly, Baldomero Sr. was a larger-than-life figure, and his standing as a local hero in the village was a hard act for his sons to follow. Baldomero, the eldest, did not attempt to. He was a quiet, pensive man who always seemed rather intimidated by the sheer magnetism of his father's presence and by his physical strength. Manuel was tougher and more independent. He was also very motivated and, but for his selfless devotion to the nurturing of Severiano's incredible talent, would almost certainly have achieved much more as a Tour player than he did. Vicente, the second youngest, was a silent, almost secretive young man. In later life he became an excellent teacher but remained an enigma, flitting about as shadowy as a moth on the edges of his brother's brilliant career. All the brothers were talented and special enough in their own way, but it was his youngest son who was the apple of Baldomero Sr.'s eye. From the very first moment Severiano picked up a golf club, he made it his life's work to encourage him and build up his confidence, and for that the boy loved him completely and without reserve. "I have to say that my father was always very optimistic," he was to remark years later. "He always believed in me. My mother was always very nice, very loving, but she has always been very pessimistic, fatalistic."

Doubtless that is true, but Doust has a theory that "great sportsmen often come from a matriarchy rather than a patriarchy. I mean, that it's the mother that worships them." A Spanish-speaker, he knew Severiano long before the drawbridge of fame came down between them and was able to get much closer to the heart of the Ballesteros family than anyone else has subsequently managed to. Severiano's mother speaks no English and Baldomero Jr. and Vicente but a smattering. Even Manuel is by no means fluent.

When Ballesteros was nineteen and the darling of all the golf world, Doust, then in the employ of *The Sunday Times*, went out to Pedreña to write a feature on him, along with sports photographer Chris Smith. Said Doust: "[We] were sitting around the house and they were having little arguments: Who's the most handsome? Who's so and so? All the brothers and the father. And they deferred always to Seve. And he was a youngster. And the mother would bring him milk—the others would be drinking the hard stuff—and she would just kind of run around at his heels. So he was spoilt hollow. But like many spoilt people, he expects the best. I think that's part of it, too [his success], being spoilt; and if you've got a pretty strong nature and you're

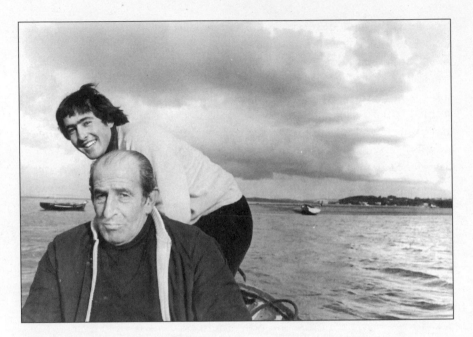

Severiano, his face a picture of happiness, relaxes on the family boat with the man who was to prove his greatest friend, mentor, and influence—his father Baldomero. (© Chris Smith)

spoilt you're better off still, because you're never satisfied because you've always just got what you've wanted. And he always got what he wanted and he was tough enough to get what he wanted when he played golf."

"That day," Doust remembers, "[his mother] was sitting in the kitchen. I went out to speak with her and she said, 'He'll be the greatest golfer in the world.' And, I mean, it wasn't vain, it wasn't anything. It was just a statement of fact. And I think he thought so himself. And it was true."

The role of his father and of his brothers who, by the time he was in his midteens, were all professional golfers, in the shaping of his career, is frequently talked of by Ballesteros. He seems more reluctant to acknowledge the assistance of Ramon Sota: "When I was a caddie, Ramon was playing outside and when Ramon retired, I was just starting. So I never have a chance to play with him too much."

Long before Ballesteros hit his first golf ball, Sota had been recognized as one of the most talented players ever to emerge from Spain, a nation which did not at that time have a long history of tournament golf. The first Spanish golf course, Club de Golf de Las Palmas in the Canary Islands, was not built until 1891, and it was 1904 before the game moved to the mainland. Twenty years later Spain produced the first of many gifted professionals, namely Angel and Sebastian Miguel, sons of a poverty-stricken laborer and caddies at Puerta de Hierro in Madrid. The former won three tournaments in Britain, two Spanish Opens, was fourth in the 1957 Open at St. Andres, played five times in the Masters, and won the individual World Cup (then the Canada Cup) title in 1958. Sota came next. John Jacobs, the eminent British golf teacher, remembers coaching both Sota and his nephew when he began giving clinics to golf professionals and teams in Spain around 1970.

"They're very strong characters, all of them [the Sotas and the Ballesteroses]. They're not easy characters. I don't mean I dislike them—in fact, I'd much rather have that sort than the person who everyone likes and then there's probably something up with them—but they could be very difficult."

Physically, there was little resemblance between Severiano and his uncle. Sota was a short, stocky figure with an unlovely but effective swing, which assisted him to victory in the Spanish, Portuguese, Dutch, Italian, and Brazilian Opens. He, too, had learned golf by caddying, and it was he who enforced the bar against caddies on the course at Club de Golf de Pedreña. One wonders, possibly completely erroneously, whether Ballesteros didn't hold this against him. Michael McDonnell of the *Daily Mail* once described him as "a repressive figure who never seems happy with the efforts of his nephews," then later said that his attitude toward them was "disparaging, perhaps intentionally so, because he knew how difficult it could be to sustain a lifestyle as a playing professional and how much heartbreak was involved."

"Seve is far more sophisticated than Ramon, as a person," says Mark Wilson, a former correspondent for the *Daily Express*. "Ramon—nice fellow—was a very basic man. Seve is a different person altogether. Were their games at all similar? No, not at all. Nothing's similar to Seve, is it? Surely Seve's got the best golf swing in the world? No, Ramon stayed with the caddie swing and very effective it was, too."

"I play a bit with Ramon," remembers Vicente Fernandez, the little Argentinean who was to become one of Ballesteros's most loyal and trusted friends. "He was a great player, too. Fantastic. But his game wasn't like Seve's. I don't think Ramon had the courage that Seve has. The difference is that

Seve has more heart. I'm not saying that Ramon didn't have heart, but Seve has more."

But while Sota had little to offer his small nephew from a technical point of view, he did do one essential thing: he showed him that a boy from a poor village in the north of Spain could go out into the world and win.

By the time he was fourteen the extent of Severiano Ballesteros's precocious talent was becoming apparent. He could regularly beat Manuel, himself a strong, experienced golfer who had played on several international teams and who ultimately sacrificed his own career for the sake of his brother's, and had won the club caddies' championship by sixteen shots. So sure was he of his own ability that, when he had caddied for his brother at the Spanish Under-25s Championship the previous year and watched Manuel perform badly, he had dumped the golf bag on the green, screamed at him for being so incompetent, and said arrogantly: "I could have done better myself." Meanwhile, his reputation as a prodigy was spreading like wildfire. Fernandez can recall Manuel telling him, three years before Ballesteros played his first tournament, that he had a young brother who was going to be great. Trevino, who played with Sota in South America in the sixties, says, "He told me he had a nephew who was going to be a helluva player. I knew about him way before he came out on Tour."

Doust, too, can remember talking to the Spanish golfers on the Continental Tour as far back as 1971 about how many good players were starting to emerge from Spain, and being told: " 'Well, there's this kid up in Pedreña who's better than any of us.' He was about fourteen then. And they all knew him and worshipped him. And he was absolutely special."

The speed at which Ballesteros developed as a player is commonly held to be due to the aforementioned influences: his father, his brothers, Sota, and, obviously, his unique gift. But he himself feels that his environment played an equal part—the proximity of his home to a golf course, the relative penury of his childhood, and the instilling in him of the work ethic.

Fernandez believes he is right. "I don't think [Seve] could have taken to golf the way he took to it if he was rich," he says. "Because first you have to love the small things about the game itself. You have to appreciate it and understand it, and you are mentally open to learn because you know that you don't have a choice to go and learn somewhere else. On the one hand, you get your experiences from books [if you are wealthy], and on the other, you have to live them. That's the hardest way but it's the way that will stay with you."

BALLESTEROS, FOR HIS PART, WAS PREVENTED FROM BECOMING AN ACTUAL MEMBER OF THE PEDREÑA COURSE BY THE "RIGID CASTE SYSTEM OF SPANISH SOCIETY."

Manuel Piñero, who, like Ballesteros, came through the Spanish caddie system that has produced such exceptional players over the years, agrees. "I think, expecially in those days, we were hungry to get money because we didn't have any. For us, golf was everything. Either we became good or we were nothing. It was our only chance to survive. And I think, when you have such a great difficulty to do something in life, and if you come through it, you will have such discipline and a strong mentality that you can beat anybody. Also, our background was very low but the people we were caddying for were very high class and we wanted to prove to those people that we can do very well. I don't say this as revenge to those people, no, no, no. It's just something that we had to prove to ourselves and to those people."

Ballesteros, for his part, was prevented from becoming an actual member of the Pedreña course by the "rigid caste system of Spanish society," and therefore concentrated all his efforts on escaping from that world to pursue his goals. Once, when he was asked how a young boy from a remote fishing village achieved those ambitions, he replied: "Well, in order to be successful, whether you play golf or you do any other thing, there's two things that you need. You have to work very hard. That's No. 1. And No. 2, you need a tremendous amount of discipline. If you have those two things, I think whatever you want you will get."

In 1973 Ballesteros effectively lost his amateur status by accepting a set of promotional golf clubs from an American army officer stationed near

Zaragoza, where Vicente was working as a club professional. The inscription on them was "Super." On New Year's Day the following year, having satisfactorily met the requirements of entry into the Spanish Professional Golfer's Association by passing a written test on the Rules of Golf, returning correct and legible scorecards, and paying a membership fee of five thousand pesetas, Ballesteros was awarded his player's card and became, at sixteen years, eight months, and twenty-one days, the youngest accredited professional in the history of Spanish golf.

And so it was that on the first day of the following April, with a thousand-dollar loan in his pocket—given to him to cover his expenses for the Portuguese, Spanish, Madrid, and French Opens by Santander-born Dr. Cesar Campuzano, a wealthy Madrid radiologist whose golf holidays were spent in Pedreña—Severiano Ballesteros shook hands with his father, hugged his weeping mother, waved to a crowd of well-wishers, and set off down the dirt track with his golf clubs over his shoulder. From Pedreña, he took a bus to Santander and then an overnight train through the mountains to Madrid. Alone, nervous and excited, but full of hope for what the future might bring, he made his way through the city to the airport and boarded a flight to Portugal. In this manner, he left Spain for the first time.

2

REBEL WITH A CAUSE

"When I was younger I used to be difficult."

Severiano Ballesteros, Royal Lytham, July 1988

October 1974, Madrid, Spain. At the end of his first season as a tournament professional, Severiano Ballesteros was bound, once again, for Lisbon. When his flight was called, he followed Gary Player, Tony Jacklin, and his brother Manuel aboard the aircraft, where he sat in his seat and stared despondently out the window, dwelling on bureaucracy and opportunities lost. All things considered it had not been a good week. Ibergolf, a course construction company, had invited nine players to compete in a thirty-six-hole event at Las Lomas el Bosque, near Madrid. In the first round, erratic driving had cost Ballesteros dearly on the heavily wooded, water-traversed course, and he had returned the worst score of the competition, a 79. But he had pulled himself together determinedly and had shot a 69 on the second day, finishing in fifth place behind Player, the eventual winner. Curiously enough, the mere fact that he had finished fifth was responsible for his melancholy air. Instead of congratulating himself on his achievement, which would have been a wholly natural and acceptable reaction in a player so young, he was remonstrating with himself for allowing victory to escape him. "Seventy-nine, 69," he thought with disgust. What a way to end his first season on the European Tour. And now there was this problem of the visa. Nobody had told him he would need a visa to enter South Africa; or if they had he'd forgotten. Of course, Player had assured him that he would use his influence to obtain the necessary documentation immediately after the embassy opened the following morning, but the delay would mean that

15

the Ballesteros brothers would miss their connecting flight and arrive in Johannesburg only hours before the South African PGA Championship was due to begin. Ballesteros glared out into the night. How could anyone be expected to play golf under such conditions?

"My brother," Manuel said confidentially to Player and Jacklin when Ballesteros's attention was thus diverted, "best young player in the world."

"Oh, Manuel," Player said in a kindly but rather patronizing way, "I don't think so."

But Manuel persisted. "You should see my brother play," he told Jacklin. "My brother is fantastic. My brother is better than all the players in Spain. You should see him hit the ball. My brother can win many tournaments. He—"

"Yeah, yeah, we know," Jacklin interrupted in a bored tone.

Manuel gave him an exasperated look. "You will see," he said stubbornly. "You will see. One day my brother will be the best player in the world."

Ballesteros had played the first round of his first professional tournament outside of Spain on April 9, 1974, the day he turned seventeen. The Portuguese Open was held at Estoril that year, on the gray Atlantic coast, and Ballesteros was encouraged by the fact that on the two practice days, playing with Manuel and the genial Argentinean Vicente (Chino) Fernandez, he had hit the ball well enough to score under par. But when the gun went off in the prequalifying round, it all fell to pieces. That morning he visited every bunker, pine thicket, shrubbery, and rockery on the 5,656-yard course, going out in 43 and coming back in 46 to finish at twenty over par. Later he was to admit that he had tried to put the ball in the hole off every tee.

"Seve, what did you shoot?" Fernandez asked that afternoon.

"Eighty-nine," Ballesteros said with a break in his voice, and when he looked at Fernandez there were tears in his eyes.

"Don't worry, Sev," the Argentinean said gently, touched at the boy's distress. "Take it easy. It's only your first tournament." And he took Ballesteros aside and talked to him for a long time about golf and about his attitude to the game. They were friends from that moment on.

A fortnight earlier, Ballesteros had played in the Spanish PGA Championship at Club de Golf de San Cugat in Barcelona, his first actual tournament as a professional. There, too, he had lived up to all of his own expectations in practice, scoring an astonishing 27 on the front nine on the opening day, but had crashed and burned when it counted. At the end of the final round he signed his scorecard with shaking hands and rushed to look at the leaderboard. He was twentieth in the 110-man field and would only earn fifteen pounds. What had gone wrong? In his heart of hearts he had believed he could win—had *expected* to win, but somehow the gods had conspired to prevent it. Worst of all, he had let Manuel and Dr. Campuzano down. Choking with fury and humiliation, Ballesteros ran for the solitude of the locker room; Manuel Piñero found him there hours later, his head in his hands, sobbing.

"I think what surprised some of us was how angry he was with himself for not doing better," says Piñero, who sat with his young compatriot, comforting him, until he calmed down. "He was so angry. I remember thinking at the time, 'This boy could be a very, very good player.' "

From Portugal, Ballesteros flew to LaManga for the start of the Spanish Open. He had already dismissed his fears of failure as groundless, recovered his high spirits, and was contemplating the tournament ahead with enthusiasm. The field was a strong one; Player, who had won the Masters in April, Maurice Bembridge, and Jerry Heard were all entered. Ballesteros relished the fresh challenge. This week, he felt sure, he would show people what he was made of.

For the most part, pressure in professional golf is self-inflicted. Ballesteros had that in common with the majority, but there the similarity ended. He didn't, as so often happens with Tour rookies, regard the halfway cut with increasing dread as the weeks went by, or allow it to assume such gargantuan proportions in his mind that he ended up being unable to think of tournaments as four-round events. He thought only of the finish line. From the very first hole of every tournament, he threw himself heart, body, and soul into trying to win, clawing and scratching at the unyielding golf course in a furious attempt to gain birdies, eagles, and even albatrosses, and getting scratched and bitten as often as not in return.

La Manga lulled him into a false sense of security. When he reached the 586-yard ninth in the opening round, he had already made eight straight pars and was beginning to think that he could take advantage of her forgiving nature. He stood on the tee and looked boldly down the fairway. Here was his chance to capitalize on his length and make a four or even a three. He set up over the ball and struck it with such force that his follow-through ended in a kind of high twirl. It flew away in a magnificent banana-shaped curve and vanished into oblivion. He teed up again. This time the ball went right, slicing smoothly out of bounds and out of sight. His third attempt (and fifth stroke) was on the fairway. Ballesteros by now was virtually apoplectic with rage. He slammed his club viciously into the golf bag and set off in pursuit of the miscreant ball, cursing and scowling and denouncing the world in Spanish. The golfing gods took a dim view of his behavior. They saw to it that his sixth shot homed in, as if by magnet, on a water hazard. Ballesteros dropped miserably out under penalty, played a poor chip into a bunker, found the green in nine, and two-putted for an 11. He scored 83 that day and 78 the next to miss the cut by a shot.

HE HELD HIMSELF ALOOF FROM THE CROWD, PREFERRING HIS OWN COMPANY OR THAT OF A HANDFUL OF SPANISH FRIENDS TO THE SOCIAL GATHERINGS INTEGRAL TO THE TOUR.

It was during this low period in his first season that subtle distinctions between Ballesteros and his colleagues began to emerge. For a start, he held himself aloof from the crowd, preferring his own company or that of a handful of Spanish friends to the social gatherings integral to the Tour. His lack of English distanced him still further. He was obsessed with the game to the exclusion of all else, and thus had an acceptance of, and even a love for, its vagaries, a quality rare among young golfers. While others grew dejected or self-pitying when confronted with the harsh reality of life on the European Tour, Ballesteros became angry or tearful, then used those emotions to fuel his desire. He set himself a punishing practice regime and disciplined himself to adhere religiously to it. Not a day went by when he didn't stand on the range until dark. Where Ballesteros was particularly unusual, however, was in his zest for watching great players work on their games. He would stay on at the golf course for the weekend, just so he could see Player practice bunker shots, Heard hit iron shots, or Peter Oosterhuis putt.

All this had little effect on his scoring. Absorbed in the contemplation of good golf swings, Ballesteros lost sight of the importance of the finer art of course management. He could not think in terms of percentages or see the advantages of tempering his game. He could not express himself but through towering drives, freakish iron play, miraculous recoveries, and audacious chip shots. His sole aim was to win every tournament he played in and win it by twenty shots. Caution was not in his vocabulary. As a consequence, he shot 84, 79 to miss the thirty-six-hole cut in the Madrid Open at Puerto de Hierro by a large margin, and 75, 75, 74 to miss the fifty-four-hole cut in the French Open at Chantilly.

When the Tour went to Britain the following week, it left without Ballesteros. Manuel had persuaded him to go home. Heartsore and travel weary, he returned to Pedreña to face the inevitable questions and inquiring glances of his friends. He felt strongly that he had let down the people who believed in him, but he saw no immediate way of remedying the situation other than through hard work. He could no more consider a life of monotony, regimentation, and toil as a factory worker, bank clerk or farm laborer than he could cut off a limb. Golf filled his dreams and his every waking hour. Without it there was nothing. Nevertheless, he had to find some way of recouping his lost earnings. To date, the young Spaniard had earned the grand total of forty pounds on the Tour. His travel expenses had come to rather more than that and his funds from Dr. Campuzano had almost dried up as a result. With no alternative on the horizon, Ballesteros resorted once more to caddying, for twenty-five pence a round.

Salvation came in the shape of the National Under-25s Championship, held at Pedreña. Ballesteros had recovered all his old self-esteem and was now certain he would soon be the best player in the world. When the tournament began he set about proving it, attacking his home course with cavalier flair and determination and, driven by pride and aided by local knowledge, swept to his first professional victory. He was overjoyed. Not only was the title a salve on all the hurts and humiliations he had suffered since surrendering his amateur status, but it had earned him five hundred pounds. Ballesteros felt ten feet tall. He finished runner-up in the next tournament, the Santander Open, also played at Pedreña, and a week later took top honors at Bilbao in the Vizcaya Open, beating Manuel and Vicente into second and third place.

In October, having regained the physical and emotional resources necessary to cope with day-to-day life on the professional circuit, Ballesteros took a flight to Venice, where the Italian Open was being held. On practice days he played with his brother Manuel and Piñero, who marveled at his prodigious length off the tee. "He was so young that it was impossible to say how far he would go in his career, but it was obvious he had a fantastic talent for the game."

Exactly how gifted he was, Ballesteros demonstrated when the tournament started. After nine holes of the first round he was three under par and sharing the lead with Johnny Miller, the golden boy of American golf, and Oosterhuis, the player who dominated the European Tour at that time. But in the afternoon, fog rose like steam from the languid green canals, and play was suspended, then halted for the day. Ballesteros whiled away the hours on the putting green, working on his stroke and smiling at Manuel's discomfiture as players came up to him and commented on his score. "It's not me, it's Seve, my little brother," Manuel would say without rancor. For as long as he could remember, he had been preparing himself for the time when he would have to take a back seat to young Severiano at a golf tournament. Now that that day was at hand, he felt nothing but pride.

As the week progressed and Ballesteros maintained his position on the upper rungs of the leaderboard—scoring 75, 73, 73 to finish five shots adrift of Oosterhuis—the winner, Piñero, was struck by his assurance and calm bearing when faced with competition of the caliber of the Englishman and the American: "He was not intimidated by playing with Johnny Miller or anybody. When he was young he watched people to learn, not to see how good they were. He was thinking: 'I'm going to beat him; I'm going to be better than him,' which is a positive attitude."

The last official tournament of the year was the El Paradiso Open in the south of Spain. Traditionally, the final event of the season is the one where those golfers who are on the borderline between success—meaning that they will be able to continue to pursue their quest for fame and fortune on the golf tour to the detriment of families, bank balances, and sanity; and failure—meaning that they may at last have to look for a proper job—make a last-ditch stand to keep their playing card. Ballesteros was in the happy position of not being one of their number, due to his fine performances in his national events. Roddy Carr, son of the famous amateur, Joe, was not so fortunate. He had to make the cut in order to finish in the top sixty on the money list. If he didn't, then he, like so many of those who follow golf's uncertain dream, would find himself washed up on the stony beach of life. Carr quashed an uncomfortable uprising of butterflies at the thought, and drove shakily off the first tee. His playing partner was a moody Spanish teenager, whom Carr supposed to be related to Manuel Ballesteros. He watched him unleash himself on his tee shot and hurry after it, muttering under his breath. Next, the youngster hit a five-iron to twenty feet and was so dissatisfied with the result that he beat his club repeatedly against the ground.

THEY WALKED TO THE GREEN, WHEREUPON BALLESTEROS MISSED HIS PUTT, LOST HIS TEMPER, AND KICKED HIS GOLF BAG.

They walked to the green, whereupon Ballesteros missed his putt, lost his temper, and kicked his golf bag.

Carr was annoyed. He fumed to himself, "Who does this kid think he is? Does he not know that this is golf and that you can't hole every forty-five footer and you can't hit every five-iron to two feet?"

This pattern continued on the second hole and on the third. Indeed, every time Ballesteros hit a poor shot, he would throw a tantrum, displaying a total disregard for Carr. At the end of the round, an angry and disappointed Carr went looking for Severiano's brother to complain to him about the boy's conduct.

"Oh, I'll speak to him, I'll speak to him," Manuel assured him nervously, and thanked Carr for not taking it any further. Little did the Irishman realize how much that small kindness would be repaid in later years.

Since golf is a game without equal in sport when it comes to sheer frustration, it is hardly surprising that it has a long and entertaining history of great players who have yielded to the temptation, having been tried beyond endurance, to violate its sacred codes by systematically destroying the tools of their trade. These men are outlaws who quickly become legends, though few quicker than Tommy Bolt, the mercurial 1958 U.S. Open champion.

Jacklin has a tale he tells about Bolt at a tournament in Santiago, California, in which the American, who had had a bad start to his round and whose temperature gauge was already in the red zone, hooked his tee shot over a cliff at the fifth hole. Smoke was coming out of his ears as he and his caddie disappeared over the brink and down the steps to look for his ball. Jacklin waited for him to reappear. Nothing happened. Silence reigned.

"He never came back up," Jacklin recalls with a grin. "I didn't see him till the next week. I said, 'Tom, did you ever find that ball down there?' He said, 'No, but I found the Eastern Airlines ticket counter.' "

Nevertheless, there is a big distinction between a player like Bolt, who was incredibly hotheaded and explosive, and one like Ballesteros, who was simply youthful and impetuous and desperate to prove his worth.

"I think with most champion golfers you'll find that in their youth they were fiery," Ben Crenshaw says. "That's what [Bernard] Darwin always spoke about. He said that if a fellow who has a fiery temperament learns to bottle it, he's going to be a dangerous fellow later on."

How much of a difference Ballesteros's temperament made to his overall results in 1974, no one will ever know, but with £275 earned for his seventeenth-place finish at El Paraiso and £1,440 for his performance at the Ibergolf Trophy at Las Lomas el Bosque, his first season as a tournament professional drew to a close. In Spain he had had two victories, two second places, and was ninth on the money list; on the Continental Order of Merit he was thirteenth; and on the European rankings (British Order of Merit), he was 113th, having played in just five tournaments. His stroke average was a poor 74.76 and his combined earnings amounted to some five thousand pounds. But these achievements were nothing when compared to the rookie years of players such as Jacklin and Player, and it was for that reason, more than any other, that those two gentlemen were so skeptical when they heard Manuel Ballesteros declare his brother Severiano to be the "best young player in the world."

May 1975, European PGA Championship, Sandwich, Kent. The
PGA Championship was Ballesteros's British debut. He had never set foot on
these Isles before and thus far it had been a baptism of fire. Soon after his arrival at Royal St. George's, Manuel, who had been looking forward to intro-
ducing his young brother to the pleasures of links golf, had led him proudly
to the front of the clubhouse and swept an arm over the bleak, unremarkable
landscape. Ballesteros followed the direction of his gaze. It was late afternoon, and the sun setting on the dull day had made the mounds and hollows
tawny with shadow. Pale grasses waved, the gray sea shimmered, and, to the
accustomed eye, the scene had a harshness and simplicity that was beautiful
to behold. Severiano's eye was not accustomed.

"Where is the golf course?" he asked in some bewilderment.

Manuel laughed. "Oh, it's out there somewhere," he said vaguely.

"It was horrible," recalls Ballesteros, who, to this day, has never been able
to find a place in his heart for Royal St. George's. "So cold, so much wind, so
much different from any other course I had ever known. Especially, I didn't
like the fact that there were no trees for my eyes to get reference. I tell you, by
the time I had played one round I didn't like *anything* about Sandwich."

His impression of its worthlessness was cemented when a Dunlop rep-
resentative came up to him on the practice ground, handed him three balls,
and told him that if he made the cut he would be given another three. "I
saw the rough was about one and a half meters high and I thought, 'These
will last me about six holes,' " Ballesteros recalls. As it turned out, Sandwich
had as little regard for him as he had for it and sent him on his way after
only two rounds, following scores of 79 and 84. Manuel, on the other hand,
led the field for most of the tournament and eventually finished fifth to
Arnold Palmer on a day when electrical storms turned the golf course into
a nightmare.

It was a relieved Ballesteros who quit the hostile shores of Kent for the
warmer climes of his native land. Almost at once he began to establish himself as the dominant player on the Spanish circuit. He successfully defended
his National Under-25s title at Sotogrande, finished runner-up in the

23

Seve often practiced sand shots off the beach near his home in Pedreña, and by the time he was nineteen, his fans would even come by boat in chilly weather to watch the young sensation. (© Chris Smith)

El Maresme Open and in the Spanish Professionals Championship, and was third in two other events. By the time July came, his experiences at Sandwich had receded into a distant corner of his memory and he was optimistic about his chances in the British Open at Carnoustie. But a week before the tournament, he injured his foot while practicing on the beach in Pedreña and, his balance and rhythm destroyed, shot 79, 80 to miss the cut by a comfortable margin. The capriciousness of links golf had defeated him once again.

Elsewhere Ballesteros had begun to demonstrate his potential. He had finished tied for sixth with Manuel in the first event of the season, the Portuguese Open—also known as the "Impossible Open" because political unrest had threatened to put a stop to it—and tied for sixth in the second, the Spanish Open at La Manga. In the Madrid Open, his third event of the season, he shared eighth place, and he was twenty-sixth in France.

At last people started to sit up and take notice of him. "Severiano Ballesteros has become the foremost of the Spanish young," Pat Ward-Thomas wrote. "Like many Spaniards, he has great flair. His swing is not

24

A child shall lead them? Well, not really a child, but in his teens Seve already was known worldwide by golf fans, including some of his own Spanish countrymen, apparently fascinated by something Seve is telling them. (© Chris Smith)

absolutely firm at the top but he attacks the ball with great confidence and appears to have a good head."

"I think he was seen very early on to be something special," Christy O'Connor Jr. says. "He hit the ball so hard he would almost run after it. Totally fearless. He was so exciting. A breath of fresh air, like a young John Daly without the control."

The intensity of Ballesteros's desire manifested itself in several ways. One was his temper, another was the amount of time he spent on the range, and yet another was his fits of pique or depression. After a day in which he had struggled on the greens, Doust can recall him punishing himself by not allowing himself dinner. "He had a bad putting round at some rinky-dink tournament, and then he putted for about an hour and a half on the putting green and went back and wouldn't let himself eat."

Dave Musgrove saw him do the same thing on a number of occasions once he started caddying for him. In the PGA Championship at St. George's in 1976, for instance, Ballesteros shot 71, 72 in the opening rounds and 76 in the third and then just went back to his room and locked himself away until morning. "He went to bed in the afternoon and wouldn't get up to eat or anything," says Musgrove, who had been staying in the same boarding house as the Spaniard. "Just lay in bed. I remember that vividly because we all kept going and asking if he was coming out. 'No!' he said. '*No!*' "

Where Ballesteros was fortunate was that he was surrounded by a small circle of close friends and relatives, who supported him through these periods. When Manuel was on Tour he acted as translator, mentor, travel agent, protector, and coach to his young brother, and, when he wasn't, his friends Piñero and Fernandez took over. "Seve was Manuel's baby brother," Bill Longmuir remembers, "and was sort of molly-coddled a bit around the Spanish players because he was so young. Everyone used to sort of look out for Seve."

This hothouse environment of nurture and encouragement did wonders for Ballesteros's confidence, and his golf game benefited as a result. His best finishes in the second half of the year were tied for eighth in the Swiss Open, third in the Lancome Trophy, and twelfth in the Italian Open. By the end of the season he was the No. 1 player on both the Spanish and Continental Orders of Merit, and was twenty-sixth on the British money list with earnings of £4,118. Manuel was twenty-fifth. He also had an improved stroke average of 73.91 and was the only golfer in Europe to have been placed in all the Continental Opens.

"I had seen many good players for the first time in my life," he said later. "I thought to myself, 'Seve, you can beat them all.' "

There are two wonderfully revealing stories about Ballesteros at that age, one of which is told by Peter Ryde, a former *Times* golf correspondent, and the other by Fernandez. In the first, Ballesteros was playing in a golf tournament in Spain. Crossing from one hole to the next, he stopped at a stand to get a drink. The vendor eyed him shyly.

"Mr. Ballesteros, I have the same name as you," he told the tall, broadshouldered young man at his counter.

Ballesteros looked at him. "How old are you?" he asked.

"Twenty-six," the surprised vendor answered.

"I am eighteen," Ballesteros said, "therefore it is I who have the same name as you."

For Fernandez, one memory stands out more clearly in his mind than all the rest: a summer's day at Fulford Golf Club in York. Ballesteros had produced a round of near-flawless golf in the first round of the Benson and

Hedges Festival. Most of his approach shots had been hit within easy two-putt range, and though he had been bunkered twice he had gotten up and down each time. Only once did he seem in danger of being over par, but disaster was averted with a long putt at the twelfth hole, and his score of 64 equaled that of Fernandez and was a shot off the pace at the end of the day. In the second round, however, his touch seemed to desert him. He slipped back into the pack with a three-over-par 75 and, despite following it with rounds of 72 and 71, was left trailing in thirty-sixth place when perfect conditions led to record scoring.

Fernandez, meanwhile, had taken advantage of the fine weather to make his move on the trophy and was occupying a seemingly invincible position at the top of the leaderboard, four shots ahead of Maurice Bembridge, when he reached the fifteenth hole on the final day. There, inexplicably, he hooked out of bounds and took a seven, while Bembridge holed a long putt to draw even with him.

As he teed up on the final hole, a tense young face watched him from the gallery. It turned as Fernandez drove the ball down the center of the fairway and it followed the flight of his three-iron to the heart of the green. Fernandez, small, wiry, and eager, carefully studied his line. His first putt ran by the hole but his second dropped for a birdie, a four-round total of 266 and victory. Hardly had the ball touched the cup when Ballesteros, black hair flying, arms outstretched, was over the ropes and racing across the green toward his friend while the gallery exploded into tumultuous applause.

"He was the first person to run and congratulate me," Fernandez says emotionally. "He took me from behind, jumping in the air. He was crying like a baby. He was in tears.

"And that's the kind of person that lives inside of Seve."

3

RITES OF PASSAGE

"When you're young you can only see the top and you just want to get there."

Bill Longmuir, Mallorca, March 1992

One bright morning in the summer of 1976 an untidy procession of red vans and blue ones and odd-colored trucks and men on bicycles or walking came bumping slowly over the narrow roads that wander through the dunes of Royal Birkdale. A dust plume charted their progress. Halting, they disbanded and threw down their loads, and with hammering and laughter soon drove away the sound of silence. The day was an infinite, azure blue. As the sun climbed higher it blazed with a fiery intensity and the air began to burn and grew languorous with the weight of humidity. Defenseless, the vast undulating greens were quickly scarred, while the rough grew dry and brittle and was bleached to the color of pale straw. The scattered men worked on tirelessly. White rivulets of sweat ran down their brown cheerful faces, as they erected steel skeletons, carted signs about, and forced the hard earth to admit ungainly wooden legs.

Toward evening, a cooling wind blew in from the sea. Salt and the smell of cut grass caught the breeze and drifted across the tented expanse. Greenkeepers gathered the bright pins; the hum of mowers ceased. As the final crossbar was being bolted onto the grandstand facing the great yellow leaderboard, Jimmy Dickinson, a caddie, prepared to go forth into the sunset to measure the course for Jack Nicklaus. Then, as sprinklers hissed and a solitary night bird called, the caravan filed slowly down the drive, transporting the weary men. Above the quiet links the canvas village

28

flapped, snapped, and billowed like a giant sail, and the flags of thirty nations streamed.

The 105th British Open Championship had begun.

Monday, July 5, 1976, Southport, Lancashire. The far end of the practice range at Royal Birkdale resounded with the crack of wood meeting golf ball with unrestrained force. Several players glanced up. Severiano Ballesteros, the nineteen-year-old executant of the shot, watched it pass the 250-yard marker on the fly and disappear over the boundary fence before turning to his gathered admirers with a toss of his black hair and a grin. Manuel nodded approvingly. The other Spanish onlookers conferred among themselves and added their comments. Ballesteros considered their appraisal momentarily, rapped his club smartly against his golf shoe to clean the blade, and, with uninhibited energy and enthusiasm, launched another attack on the ball.

Walking by, Christy O'Connor Jr. received an impression of youth, strength, wildness, long hair, and flares. A year earlier Dave Musgrove, the dry-humored, razor-tongued Midlander who was to become Ballesteros's regular caddie, had been struck on first sight of the young Spaniard by the length of his legs and by his large hands. To defending champion Tom Watson, pausing in practice to see him hit the ball, Ballesteros's strength was nothing less than awesome. "I remember how hard he swung at the ball—how he just lashed at it, hit it with all his might."

The Ballesteros brothers had already spent several days at Royal Birkdale. On the previous Saturday Severiano had caddied for Manuel in the thirty-six-hole British Open qualifying at Southport & Ainsdale, where he was among 650 players on five courses attempting to gain entry to the tournament. Manuel had played well enough to get into the play-off but was then unfortunately beaten, whereupon his young brother had abandoned him without a word and marched disgustedly back to the clubhouse, Manuel trailing miserably in his wake.

29

But it was not the Spaniards who made news the following morning. As Pat Ward-Thomas remarked in the *Guardian*: "Whether or not Nicklaus, Palmer, Watson, Miller, and the rest had arrived at Birkdale for the British Open Championship seemed for a while to be of little account when the extraordinary story of Maurice Flitcroft, a crane driver at Vickers in Barrow-in-Furness who had entered as a pro, came to light. In the first qualifying round at Formby, he fashioned a matchless score of 121." Flitcroft, it transpired, had never played eighteen holes in his life before but had somehow slipped through the R&A's net of entry restrictions. The game up, they dispatched the culprit speedily, with a flea in his ear.

The weather throughout had been hot and close. Inevitably, the conditions had baked the fairways of Birkdale to the consistency of concrete and it was playing far shorter than it otherwise would, but even if it remained so, the quality of the tournament would be unlikely to be diminished. Nicklaus observed that there would not be a fluke winner of the British Open—nor has there ever been.

Late afternoon Johnny Miller arrived for a practice round. Seeing Ballesteros in the locker room, gazing enviously at the clubs and clothes of other players with his dark, expressive eyes, he greeted him cordially, for they shared a manager. The American's British Open record was astonishing: a second place, a tenth, and a third in the preceding three years. In 1975 at Carnoustie he had hit his tee shot into a fairway bunker on the final hole, heard the gallery on the seventeenth roar and assumed, incorrectly, that either Watson or Jack Newton had birdied the hole and that he would need a birdie at the last to tie. He took a five-iron out of the bunker, left the ball in the trap and missed the play-off by a shot. As far as he was concerned, he had come to Royal Birkdale to fulfill a date with destiny: "I've paid my dues. This year it's going to be my turn."

Tuesday, July 6, 1976. The British golf writers, cowed, like British golfers, by years of American domination, were all doom and despondency as to the tournament's eventual outcome. "It would be stretching optimism to its limits to say that a British victory is likely," the *Guardian* said pessimistically, and other papers followed suit. Only two European players had won the Open Championship since the early fifties—Max Faulkner in 1951 at Royal Portrush and Tony Jacklin in 1969 at Royal Lytham and St. Annes, and in the interim honors had been divided between Argentina (once), South Africa (five times). No Continental player had triumphed in the Open since Arnaud Massy lifted the claret jug at Hoylake in 1907 with a score of 312.

It had never been an obsession of Ballesteros's to become the first Spaniard to end the European drought. As a boy he did not, as other golfers claim they have, dream of becoming British Open champion and occupy a fantasy world where he regularly putted for victory at St. Andrews. He simply wanted to be the best. Now that the time had come for him to prove that he could be, he didn't shy away from it, but looked forward to it with a singular relish. Having devoted the morning to altering the loft and lie of his golf clubs to suit the conditions at Birkdale, he spent the afternoon playing a practice round with Manuel and the Argentineans Roberto De Vicenzo and Vicente Fernandez in the shadow of the thunderheads, testing the brisk wind and the smooth shining greens, and watching how the ball flew from the saddle of one mound but rolled through the valley of another, until at last he felt that he would come to love and understand links golf the way he did the courses of his native Spain. Thus prepared, Ballesteros scorned the conventional European attitude—which said that all American players were superior beings whose right to the British Open trophy was preordained—and turned squarely to face the dangers which the morrow would surely bring.

Wednesday, July 7, 1976. The long breathless days and indigo skies had brought Royal Birkdale to the point of spontaneous combustion. At midday it succumbed to the inevitable: beside the first tee, a bush burst into flames. Spectators were evacuated, fire engines wailed, and the opening round was held up for thirty minutes while the small conflagration was subdued. There was an air of comic absurdity about the scene, and for an hour or two the general attention of the public, and of a few players, was concerned with things apart from golf. It was then that two unknown names appeared on the leaderboard and made their way inexorably to the top. Joining Irishman Christy O'Connor Jr., who had returned a three-under-par 69 to finish leader in the clubhouse, were Norio Suzuki, the diminutive Japanese player, and Ballesteros.

They say that fortune favors the brave. The previous afternoon, U.S. Open champion Jerry Pate had emphasized the importance of precise tee shots, especially for long hitters, because of the risk of running out of fairway. Willfully, and because he had never played any other way, Ballesteros took his driver from the bag on the very first hole and, with joyous abandon, smashed it as far as he possibly could. On the next tee he again lashed at the ball with his wide, free swing and again lost nothing to par. At the third, his aggression was rewarded. Fine attacking iron play won him a birdie three there and a two at the 150-yard seventh. Before long the record galleries began to drift from the failing greats to take up with the young Spaniard. He responded by flirting with peril more outrageously at the eighth. By the time he had reached number nine, they were fast warming to his ready smile and devil-may-care golf game, and were sorry to see him take three putts to turn in 33.

BALLESTEROS CONTINUED TO BOLDLY COURT DISASTER. HIS FREEDOM OF SPIRIT WAS INFECTIOUS.

There is an element of caprice in the nature of every links course which is subtly influenced by the wind. A stretch of holes that is no more threatening than an aged spaniel during a southwesterly will be transformed into the Hound of the Baskervilles by the slightest shift in the direction of the breeze. So it is in the case of Birkdale. When from the ocean the wind helps the thirteenth, seventeenth, and eighteenth, and they can play too short for genuine par-fives. Now it became a sirocco and gusted around the easternmost holes of the course, so that the drives were more exacting and the greens out of range for all but the strong. Ballesteros continued to boldly court disaster. His freedom of spirit was infectious; the gallery was carried along by it and derived a certain vicarious pleasure from his adventures. They delighted with him at the twelfth, where he secured a birdie after holing a monster putt, and at the thirteenth, where he was home in two with a one-iron, but were as downcast as the Spaniard himself when he dropped a shot at the next par-three, taking two to recover from a greenside trap. A stiff breeze made the closing holes especially difficult, and it is a measure of his strength that he was green-high with a one-iron at the last, and could get up and down for a birdie four and a back nine of 36. His score of 69 brought him level with O'Connor Jr. and Suzuki at the end of the first day of play. Brian Barnes, Tom Kite, and Jack Newton were a shot further back, with Player and Miller at level par.

Afterward, Ballesteros was disarmingly unaffected and cheerful. "If I play like this I have very good chance. My driving is very good. Maybe I win. But if the wind blows I make 80 tomorrow, perhaps."

Thursday, July 8, 1976. A gambling man would not have placed money on Ballesteros to retain his position at the top of the leaderboard after two rounds. It is traditional for the first day of the British Open to be dominated by the heroics of journeymen and pretenders to the throne; this is their moment of glory and no one denies it to them. After that, the established stars will usually pull up their shirt sleeves and set to work, then it is business as usual on the links. Not so at Birkdale. Miller, a charismatic figure with flying gold hair and a tall, slender frame, had taken the early lead after Ballesteros dropped two strokes to par on his outward half. The American played the front nine in 36, but took full advantage of the back nine which had been made benign by a sudden change of wind. At fifteen, the longest par-five, he pulled his tee shot into heavy rough and could do no more than hack the ball out sideways with a wedge. With 240 yards to go, he hit a long-iron to the heart of the green and sank a fourteen-foot putt for birdie. Prudent use of the one-iron netted him birdies at the fourteenth, seventeenth, and eighteenth holes, so he was four under par for the last seven holes and ended with a 68 and a total of 140.

Now Ballesteros entered the fray. His gallery was growing larger by the hour, drawn to the pervading atmosphere of gay drama that surrounded his match. They crowded quickly after him, as he struck fearlessly off the tee, ran to follow the flight of his ball as it departed the fairway for the dunes, then strode through the rough like a beagle on the scent with an alert and confident stride. "A Spaniard in Lancashire," a watching commentator remarked. "Everyone enjoying him and waiting for him to vanish from the leaderboard." Ballesteros, of course, had no intention of obliging. Gathering himself for the finish, he began to fire at the pins with crisp and powerful iron shots. At the eleventh he was rewarded with his first birdie and earned another two holes later. The fifteenth, seventeenth, and eighteenth were reached with a one-iron, three-iron, and five-iron, respectively, for his second shots. At the close of play his score of 69, for an aggregate of 138, six under par, gave him a two-stroke lead over Miller, with O'Connor Jr. and Ken Brown next, followed by Barnes, Tommy Horton, and Raymond Floyd.

At all of Ballesteros's postround interviews, Manuel acted as translator. His brother's broken English was not yet equal to the demands of press conference dialogue and in this, as with everything, Manuel liked to be by his side to protect him from harassment and unnecessary pressure. Bilingual debates at golf tournaments tend to degenerate fairly rapidly into mini-circuses, and Thursday's was no exception. Eventually, Ballesteros gave one Spanish reporter a reply that was so convoluted it went on for five minutes, and provoked much hilarity among the Latin contingent of golf writers.

"What did he say?" a member of the British press said impatiently to Manuel when Severiano finally came to a stop. "Well," Manuel replied seriously, "he said: 'No.'" And brought the house down.

The Ballesteros brothers had found accommodation at a small guesthouse in Southport. Neither of them could drive, and it was before the days of courtesy cars, so they relied on Musgrove and his friend, Constable Dick Draper, to fetch and carry them from the golf course. Musgrove, who later became famous as Sandy Lyle's caddie and co-author with John Hopkins of the book *Life with Lyle*, had worked on a casual basis for Ballesteros since 1975 but, because he traditionally carried Roberto De Vicenzo's bag in the British Open, he had suggested to the young Spaniard that Draper, a five-handicapper from his hometown of Kirkby with previous experience of caddying in the British Open, work for him at Birkdale. Ballesteros agreed straight away; like most Spanish players, he revered De Vicenzo, the 1967 British Open champion. The respect was mutual. Later in the week the Argentinean remarked to Musgrove that in his opinion there were only three golfers in the world that mattered: Miller, Tom Weiskopf, and Ballesteros. "They are in a different class to the rest of us."

Friday, July 9, 1976. The third round brought rain, heavy and disagreeable, drenching the rainbow gallery and transforming the narrow footpaths into twisting rusty streams. When it cleared the wind had moved for the first time to the southwest, the true direction for the course and, in doing so, had induced a schizophrenic change in the character of several key holes.

Ballesteros and Miller were the last of the field to tee off. At his press conference on Thursday evening, the Spaniard had been asked whether or not it would bother him to play with a golfer of the Californian's repute. "Where is Johnny Miller?" Ballesteros demanded. "Come, you tell him we can go and play now." This morning as he drove from the first, he was no less assured, but with his spontaneous smile, canary yellow shirt, and sky-blue waterproofs brought a welcome ray of sunshine to the air of prevailing gloom. Two holes later, he was looking slightly crestfallen. His eagerness to make Royal Birkdale conform to the way he wanted to play the game, rather than to try and adapt his golf to suit the course, had resulted in a clash of wills in which Birkdale came out on top. It was Miller's turn to suffer at the next, where he took a bogey five. But he retaliated with a tee shot to four inches at the 206-yard fourth, while Ballesteros missed the green and became entangled in heavy grass. On close inspection of the lie a lesser player might have written the hole off as lost, but young Severiano never hesitated as he lofted the ball smoothly and easily to two inches for a par, grinning at his caddie's astonished face as he did so. The period of grace was not a long one. A par at the fifth was followed by further punishment at the sixth and seventh, so that when he reached the ninth hole, Ballesteros was four over par and Miller was leading the tournament.

Then the wheel of fortune began to turn in the young Spaniard's favor. He persisted in lashing away from the tee, but with remarkable recoveries survived the consequences of his wildness. At the eleventh, where he fired his drive so far left that it vanished over a sandhill, a double bogey or even quadruple seemed imminent. There was no need for concern. Ballesteros disappeared into the undergrowth and disbelieving fans heard a crack and saw the ball rise toward the green. Miller was not amused. His own

35

approach from a good lie had finished short and left, and he took three more to get down. Ballesteros required only two putts for his par. On the short twelfth the Spaniard again explored uncharted territory when his tee shot flew over the dunes. Miller waited smugly on the putting surface for him to reappear. Over the hill came another ball; Ballesteros was still fighting and put his recovery close enough to get an impudent three. Even for a player of Miller's experience the sight of these Houdini-like endeavors was disconcerting. "It was very frustrating," he admitted. "It would not have been so upsetting if we had both got a share of the luck, but he seemed to have got both our rations."

Witness the fifteenth. Miller's tee shot on the 542-yard par-five rivaled Ballesteros's for waywardness, and they both played provisional balls. But where Miller was forced to drop out under penalty and so notched up a bogey six, the irrepressible Spaniard escaped unharmed, holing a twelve-foot putt for par to increase his lead to two shots. At the next, the pattern continued. Miller, who was on the fairway, hit his approach to twenty feet with a high and beautiful swing. Ballesteros, who wasn't, missed the green altogether, but took a putter from the short rough and almost holed it for birdie. Then Miller's ball lipped out for par. As the *Daily Mail* recorded, "One of the most delightful sights of this championship was that of Miller, one of the world's highest-paid sporting superstars, kicking his hat in disgust by the sixteenth green, then throwing his ball angrily into the bushes because it had refused to drop for a birdie. . . . What maddened Miller more was that every time Severiano pulled off one of his escapades, he smiled apologetically and with reverence at the man he acknowledges as one of the golf masters."

At the seventeenth, Ballesteros added insult to injury, making eagle from the rough to get to five under par. Miller closed with two birdies but the Spaniard's score at the end of the day, a 73 for an aggregate of 211, left him two strokes ahead of his playing companion, four ahead of Horton, and five ahead of Nicklaus and Floyd.

All the golfing world now wondered whether Ballesteros could become the youngest player since Tom Morris a century before to win the British Open Championship. Whatever the outcome of the tournament, however, one thing was for certain: Ballesteros's simple charm off the course and appealing dash and flair on it had earned him lasting respect and admiration. "Seve was almost made to entertain people through golf," said Miller. "He is a very unique player. He is a genius. He has got charisma, he's got power, he's got flair, and he has a passion which people can feel."

Nevertheless, it was almost impossible to believe that Ballesteros would continue to elude capture if he persisted in employing the same strong-arm tactics he had used all week on the final day. Miller drew parallels between their golf games: "Seve had a big swing, swung hard, went for the pins, and had a lot of emotions—*I* had a lot of emotions on the golf course. I could relate to him and I think he could relate to me, and I respect his game and he really respected mine." Miller also said that Ballesteros only had one shot in his bag. "You need patience over here," he commented to reporters. "You can't throw everything at the pin."

Ballesteros scoffed at the Californian's cautionary words. "I am still young," he declared. "When I am older there will be time to be careful."

Ever since Ballesteros had arrived at Royal Birkdale, he practiced when he had come off the course, slept for a couple of hours, then behaved like any other teenager in the evening. He and his brother did the rounds of most of the nightclubs in Southport that week, and he can still recall walking through the town and laughing as passersby congratulated Manuel on his marvelous performance in the British Open.

"SEVE WAS ALMOST MADE TO ENTERTAIN PEOPLE THROUGH GOLF," SAID MILLER. "HE IS A VERY UNIQUE PLAYER. HE IS A GENIUS. HE HAS GOT CHARISMA, HE'S GOT POWER, HE'S GOT FLAIR, AND HE HAS A PASSION WHICH PEOPLE CAN FEEL."

"Was Severiano very excited at the prospect of vying with the best players in the world for the British Open trophy?" a reporter wanted to know.

"I am not excited and I am not nervous," Ballesteros said with calm authority. "I will play to win and, if I have a three-foot putt to win the British Open Championship, I will know that anyone can put it in and anyone can miss it."

Saturday, July 10, 1976. Severiano Ballesteros stood on the tee at Birk-dale in the final round of the British Open looking as exuberant and happy as a boy at his first funfair. The pressure that had been talked about at length since the start of the tournament had failed to touch him and, as he smashed the ball from the tee and trotted joyfully down the fairway after it, it seemed that he had rarely enjoyed himself more. "The nicest smile that I ever saw in golf," recalls Puerto Rican Chi Chi Rodriguez. "He was very colorful. I don't say handsome, because I never have seen a handsome man or an ugly woman, but I really liked what I saw, you know—strong guy, Spanish, the smile, the drive, the way he walked. He walked like a champion."

Miller, by contrast, was preoccupied with the task before him. He watched Ballesteros's tussle with the rough and subsequent shots to the green expressionlessly. His own ball was four feet from the pin and waiting to be tapped in for par. When the young Spaniard came striding onto the putting surface, he simply lined up his putt and stroked it in from twenty feet for a four. Miller's face registered utter disbelief. He walked to his ball like a man in a dream and missed the short putt for bogey.

But on the next it became apparent that Ballesteros's luck had run out. He hooked into the willow scrub that grew along the sandhills, put his re-covery into a bunker some forty-five yards short of the green, splashed out to fifteen feet, and made bogey; Miller sank his putt for birdie and claimed two shots back in one hole. Nicklaus and Floyd, too, were closing in on the lead. They had had two birdies apiece in the first five holes when they reached the 468-yard sixth—a notorious dogleg par-four that had already cost O'Connor Jr. a seven, Graham Marsh a six, and Horton a five. There, their hopes were dashed. In trying to avoid the cross-bunkers, Nicklaus walked off the green with a six on his card. Ballesteros visited the bushes Nicklaus had just va-cated. Having located the ball, he could do little more than nudge it out with a putter, whereupon it caught the top of a bunker and fell in. He took a double bogey from seven feet, while Miller made par from four. Two holes later he was in trouble once again, after hitting a reckless tee shot into the dunes. His ball was nestled snugly against the trunk of a small bush and his only option was to move it farther along the sandhills—which he did, then pitched to twenty feet. By now he was tried beyond endurance and his shoulders were bowed with the weight of despair. When he missed the putt and saw Miller go three ahead, he was near to tears. He passed a hand across his eyes and trailed miserably after the confident Californian.

Disaster followed disaster. On the eleventh he lost heavily in yet another encounter with the dunes, and took a triple-bogey seven. At the short twelfth, he was forced to drop out and made a bogey four, while Miller hit a four-iron to ten feet for birdie. But still Ballesteros refused to compromise. At every tee he swung at the ball so furiously that he actually walked after it. Then he would search for it among the hills and scrub and, having found it, would try to hole it.

Miller put an arm around the boy's shoulders as they walked to the thirteenth. "I said: 'Seve, why don't you put on a real strong finish and see if you can finish in second place?' I didn't really mean to make a big deal of it, but I genuinely knew I had the tournament won. It's easy to be nice when you've got a six-shot lead. I was feeling bad because he was struggling. He's such a pusher, you know, he's so competitive. And I was basically just saying, 'Why don't you regroup and get it together?' "

At the fourteenth Ballesteros began to fight back, hitting his third shot from the rough to two inches and making his second consecutive birdie. Then Miller chipped into the hole for eagle, after missing the fairway from the tee, and his partner's name slid even further down the leaderboard. "After such a promising beginning," a commentator said sorrowfully, "now destined to finish among the also-rans." Proof positive that nothing was further from the young Spaniard's mind, and that he was once more relaxed and focused on the challenge before him, was provided at the next hole. Finding himself in trouble off the tee, he paused, bent down to inhale the scent of a flowering bush of yellow bracken, and only then considered his lie.

In the waning afternoon the sky had cleared to a brilliant cobalt blue. A fresh wind blew silvery waves through the pale grass, whipping at the clothes of the gallery as it surged over the sandhills and deserted fairways like a swarm of marauding locusts. Nicklaus had finished as the leader in the clubhouse at 285. Aware that something approaching a miracle was needed if he was to lift himself clear of the chasing pack, Ballesteros sank a twenty-five-foot putt for eagle on the seventeenth and found that now he needed only a birdie to tie Nicklaus. He had regained his eagerness and cheerful demeanor, and responded to Miller's handshake as they walked to the final tee with a sudden smile of pure pleasure.

For the last time at Birkdale, Ballesteros unleashed himself on a drive. He had hit only three fairways from the tee all day and the eighteenth, unfortunately, wasn't one of them. As Miller said: "He was so bold but his driver killed him." The Californian's approach was perfect. When he had played it he stood in the center of the fairway, arms raised heavenwards, as the crowd acknowledged him as British Open champion.

The Spaniard's second shot flew into the left rough and finished just short of the putting surface. He threw up his hands in a typically Latin gesture of annoyance at his mistake and the gallery flocked around him, racing to jostle for position by the green. With some difficulty, he and Draper fought their way forward through the throng. The ball was resting in trampled yellow grass, some fifteen yards away from where a hard path rode the crest of two bunkers and ran up to the green. Draper gave the matter but a minute's consideration. To him, only one shot was even remotely possible: a sand-iron over the bunkers. After weeks of continuous sunshine, the putting surface bore an uncanny resemblance to a downhill section of motorway. Ballesteros was not so hasty. In his mind he was trying to envisage a shot so perfect that it would flit as lightly as a feather over the scorched and rumpled earth, neatly evade the hazards and run smoothly into the hole for eagle.

The atmosphere was rigid with tension. Only the creaking of the great stands as the gallery craned expectantly over the railings broke the cathedral-like silence of the eighteenth green. Ballesteros put out his hand for the nine-iron. Draper handed it to him and moved away, the golf bag scraping on the ground. Then, with scarcely a pause, the young Spaniard stepped forward and played one of the lightest, most delicate little chip shots conceivable. Years on, he still considers it to be one of the most important of his life. The risks attached to it were considerable. If he had caught it too heavily, he would have left it in the rough and taken bogey; if he had put it in the trap, he would have taken a five or worse; and if it had run right over the green, he might have lost everything. Instead, he banished every negative thought from his head and committed himself to the shot. The ball bounced onto the path, skipped gaily up to the peak of a mound and over the other side, rolled smoothly along the green and finished four feet from the pin.

John Jacobs, who was watching it on television in Hampshire, leapt to his feet and said: "This boy is a genius. If he ever learns to play, he will be unbeatable." Lee Trevino, recovering from a back injury in Texas, laughed out loud at the audacity of it. "I thought he might have won that golf tournament if he'd had a little bit more experience. He took too many chances. He was going at the flag all the time. But what a wonderful short game he had. He could do anything he wanted with a golf ball."

Miller's first putt shaved the hole, but he was sporting enough to tap it in for victory and a nine-under-par score of 279, thereby allowing Ballesteros to play the last stroke, an honor usually reserved for the champion. The Spaniard sank his birdie putt with aplomb; then he threw his ball as high as he could into the grandstand, lifted his hands to the acclaim, and beamed up at the people who had taken him into their hearts. Afterward, Draper recalls Ballesteros being very calm, collected, and contented, but not in the least bit emotional. He had finished tied with Nicklaus for second place, while Floyd was third, and Mark James, who recorded a course-record 66, was tied for fourth. He knew what an achievement it was, but still said to himself: "I should have won this championship."

In his press conference Miller was generous in his praise of the young Spaniard, and admitted that if Ballesteros had used a one-iron off the tee he would probably have won. "Don't get me wrong," he said, "but I think it was a good thing for Seve that he didn't win. Day in, day out, he wouldn't have been able to back it up. He might have been swamped by the resulting pressures. Now lots of lovely things can happen to him just because he's come second. Just like me: best thing that happened to me was not winning the Masters in 1971. It gave me time to prepare myself for winning a big one. No, the best thing for his career was to finish second. His day will come."

FAME AND MISFORTUNE

"He was a bit like the Kennedy family: you were either for him or against him."

Doust, on Ballesteros's first years on Tour, July 1992

At the time the Ballesteros brothers embarked upon their journey to the Southern Hemisphere in 1974, the interests of all South African pro golfers and many foreign players were watched over by George Blumberg, a gentle and benevolent man. Blumberg, or Uncle George, as he was universally known, was a retired paper millionaire whose consuming passion was golf. He traveled the fairways of the world in search of new talent and, when he found it, would nurture it until it yielded up its potential. This he did both for his own pleasure and for International Management Group (IMG), on whose board of directors he sat and for whom he recruited likely champions. A Churchillian figure who puffed great cigars, he gave freely and generously of his time and money, and it is said that he was almost single-handedly responsible for the financial support of some of the finest players ever to emerge from his country—including Gary Player (although there is some dispute about this), Dale Hayes, Bobby Cole, and the Henning brothers—as well as several British players, such as Clive Clark and Warren Humphries.

The golfers whom Blumberg helped returned his love and admiration a hundredfold. In the autumn of his years, they made him an honorary member of the South African PGA, and it was in this capacity that he first encountered Ballesteros. He was collecting scorecards during the Toro Classic at Glendower Golf Club, near Johannesburg, when he came across those of Ballesteros; who had recorded identical sub-par totals on all four days.

Observing to himself that the unknown Spaniard must be the very model of consistency, Blumberg ran his finger down the numbers. There was hardly a par to be seen. There were flocks of birdies, aviaries full of eagles, and an arresting number of bogeys, double bogeys, and triple bogeys, but few pars. Blumberg could not believe his eyes. Further inquiries into the boy's background convinced him he was not mistaken. It was obvious that here was a player bold enough to go for the ultimate shot, confident enough to take the consequences, and skillful enough to reap the benefits.

Shortly afterward, Blumberg sent an impassioned letter to the directors of IMG in London. "I have seen what I consider to be the most exciting prospect in the world for the next ten to fifteen years," he wrote.

When the answer came back it was simply: "We're not interested."

From time to time one hears of record companies, film studios, and like institutions making monumental blunders. This one turned down the Beatles, so and so rejected Elvis, and Dunkin' Donuts sacked Madonna. With Ballesteros, IMG made theirs. They are still paying for it. Repeated attempts to lure him away from his various managers have resulted in only one reply: "I'm not interested." Somewhere along the line, Ballesteros found out that IMG had rejected him and his pride has never allowed him to forgive them.

In September 1975 Ballesteros played in the Double Diamond International at Turnberry in conditions scarcely fit for polar bears. When the full fury of the gale hit the tournament on the final day, tents were ripped from their moorings, and rain hailed down upon the golfers without mercy. Ballesteros was in the Rest-of-the-World side that week, along with Player, Hayes, Jack Newton, and Bob Charles. Incredibly, given that he still had relatively little experience of playing golf in unplayable weather, he managed to beat Guy Hunt 3 & 2 and Craig Defoy 5 & 4, only losing 3 & 2 to American Jim Colbert. His performance was so outstanding that it attracted the notice of Roberto De Vicenzo, the 1967 British Open Champion and winner of more than 170 tournaments worldwide. De Vicenzo, who was and still is the hero of every Spanish pro golfer in the world, thought highly enough of

Ballesteros as a player to take the trouble to call his own manager, an American by the name of Ed Barner, with a testimonial.

"I am going to tell you something important," De Vicenzo told Barner earnestly. "This Spanish boy, Ballesteros, he can hit the ball. He will be a great player. You should keep an eye on him."

Barner was never slow to pursue a lead on a possible client and he immediately asked Billy Casper to play a practice round with Ballesteros at the Lancome Trophy the following week. Ballesteros then went on to win the pretournament long-hitting contest, with a drive of 293 yards, and finish third behind Player in the main event. Casper, one of the most talented players in the game in his day, was unstinting in his praise of the young Spaniard. "Severiano is not only a gorilla off the tee," he enthused to Barner, "he also has the finest short game I have ever seen in my life."

Billy Casper had in fact been one of the founder members of Uni-Managers International (UMI), along with Barner, a former show-business promoter. Until the U.S. PGA Tour required him to divest himself of all his interests in the company—for it was considered ethically unsound and a conflict of interests for one professional golfer to represent another playing in the same event—Casper assisted Barner in the recruitment of players and the running of the business. When he left UMI in 1972, he sold his shares to a law firm in Los Angeles; whereupon Brent Turley, an attorney with that firm, joined UMI as general counsel and director, and Barner took up the reins of the company. UMI had already built up a strong client base. Both Barner and Casper were Mormons (or Latter-day Saints), which had been an incentive for Johnny Miller, who was born and raised in the church, to join them in 1970, and Miller had brought in several of his friends—players like Jerry Heard, Lanny Wadkins, J. C. Snead, and Dave Hill. Sam Snead, De Vicenzo, and the 1969 U.S. Open champion, Orville Moody, had been with UMI from the outset.

Barner now became intent on signing up the prodigiously talented Ballesteros. At the Lancome Trophy, he approached Severiano and Manuel with a proposition. He would pay their airfares to Como for the Italian Open and cover the cost of their accommodations; organize invitations for them both to play in the Walt Disney World National Team Championship in Florida; pay for their travel and living expenses while they were in America; and give them return tickets to Spain. He would do all of these things with no strings attached, provided Severiano would go to the U.S. PGA Tour

Older brother Manuel Ballesteros was the first golfing star of the family, but he gladly handed the baton to Seve, eventually serving as a caddie and translator for his younger brother. (Peter Howe photograph, Globe Photos Inc., 1997)

Qualifying School and attempt to win his card. After that, well, maybe then they'd talk about him representing them.

A fortnight later the Ballesteroses flew to America for the first time. As soon as they found their bearings, they made their way out to the Lake Buena Vista course, where they were told they had missed their tee-off time. Indeed, it was only through the intervention of Jim Colbert, an eventual winner with Dean Refram, that they were allowed to play at all. Both failed to qualify. Barner, meanwhile, had drawn up a contract for Severiano but not for Manuel. He arranged a meeting with them. Five hours after the pre-arranged time, he was still waiting. The brothers had fallen into conversation with Moody, a Spanish speaker, who was giving them chapter and verse on the iniquities of managers as a species and on his own unhappy dealings with Barner. When they finally knocked on Barner's door, they were in mutinous frame of mind. They wanted him to prove that he would be able to make Severiano the kind of money he claimed he could and obtain the contracts he promised. If not, they weren't interested.

"Look," Barner said, struggling to control his temper. "Nobody here has ever heard of Severiano Ballesteros. One day, maybe, everybody will have, but right now I can only make money if *you* play well. I can't sell a loser."

There is no question that Barner was talking from a position of strength. He had a great deal of personal charm and a pleasantly reassuring manner and—aided by the obvious advantages that a professional salesman has over two naive Spaniards in a foreign land with little English and hardly any business acumen between them—easily won them around. He readily agreed to them taking the five-year contract back to Spain to be examined by a local attorney. Severiano, his guard lowered, then agreed to sign on the dotted line, but not until he had mulled over his alternatives. Miller is positive that when he did so, he brought Miller into the equation.

"I really believe that Seve admired me a lot," Miller observes. "I know that he watched me at the World Cup in '73 at Nueva Andalucia, Spain. I was a young, sort of dashing player, swung hard, and I won the individual title. I'm not saying that I was his idol, but I took him a little bit by storm. I wasn't just a guy he'd read about; he had actually seen me in person. So when I met him, he knew what kind of player I was. I think I had an impact on him because we've always had a very special relationship. There was always a bond between Seve and me. Maybe it was because he was so young and I was in my prime . . . but it's always been there, to this day. We've always been close. Not close in that we go out per se, but when he went to UMI I really believe that he went with UMI because I was with UMI. One reason. Not all the reasons. But one good reason was, 'Geez, if it's good enough for Johnny Miller, maybe it's good enough for me.' And Ed Barner was a genius at selling himself."

From Florida, Ballesteros went to the U.S. PGA Tour Qualifying School to try for his card. There is not much difference between it and the PGA European Tour Players' School now, in terms of actual degree of difficulty, but seventeen years ago it was unrivaled as the most grueling academy of skill and nerve in sport. Held over six days, its sole purpose was, and still is, to determine which players are most likely to survive the competition on the Tour. Thus, around four hundred golfers fight for forty or so spots.

Ballesteros found himself hurled into this maelstrom without warning. He shot 77 and 75 in the opening rounds before finding his feet. On the sixth day he came within a hair's breadth of winning his player's card; but inexperience got the better of him and, after an outward 33, he took 40 over the back nine and missed qualifying by four strokes. When it was over, he was anxious to return to Europe. Barner had other plans for him. He wanted Severiano to return with him to California, where UMI would begin grooming him for stardom. Reluctantly, Ballesteros complied. They traveled to Los Angeles, where Ballesteros was to spend nearly two months in total at the home of Barner and his wife, studying English and playing the great Californian courses.

"It was a tough time for Seve," Barner admitted later. "I think he is still uncomfortable remembering those days at our house, alone and without his family."

When the news came that Franco had died, Ballesteros locked himself in his room and cried.

Brent Turley, who accompanied Ballesteros to Japan in November that year, where he tied seventeenth in the Dunlop Phoenix, remembers him as being very young and very lonely. "He kept his own counsel. Very impressive in a sense of his talent, although maybe he did not know then how good he was or how difficult it was. Nice kid. He was apprehensive about things around him. His brother Manuel was very much involved in his life, helping him make certain adjustments, but he wasn't with him in Japan and he wasn't with him for a good period of time when Ed had him in Los Angeles learning English and doing all these things to help him bridge the cultural and language gap."

When UMI had signed Miller who, as a nineteen-year-old university student, had rocked the golfing establishment by finishing eighth behind Casper in the 1966 U.S. Open, Barner's first action had been to alter Miller's name. John, he maintained, was bland and boring, while Johnny had an appealing boy-next-door quality about it. Miller was opposed to the change. Barner persuaded him to accept it by explaining to him the potential commercial benefits of such a decision, but to this day Miller still signs his name "John ny," leaving a space between the two n's.

Now Barner turned his attention to the Spaniard. He had already decided that something had to be done about the boy's name. S-e-v-e-r-i-a-n-o B-a-l-l-e-s-t-e-r-o-s, spelled out, added up to twenty characters. "How could they get that in a headline?" he reasoned. "How could they fit it on the head of a golf club? How many sports commentators would manage to say it?"

"What do they call you at home?" he asked the boy.

"Seve," Ballesteros replied.

"Sevvy," Barner mused. "And what was your mother's maiden name?"

"Sota."

"What do you think about using Sevvy Sota?"

Ballesteros saw red. He refused point-blank to even contemplate such a thing. Sevvy, or Seve, he would go along with, but as for Sota. . . . ? The very idea was anathema to him. So Seve Ballesteros it became; and Barner adopted the same, peculiarly proprietary interest in the young Spaniard as he had in Miller.

August 5, 1976, Dutch Open, Holland. "The name Severiano Ballesteros is beginning to take on an ominous ring. It does not yet carry the same charge of awe as, say, Walter Hagen did in the minds of his contemporaries, but things are moving that way."

So wrote Peter Dobereiner after Ballesteros had shot a course-record-equaling 65 in the first round of the Dutch Open. A fortnight had gone by since the swashbuckling young Spaniard, with his dark eyes, flashing smile, and absolute abandon on the golf course, had exploded into history at Birkdale, and still the shock waves had not yet abated. Huge galleries had flocked to see him in Scandinavia, where he was struck by lightning but finished third; in Switzerland, where he was runner-up; and they poured across the links-like fairways of Kennemer, desperate to catch a glimpse of the boy who was being hailed as a golfing genius. He did not disappoint them. Recklessness cost him a 73 and the lead in the second round, but he responded by attacking the course with still greater fervor and, in the final round, left the entire field standing as he swept to an eight-stroke, record-equaling victory of 275, thirteen under par.

"YOU CANNOT BELIEVE HOW WOMEN LOVED THAT GUY. THERE WERE SIX HUNDRED, SEVEN HUNDRED GROUPIES AT EVERY TOURNAMENT. ALL AGES, TOO!"

"That's the only way he knows how to play golf," Dobereiner concluded admiringly, "full steam ahead and damn the torpedoes."

After that it was as if somebody had opened a floodgate which once released could never ever be shut again. Ballesteros, like a helpless rock star being hoisted above the heads of a screaming crowd, was seized by the publicity machine and carried along on an increasingly frantic vortex of media attention and public adoration. Sponsors beat a path to Barner's door, and scores of teenage groupies, a phenomenon hitherto unheard of in European golf, followed him around the course and clamored outside his hotel room.

"You cannot believe how women loved that guy," former European Tour player Simon Hobday says enviously. "There were six hundred, seven hundred groupies at every tournament. They were just after Ballesteros. All ages, too!"

Once, when a reporter asked a group of teenage girls at a tournament which pop star Ballesteros reminded them of, one of them replied, "We have been here every day to see him this week. He's better looking than anyone in pop."

"He had a following from '76 on," Doust recalls. "Gary Hallberg told me he was at a fraternity house in North Carolina, and when Seve nearly won the British Open in '76 they went absolutely bonkers. So immediately he had a constituency that stretched around the world. He was pretty sunny [by nature] and he was very funny and he was something unique. On the circuit here we hadn't had a magic figure since Jacklin. We had some very, very good players, like Neil Coles—wonderful golfer, wonderful striker of the ball—but no magic. And nobody was magic. And, I mean, for someone like Seve to come along, who was very good-looking and played the shots he played and was so good, I think he was worshipped, in a way, and loved."

Ballesteros's impact on the whole of Europe, even at that early stage of his career, was that of a "Continental Jacklin," as Ken Schofield, the executive director of the European Tour, has described him, for the spiraling myth which surrounded him effortlessly transcended political and geographical boundaries. "Seve is big news all over Europe," Bernhard Langer said in the autumn of 1976. "Even in Germany, where golf does not often get into the newspapers. What he has done is a tremendous inspiration to other Continental players."

"If you got Seve competing for victory against an English player, or a Scottish or Irish player in Britain," golf writer Alan Booth recalls, "they were all rooting for Seve. And that, to me, is strange in a way. But I felt the same way. I was rooting for Seve even if it was against Sandy Lyle. It's a peculiar sort of attitude you get. You want Seve to win. Why? Because he's different. He's a one-off. You can't compare him with any other player that there's ever been."

"You were *fascinated* by Seve," remembers Mark Wilson, now consultant to Schofield on the Tour. "Every time you talked with Seve you became more and more fascinated. He went through that phase where he was desperate to learn English. I remember one time he came to me and he was very upset—he was very upset often—and he remonstrated with me quite fiercely, because he was asked at Birkdale, 'How do you feel now?' and he said, 'Mucho Contento,' and the newspaper I was working for saw this as a great headline and they put it right across the back page. And Seve came looking for me and he was not happy. Because, he said, it highlighted and exaggerated his lack of English. It was at that stage he declared that he would learn and speak English perfectly. Then came that phase when he had a marvelous grasp of English, not as we understand it, but he was literally translating Spanish into English. He didn't have colloquial English at all. One day he shot 74 and he came in and we asked: 'Seve, how could you shoot 74?' He said: 'Some days you wake up and you open the eyes and all is bright. Some days you wake and you open the eyes and all is dark. Today all was dark.' "

Ballesteros, who could hardly have been less affected by his runaway victory in the Dutch Open, whirled on through Europe like a hurricane, notching up a third place in the German Open, a fifth place in the Irish Open, a win in the Donald Swaelens Memorial Trophy in Belgium, and a share of eighth place in the Benson and Hedges International. By the time he reached Paris for the Lancome Trophy he was, as Pat Ward-Thomas noted, "riding a crest of rare confidence." That is not to say that he had become conceited or full of himself. Indeed, Hobday says, "He didn't become big-headed at all. He became more confident, yes, but he didn't become big-headed. You take a guy like Faldo, for example. Dear, oh dear, oh dear, oh dear. Faldo suddenly thought he was God's gift. Mind you, he was."

"He was one of the most confident sportsmen I ever met when he was eighteen," Doust remembers. "But I didn't find it very offensive. I don't think anybody found it offensive. He was very aloof sometimes. He was a bit like the Kennedy family. You were either for him or against him, and if I wrote anything critical of him he thought I'd let him down. And that was the only problem we ever had, really, is that he expected me to be—not his mouthpiece, but his cheerleader."

The extent of Ballesteros's self-belief at that age is simply illustrated by the fact that he composed his winner's speech on the eve of the final round of the Lancome Trophy when he shared the lead with no less a personage than Arnold Palmer.

Palmer, at forty-six, was no longer at his peak, but he was still a champion and still capable of drawing huge galleries. Thus, when the maestro and the prodigy who had elicited so much comparison with him teed off the following morning, a vast crowd of excited spectators surged after them. It was Palmer who drew first blood. Hitching up his trousers and smashing the ball powerfully down the fairway, he went out in 34, opening up a four-stroke advantage over the Spaniard. The writing, it appeared, was on the wall. But Ballesteros was not finished yet. Gathering himself for the fight, he began to attack the course with fearless iron play and flawless putting, in a way reminiscent of Palmer's own famous back nine charges, birdying five of the last eight holes for an inward half of 31 and victory.

Henry Cotton, reviewing the tournament, observed that he "is now the top European golfer and not afraid of any player in the game. I heard some of the golf stars here this week talking about him—they can't avoid doing that because he is here to stay—but I do not agree that he is a seven-day wonder. There may be better strikers of the ball, more mechanical players, but he was the best golfer, even though he won by the minimum."

Toward the end of the season two rather galling incidents occurred, though neither of them detracted in any way from the glory of Ballesteros's achievements in 1976 when he became, ultimately, the youngest player ever to win the Order of Merit, with earnings of £39,504, and the first Continental player to do so since Flory van Donck in 1953. He was also named Sportsman of the Year in Spain by *El Mundo deportivo de Barcelona*.

The first incident took place at Wentworth during the World Match Play, where Hale Irwin, who was playing Ballesteros and who was irritated by a rule which existed in Europe at that time but not in America allowing the tapping down of spike marks, accused the young Spaniard of trying to repair his pitch marks instead. It was all very unpleasant and resulted in Ballesteros losing both his temper and the match.

The second thing that happened also involved a rule and took place at the World Cup in Palm Springs, California. Ballesteros and Manuel Piñero were paired with Dave Stockton, the U.S. PGA champion, and Jerry Pate, winner of the 1976 U.S. Open, on the second day of play. At the sixth hole Piñero's approach shot finished three feet short of the green and Ballesteros's about six, so that the former's ball interfered with his partner's line. "Manuel, can you move your ball?" asked Ballesteros. Piñero obligingly marked his ball, picked it up, and dropped it into the palm of his black caddie Victor who, because he was going to clean Piñero's ball as soon as it was on the green, had a towel draped over his hand.

"*That is not allowed!*" shouted Pate, who was watching Piñero like a hawk.

In that instant both Ballesteros and Piñero realized that they were about to violate what is now Rule 21c (then 23), which states that "a ball may be cleaned and lifted [off the putting surface] except when it has been lifted: Because it is interfering with or assisting play (Rule 22, formerly 23)." Piñero snatched his ball out of Victor's hand before the caddie moved a muscle and before the two referees who were following the match knew what was happening. They played out the hole in silence. On the seventh tee Pate started saying that the Spaniards should be penalized two strokes.

"Who was the caddie?" a referee demanded.

Piñero claims that Pate then said something to the effect of "the caddie's that black guy." But he didn't react immediately, not having understood what Pate meant. When some Spanish friends who had overheard it translated it for him a few holes later, he was furious. "When I left the eighteenth green, I was out of my mind with anger," Piñero recalls. "Seve was the same. I said to him, 'If they penalize us two strokes, I'm going to hit Pate.'"

He tried to sit down next to Pate when the players went to sign their scorecards, but Ballesteros took the chair away and sat in it himself. The Spaniards had managed to better their opponents by three strokes after Piñero had birdied the seventh hole while Ballesteros had eagled the ninth. The American cause had been weakened by Pate who had dropped three consecutive shots from the seventh. At length, the referees appeared and informed them that the Spaniards wouldn't be penalized in view of the fact that nobody had actually seen the caddie clean Piñero's ball. The Americans were outraged.

"That incident at the sixth hole affected my whole round," Pate said, forgetting that it was his score of 69 that had prevented Spain from taking control of the tournament. "I played badly because of it."

Ballesteros fixed him with a cold stare. "You were not affected because you never played well anyway," he said clearly, putting an end to any further discussion.

The following day Ballesteros and Piñero stormed to an emotional two-stroke victory over the United States with an aggregate score of 574, becoming the first Spaniards and only the second European team to win the World Cup.

Back in Britain, IMG had belatedly woken up to the realization that a star had been born. Roddy Carr, who is now chief executive of Amen Corner, one of Severiano's three companies, but who was then responsible for the recruiting of young players for IMG, remembers the young Spaniard as being "absolutely exceptional. Absolutely. I mean, he was what I'd consider a matador, the ultimate matador of golf...the way he attacked the game, the contempt [with respect] and the aggressiveness. No matter where it was, where it went to, what lie, what position he was in, it was just go for it. And it was wonderful."

"Well, he'd be the ultimate guy you'd want to manage at that stage," says John Simpson, Nick Faldo's manager and friend at IMG. "One of the best, if not the best golfer for many, many years. Good-looking, modeled his clothes well, was good with people. He was confident, but a very, very nice guy. Very sympathetic. He always had a good heart. He would always see other people's point of view. Loved kids. He had a good feeling for other people, which I always thought was a very nice attribute to have. Everybody loved Seve. And he could play like hell, you know. So he'd be the ultimate golfer you'd want to have, and we could have done a helluva lot for him."

It was for all of these reasons that Mark McCormack, head of IMG, was so annoyed at having been pipped at the post by Barner and so determined that Ballesteros should be lured away from him. Doust claims that "the Spaniard became the central figure in McCormack's plan to dominate and control tournament golf on the continent." He cites as an example meetings held in October 1977 between McCormack and a dozen members of his team, the minutes of which were published in *The Sunday Times* and read: "It seems that Ballesteros is unhappy with Barner, and now may be the time to approach him. The stronger we become in golf, the more Barner is able to do for Ballesteros, so it is important to have Ballesteros. It was felt that an investment in hiring the person closest to Ballesteros to work for us in Spain [e.g. Manuel Ballesteros or Jorge Ceballos, chief executive of the Spanish PGA] should be considered if this would guarantee us Severiano Ballesteros as a client. At present, Ceballos is an obstacle in our way. He certainly has a big influence on [Antonio] Garrido and we think he is trying hard to influence Ballesteros as well."

All of these advances came to naught. "I can say this," Carr comments, "that the strategy of IMG to get Seve would have probably been the most aggressive strategy of all time. But the bottom line is that Seve was never going to be an IMG element, anyway. Never. It's just not him. He was always going to control his own destiny. IMG would have been a helluva lot better than Ed Barner was. IMG is the best in the business, really, and at that stage, Ed Barner was nothing. Nothing. He had no real qualification in that particular area, in my opinion."

One thing Ballesteros couldn't control, couldn't even staunch the flow of, was his rising tide of popularity. "When I became famous," he told me, "I feel like I lost a big part of myself. And this is the most difficult thing that can happen to anybody. I would say—"(he paused, searching for words)—

"it's not good to be famous. I think it's good to be recognized but not to be famous because it's like carrying a big stone on your shoulder all the time and it's difficult. Now I beat the pressure, but before I went through a very difficult time."

Piñero nods compassionately. "Seve was afraid of people when he was young—afraid of being with people—because he comes from a very small village. I don't think he actually likes publicity, and he had to live with it. Seve likes to be alone with a few friends. Now he's more outgoing but before he was introvert. When he was eighteen or nineteen he had to have dinners with old people, dinners with presidents of companies, and when he went to restaurants everybody knew him. So it was a very, very difficult life. But to explain that in Spain is impossible. I have a lot of friends and I have private conversations about it and some of them say, 'Seve is not a friendly person.' I say, 'He can't be. You don't understand what he's going through. He can't be, because he's got so much pressure inside himself.' To people on the outside, it will seem like he's always apart, but in a way, for his career, it is good that Seve wasn't a diplomat. Seve wouldn't be the same if he tried to change his attitude. It would affect his game. Seve has to be tight on the course—he needs to be nervous. He's like a car. He needs to be in overdrive."

Ironically, the sensation Ballesteros was causing throughout the Continent went almost unnoticed in his own country. "Seve has never had very good publicity in Spain," explains Piñero, "because in Spain we have a very peculiar way of seeing things. Fifteen years ago nobody knew what a golf professional was. Seve was the center of attention in the golf world when he was eighteen, but in Spain he wasn't. He was the best player, but they didn't understand what that meant. And I always, in private and in public, excuse Seve for the early years. To me, it doesn't matter what he did. He was allowed to make a lot of mistakes because he was in a situation where very few people would have the character to take it. He was put in a situation where, when he was sixteen, he was caddying for a hundred pesetas a day, and when he was nineteen, he wouldn't pour the tea for less than ten thousand pounds. *In two and a half years.* You cannot go from one extreme to the other in that time. It's impossible."

" 'Course he found [fame] difficult to deal with," Dave Musgrove says abruptly. "You can understand that, can't you? He had no background to it. That was obvious at the time. He didn't like it. He didn't like being mobbed for autographs. He didn't like having to go to receptions and presentations and all that crap."

"Well, it's very difficult for somebody like him, at the age of nineteen, to become so responsible for everything," says Chino Fernandez, Ballesteros's most steadfastly loyal friend. "A person of his age having to sit with people maybe three times older than him, and even though they speak the same language, they don't speak the same language because of the difference between their ages and everything. So he have to mature very quick. And I think he avoid one step of his life because he became famous very young. He didn't live one part of his life. And it was very tough for somebody of his age. Sooner or later, it gets you."

"So now I think his attitude is one of self-defense. He wants to be by himself. That's why for people who never live the same way, it's difficult to understand. He didn't live from eighteen to twenty-five. He wasn't allowed to be young. He was under the focus of the world at that age."

5

FIRE AND ICE

"No man is a hero to his valet."

Mme. Cornuel (1605–84)

Scientists, who have a label for everything, describe a person or thing that precipitates a change while remaining unchanged itself as a catalyst. Dave Musgrove was such a person. He walked into Ballesteros's life in April 1976—a thirty-two-year-old Midlander with grizzled hair, beetling brows, steely gray eyes, and wit like a scimitar—and for four seasons was the calm eye at the center of the storm that is the Spaniard. Musgrove is, and always was, unshakably down to earth. Ballesteros, at the age of eighteen, was intense, explosive, and overemotional. Doust described their relationship as "a marriage of strong wills." Ultimately, it ended in divorce.

Musgrove had begun his caddying career some twenty years before, at Hollinwell, a Nottinghamshire golf course close to his home in Kirkby-in-Ashfield, near Mansfield. He had continued to caddie throughout his teens and, when he became a draughtsman for the National Coal Board, had habitually taken his annual vacation during the British Open Championship so that he could try to find a bag. In 1972, by which time he had left the Coal Board for the aerospace engine division of Rolls-Royce, he was offered voluntary dismissal. He took it. Years later, when he was asked why he had done it—what the appeal was in caddying, he said it was the call of the open

57

road. "The chance of a big check and the freedom of the road. And if you've ever worked in an office you'll know the difference."

By then Musgrove had already worked for several of the top players, including Roberto De Vicenzo, through whom he had come to know Manuel Ballesteros and Chino Fernandez. He was caddying for the latter in the PGA Championship at St. George's in 1975 when he first saw Ballesteros. "I saw this lad practicing away and the first thing I noticed was he had legs longer than his body and a great big pair of hands. He stood a long way from the ball to give himself plenty of room to swing. I looked at the golf bag [a Dunlop] and it said 'Ballesteros.' So I said to Fernandez, 'Is he any relation to Manuel?' 'Yeah,' he says, 'he's his brother.' "

If Musgrove was impressed then, he soon became even more so, for the young Spaniard improved markedly during the course of the season. But it did not occur to him to try and caddie for him until almost twelve months later, when he arrived at the French Open at Le Touquet to discover that Fernandez had hurt his finger and withdrawn. It was not a catastrophe. The competition for bags then was not as stiff as it has become, and Musgrove simply settled down in front of the clubhouse to wait until a player without a caddie happened by. Before long, Manuel appeared.

"Need a caddie?" Musgrove said hopefully.

Manuel hesitated. "Best thing you can do," he said, "is wait for my brother to come. He's playing good."

So Musgrove waited. When Ballesteros came striding up the path, he remembered the Englishman and greeted him shyly.

"Do you want me to caddie for you?" Musgrove asked, coming straight to the point.

"You—work for me?" Ballesteros said, making sure he understood the question.

"Yeah."

"Okay."

"So we set off," Musgrove says, describing their first round together. "He'd never seen the course before. He chipped up for a four on the first hole, birdied the second, birdied the third, hit a great drive on the fourth, a par-five, and then hit a three-iron on the green and missed the putt for eagle. I thought, 'This is all right for a nineteen-year-old.' The next hole, a par-three, he hits it middle of the green and missed it from about twelve feet. But he went off his head. Shouting and screaming. Anyway, he shot 66 and won the pro-am and didn't seem to think a lot of it. Didn't think it was a big deal, I don't s'pose. Very hot that week. Incredibly hot. He played all right, but every time he hit a bad shot or got into trouble his head would come off. I don't know where he finished—not bad [tied for eighth with earnings of £569]. 'Course there was no money in those days."

After the French Open Musgrove started to work for the Spaniard regularly, only surrendering the bag to his friend Dick Draper at the British Open at Birkdale because he didn't want to let Roberto De Vicenzo down. But by the time Ballesteros swept to his first European Tour victory in the Dutch Open, Musgrove was running low on funds. He informed his boss that he was returning to England to earn some money with which to subsidize his caddying.

IF BALLESTEROS CAN BE SAID TO HAVE ONE MAJOR FLAW IN HIS CHARACTER, IT IS AN OBSESSION WITH MONEY.

"Aren't you going to go to Germany?" Ballesteros said, aghast.

"I said, 'I've got to work,' " Musgrove recalls. " 'Course, he never would pay any more money."

If Ballesteros can be said to have one major flaw in his character, it is an obsession with money. Tales of his meanness are legion. Given the circumstances of his childhood it is understandable, if not excusable, but it has, nonetheless, been the source of a great deal of heartache and controversy during his career. Not surprisingly, it has been the men who have carried his bag who have complained longest and loudest. Most caddies feel, quite reasonably, that they play a valuable part in the success of their player and that, when the said player becomes a very rich man through their combined efforts on the course, he should allow more than a few crumbs to fall from his table. Musgrove, for instance, says he was paid a "minimum wage and 5 percent. Well, minimum is what he paid, which happened to be better than normal. But it could never be described as good."

Minimum wage on Tour these days is around £250 per week, but in 1976 it was less than £120, plus 5 percent, while Draper received £250 for his week's work at the British Open in 1976.

"A lot of people ask me how much money I got off him for winning the Open in 1979," Musgrove says. "And I always say, I was there for ten days and the total amount of money that changed hands was, I had to lend him a fiver. Which he paid me back."

"I've had my ups and downs with him on money," comments Ian Wright, who caddied for Ballesteros in 1988 and 1989. "I don't think generally he's a mean person, he's just careful. I felt, in the position he was in, he could have paid for a few more of the flights and things, particularly when the bad years came. You always felt . . . that he could have provided flights to the States, which is what other players do for their caddies. But he always paid a fair wage and a good percentage, so one balances out the other, I suppose."

In January 1977 Ballesteros experienced firsthand what it was like to be underpaid. He was drafted into the Spanish army, where he earned the princely sum of two pounds a week as a private. In Spain, national service is compulsory. But where a conscripted serviceman has to serve up to twenty months, a volunteer, provided he has a primary school certificate, can choose his own posting. Ballesteros, of course, didn't have a certificate. He was too proud to sit for an army examination either. "I will not go through any examination whatsoever," he told Jorge Ceballos, who later became his manager. "Not even the U.S. Qualifying School that the Americans want me to do. I have nothing to prove in golf and I do not regret not having as much culture as other people. I shall learn my own way through life." However, it was some months before the authorities who wanted him to undergo written tests relented. At Birkdale it was announced that he had been assigned to the staff of a Spanish general on a U.S. base in Saragossa, but he ended up serving most of his time at a small nine-hole golf course outside Madrid, the Centro Duportivo Barberan; where he gave exhibitions and instructed air force officers in correct backswing technique.

"He only pretended to [go into the army], didn't he?" Musgrove says sourly. "Well, he didn't do a great deal, did he? It never stopped him playing. Just did a bit of time in the winters. He never did a great deal in the army. Basic training, that was about all. He never did as much as Elvis."

Doust, who went to interview him for *The Sunday Times* the week before he was sworn into the Spanish air force, observed that since he had turned professional Ballesteros had grown enormously strong and was filling out almost daily. "He is six feet tall and weighs twelve stone, eight pounds [approximately 176 pounds, American] a stone up on last year. [His 1996 weight was listed in the PGA Tour media guide as 195 pounds.] He can carry eleven golf balls in one hand and the air force doctors found he could expand his massive chest from the normal 95 to 105 centimeters in one searing breath." He was also struck by how natural and at ease Ballesteros seemed in his own environment, how little affected by the successes of the previous season. "Spoilt, yes; confident and magisterial, yes. Subject to some of golf's blackest moods, Severiano Ballesteros remains a warm and friendly boy, generous of his time and amazingly untouched by fame or fan mail."

By spring Ballesteros was ranked tenth in the world—Nicklaus and Crenshaw were No. 1 and 2—and had been given extended "leave" by the Spanish military to play in the U.S. Masters and on the European circuit. Those players and journalists who had spent the early part of 1977 commenting wistfully on what a shame it was the Europe's best player was confined to barracks and would be unable to defend his position as leading money winner, were thrown back on their heels as Ballesteros suddenly laid down his rifle, combat jacket, and boots, and embarked on a crusade far more important to him than defending a country not at war. In his first Tour event, the Spanish Open at La Manga, he showed glimpses of his best form and finished tied for third.

Ballesteros followed this performance with a rather poor thirty-fifth-place finish in the Madrid Open, but recovered almost immediately and was placed fifth in the Italian Open. After that, there was no stopping him. He won the French Open at Le Touquet, was twentieth in the European PGA Championship, and then overcame Faldo at the first extra hole of a play-off for the Uniroyal International, despite being plagued by back trouble and receiving painkilling injections all week. Then in July he was fifteenth at the British Open Championship at Turnberry. "He was going nicely and then he blew it toward the end of the third round," Musgrove recalls. "The last round he was thumping his driver on the floor and bent it, and he was trying to straighten it up again and it broke. So he had to drive off with a three-wood. He said: 'These holes are playing long.' I said: 'This is where normal people play from.' "

The next week Ballesteros overcame further back problems to finish three shots clear of the field at the Swiss Open. He swept all before him in Japan, where he won the Japanese Open and the Dunlop Phoenix, and in New Zealand, where he won the Otago Classic. Finally, in December, he teamed up with Antonio Garrido in the Philippines to bring glory to Spain for the second time in the World Cup. By the end of the season he was Europe's leading money winner once more, had gone fifteen straight tournaments without once three-putting, and had a stroke average of 71.06. Only Byron Nelson, Ben Hogan, and Sam Snead had triumphed so often in a single year, and no player had ever won in seven different countries in a season. In Europe he was a phenomenon, and his ability to compete at an international level was indisputable. All that remained now was for him to prove that he was a world-class golfer by contending with, and beating, the world's best players: namely, the Americans.

Sunday, April 2, 1978, Greater Greensboro Open, North Carolina. Severiano Ballesteros took three putts to get down on the final green of the tournament today, but it couldn't have mattered less. Victory was his by a shot. Long after he had signed his scorecard, having established an unassailable lead, America's finest were still limping off the golf course. One by one they would gather their wits, dust themselves off, pause before the leaderboard to shake their heads in puzzlement, and then head for the locker room like broken men.

The cause of all this devastation was in the press center, wreathed in smiles. "I was lucky," Ballesteros said feelingly. "Everything went wrong for me but it all came right in the end. I don't know how I win tournaments. I came here and my game has no confidence. I was very worried that I miss cut. No one likes to do that. The last two rounds I get confidence and I do my best, but I never think I win."

The facts of the matter were these: that Ballesteros, exactly one week before his twenty-first birthday, had just become the first foreigner to win his first regular U.S. Tour event he entered—previously he had only played in the Masters, which is a major; the first nonmember to win on the U.S. Tour since Harold Henning at the 1966 Texas Open; the first player ever to win after only qualifying by one stroke; the first player to win his first regular Tour event entered since Crenshaw (1973 Texas Open) and Marty Fleckman (1966 Cajun Classic); and the third-youngest player to win a regular tournament, being a few months older than Raymond Floyd was when he won at St. Petersburg in 1963 and Horton Smith had been when he won the 1928 Oklahoma City Open.

"Everything went wrong," reiterated the young Spaniard, who was explaining in his halting English why he considered his achievement to be more incredible than all the dry statistics in the world could show. "My plane left Madrid last Saturday at 1:00 P.M., but after three hours, in the middle of the Atlantic, the captain tell us that an engine give trouble and we turn back. I was very frightened. We land again in Madrid and, I tell you, if there had been a tournament in Europe I would have gone there. After six hours' wait we set out again in another plane and land in New York at La Guardia instead of Kennedy. There is a further four-hour delay before I connect to Greensboro, and I arrive Monday morning nearly twenty-four hours late and very tired."

"HE PLAYED SO INSTINCTIVELY AND HE PLAYED REALLY TO JUST SLASH AND BURN EVERY GOLF COURSE HE COULD PLAY. TO ME, HE'S BEEN THE MOST EXCITING PLAYER THAT I'VE EVER SEEN BESIDES PALMER."

Subsequently, Ballesteros had recorded scores of 72 and 75 in the opening rounds to scrape through the qualifying and, after following them with a 69, had been five strokes off the pace going into the final day. Then, on a lightning-blue day, when temperatures went soaring into the high eighties and humidity sapped the resistance of the strongest, the raven-haired Spanish youth blazed a fiery trail to glory, going out in 31 and demolishing Fuzzy Zoeller and Jack Renner en route. Counting those in 1977, it was his sixth consecutive tournament victory, for he had won the Kenya Open at the beginning of the new season.

Of all the American players, perhaps Crenshaw, who had first played with Ballesteros at the British Open in 1977, was most overwhelmed by his brilliance.

"He played so instinctively and he played really to just slash and burn every golf course he could play," says Crenshaw, himself one of the gentlest, kindest, most-gifted players the game has seen. "He played with total abandon. To me, he's been the most exciting player that I've ever seen besides Palmer. I've always been an admirer of Seve's. He's an artist, he really is. To watch him try to figure out problems is fantastic, because when he's in a little bit of trouble he has great facial expressions. He really does wear his heart on his sleeve. He's got just an incredible imagination, and you can see what he's trying to do to the shot. All the time, he's working on something. I've seen him pull off some of the darndest shots I've ever seen.

"His instinct is incredible. And he looks so good. His hands go on the club and the way he sets up to the ball, he looks like he was born with a club. It's magical. But he's a fierce competitor, and I think he's very funny. I think he's got a great sense of humor. He gets down, like the rest of us, but he fights his way out of it. He's great for the game. *God, he's great.* I think he's marvelous, I really do. I always have."

Two days after his victory at Greensboro, Ballesteros was offered his U.S. Tour card. Ordinarily, he would have had to go through the rigors of the Qualifying School just like any other player but, in an unprecedented move, Deane Beman, the PGA Tour commissioner, said that the Spaniard had proved his ability and would have sixty days to accept the offer. This met with mixed response. Many of the American pros were outraged that Ballesteros should be made an exception of, and called for the decision to be rescinded. Frank Beard, a U.S. Tour pro, reminded everyone that the whole purpose of the Players' School was to prove that a professional was a good enough player to compete, and pointed out that neither Graham Marsh [twenty-eight wins worldwide] nor Oosterhuis [four times the European money-list winner] had been given an exemption. "So why Ballesteros?" he asked. Obviously, Ballesteros himself felt complimented but there were rumors that, because U.S. Tour regulations stipulated that all members had to play a minimum of fifteen events on their own circuit and no more than three elsewhere, Ed Barner was trying to negotiate a deal with Beman whereby the card offer would remain open indefinitely, and would also allow the Spaniard to fulfill his commitments in Europe.

Nothing has quite such a bracing effect on Ballesteros as antagonism, and he responded to the American cold shoulder by surging into the lead at the Tournament of Champions, at La Costa, a fortnight later. Indeed, he played so well that after three rounds he had a four-stroke advantage. Then, incredibly, he lost.

Now, if Ballesteros had been just another twenty-one-year-old golfer and had been subject to all the usual pressures and fears which govern the performances of young players, this loss would simply have been put down to inexperience and forgotten about five minutes hence. But he wasn't. He

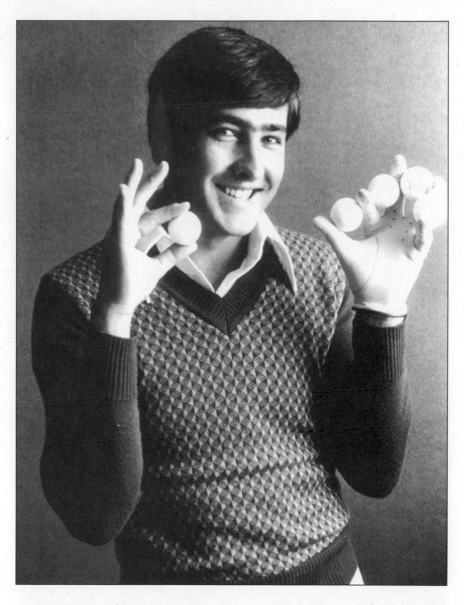

At twenty-one, one of the youngest competitors in international golf, Seve has just learned that he has been officially exempted from the PGA Tour's Qualifying School by Tour commissioner Deane Beman. America is about to be introduced to Spain's whiz kid. (Peter Howe photograph, Globe Photos Inc., 1997)

was absolutely unafraid. Yet, in his final round, on a sunny, breezy day perfect for golf, he dropped two strokes at the relatively easy opening hole when he drove into a bunker, another stroke at the fifth where he was in the water, and another at the sixth where he failed to get up and down. Altogether, he had a miserable outward half and the tally at the end of it was 40. Gary Player, meanwhile, the Masters champion, who had been seven strokes behind at the start of the day, had gone out in 32. The tournament was won and lost on the front nine, and the only clue to Ballesteros's collapse might lie with his playing partner, Trevino. It seems the Mexican held an animated conversation (or monologue) with him the entire length of the first hole, while Ballesteros tacked his way from tee to green, but that for the remainder of the round a deathly hush hung over their little group.

A week later he was in contention again. As Musgrove says, "He don't give up, you see, he's very intense. He never gives up. But then it takes a lot out of him." Ballesteros showed no outward signs of weakening at the Madrid Open when he shot an opening 66 to establish a three-stroke lead, but he did admit that after playing seven seventy-two-hole events in eight weeks he was feeling the strain, not only of golf but of the increasing number of interviews that the Spanish media, who had lately woken up to the concept of a golfer as a star, were demanding of him. But Faldo, who partnered with him, said, "It was as if he had a 66 written on the board before he went out, so easily did he do it." Ballesteros credited his fine round to a tip of Musgrove's. "Dave is a very good caddie. I have confidence in him and if I go to America next year, he comes with me."

A trio of three-putts on the back nine cost him the title, but he still finished third and followed his fifth-place finish in the Spanish Open with a second in the French, which the South African Dale Hayes won by an astonishing eleven strokes. At last he reached Britain, where he overpowered Faldo and marched confidently to victory in the Martini International. There is a lovely story of how, on that day, all the Spanish restaurant staff in London, among whom the bold young Severiano had become a folk hero, deserted their posts and drove up in convoy to the RAC Epsom to support him. Whether or not it is true, it conjures up delightful pictures of Ballesteros, like a Latin pied piper, leading a band of merry chefs and waiters, all in their white uniforms and hats and carrying their cooking utensils, along the fairways. Whatever—he entertained the galleries with a succession of magical shots, the most singular of which was a two-iron approach to the difficult eighth, a kidney-shaped green which falls away sharply on three sides, which he holed for an eagle two from 150 yards.

It was not long after this that he and Faldo, by now his chief rival in Europe, gave the following illuminating interview to Renton Laidlaw, in Europe's *Golf World*:

RL: Do you really think you can do justice to your [ability by] splitting yourself between two major world circuits?

SB: It will be tough for me. It means a demanding schedule but I have been offered my card and I have enough confidence in myself to feel I can cope successfully as long as my program is carefully worked out.

NF: I think you are going to find it extremely difficult to play well on both sides of the Atlantic. Will you be getting any special treatment over there to make it easier for you? There are so many rules—I mean, having to play fifteen tournaments to retain your card—that sort of thing.

SB: We are trying to arrange the whole thing with Mr. Beman, the U.S. commissioner, at the moment, and I think it will work out all right. I'm hopeful that I can get the type of deal which will enable me to become a transatlantic golfer without tiring myself out.

RL: What lessons have you learned in the past twelve months that have helped you become a better player, Seve?

SB: Before this season I played good some rounds, bad others. This year I play much more steadily. Before, I tried to attack the golf course with every shot. Now I attack when it is best to attack and I play safe if that is best. I'm not so impetuous. I think my way around better.

NF: What he means is that in the past year he has moved from being good to being bloody brilliant!

RL: How worrying is your back trouble?

SB: It's worrying enough for me to have seen several specialists, but I think it is okay if I do not overdo the practice. . . . I can live with the problem. It's okay and, after all, I am not as bad as Lee Trevino, who has to hang upside down every morning to get himself into shape.

RL: Any golfer as successful as you, Seve, is very much in demand. How do you cope with the pressure?

SB: You just have to. There is far more to professional golf than just playing in tournaments. There are regular meetings with the press, photographic sessions to fit in. . . . I suppose I have to be choosy up to a point, but I try to please most people. I'll admit that it can be tiring at times, but it's part of the price you pay for success.

NF: I agree with Seve. You certainly cannot afford to get fed up with all the extra demands. The hassle of interviews for the newspapers, radio, and television is something we can all live with and all want to live with because it is a measure of success, and being successful is a nice feeling.

RL: How much has Severiano helped you?

NF: We are good friends, as you know, off the course—although we thump each other in private. No, seriously, there is a lot of rivalry between us and it's great. . . . Seve has a tremendous feel for the game. . . . but what impresses me most about him is the way he works the ball. There is not a shot that he cannot hit. . . . He's exciting to watch. . . . All he ever sees is the pin and the hole. He is dedicated to winning, is super-confident, and will win many more events in the next few years. Didn't Lee Trevino say recently that every fifteen years a player of Nicklaus's class is born and he believed Seve was the latest Nicklaus? I agree with that view. That's how highly I rate him.

RL: Is it true that you don't like America, Seve?

SB: Maybe. I'll whisper it—'Yes,' for various reasons. . . . I cannot ever see myself full-time in America. . . . One of the big problems I have faced in America is that you have far too much time to think. Sometimes you play in the morning at seven o'clock, are finished by noon, and are not playing again until two o'clock the next day.

RL: What's your one big burning ambition?

NF: Winning the Open Championship would be the greatest thing that could happen to me.

SB: I'd like to win the British Open. That's my ambition. Coming second to Johnny Miller in 1976 at Royal Birkdale is a bigger career highlight than some of my victories—that's how important I consider the Open.

The British Open in 1978 was at St. Andrews. Ballesteros was in peak form when it came around and more contented and at peace with himself than he had been in ages. "Ballesteros never stops smiling," Frank Keating remarked in the *Guardian*. Nor did he. And at press conferences he engaged in teasing skirmishes with his critics, saying, in heavily accented English, "You cannot write all the time about me in the rough, because there's no rough here." He was even happier after scoring 69 in the first round to share second place with Jack Newton, Floyd, and Weiskopf, one stroke behind Japan's Isao Aoki.

"In 1978," British professional Ken Brown says, "he was playing absolutely brilliant golf. I played the first two rounds with him and he played almost fearlessly—much more aggressively than he does now. I was singing his praises and Jerry Pate, who we were playing with, was trying to say that he wasn't that good."

Unfortunately, Ballesteros's boldness and derring-do robbed him of the chance to win his first British Open a year sooner than he did. In the second round he stood on the tee of the infamous Road Hole seventeenth and, like Palmer before him, curved a 325-yard drive far into the crowd in front of the Jigger Inn. All he had needed to do was to par the final two holes in order to gain a two-stroke advantage, and the assumption was that he had elected to go for maximum length rather than safety. But Brown says that it was the wall of photographers in front of the tee, all clicking and shirring at the wrong moments, that put him off. His second shot from the tee was played with great ferocity—"the stroke of an angry young man," someone said—and traveled some 350 yards into the great unknown. From that position, he managed to reach the green with a four-iron and two-putted from thirty feet. He shared the lead with Crenshaw and Aoki at the end of the round at 139, and was only four strokes off the pace going into the final day's play. But after his third-round 76, a closing 73 left him tied for seventeenth place.

"He should have won," Musgrove says firmly. "He played a lot better at St. Andrews [than he did at Lytham], but he hadn't learned to play the course. He should have walked away with it. It was like five in the afternoon and he was seven under par for the tournament, turned for home, and the wind dropped, and, by the time he got to the seventeenth, he'd realized what chances he'd missed. So he hit one out of bounds, the other side of the hotel—to the *right* of the hotel—and lost his rag. But he played incredibly."

It is only when one looks at Ballesteros's record for a season such as 1978, when he finished at the top of the money list for the third consecutive time, that one can see why it is that people talk about him being in a slump when he goes for three tournaments without being in the top ten or for a month without a victory. Between leaving St. Andrews and arriving at Walton Heath for the European Open, he finished first, first, tied for fourth, tied for second, and first. His initial victory was the German Open which, by all rights, he shouldn't have been attending. In April he had been honored with an invitation to play in the U.S. PGA Championship at Oakmont, the first official exemption ever issued to a foreign player, but, having been mistakenly advised by Barner that the U.S. PGA was not one of golf's major events, had graciously turned it down.

"It's the major that he's usually prone to miss the cut in," explains Joe Collet, one of his managers, "and he had very good commercial possibilities in Europe at the time. It wasn't just the fact that he got an appearance fee, but I think it meant pushing an endorsement deal . . . with Braun [the tournament sponsor], which was a clothing company. They [the press] criticized the management [UMI] for doing something which, arguably, was detrimental to his career in the record books, but on the other hand it was financially rewarding and he was an important guy and he played in an event whose field was vastly improved by the fact that he was playing in it. I don't feel bad about it. I'd feel bad about it if it happened five years ago when he was at his peak, and he gave up a major to chase money which he didn't need. But at the time he was very young and the PGA wasn't a very big deal. It still isn't as important as the Masters or the Open Championship."

While Collet is unquestionably right about the U.S. PGA Championship's inferiority to the other three majors—he is wrong about how little it probably mattered, given that Ballesteros was still young and not yet the force to be reckoned with that he later became. Ballesteros was at the top of his game when he reached Cologne for the German Open, and if he had gone to Oakmont instead, who knows what he might have achieved. He had a four-stroke lead at 131 after two days' play and, in his final charge for victory, reduced the 594-yard ninth, one of the longest holes in golf, to a drive and a three-wood.

"Can you believe that?" asked Gary Player, who was in the field, with a theatrical expression of awe. "The Ballesteroses of this world will be shooting regularly in the 50s in years to come. Thank goodness I've got my titles won."

The following week Ballesteros, told by Musgrove that he needed to shoot 32 on the back nine at Vasatorp to win the Scandinavian Open, proceeded to do exactly that to defeat Hayes by a stroke. It was his eleventh victory in eight countries and on four continents in sixteen months. A fortnight later he won the Swiss Open.

Through that period of his life Ballesteros can only be described as a phenomenon. Weiskopf said that he was the most charismatic player that he had seen since Arnold Palmer, and Jack Nicklaus and Roberto De Vicenzo predicted that he would win the Masters several times. Everywhere he went he left a lasting impression.

"The first time I saw him was at the 1978 Madrid Open," recalls Nick Price, the U.S. PGA and British Open champion. "He was hitting five-iron shots on the practice tee that day and they were probably going the same distance as my three-iron was. I just couldn't believe how strong he was. He swung the club with such ease and grace, and you couldn't figure out where all the power came from. I think the thing that was so outstanding in those days was the way he could get up and down from anywhere. He hit shots that most of us couldn't even dream of. He hit these little finesse wedge shots and little bump and run eight-irons and things. He just had wonderful hands and wonderful hand-eye coordination. I think what he did with his game [in later years] was to try not to hit the ball as far and he became a better all-round player. He may not have that kind of eye-opening game that people used to enjoy, but golf's not about that, unfortunately. John Daly's in that league now, in that if he wants to have any longevity he's going to have to throttle back."

"I feel very privileged to have seen him play in those years," Irishman David Feherty says. "There are a lot of parallels between him then and John Daly now, because it is a very expensive way to play the game, giving people what they want. You can't afford to give people what they want in this game. 'Hit the driver, hit the driver,' they'd all shout, and he'd get the driver and have a lash at it. His game was extraordinary in that he hit the ball in the middle of the clubface a lot, even when he hit it a long way wide, and that's always, I feel, a sign of a player that's committed. You know, when he does start to swing well, he's going to be very, very good."

In Liz Kahn's biography *Tony Jacklin: The Price of Success*, Jacklin observed: "Ballesteros is a shot in the arm. He is just something else. He plays the game in the right spirit—smashes it long, ambles after it, looks for the hole, *whack!* and it all looks such fun. He gives you the feeling that he's actually enjoying it, and he is. He's won in America, which is great, and it will be interesting to see what he will do there in the future. At the moment, he's doing it all and enjoying it all, but when it gets too much, for whatever reason, that's when the problems start. He'll not be human if he doesn't go through some form of what I've been through."

There was no doubt that Ballesteros did give the impression he was enjoying himself. And why shouldn't he have been? He had everything a young golfer could ever dream of. He had fame, he had wealth, he had an adoring following, and he had a divine talent for the game. He should have been the sunniest, most contented man alive. The fact that he wasn't has a lot to do with the fact that nothing in this world is ever entirely what it seems. Take, for instance, the Hennessy Cup, a biennial match between Europe and the British Isles. Ballesteros played a shot there which had deservedly gone down in history. He came to the tenth hole of the Brabazon course at The Belfry, one up in his match against Faldo, and stood looking contemplative while the Englishman struck a mid-iron off the tee. Faldo was not being particularly cautious, nor was he playing safe. He was just doing what any rational golfer would do when faced with a 255-yard par-four, with water down the right and the green tucked in the midst of a ring of trees, around a corner and across a pond. As a consequence, he was startled when the Spaniard plucked the cover from his driver. So was the crowd. They strained against the ropes to obtain a better view. Ballesteros smashed the ball toward the distant flagstick. It soared out into the pale sky, carried a fifty-foot tree some 250 yards from the tee, faded into a cross-wind and dropped onto the green, ten feet from the pin, as easy as you please. There is a picture of Faldo walking open-mouthed from the tee. It was truly a marvelous golf shot and merits the comparison it had with Gene Sarazen's fairway wood for an albatross at Augusta.

HE HAD FAME, HE HAD WEALTH, HE HAD AN ADORING FOLLOWING, AND HE HAD A DIVINE TALENT FOR THE GAME. HE SHOULD HAVE BEEN THE SUNNIEST, MOST CONTENTED MAN ALIVE.

The shame was that Ballesteros's performance on the golf course that week was slightly marred by two things, one of which was the comments of Angel Gallardo, the captain of the Continental side. "Gallardo," wrote Mitchell Platts in *Golf World*, "the much-respected Spaniard who had tugged at our sleeves four years earlier to go and witness a boy he regarded as a golfing genius, insisted [that]: 'Seve thinks only of money. He does not think enough about the team.' " The young Spaniard . . . had stated that summer that he might not play. "But Gaetan Mourgue d'Algue, much involved at that time in organizing the match, intervened. He offered to increase the appearance money from twenty-five hundred pounds to four thousand. Seve played but Gallardo was unamused by his compatriot's attitude that week."

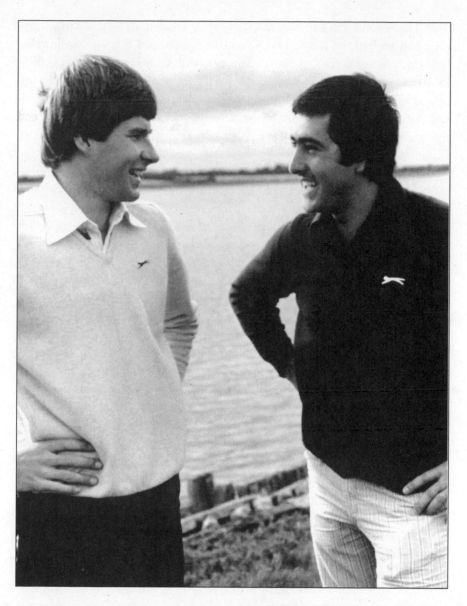

Friends, foes, and legends-to-be: Nick Faldo spent the early part of his career "hoping there was going to be some competitive rivalry" between himself and the Spaniard, but "Seve was too good." The two future international masters are shown during a magazine interview in 1978. (© Phil Sheldon)

The second incident was the bombshell Ballesteros dropped after Europe lost to Britain, 17½ to 14½, when he announced that he wouldn't be helping Spain to defend its World Cup title that year. He said it was ridiculous for a professional to be asked to play for a return of one thousand pounds. When it was put to him that many players considered it their patriotic duty, he declared that Spain had never encouraged him and neither had the Spanish Golf Federation. He said that he felt more loyalty to his fans in Britain.

Manuel Piñero, his first World Cup partner, who feels that "one of the most important things for a professional in any sport is to play for your country, and if you refuse to play for your country I'm not happy with you," was livid and told him so. "I have a great admiration, not only for Seve but for all the Spanish professionals, because of our background," Piñero says, "because of what we've come through. And because of that I will not accept anybody who tries to keep my opinions quiet. When it comes to important decisions I think that Seve feels that he can come to me and say, 'Manuel, how do you feel?' I will give always my honest word. But sometimes my honest word—and it did happen twice—is not to say 'Yes' or to say 'You are the best and you have the reasons.' Sometimes my honest word has to be, 'Seve, you're wrong and you have made a mistake.'"

Musgrove had a very similar relationship with Ballesteros at that time, if rather more stormy, as was apparent at the European Open. On the eve of the tournament at Walton Heath, Musgrove was standing beside the practice green waiting, slightly impatiently, for Ballesteros to finish putting. He was anxious to get home. Only one of the headlights on his car was working and he was worried about driving after dark. Musgrove cast a glance at the Spaniard's bowed head and his rhythmic stroke. He was convinced that nothing would be gained by owning up to his predicament, and even thought that Ballesteros might deliberately extend his practice session out of spite. So when twilight drew its silvery cape across the course, Musgrove simply took the clubs, put them beside the Spaniard's street shoes in the clubhouse, and left the course. The following morning he was standing in the car park, as usual, when his employer whisked in.

"Fetch the clubs," Ballesteros ordered when he spotted his caddie.

"*I* haven't got them," Musgrove said coldly. "I left them with you last night."

Ballesteros stared at him. "You have got them," he insisted. A rather fruitless row ensued, followed by a frantic search for the missing golf clubs. They were nowhere to be seen. Ballesteros, his face a picture of misery, was forced to borrow a set from the local pro and "played badly, scored badly, played as best I could, but what can you do?"

The irony was that after six holes PGA European Tour tournament referee George O'Grady came out to tell them that the clubs had been found. A well-meaning official had seen them in the clubhouse the night before and had put them in a member's empty locker for safekeeping. There was nothing Ballesteros could do. Under the Rules of Golf he had to complete his round with the borrowed set, which he did and scored 75.

Earlier in the week there had been another clash between the two of them. Ballesteros's practice session had not gone well and, eventually, after a series of imperfect shots, he rammed his club back into the bag and stalked moodily off the range. Musgrove glared at his departing back and began to gather together balls, clubs, tees, and towels. At last he heaved the bag onto his shoulder and swung round in time to see the courtesy car which had been waiting for Ballesteros start forward.

"*Hey!*" Musgrove screamed at the top of his lungs.

The driver stopped in confusion. Musgrove marched menacingly up to his window and swore at him. "What d'you do that for?" he demanded.

The man shrank back into his seat, alarmed. "He told me to," he said pleadingly, jerking a thumb toward the passenger seat.

Musgrove threw the clubs into the car with some force and climbed in after them. "Well, you're a right bastard," he said to the back of the Spaniard's head. Ballesteros kept his eyes fixed on the road.

"So I got fired again," Musgrove says dryly, "and re-employed the following morning at a pound extra a week."

He turns his gray gaze on the horizon. "People would never believe me what a bastard he was."

Doust can: "He was very, very, *very* tough on caddies. I mean, really cruel."

Nick de Paul, who caddied for Ballesteros when he won the British Open in 1984, agreed. "Seve gives you hell every other hole out there, complaining about everything from golf to life in general. But you have to take the abuse—that way he's not battling on his own—which is all part of the business."

In the book he cowrote with Musgrove, Hopkins says that, "after several tumultuous years with Ballesteros [Musgrove] could no longer tolerate the abuse that was heaped upon him at, it seemed, almost every turn. Caddying for Seve at the Open at Lytham was hell, he was to say later. 'Three weeks later he was still chewing me out. But there were also wonderful moments with Seve. He is so gifted it's not true.' "

By the end of 1979 they had parted company. "I'd had enough of him and he'd had enough of me," Musgrove admits. In 1978, however, any rocky patch in their relationship was just another thing for Ballesteros to store away in his memory and, like an oyster with a grain of sand, used to spur him on to still greater achievements. He has a memory like an elephant when it comes to remembering snubs, and has a habit of bringing them up months or even years later without prior warning. In the middle of that season, for example, he was having a relaxed conversation with several journalists in the lounge of a Southport hotel when he suddenly brought up the subject of the Tournament of Champions, which he had lost by shooting 79 on the final day. "They [the Americans] all come over to me, smile and say I have bad luck. They pat me on the shoulder. But they are happy and I see it. Why they not want me to win?" He gave a short laugh, the way he does when he is very hurt or bitter. "Everybody said how sad it was. I led for so long, then I shot a bad last round. They say it was too much pressure for me. Not true. I lost because I was never meant to win." Then he smiled.

"But let me tell you something else. In my *destino* there are many wins to come."

CAR-PARK CHAMPION

"They all kept trying to say he was lucky, but Jack Nicklaus holed in one on the first day."

Dave Musgrove on Ballesteros's 1979 British Open victory,
March 1992

It is not unreasonable to assume that most golfers who have scaled the slippery ladder of success on the professional circuit have arrived, through trial and error at a less costly time in their lives, at the conclusion that if they have a less than one-in-ten chance of making a birdie from a position where they could just as easily make an eight, there is likely to be more profit in playing safe.

Ballesteros is not among them. At a very early age he developed the ability to stand on the tee of a perilous golf hole and, where another player might find his view to the green interrupted by an impenetrable forest of dark, forbidding pines, or even a greedy lake, see only the fairway stretching like a shining verdant carpet to the foot of the distant flagstick. All hazards were invisible to him. They did not exist. After a period this sleight of mind became second nature and, when he reached the eighth hole at Torrequebrada in the first round of the Spanish Open in April 1979, he had mentally obliterated every obstacle in view before fully realizing that, in the intervening months since he had successfully cut the corner off the dogleg and made birdie in each of the four rounds of the Spanish Under-25s championship en route to victory the previous year, a steep mountain of wilderness, trees, and boulders had sprung up and rendered that route impassable. He held a brief consultation with a two-dimensional sketch in Musgrove's yardage book. It confirmed to him that if he took the flight path preferred by crows to the green, a distance of 310 yards, he would be shaving as much as 86 yards off the total length of the par-four. Obviously, there was no choice. He measured two club lengths back from the markers to give himself the optimum target line and prepared to drive. Musgrove, who had tried vainly to dissuade him, was watching from the skyline, muttering under his breath.

Ballesteros launched himself into the ball with conviction. It soared out over the trees and vanished, and the sound of disintegrating wood was heard. The Spaniard's face clouded with dismay. He set up over a provisional ball and smashed it in the same direction as the first. For an instant it hung provocatively above the horizon, tantalizingly near its destination, then gravity impelled it downward and it ended among the rocks. Ballesteros was fuming. He refused point-blank to hit another shot and went storming off up the slope in search of the last two. Naturally enough, given the depth of the scrub and the prevalence of bushes, any balls to be found were not his own. He had no option but to return to the tee, which he did with a countenance as black as thunder, and play a safe one-iron up the fairway.

"Next time you watch where ball go," he said angrily to Musgrove as he put down a nine on his card.

There is no doubt that Ballesteros is a compulsive gambler. Like all of his breed he occasionally suffers heavy losses, but these are counteracted by windfalls, which happen often enough and are lucrative enough to make the risk-taking worthwhile. The English Classic, held at the Belfry, provides a fine example.

Until that tournament Ballesteros's season had been singularly uneventful by his own high standards and had been marred by his experiences at the French Open at Lyon, where something happened which was to cast a shadow over his young life for some considerable time. His good friend Salvador Balbuena died.

The fact of Balbuena's death was shocking in itself, for he was a gifted player of just twenty-nine who had a chance of making the next Ryder Cup team. But the circumstances of it were worse. At dinner on the eve of the tournament he suddenly said: "I have a pain in my heart. I am going to die." Piñero, Jose Maria Canizares, and Antonio Garrido, who were with him, at first were astonished, then thought he was joking. Moments later he fell dead of a heart attack on the street outside the restaurant. His stricken comrades withdrew instantaneously. The remaining Spaniards decided to compete and donate their prize money to the widow and her two children. Ballesteros, who was among them, was almost inconsolable with grief, breaking down several times in public; but for the sake of Marcia Balbuena he composed himself sufficiently each day to be able to play and hand in his card, and eventually finished third.

Nevertheless, he was out of form and out of humor for several weeks after the French Open, and inwardly miserable for much longer. In June he failed to qualify at the U.S. Open in Toledo, Ohio. He walked off the course and, fighting back the tears, went straight into the locker room. There he sat, with his head in his hands, looking disconsolate and lonely. "This year in the winter I practiced harder than ever," he mumbled, more to himself than to anyone else. "I run every day. I train. But for what? Look what happens—nothing."

It didn't help that his back was causing him a great deal of discomfort, and that the American specialists he had seen had made gloomy predictions about his future as a professional sportsman. To reporters, Ballesteros commented that he should make his fortune quickly lest his career didn't last as long as he might wish it to. On the subject of his indifferent form, he also said that "the difference between a 65 and an 81 is this"—and held up his hand with his thumb and forefinger about half an inch apart.

But his spirits lifted with his return to Europe, and when he arrived at the Belfry he was lean, smiling, and hungry for confrontation. The opportunity came sooner than he expected. During the first three rounds of the tournament he scored 73, 71, 71, and it gave him the edge over his opponents. This was somewhat blunted by the capriciousness of the wind and the unpredictability of his driver at the outset of the fourth day, and, upon reaching the eighth hole, he discovered that his pursuers were closing in on him and that Faldo was only a stroke behind. Ballesteros was not pleased. He stood on the tee of the 460-yard par-four and regarded the distant flagstick with grim resolution. It was high time he laid his cards on the table. A par at this hole was unacceptable; nothing less than a birdie would do. That the lake might enter the equation did not occur to him. He had erased it from his mind's eye. Musgrove recalls the situation well. "It was cold and the course was in crap-arse condition because it's a crap-arse golf course. The anti-golf course. I mean, I can remember when they used to play the Ryder Cup on golf courses, but they gave that up."

The Spaniard drove the ball powerfully away. Faldo, who had just putted out on the eighth green, saw it depart in an ugly arc toward the water. Its owner came striding after it, gesticulating to Musgrove. But Ballesteros's consternation turned rapidly to joy. Destiny had dealt him an ace. An up-turned greenkeepers' boat had deflected his ball onto the bank, where it was now sitting pertly, a mere yard from the brink. Ballesteros was thrilled to find it in play, and promptly struck an eight-iron to twelve feet and holed it for birdie. Poor Faldo, wandering down the ninth and expecting the Spaniard to have dropped a shot, could hardly believe his eyes when the leaderboard made clear that he had in fact gained a shot.

The scales of fortune tilted in his favor, Ballesteros swept to a six-stroke victory, overcoming Neil Coles and Hobday with a final-round 71 and an aggregate of 286. Faldo and Lyle shared third place. As Ballesteros observed, the season's first triumph could hardly have come at a more opportune moment with the British Open a little more than a fortnight away.

"I needed it for my confidence," he admitted.

Wednesday, July 18, 1979, British Open Championship, St. Annes-on-the-Sea, Lancs. A watery sun was climbing unconvincingly into the sky where Ballesteros, his face ruddy with cold and excitement, crunched along the road to the practice range before teeing off in the first round of the British Open. Musgrove toiled behind him. Once there, he selected a space, pulled on his glove, and began to warm up, twisting and stretching in an effort to ease his aching back. The frozen crowd pressed closer to the barrier. Their breaths rose like cartoon bubbles into the air. After a while Ballesteros paused, flipped the ball bucket over with the end of his sand wedge, and stepped into the bunker. He hit a few shots. Musgrove, who was polishing the Spaniard's golf clubs, watched them land with something akin to pleasure. Earlier in the year he had remarked to Ballesteros that great bunker players, such as Player, Jacklin, Bob Charles, and Peter Thomson, always won at Lytham. And Ballesteros had replied, with no small amount of pride, "I am the best bunker player."

In practice rounds his performance had been encouraging if erratic. Every morning De Vicenzo had waited for him on the putting green and they had worked on their strokes together before playing the course.

Essentially, De Vicenzo's lessons were these: (1) The foundations of a low score at Lytham must be laid on the front nine; (2) Patience is a virtue in major championships; (3) A draw is more helpful than a fade at Lytham because most of the trouble is on the right; (4) A long hitter with the courage to bypass the conventional routes to the green might find "loopholes" in the rough, i.e. bald patches, which give a better angle of approach; and (5) The transient nature of seaside climates means that all links holes have split personalities.

Ballesteros did not employ his apprenticeship to good effect immediately. In the opening round, playing with Ken Brown and Trevino (who was so fearful of catching his death that he wore pajamas under his clothes) in gales of more than twenty-five miles an hour, he shot a two-over-par 73, which left him a tie for sixteenth place at the end of the day. The inclement weather was partially responsible: If Mark Twain had visited Britain for an Open he never would have dreamed of saying, "The coldest winter I ever spent was a summer in San Francisco." Nevertheless, Bill Longmuir, a little-known player from Basildon in Essex, proceeded around the golf course as though it were a fine spring morning, making six birdies in the outward half to turn in 29. By the twelfth hole he was eight under par and practically lapping the field, and his sole objective was to score 59. "I felt so good with the putter, I thought, 'I'm going to shoot an unbelievable score here and nothing's going to stop me.' " A fraction less zeal on Lytham's cruel back nine and nothing might have. But after making bogeys at the fourteenth and fifteenth holes, Longmuir lost some of his momentum, and his sixty-five-foot putt at the last lipped out for a 65, which equaled the course record and led by three strokes at the close of play.

Thursday, July 19, 1979. After the first round Ballesteros switched drivers. He had not felt comfortable on the tee all year and had thus rotated six or seven of these woods on a weekly basis in the hope that one of them might prove superior to the rest. Wednesday's club actively contributed to the Spaniard's 73 and caused him to think, with irrefutable logic: "Well, I can't hit fairways with this one, so it can't be more difficult with my old one." Fairways, unfortunately, showed themselves to be every bit as difficult to hit in the second round—indeed, as they had done since the beginning of the season—for the simple reason that it was the swinger of the club rather than the club itself who was at fault. No one was more aware of this than Ballesteros. Some months earlier it had become a matter of such concern to him that he had sought help from John Jacobs. "Because," he said worriedly, "I can only slice the ball."

Jacobs was delighted to oblige: "I can remember exactly what I said to him, and that was that he'd got the club too strong and was too much underneath. In other words, his five-iron was sitting rather like a four-iron. That, in itself, tends to take the club back too straight, and the shoulders get too tilted and the club comes underneath the ball. I had to make the club weaker and get him to turn away from it."

SO BALLESTEROS WAS CURED OF SLICING, BUT NOT OF WAYWARDNESS. NO AMOUNT OF PRACTICE OR SELF-CONTROL COULD HOLD HIS VAST SWING IN CHECK.

So Ballesteros was cured of slicing, but not of waywardness. No amount of practice or self-control could hold his vast swing in check. In the opening rounds at Lytham he relied on the teachings of De Vicenzo and his own courage to save him as he lashed mightily from the trees, forcing the galleries to run for cover, then attempted to retrieve his ball and to play it from a variety of unorthodox lies. His wildness was accentuated by the blustery conditions. At the tenth hole on the second day, Ballesteros hit a drive so far off line that Trevino felt compelled to point out the cause. He did so in Spanish, explaining that his erratic driving was due to the fact that he was not clearing his left hip adequately before following through. In fact, this was a violation of Rule 8-1, but nothing was done about it. Ballesteros was excessively grateful. His tee shot at the eleventh flew miles over the fairway bunkers and set up a birdie chance, and further strokes were snatched back from par at the fourteenth, fifteenth, and seventeenth holes. Then a driver and a superb five-iron, punched from the downhill slope of a grassy knoll to four feet at the eighteenth, earned him his eighth birdie of the round.

"One hesitates to say vintage stuff at the age of twenty-two," Peter Alliss said, as Ballesteros acknowledged the acclaim of his fans, "but, my word, vintage stuff indeed."

Alliss later wrote that the true par of the last five holes on that day was considered to be 4, 5, 4, 5, 4; because of the prevailing westerly wind. Ballesteros's figures were 3, 3, 4, 3, 3. Before the close of play, they had helped to lift him into second place at 138, two strokes behind the leader Irwin and one ahead of Longmuir. The American had played some of his best golf for a 68—although his driving had been adversely affected by the multitudinous layers of clothing he wore to prevent hypothermia—and was astonished when he heard that the Spaniard had not only matched the course record with a 65, but had completed the back nine in 32 strokes. "What did he do?" he queried. "Cut across?"

Ballesteros was typically wry in his press conference afterward. Regaling reporters with stories of his adventures on the golf course, he confessed that his ball had finished in the rough so often that in the end Musgrove had said sardonically: "Why don't you close your eyes and hit it? Maybe then you'll put the ball on the fairway."

"I always play for the fairway, though," Ballesteros said, "but I never go there."

Asked whether he would like to see the fairways made wider, he responded, tongue in cheek: "No, I would like to see the fairways more narrow, then everybody play from the rough. We should play one time the Open with no fairways. Then maybe I come close to winning."

Friday, July 20, 1979. Rarely have two golfers provided a sharper contrast of manner, appearance, and style of play than Ballesteros and Irwin, paired together in the third round. Jekyll and Hyde had more in common. If this was not readily apparent, it soon became so. The second hole at Lytham is a beguiling par-four of some 436 yards, with a railway running the length of it. It tests a man's mettle by encouraging him to flirt with the tracks and thus open up a better line to the green. Irwin, tall, upright, and bespectacled, drove first, electing to place his ball safely in the center of the fairway. His swing is high and classic, his forte is target golf. Straight driving and accurate iron play allow him to plot his way around the golf course like a chess master.

Then came Ballesteros, swarthy and handsome, his white smile flashing as he asked Musgrove his opinion, then selected a one-iron. With youthful bravado, he whipped the ball away to the right. A train clattered down the line; the gallery moaned; the ball disappeared out of view. The Spaniard looked faintly disbelieving. A provisional was played and he and Musgrove went to hunt for the original. They located it deep in the bushes. It was quite unplayable and, there being nowhere within two club lengths to drop, he was unable to continue with the provisional as he would have done if the ball had been lost or out of bounds, and had to walk back to the tee all alone, swinging his golf club self-consciously. He played his third shot onto the fairway, his fourth into a bunker, his fifth onto the green, and he sank a tricky putt for a double bogey (the only one he made during the championship). At the next hole, also a par-four, he dropped a third shot. He stayed remarkably calm. On another day he had said, "You have to be very patient on this course because it's very easy to make bogeys, and bogeys and never stop. Here you have to wait. When you attack the golf course, the golf course kills you." He continued to observe his own rules and was rewarded with birdies at the sixth and eighth holes.

The Golden Bear was up ahead and had made his move, holing a wedge shot at the third and birdieing the seventh to turn in 34. But Lytham's finish is notoriously impregnable—only Ballesteros had managed to break through its defense—and it defeated him then as it had in the first two rounds, when he had gone out in 32 and 30 and come back in 40 and 39, respectively. This time he notched three consecutive bogeys beginning at the eleventh, for an inward half of 39 and a one-over-par aggregate of 214. Watson, the pretournament favorite, and Longmuir, who had had a 77, were two strokes further behind.

Out on the golf course it had begun to pour. Spectators huddled together beneath umbrellas. Ballesteros pulled on his rainsuit and Irwin rubbed unhappily at his glasses. Until then the American had been in control, his methodical, accountant-like approach to the game paying dividends.

But icy gusts of wind and rain affected his concentration, and he dropped shots at the tenth and eleventh before coming to grief at the penultimate hole where his tee shot missed the fairway, his three-wood recovery plugged in a bunker, and he took four more to get down for a double-bogey six. Ballesteros had problems of his own. As Irwin had distanced himself on the leaderboard, he had grown increasingly agitated, finally throwing caution to the wind and playing with a passionate fury that was beautiful to behold. It did, however, cost him dropped shots at the fourteenth, fifteenth, and seventeenth holes, but at the end of the day he was in contention with Crenshaw and Robert Byman at 215.

Ballesteros and Irwin, as diametrically opposed as an Arabian sheik and a county librarian, came to the eighteenth hole still separated by two strokes—the same number that had divided Tony Jacklin from Bob Charles in the final round of the 1969 British Open before the Englishman had hit the perfect tee shot far beyond all danger and settled the contest. Player, too, had brought drama to the final hole, playing his third shot left-handed with a putter from against the clubhouse wall in 1974 to win the championship for the third time. But in the event the fifty-fourth hole did not prove as important for Ballesteros and Irwin in the grand scheme of things as it first threatened to when the American hit his "worst drive of the championship" into the rough; for both he and the Spaniard then overflew the green and had to get up and down for par and matching scores of 75. The gallery could not have cared less. The only thing that mattered to them was that their hero had lived to fight another day, and they communicated this with such tumultuous clapping and cheering that Ballesteros, obviously pleased, took off his raincoat and waved it gratefully above his head.

In his postround interview he was quietly confident. "I was not much lucky today," he said. "Maybe I save the lucky for tomorrow. If I start well on the first four holes, I think I have a chance to win."

Saturday, July 21, 1979. The windows of the men's locker room at Royal Lytham provide an unparalleled vantage point from which to observe

British Open Championship drama, positioned as they are behind the eighteenth green. During the course of the tournament one can occasionally see professional golfers or caddies gazing from them with rapt faces. Now, however, no one was there. Everyone who could be outside was, braving the drizzle in order to pay tribute to the Spaniard marching so triumphantly up the final fairway.

No gulf in professional sport is wider than that between a good player and a major champion. Talent alone is not enough to bridge it, nor is desire, stamina, physical strength, or mental resilience. "Hitting the ball," Player says, "is just one piece of the puzzle. Nicklaus had the complete puzzle filled in, and I think I had it filled in pretty well, otherwise I couldn't have won nine major championships."

As far as Jacklin is concerned, the first time that Ballesteros showed that he might have that delicate balance of fire, humility, audacity, patience, intrinsic wisdom, and absolute simplicity inherent in all major champions was when he fought so long and so brilliantly at Birkdale in 1976. "He showed he could handle the pressure, and when you've done it once you can always build on it." Jacklin watched and took note, knowing that "there are a lot of people with a lot of ability, but some of them haven't got the right sort of intelligence—common sense—to make it happen for themselves. To recognize that golf isn't just about hitting the ball and having a pretty swing. It's about much, much more than that—adjusting to different environments and circumstances, feeling comfortable wherever you go, never letting anything get in the way of your determination to succeed. . . . "

Ballesteros had spent a restless night dwelling on every one of the above and on his golf swing in particular. He was worried about his driving. It still wasn't right, and he feared that any technical weaknesses in it were being exacerbated by his back problems. Thus far, the latter had been relieved by treatment. Every morning since the British Open had started, Ballesteros had woken up, partaken of his favorite breakfast of scrambled eggs, toast, and milk (he rarely drinks tea or coffee), and driven down to the local physiotherapist for a swim and a massage. On Saturday he decided against it. He didn't want the time of the appointment on his mind.

At midday he left the house he had been sharing with Baldomero Jr., Jorge Ceballos, and Ed Barner and Joe Collet and their two wives, and went down to the golf course to begin his preparation. It was a bleak, stormy day. Clouds scurried across a sullen gray sky, while the nor'wester which drove them turned the back nine into an ordeal. Ballesteros pulled on a navy blue sweater and strode briskly through the milling crowds to the range. The other contenders, Rodger Davis among them, glanced up involuntarily when he appeared. "He always had this aura about him," the Australian recalls. "The way he walked was a very confident walk. The way he talked was always very confident—nothing negative came out of him. And in some ways . . . he was a little bit intimidating to other players, because he just gave off that aura that he was going to win. And you had to try and stop that somehow in your mind. I think if you could say Seve had a weakness in his bag, it would have been his driver. Nearly every great player has had a weakness, and I'd say Seve's was his driver."

At 1:10 Ballesteros went to cross from the practice green to the first tee. De Vicenzo, his friend and mentor, stopped him. "*Tienes las manos. Ahora juega con tu corazon*," he said fervently to the young Spaniard. "You have the hands, now play with your heart."

Royal Lytham is unusual among the British Open courses in that it begins with a par-three. Ballesteros teed off first, striking a seven-iron to fifteen feet. Irwin's shot was more tentative and only just limped onto the putting surface, from where he two-putted for par. With scarcely a pause, Ballesteros stepped up his own ball and stroked it swiftly across the green for a birdie. It was like a knife in Irwin's heart. One hole played and half his lead gone. His expression was an exact mirror of Miller's at the same stage in the final round of the 1976 British Open, after his young rival had made one of his vintage pars. But on the next hole his face grew long. Ballesteros had no intention of repeating his experiences of Friday, so he played a safe two-iron down the fairway and made a conventional four. Irwin selected a three-wood, pushed it out to the right, left his second shot miles short of the green, hit his third to the back edge, and three-putted. A six was marked down on his card and he surrendered the lead for good.

Davis was the first to challenge the Spaniard's one-stroke advantage, taking a share of the lead when Ballesteros bogeyed the fourth, then birdieing the next to seize control of the tournament. Elsewhere in the field Crenshaw, Nicklaus, James, and Aoki vied for position on the upper reaches of the leaderboard. The Japanese toppled soonest. He had birdied the third, fifth, and sixth holes to turn in 33 but, like James, was unequal to Lytham's grueling finish. Crenshaw, aware of the struggle to come, concentrated on gathering birdies, whipping the ball cleanly into the air with his smooth and stylish swing, and gaining strokes at the sixth, seventh, and ninth holes to move into second place. Ballesteros, meanwhile, had dropped another shot at the sixth. On the seventh tee he remembered De Vicenzo's words and drew courage from them. "It's the one with the biggest heart who will win," he confided to Musgrove. And made birdie. When he reached the turn he was one under par and co-leader once more, while Irwin was two over.

All of this time Ballesteros, though he lashed fearlessly off the tees, uncaring of retribution, was holding himself in check, remembering not to press—to wait. Afterward he said: "The only real time I attacked is on the thirteenth. I was watching the scoreboard to see how is my position . . . and I told my caddie that maybe we can hit the green."

He came to the 339-yard dogleg par-four—the beginning of Lytham's brutal closing stretch—after making two crucial putts, one to save bogey at the tenth and one for par at the twelfth, and the adrenaline was still rushing through his body. Standing on the tee, his face taut with concentration, he looked strong and unyielding. "He will not be afraid if he gets the chance," Musgrove had said. The conventional way to play the thirteenth is to take a long-iron off the tee and hit a wedge into the green. But De Vicenzo had told Ballesteros always to hit driver and chance falling foul of the fairway bunkers. Curiously enough, the Spaniard had resisted the temptation all week. Now, with a gale at his back and his name at the top of the leaderboard with Crenshaw's, he gave in to it. "We'll go for it today," he told Musgrove.

"You could say thirteen was a bit of a birdie hole," remembers Davis, who by then had blown himself out of the championship with a double bogey at the fourteenth and bogey at the fifteenth, "but, you know, the wind was so strong there was really no birdie hole out there."

Ballesteros set up over the ball and stared at the flagstick. To have even a prayer of making the green he had to carry the ball three hundred yards over a trap. It was not easy, but then again it was not impossible. Summoning all his reserves of power and skill, he smashed his drive from the tee and, like the ballplayer Carlton Fisk hitting his memorable game-winning home run in the 1975 World Series, tried "to will the ball to stay up there and never come down." It almost worked. A degree less wind, a millisecond longer on the clubhead, and the ball would have carried the extra yard it needed to clear the bunker. Instead, it flew an incredible 298 yards, caught the top of a mound and toppled into the sand. By the end of the British Open he had been in fifteen bunkers and had gotten up and down from fourteen of them. "The sand wedge was the key to my win," he said later, "certainly not my driver." Now, however, with sixty-eight yards to the pin, he took a wedge, hitting it down hard on the ball to force it over the high wall of the trap.

BALLESTEROS SEEMED TO SENSE THE END WAS NEAR. HIS STRIDE QUICKENED AND BECAME MORE JAUNTY; HIS FACE WAS DARK WITH INTENSITY AND A FIERCE JOY.

"I hit it just about perfect," Ballesteros recalls, "but the spin pulled it off the green to the right."

That's when *destino* laid a hand on the young Spaniard's shoulder. He had a ten-foot putt for birdie and it never for one second looked like missing the hole. It positively flew in. And if ever victory shone in the eyes of a player it did so now, as Ballesteros, black hair flying, putter thrust forward like a sword, charged across the green like a matador, punching the air with his fist. "All week," Davis says, "Seve had been just flowing along, flowing along. . . . And if you looked at his face there, he was the winner. . . . When that happened, all of a sudden everything just lit up and nothing was going to beat him."

Ballesteros seemed to sense the end was near. His stride quickened and became more jaunty; his face was dark with intensity and a fierce joy. The unruly gallery surged after him, trampling the barren landscape and buffeting his forgotten partner in their frenzy to see him play. Irwin was too drained and demoralized to put up a struggle. His entire round had been a chapter of disaster, and he watched the Spaniard's three-putt at the fourteenth and magical thirty-five-yard chip for par at the fifteenth with a jaundiced eye. Even Ballesteros's next feat, his most spectacular yet, failed to elicit a response. He simply walked to the green with the air of a man who had been called upon to witness more improbabilities in one day than most men could reasonably be expected to in a lifetime, and leaned dispiritedly on his putter.

Few shots have cast as long a shadow over a champion's career as Severiano Ballesteros's into the car park beside the sixteenth fairway in the final round of the British Open. It was viewed, especially by the Americans, as symbolic of his entire performance that week—wild and outrageously lucky (he hit eight fairways in the first three rounds and one in the last)—and it earned him the nickname, "The Car-Park Champion." Even Irwin, who finished with a 78, said afterward, "I can't understand how anyone can drive as badly as that and still win an Open Championship." Actually, that particular tee shot was premeditated. Ballesteros *intended* it to finish where it did—some twenty-four yards from the fairway and sixty-four yards from the green. "I drove to the right because the wind was helping from the left," he insists, "which meant an approach from the fairway—with the wind behind—would be very difficult and an approach from the right rough, almost into the breeze, much easier. I knew the rough out there was not bad because the spectators had trampled it down, and that if I hit a big drive I could get close to the green and make a birdie. I also realized that if my ball finished among the cars I would get a free drop."

As he marched hurriedly from the tee, the crowd stampeding past him, he felt a flicker of alarm. What if he had miscalculated? What if he had overcompensated for the wind? A moment later his fears were allayed; his brothers Vicente and Baldomero shouted urgently to him: "Don't worry, you are two strokes in front." Crenshaw had just double-bogeyed the seventeenth. "When I realized that, I told myself just to make par," says Ballesteros, who, under special tournament rules, was allowed to drop clear of the car he found his ball underneath, without penalty. He paced off the distance to the green himself, selected a target about fifteen feet away from the flag which was slightly softer than everywhere else, and hit a perfect sand wedge to that precise spot. Then he holed the putt for birdie to lead the British Open by three strokes with two holes to play.

The rest, as they say, is history. After parring the seventeenth from a bunker, Ballesteros played a conservative three-wood from the tee at the last, deliberately aiming away from the fairway to avoid the treacherous bunkers. It hooked out over the rough and disappeared from view.

"What's over there?" he asked Musgrove anxiously.

"I don't know," came the droll reply. "That's the one place we haven't been this week."

But the ball had found a perfectly playable lie and the Spaniard hit an easy five-iron to the front of the green. With that, any sense of decorum that the crowd might have had was lost and, like a river bursting its banks, they poured down the stands and over the fairways, engulfing Ballesteros in a tide of warmth and adoration, just like they had with Jacklin ten years before him, and carrying Irwin and the two caddies helplessly along with them. When the American had fought his way free he was waving a white handkerchief in surrender—to the people as well as to the British Open Champion.

"You always know what a guy feels when he's winning his first major," Jacklin says. "You never forget, because you're so incredibly nervous and keyed up. You just feel so unbelievably full and nervous and aware and, *God!*—your senses are so sharp. You're just flying by the seat of your trousers, basically learning the whole thing. You've got to have a lot of courage to see it through."

Few men have as much of that precious resource as the young Spaniard who broke through the gallery that summer's evening, arms held high in a victory salute, and a smile of unalloyed happiness on his face.

"So much was made of Seve's wildness that week," says Crenshaw, who finished tied for second with Nicklaus. "You know, he hit some errant shots and everyone will agree, but the only thing that counts is your name on that big board and the score. He shot the lowest score. I don't think there's any question that Seve wasn't hitting the ball anywhere like he'd like to, but it takes a champion to overcome that and to learn to get out of places like that and make a score under British Open Championship conditions. That's what's important. And that's an impressive victory."

"I won by three shots," Ballesteros says summarily. "I won because I played better than anyone else, not because I was luckier than everybody else. I've watched the video many times and I don't see any luck there at all. Luck is when you hit a tree and bounce out onto the fairway."

Musgrove's only concern was that Ballesteros made a four at the last to be the only player under par with a total of 70 and an aggregate of 283. At the edge of the eighteenth green the Spaniard had told him proudly: "I can take four putts from here and still win."

"No, you can't," Musgrove retorted, "because I've got a bet on with one of the caddies that the winning score will be under par."

Ballesteros holed out for a par. As he did so, there was a scuffle in the gallery, then first Baldomero Jr. and then Vicente raced across the green and embraced him. They clung to each other, weeping, until officials led Severiano away to sign his card. Manuel, who was in the clubhouse, watching it on television, was no less emotional: "I could not bear to be near the green itself. I felt the pressure of that last hole a hundred times more than if I had been playing myself."

"Was great emotion," Ballesteros confessed with an unashamed grin in his press conference afterward. "Will be very difficult to forget that time. Very, very difficult. My brothers just cuddle me, and it was very emotional, especially for the oldest one. He tell me after the third round, 'I can't watch you putt because my heart was bang, bang, bang,' and he was very, very happy."

When the prize-giving ceremony was over, there was a small cocktail party held for the British Open Champion in the R&A caravan. Afterward, Ballesteros was walking across the putting green carrying some champagne he had been given, when he spotted Michael Williams, the *Daily Telegraph* golf correspondent. Much to Williams's astonishment, he immediately went over and handed it to him. "Take this," Ballesteros said with a smile, "and have a drink with all the other writers for all the nice things they've said about me."

Later, he went back to the house where he had been staying to celebrate, accompanied by Mark Wilson. "It wasn't a wild party but there were certain people enjoying themselves," Wilson recalls. "I'm guessing there were no more than twenty people in the house. *He* certainly did not join in the celebrations. Everybody else could celebrate, but not Seve. He was going to be playing golf the next week and that was it. I don't know of Seve ever breaking the strict training rules. I've never heard of Seve going wild, I've never heard of him having a bender, I've never heard of him having a night out. Which is amazing because they all go off the rails occasionally. But he suddenly went into a corner on his own and he was talking. He just wanted to talk, he didn't want to drink. As you know, he doesn't. And I remember I said, 'How much is this going to change your life?' And he said: 'It won't.' He was a young man, and I laughed. Because it changes everybody's life. And almost every player, like a [lottery] winner, says: 'It's not going to change my life.' And you know damn well it will. And he suddenly looked at me—he was very serious—and he said, 'If you think I change, you come to me and you stand in front of me and you say: "Where is Seve Ballesteros?" "*Where is Seve Ballesteros?*" And I will know what you mean.'"

7

THE GREEN ROAD TO GLORY

"A man conscious of enthusiasm for worthy aims is sustained under petty hostilities by the memory of great workers who had to fight their way not without wounds, and who hover in his mind as patron saints, invisibly helping."

George Eliot, *Middlemarch*

In the spring of 1977 Ballesteros made his first trip to Augusta, Georgia. He had just emerged from the Spanish air force and, with his military haircut and tanned good looks, resembled no one so much as a young Elvis, leaning eagerly out of the window of the Cadillac, impatient for a glimpse, however fleeting, of the sacred turf of Augusta National Golf Club. As far back as he could remember he had imagined this moment. A decade ago, at least, he had sat at the feet of Ramon Sota, a small intense boy with a pensive, wistful face, and listened enraptured as his uncle, who had played Augusta half a dozen times between 1964 and 1972, finishing sixth on his second visit, talked of the golf course that was home to the U.S. Masters Tournament: of wide fairways lined with rare and beautiful trees; of hidden perils which visual splendor belied; of greens so swift, so undulating, and so mysterious that a man might play them all his life and never master them; of great champions who won there and broken men who fell; and of memories, achingly sweet or bitter as gall, that remained indelibly etched on every golfer's mind for the rest of his natural life.

The driver of the Cadillac slowed and turned down Magnolia Lane. Ballesteros sucked in his breath sharply. Vistas of sky, clouds, and emerald foliage flashed across the windshield as they swept along the cool, fragrant tunnel and up to the stately white clubhouse. For a moment Ballesteros sat unmoving, entranced by the magnificence of it all. Then he was out of the car and running swiftly to see the golf course. It was a warm day. A faint-blue haze had settled on top of the towering pines and below it golfers moved about lazily, like ants in slow motion. The fairways dropped away from the clubhouse in a series of low curves, as closely shorn and perfect as Astroturf, artistically striped and dotted with snowy bunkers. Spectators flowed in a river of living color across the jewel-green grass, a slender ribbon of creek shone through the trees, and everywhere there were flowers: jasmine, azalea, and dogwood. Ballesteros gazed with childlike wonder at the loveliness of the scene. He had a strong feeling of déjà vu. There was something familiar about it all, something that reminded him of Pedreña. "Seve," he said to himself, "one day you will win this tournament."

But 1977 was not to be Ballesteros's year. Even if Augusta had not been one of those courses where experience means everything, he would still have been disadvantaged from the start. His stint of national service meant that he was suffering from lack of competitive practice and, as a consequence, while lashing furiously at balls on the range before the tournament even began, he strained a muscle in his back. This did not put him in the best humor. He had already formed the notion that the hierarchy at Augusta were conspiring against him, something which had become clear to him when he saw he had been paired with Nicklaus in the opening round, and the least negative sign served to enhance this impression. He was convinced that he was being tested, deliberately put under pressure.

Nicklaus, of course, was blind to this resentment. It would never have occurred to him that the Spaniard might regard their partnership as anything other than an honor of the highest order, and he read nothing into his silence, contemplating his swing in an abstract manner and reviewing it favorably on another day. Said Nicklaus: "I saw this sort of long, flowing golf swing that I liked very much. I saw a fella that had trouble controlling the ball at times yet didn't worry about it because he was very long, which was much the way I played when I was young. I liked that. I liked his aggressive enthusiasm for the golf game and I felt like he would become a very, very good player."

Ballesteros's initial scores at Augusta reflected his state of mind. He shot 74, 75 in the first two rounds and came within a whisker of missing the cut. During the weekend he acquitted himself rather better, finishing thirty-third behind Tom Watson with a score of 291, three over par. Joe Collet, a brilliant young lawyer who had joined UMI in January and whom he had only just met and was sharing a house with, strolled companionably around the fairways with him every day, finding him quiet and serious off the golf course. Said Collet: "He was really not very talkative because my Spanish wasn't very good and his English wasn't very good, and I didn't know a whole lot about golf and he wasn't interested in a whole lot of other things, but we became friends because I was somebody there that he could talk to." Together they went to the cinema and out to dinner most evenings. On Ballesteros's birthday (which falls during Masters week), Collet and Ed Barner baked him a cake. "We invited some of his Spanish friends over and had a little party, which he wasn't too thrilled about. Never has been thrilled about having his birthday that week. He was very gracious and appreciative, but . . . okay, that's fine, let's eat the cake. Now that's over, let's watch TV."

HIS LOVE AFFAIR WITH THE COURSE, UNTAINTED BY HIS UNEASY RELATIONSHIP WITH MASTERS OFFICIALDOM, HAD DEVELOPED INTO AN OBSESSION.

Later in the year, when relating his experiences at the Masters to Dave Musgrove, Ballesteros revealed that he had been forced to play the final round of the tournament with old balls because he didn't have any new ones.

"Well, he wouldn't go and buy any, would he?" Musgrove says sardonically. "Years afterward I reminded him of that. He says: '*How you know this?*' I said, 'You bloody told me!' "

The following season Ballesteros finished tied for eighteenth at Augusta and in 1979 he was twelfth. His love affair with the course, untainted by his uneasy relationship with Masters officialdom, had developed into an obsession. What De Vicenzo had prophesied—"Seve won't win the Masters once, he will win it many times"—Ballesteros fervently believed. He was certain that, with the right preparation, the green jacket could be his in 1980. Accordingly, he devised a new winter practice regime. Instead of merely hitting thousands of balls into oblivion each day, he began to work on his draw, the essential shot for Augusta. That done, he would walk down to the beach at Pedreña as the sun was going down and, for the first time since he was a boy, plant a makeshiff flagstick above the watermark and practice his putting: At low tide the sand had the same glassy quickness as the greens at the Masters. Lastly, before going to bed, he would stand before a full-length mirror in the stables and study his takeaway. Something Jacklin said to him shortly after his victory at Lytham had stuck in his mind. He and the Englishman were friends and often played golf together. Once, when they were driving to St. George's Hill to get their clubs repaired, Jacklin said to him, "You know, you're never really going to be as good as you want to be until you learn that you can't hit the ball flat out all the time. For what it's worth, I'm telling you, you've got to learn to control the ball and you've got to learn to control yourself. It's no use taking your anger out on the ball, because you can't win every tournament hitting it into car parks all the time, like you did at Lytham. You will *not* last. Nobody's nerve can stand that. You've got to learn to go at 85 percent and put it on the fairway all the time."

Ballesteros set his jaw stubbornly. "But I am not like that," he said proudly. "I have to go for everything."

"Seve," Jacklin said with quiet emphasis, "you won't be there to go for everything if you don't learn not to put yourself under such extreme pressure."

Looking in the glass at his reflected golf swing, Ballesteros had to admit that Jacklin had been right. If he wanted to achieve the level of consistency necessary for victory in the Masters, or indeed in any other major championship, he was going to have to shorten his backswing and learn to take the club back more in one piece.

Tuesday, April 8, 1980, Augusta, Georgia. There has long been a tendency among the higher beings whose domain Augusta National is, to consider the home of the Masters as the very axis upon which the rest of the world turns. They have scant regard for the conventional rules of modern society, believing them to have no application whatsoever to themselves, and instead create laws of their own which the combined might of the Vatican and the White House could not have repealed.

In 1980 one of their more notorious policies was their racial one: Until 1983 no white man carried a bag at Augusta and it was 1975 before a black man (Lee Elder) played. As a result, Ballesteros came alone and simply enlisted the services of his regular Masters caddie, Marion Herrington. Herrington duly made preparations to go out and measure the golf course. Ballesteros stopped him. Herrington, like Musgrove and most of his other caddies, only worked in yards. To this day, Ballesteros finds it impossible to think in anything but meters. "I will do all by myself," he declared, and set off armed with pencil and pad to carefully pace out the distances from the fairways to the greens, from the bunkers to trees, and from other landmarks, such as mounds, to possible pin placements. Then he padded for several hours around the putting surfaces, studying every undulation, slope, and borrow.

When he had finished he stood behind each one, as he had seen Nicklaus do, and looked back up the fairway—playing the hole in reverse in his mind—so that he could see where his approach shot should come from, for the secret of Augusta's treachery lies in the allure of her spacious fairways. "Augusta," Crenshaw says, "is the most tempting golf course I think I've ever seen. It *goads* you into trying different shots because there's so much to gain. If you're right on your game and you live dangerously for a day and you can just skirt the trouble here and there, you can come off with a brilliant score. But if you're not, that's when it's really punishing. . . . I think people tend to overlook how you must be good with your irons that week if you expect to win, because if you can't position your approaches you play defensively all week. It's very difficult to keep the ball below the hole, but that's the idea. You're rewarded when you do. Every time."

In practice Ballesteros played with Trevino and Graham Marsh, who observed that the Spaniard was putting exceptionally well. Michael Williams walked with them to the second green.

"How long have you been here?" he asked Ballesteros.

"A year," Ballesteros replied cryptically. In spirit he felt he had. Afterward, he remarked to the press that he felt more in control of his golf swing than he ever had in his life.

The Masters began on one of those crisp, sparkling blue days reminiscent of the best seaside holidays. A fresh wind gusted through the pines, searching for, but not finding, sandwich wrappers and drink cartons, and toying instead with the psyches of hapless competitors. Ballesteros teed off at midday with Craig Stadler, the aptly named Walrus. In contrast to his playing partner, Ballesteros was in a buoyant mood, further improved by birdies at the second, third, sixth, and eighth holes, and was not discouraged when he dropped a shot at the fourth, where he had missed the green with a one-iron. The back nine, too, asked no questions he couldn't answer. He gathered birdies at the eleventh, thirteenth, and seventeenth holes and was unlucky not to card two more.

"This is the best I have played at Augusta," he said delightedly when he came off the course. His score of 66, six under par, gave him a share of the lead at the close of play with Australian David Graham.

Friday was a gloriously hot and still day. Ballesteros, who was off early, went out in level par. This tends to suggest that he recorded a commendable string of threes, fours, and fives, but appearances, as we know, are often deceptive. In reality, he was up to his old tricks again. Whether for the benefit of Larry Nelson, his playing partner and old Ryder Cup rival, or for the sheer pleasure of kicking over the traces, he thrashed at his drives with such force that he was almost carried after them. Thereafter, he would pursue the ball into forests and flowerbeds, tearing the heads off azaleas in his efforts to salvage pars. But on the inward half his philosophy of "an eagle or a seven" began to pay off. He made threes at the tenth and eleventh and birdied the thirteenth and fifteenth with two wonderful long iron shots into the green.

At the sixteenth he called for his eight-iron. Herrington shook his head. "It's a seven-iron," he said. Ballesteros hesitated but took the caddie's choice of club anyway, and hit his tee shot eighty feet past the pin. Herrington was aghast. "I'm so sorry, I'm so sorry," he kept repeating.

"Don't worry," Ballesteros said magnanimously. "It was not your fault. It was mine for listening to you."

He teed up on the par-four seventeenth, seething with suppressed anger. All his aggression was channeled into his next shot, which snap-hooked off the tee at an angle so extreme that it flew through the top of a pine tree, bounced on to the adjacent seventh fairway, rolled between two bunkers, and came to rest some ten feet away from the flagstick on the seventh green.

"Where did that other ball come from?" Graham queried when he reached the green to find a strange ball on his line to the hole. "No one's playing mulligans, I trust? Oh, it's Seve's ball, is it? Well, good enough, that explains it."

Ballesteros emerged from the trees, looking slightly embarrassed. "Nice drive," Graham commented with some sarcasm. "Would you like to play through?"

"I am a good driver, yes?" Ballesteros snapped, his temper flaring. "This is the first time I hit the seventh green today. I missed it the other time."

"I'd trade balls," Graham said dryly. "Yours is closer to the hole."

Ballesteros marked his ball and, as soon as the green was clear, took a free drop nearby. He was now faced with a shot of extraordinary difficulty. Before him, and completely obscuring his view of the green which lay 150 yards away, was a vast scoreboard, a large mound, and several pine trees. While marshals scurried about, Ballesteros considered his options.

"Are you going to make a birdie?" a southern wag shouted.

"Yes," Ballesteros said positively. He selected a seven-iron, settled over his ball and swung through it with one of those exquisite swings of his which are all feel and no hit. A roar went up from the green. Ballesteros was off and running, the gallery surging after him. He found his ball fifteen feet from the pin and rolled it in for birdie. Nelson was rendered speechless. Ballesteros finished with a par for a 69 and a halfway total of 135, three strokes ahead of Rex Caldwell and Graham.

The latter, who had been proceeding with less caution than he perhaps ought to have, had fallen horribly from grace at the twelfth, the same hole where Weiskopf chalked up a 13 the previous day after putting five balls in the creek, and had squandered his chance to equal or better the Spaniard's lead.

In any tournament, regardless of whether or not it calls itself a major, it is impossible to predict with confidence the eventual outcome when only two rounds have been played. The Masters is no exception. Ballesteros might well have had a three-shot margin when he teed off on Saturday, but three shots is a reserve parachute barely worth its weight around Amen Corner. Six would be more reasonable. Nevertheless, there were now two distinct camps of anticipatory opinion at Augusta: those who thought Ballesteros was a great golfer who was playing well enough to win, and those who thought he'd be lucky to. The second brigade were already clapping their hands together in glee and saying "I told you so" rather tiresomely when Ballesteros reached the sixth hole. Certainly, his start had been erratic. He had gone bogey, birdie, bogey, par, before his drive at the par-four fifth had ended in a stand of pines. Fortunately, his ball was lying in the very place where a tree had recently been uprooted. Unfortunately, he had no clear line to the green. This realization came together with a new and sobering thought: "A bogey or even a double bogey was inescapable." Indeed, a six would reduce his lead to one.

Afterward, he said that it was a lesson from his childhood that had helped him at such times. "If the water is rough in Santander Bay, you must fight harder in the boat and not give up, not worry about sinking. That's what I learned from my father. Others worry about sinking and they are finished."

He counseled himself to remain calm at all costs, selected a sand wedge, and lofted the ball high over the trees and back on to the fairway. When he walked off the green he was thankful he had done no worse than bogey.

In light of the ensuing drama, there can be little doubt that the par-five eighth played a crucial role in turning the tide of the tournament, even in those early stages of it. Up until that point Graham, who was partnering Ballesteros, had been slowly gaining ground on the Spaniard and, psychologically at least, felt he was virtually in the driving seat. That was his first mistake—and his last. Ballesteros, having driven powerfully up the fairway, consulted his yardage book and decided to go for the green, some 245 yards away. A three-iron was chosen for the task. He set up over the ball and sent it soaring into the blue. It came to a stop six feet from the pin. Before Graham's incredulous eyes, Ballesteros stroked the putt in for eagle.

The Australian was visibly shaken. He immediately took six and, despite the fact that he was in third place tied with Jack Newton, Andy North, and J. C. Snead at the end of the day, never really threatened again. Ballesteros turned in 35, one under par, and came home in a relatively steady 33, for a score of 68 and a total of 203. His nearest challenger was the robust American Ed Fiori, a distant seven strokes away.

For a young man poised on the brink of history, Ballesteros was inordinately composed and unexcited. He knew that victory on the morrow would make him the youngest winner of the Masters ever—Nicklaus was eighty days older than the Spaniard's twenty-three years and four days when he marched to glory at Augusta in 1963—and that he would become, along with the Golden Bear, Francis Ouimet, and Bobby Jones, one of the elite group of players who had won two or more major championships by the age of twenty-three. As such, he responded to the attention received with grace and goodwill, but slipped quietly away as soon as he was able. He had invited a handful of his Spanish friends and an American woman journalist over to

The personal celebration already appears to be underway as Seve putts out at Augusta's eighteenth, where he completes the third round of the 1980 Masters Tournament with a seven-shot lead over Ed Fiori. (© Phil Sheldon)

his house for dinner. When they arrived they found him in an ebullient mood, determined to be the perfect host. He supervised the buffet meal and was, by turns during the course of the evening, amusing, entertaining, and an articulate conversationalist. Later, needing the cool comfort of solitude, he left his guests and watched *Saturday Night Fever* in another room. By ten he was in bed. For a while he was restless and lay with his headphones on, staring wide-eyed into the night; but the gentle tones of his Barcelona psychologist filled him with confidence and allayed his fears, so that when sleep finally drew him into its dark embrace, there wasn't a shadow of self-doubt in his mind. He believed he was the best and, he told himself, when day broke he would prove it.

IN THE MORNING A WOOLLY BLANKET OF CLOUDS HUNG IN LOOSE FOLDS ABOUT THE TOPS OF THE TALL PINES OF AUGUSTA.

In the morning a woolly blanket of clouds hung in loose folds about the tops of the tall pines of Augusta, enveloping the golf course in a congenial, motherly warmth. Ballesteros was off at twelve minutes to two. At a quarter before the hour, he walked from the putting green to the tee with Jack Newton. Outwardly, he was the epitome of tranquillity, but inside the butterflies were flapping around like eagles. "Everybody gets nervous," he admits. "I think any time you don't have any nerves out on the course it's because you are not interested in the game." He was relieved when he had hit his opening drive on the fairway and even more so when he had pitched up to six feet for birdie. At the third he was closer still, holing from five feet to steal another shot from par, and on the fifth he sank a big, swinging putt right across the green. When he reached the tenth, he was three under par for the day and leading by an incredible ten shots. Victory, it seemed, was a foregone conclusion.

Then, for the first time since the tournament had begun, Ballesteros faltered; he three-putted the tenth. Newton saw his chance and grabbed it, making a four there and a birdie at the eleventh to close the gap between them to eight strokes. Ballesteros was unperturbed. Provided he didn't lose another shot to par, no harm was done; besides which, for the bold player there were still plenty of birdie opportunities to come. He stood on the twelfth tee calmly reflecting on this, and considering his next move. Ahead of him lay one of the toughest par-threes in the world. The slick green is bordered by Rae's Creek, the graveyard of a million hopes, and guarded by one cavernous bunker and two smaller sand traps. A wall of trees stands behind them, and herein lies the danger, for they trap and deflect the wind, causing it to swirl unpredictably above the putting surface. Contemplating them now, Ballesteros decided to aim to the left with a six-iron and let the breeze bring the ball in to the pin. Then he did something utterly out of character; he changed his mind at the top of his backswing and tried to hit the ball straight at the pin. It sailed right, hung suspended for an irritating age in the air, then plopped unceremoniously into the water. Ballesteros was shaken. He slammed his club into the ground. After a moment, he stalked to the water's edge to drop another ball, peering into its murky depths with a black scowl. One chip and two putts later and he had notched up a double bogey. Newton, meanwhile, had birdied to reduce the Spaniard's lead to five.

On the thirteenth Ballesteros teed up and launched himself into his drive. It drew pleasingly around the corner of the dogleg. The green was now just 180 yards away, tucked against Rae's Creek. "Three-iron," he ordered. Herrington was sure it was a four, but didn't like to say so. He watched Ballesteros line up over the shot with some concern. Then . . . calamity! The Spaniard hit the ball fat, striking the ground inches behind it. It climbed weakly into the air, dropped short on the grassy verge of the green, paused, then tumbled into the creek with a splash. The gallery gasped. Spreading rings of ripples chastised him silently, while ten thousand pairs of eyes swiveled and pinned on him in horror. Ballesteros felt the cold fingers of fear clutch at his heart. Sweat pricked his skin. He started toward the green with the heavy-limbed languor of a nightmare. The drone of the disturbed crowd grew louder and louder as he walked. They hummed like killer bees. He bent to lift his ball from the tepid water, feeling persecuted, and dropped it over his shoulder. The referee was not satisfied and told him to drop it again. Rage bubbled up inside Ballesteros and threatened to overflow. "This man is trying to put me off," he thought, and he stared icily at the referee.

"Are you sure, *sir*?" he asked menacingly.

Then, hurtling through his subconscious came a flash of memory, vivid and arresting. With picture-book clarity, he could recall the spring of 1978. He had been striding down this very fairway in the final round of the Masters when Gary Player, whom he was paired with, suddenly turned to him and said: "These people don't think I can win." Ballesteros had stared at him in surprise, then turned to look at the gallery. There was little doubt that that conclusion had indeed crossed the minds of several of them. They had begun to chatter among themselves and drift away disinterestedly. Ballesteros, who had started the day seven strokes behind the leader, Hubert Green, was heading for a 74 and playing that way, but Player had done better. He had reached the turn in 34 and had since picked up two birdies. Nevertheless, the inalterable fact was that he was still a distant three shots adrift of Green entering one of the most treacherous stretches of holes in golf. The crowd regarded the little man in black with pity. "What prayer does he have?" was their collective thought.

Player felt them write his chances off as keenly as if it were a lash across his shoulders. He responded to it with a sudden flash of rage. "These people don't think I can win," he said resentfully to Ballesteros. "You watch, I'll show them."

There followed one of the greatest back-nine performances in the history of major championships. Player scored 30 on the inward half at Augusta and rimmed the hole with putts three times. "Had they dropped, I would have shot 27," Player says. He grins. "I would never have been invited back." An incredible seven birdies in the final ten holes allowed him to overcome Green, Watson, and Rod Funseth by a stroke.

"I'll never forget," Player says, "and I want you to put this in Seve's book, because it's a good thing to spread a little love around the world because so many people spread bloody nasty things, but I'll never forget as long as I live the way he hugged me when I won the Masters. He came up to me on the eighteenth green in front of two hundred million viewers and he hugged me. Which is fantastic. And he was very complimentary because he said I taught him to win the Masters."

Few things have had as much influence on the course of Ballesteros's destiny as Player's words that day on the thirteenth fairway. Now, as he dropped his ball for the second time, he remembered them, and also the note he had found in his locker just before teeing off. "*Buena Suerte*," Player had written. "Good luck, I'm pulling for you." Ballesteros selected a sand iron and chipped onto the green. But despite his best efforts he could do no better than bogey, while Newton holed out for a four. Ahead of them Gibby Gilbert made a three at the fourteenth to move to within four strokes of the Spaniard.

Ballesteros was still smoldering when he drove off the next tee. "So stupid," he said to himself. "What are you doing? Now you must try very hard or you lost the tournament." A spectator's voice forced its way into the mael-strom of his thoughts, loud and jangling. "Come on, Jack!" it shrieked. Ballesteros went white with fury. He threw the man a murderous glance. Adrenaline, thick and heady, coursed through his veins. These people don't think I can win, he thought rebelliously, "I'll show them." He took out a six-iron and hit a magnificent shot out of the rough and onto the green. It ran to twenty-five feet and he two-putted for par. Later, Newton said he believed that approach to have been critical to the Spaniard's success. "Seve had to get it on the green, but also to the right place on that big rolling green. From anywhere else he could have three-putted."

By now Ballesteros had marshaled his thoughts and was ready for the final challenge. "Slow backswing, very important" he said to himself as he addressed the ball on the fifteenth. Then he powered a drive down the fair-way and hit a four-iron over the water to twenty feet. When he reached the green, he glanced at the scoreboard. Gilbert had birdied the sixteenth and was only two strokes behind. Ballesteros leaned with some trepidation on his putter while he waited for the Australian to putt out. But the green was far quicker than either man had judged, and Newton ran his ball ten feet past the hole. Ballesteros watched and learned. His own putt was lagged to four feet and he tapped it in for a birdie.

Only the sixteenth now stood between Ballesteros and the U.S. Masters title. The seventeenth and eighteenth were certain pars, but the sixteenth is a daunting par-three of 170 yards with water running from tee to green. Ballesteros, however, was done with heroics. He took a six-iron for safety and two-putted for par.

"It's finished," he said to Herrington. "The tournament is ours."

Monday, April 14, 1980, London: *Daily Telegraph*—"On the day Sev-eriano Ballesteros clinched the U.S. Masters golf title, Spain's national radio began a news bulletin with a Spanish swimming record. No mention was made of the Spaniard who became the youngest winner of the Masters with a thirteen-under-par total of 275."

A beaming Seve Ballesteros adorns his first Augusta green jacket, symbolic of his 1980 Masters Tournament victory. Helping Seve with his coat is 1979 Masters victor Fuzzy Zoeller. (AP/Wide World Photos)

Thursday, April 17, 1980, La Costa, California. The days following Ballesteros's victory at Augusta were so frantic and filled with activity that in no time at all they had merged into a confusing reel of places, colors, and strange ingratiating faces, like half-remembered scenes from the windows of an express train. First, there had been the prize giving and a lengthy and demanding press conference, at which he had been more or less asked to quantify the exact proportions of luck and good judgment used in his triumph. Newton, who had finished runner-up to Ballesteros with Gilbert, took issue with the blind insistence of American reporters that fortune was the overriding element in the Spaniard's successes at Augusta and Lytham. "It takes a lot of guts to win a major championship," he said shortly, "and Seve has won two of them. Here is a superstar and it's about time everybody realized it."

That evening there was an honorary dinner at the golf club, where, Ballesteros complained, he was given a steak scarcely bigger than a peseta. Then, of course, there were the inevitable celebrations. It was 5:00 A.M. when he finally went to bed and he was up again by eight to catch a plane to Atlanta. At eleven o'clock he was collected from the airport and whisked away to a photo session. After that, he was rushed to a television studio for the Mike Douglas chat show, put on a flight to Los Angeles where he was meeting Ed Barner for dinner and, at length, shown a televised rerun of his Masters win. No sooner had he caught his breath than he was back on an airplane and winging his way to the Tournament of Champions at La Costa, California.

Upon reaching the golf course, he collected his credentials from the players' registration desk. The official dispensing them beamed. "Your mother called from Spain," she informed him.

"My mother?" Ballesteros said in puzzlement. "She spoke English?"

"A little."

The slow light of comprehension dawned across his face. "Not my mother," he told her with the sly grin of a man not unused to getting calls from women purporting to be near relatives.

"Well done, Seve," Trevino said as the Spaniard passed him, clapping him on the back. "Remember me telling you to go to Augusta a week early?"

Ballesteros had not forgotten. "How do I win the U.S. Open?" he asked hopefully.

"Get them to cut down the rough," Trevino laughed.

Eventually, after disentangling himself from two persistent salesmen who were determined that he should endorse their shirts, Ballesteros went out to play a practice round, alone but for his caddie and a dozen spectators. Coming off the third green he was stopped by a television crew. They only wanted to ask the same questions he had heard a hundred times before, but he was patient and tactful and gave them as much time as they needed. That night he wandered down to the clubhouse restaurant and had supper with Doust and Williams. He said three things of note during the meal: (1) The Swiss Open was one of his favorite tournaments because he loved to go to the local disco; (2) Sandy Lyle would one day win the Masters; and (3) Appearance money was essential to the European Tour.

When the tournament was over and Ballesteros had finished eighteenth behind Watson, he flew to Spain for the Madrid Open. There he was greeted as a conquistador by his comrades but went almost unnoticed by the nation at large. Piñero had spent the night after the Masters on the telephone to every newspaper in the country in an effort to establish whether in fact Ballesteros had won, but to no avail. "Severiano who?" they had echoed blankly. But, from those people who did know him and who did understand how momentous his victory was, Ballesteros received a deluge of congratulatory telegrams and phone calls. King Juan Carlos and Adolfo Suarez of Spain both wrote letters, Bob Hope requested a round of golf with him, and Muhammad Ali rang to tell him he was the greatest.

On the surface, all of this left him unaffected. His family had come down from the north to welcome him home, accompanied by a coachload of excited villagers driven by Ramon Sota, and he was drawn willingly back into the warm and familiar cocoon of friends and relatives—simple, generoushearted people with simple values—experiencing a strong sense of relief as he did so, rather like a cat that has been too long in the cold snuggling into a sheepskin rug on the hearth. But inwardly he was beginning to alter beyond all recognition. The incessant demands of the public and of sponsors, and the constant pressure on him to perform, made him increasingly moody and withdrawn. Away from the golf course, during those sultry Madrid evenings, he was able, for a few hours, to forget who he was and what he stood for; but when the harsh light of morning returned it always brought the tournament, and along with that came the probing glances and intruding questions of strangers intent on invading his private world.

On the first practice day of the Madrid Open, Ballesteros went hunting for Musgrove. Musgrove, however, was caddying for Michael King and refused to change bags. He had not heard a word from the Spaniard over the winter and didn't see why he should. There was a small confrontation of wills. Ballesteros's brown eyes were the first to drop. He knew he was in the wrong—not that he would ever have dreamed of admitting it. "I didn't tell him to go," Seve said defensively to journalists. "Last season he got very excited towards the end and he talked too much on the course. That was not good." Baldomero, his brother, was then prevailed upon to caddie for him.

In the second round Ballesteros shot a career-best 63. It was the triumphant result of a personal ambition to make everyone he felt had insulted him eat their words: Musgrove, for instance, had been palpably rude and quite scathing when rejecting his offer of employment; the Spanish media had failed to recognize the enormity of his achievement at Augusta; and the Americans continued to doubt his ability to win major championships without divine intervention. Pursued by these imaginary demons, Ballesteros played like a man possessed. He strode along the fairways, eyes fixed on his target, muttering to himself over and over again: "I can win every tournament in the world, I can win every tournament in the world." The spectators stared at him curiously but shrank back when he glowered at them, and once or twice when Baldomero made an incautious remark he had his head snapped off.

"You have a 30, six under par," he had pointed out to his young brother at the turn. But Ballesteros's mood had been further blackened by an eight-foot putt missed at the ninth, and he only said irritably: "It should have been a 29."

On the back nine Baldomero told him that the King of Spain was in the gallery. Ballesteros didn't glance up—didn't hear him even, so absorbed was he in the task that he had set himself.

In the third round the young Spaniard scored a 70 to Piñero's 69, gaining a four-stroke advantage and the upper hand psychologically going into the final day. Piñero, however, is long on courage and fortitude, and had closed the gap to a shot by the time they reached the sixteenth hole. There, Ballesteros showed his mastery. He extracted a seven-iron from a desperate lie among the pines, putting it six feet away from the pin for birdie, while Piñero, who is not blessed with magic powers, had to chip out onto the fairway for bogey. Ballesteros eventually won by three shots with a score of 69 and an aggregate of 270, eighteen under par. It was his first major triumph in his native land.

The subsequent festivities were entered into with gusto by the gathered clan, but were cut short by the collapse of Baldomero on a street corner in Madrid. "Baldomero is a very nervous person," Ballesteros explained, "and he is not used to carrying a golf bag that weighs twenty kilos up and down hills for four days. Eight kilometers a day for a man thirty-three years old made him very tired. His nerves, plus the pressure, plus all the eating and alcohol and smoke . . . Baldomero just . . . stops breathing." For an instant Ballesteros was paralyzed with fright at the sight of his older brother lying motionless on the pavement, but soon recovered himself and was about to give him mouth-to-mouth resuscitation when he revived. Baldomero was taken to the hospital for examination, kept in overnight for observation, and released the following morning.

Two days later Ballesteros was already in rehearsal for the Spanish Open, his third consecutive tournament after the Masters. Contrary to all expectations he showed no outward signs of fatigue but, rather, was bursting with vitality and good health. His presence at El Escorpion had been guaranteed by Benson and Hedges, sponsors of the event; who, having paid him forty-seven hundred pounds to play at Torrequebrada the previous year, where he had promptly missed the cut, now found themselves writing checks for two thousand pounds in appearance money, two thousand pounds if he qualified for the final two days, and an additional two thousand pounds if he won the seven-thousand-pound first prize.

Ballesteros secured the first and second parts of the bargain easily enough, scoring 68, 72 in the opening rounds, but his temper and Eddie Polland, the former Ryder Cup player, cost him the third. "In contrast with Ballesteros, who could frequently be seen beating his club on the ground in frustration," Williams wrote in the *Telegraph*, "it was refreshing to find Polland accepting any minor unintentional shots without a tantrum and, instead, a rueful smile." Polland won by five shots over the Spaniard and Mark James.

In retrospect, Ballesteros's achievements in the early part of 1980 are nothing less than extraordinary. Beginning with the Tournament Players Championship in March, he finished third, first, eighteenth, first, second, and first—the last being the Martini International, where he beat Brian Barnes. Throughout that period he maintained an air of youthful defiance and invincibility, the only indication that he might be succumbing to the inevitable strain of contending every week being the European PGA Championship at St. George's, where he was suffering from a chest infection, and informed the media morosely: "Winning is very difficult in any company." He then proved it by finishing thirty-second.

Five days before the U.S. Open Championship was due to start at Baltusrol, Ballesteros flew to New York to begin his preparations.

Friday, June 13, 1980, Baltusrol Golf Club, Springfield, New Jersey. The existence of newspapers is proof that no two people can ever tell a story in exactly the same way. Human nature doesn't allow it. One can hardly be surprised, therefore, at the number of variations on a theme one hears of the following events—particularly when some of the storytellers are given to sensationalism and others are hoping to absolve themselves of blame. Suffice to say that they began, in Ballesteros's version, at least, when he experienced a premonition on the flight from Madrid to New York. One minute he was looking distractedly out the window, and the next he was overcome by a sensation of impending doom.

"Seve," he said to himself, "you should not be going to the U.S. Open. Something bad is going to happen."

Things began to go wrong almost immediately. Upon registering for the tournament Ballesteros was given a player's badge and a caddie's badge, the latter being for his brother Baldomero. He then discovered that Baldomero was not allowed beyond the locker room, let alone into the dining room, and an acrimonious discussion with a USGA official ensued. But in vain. The official could not be swayed. Ballesteros stamped off crossly to find his golf clubs, encountering Irwin en route; who, though there had been little love lost between them in the past, invited him out for a practice game. Ballesteros accepted, played well, and had a thoroughly enjoyable time, finishing two, four, four—all birdies. Irwin remarked to journalists that the young Spaniard was "driving respectably and swinging the club both smoothly and slowly."

When he came off the course he had recovered his humor and was smiling. It was but a fleeting phase. Soon he was in conflict with Barner, who was insistent that he should attend a cocktail party half an hour's drive away in New York City, because UMI was negotiating a new contract for him with Rolex. Ballesteros refused point-blank to go anywhere. Barner used a variety of pleas, ploys, and entreaties to try to persuade him, but in the end Ballesteros had his own way: He stayed in his hotel room. As it turned out, it wouldn't have made a blind bit of difference if he had gone to the cocktail party or even if he had made a comprehensive tour of the nightlife of Manhattan afterward. The following day he recorded a dismal 75, five over par, and drew perilously near to missing the cut.

It is at this point that the stories of the people involved in this incident start to diverge. Ballesteros has an excellent memory, there's no question about that. According to Joe Collet, who was taking care of the Spaniard that week: "He has such a good memory that sometimes he thinks he's the only one that remembers it in the way that it was. But he does have the same frailty that a lot of us have, that [his] perception of reality is not always what everybody else's perception is. He has his impression of what happened [at the U.S. Open] and I have mine."

THE COLOR DRAINED LIKE A SPONGE FROM BALLESTEROS'S FACE. IN AN INSTANT HE WAS IN A COURTESY CAR AND SPEEDING DANGEROUSLY THROUGH THE TRAFFIC.

Collet's impression is this: Because Ballesteros wasn't yet fluent in English, Collet had always made it his job at the beginning of every tournament to search out the draw, take it to the Spaniard, and check that he knew his tee times. The U.S. Open was no different. On Wednesday evening he had taken a starting sheet from his briefcase and said to Ballesteros: "Do you know what time you are playing on Thursday and Friday?" After Ballesteros had reeled off the times confidently, Collet had not given the matter another thought. But on Friday morning when he was walking through the hotel lobby, on his way to get a courtesy car, he caught sight of Ballesteros wandering aimlessly out of the dining room.

"Seve!" Collet cried in amazement. "You're off in a few minutes! What are you doing here?"

Ballesteros was taken aback. "Oh, no," he said, "I don't go off for another hour."

"You go off right now," Collet said in a chilling tone.

The color drained like a sponge from Ballesteros's face. In an instant he was in a courtesy car and speeding dangerously through the traffic to the golf course. He was out of the door before the car stopped and running to fetch his shoes and clubs, but by the time he reached the first tee, seven minutes too late, his playing partners had hit their second shots. USGA official John Laupheimer had no choice but to disqualify him under the Rules of Golf for the breach of Rule 37-5.

Dudley Doust's interpretation of events is totally different to Collet's, and yet they were the only two people allowed into Ballesteros's hotel room after he had returned from the course. He claims that it was Collet who failed to remind Ballesteros of his starting times, and that when Ballesteros and his brother had set off that morning at 9:25, for what they thought was a 10:45 tee time, they had done so in a relaxed fashion, laughing and joking all the way to the course and taking no notice whatsoever of the lines of rush-hour traffic. It was only when they had pulled up at the club and a British journalist came rushing over to tell Ballesteros that he was due on the tee, that they had realized anything was amiss.

Another story is that Baldomero was supposed to have checked the starting time and told Ballesteros, and that there had been some breakdown in communication between the two brothers. But Collet says he has talked to Baldomero about it and that Baldomero just answered tersely: "I know how to read. But Seve had it set in his mind that it was another time and, because he seemed to know, I didn't question him." No matter. The end result of all these scenarios was the same. When Ballesteros heard he was to be disqualified he flew into a terrible rage and pleaded for a reduced sentence. However, the rules of the game are specific. Ballesteros had to swallow his medicine and, not liking it one little bit, went snarling to the clubhouse to empty his locker and left the course at speed.

"Of course, it was big news," Collet continues. " 'Europe's Order of Merit leader makes idiot mistake.' And there were reporters hanging about the hotel trying to get pictures and interviews and, of course, he just wanted to hide. He was so embarrassed, it was terrible. A good friend of ours, Susan Minkley—she was very fond of Seve—just felt terrible about it. She had a Cadillac and she offered to help get us to the airport. And I'll never forget, I had the room next to Seve's, and I was looking out the window and all the reporters were hanging around the car park. So I said, 'Baldomero, you go down to the lobby like you're expecting Seve to follow. Susan, get your car and sneak around the back. Then we'll go down and drive off and avoid all the confrontation.' It almost worked. Everybody went to the lobby when they saw Baldomero, and Seve and I bolted down the stairs. But just as we were jumping in the car, a couple of them got wise, and came around and

Don't be fooled by the smile: A boiling Seve Ballesteros heads to the airport after being disqualified from the 1980 U.S. Open for missing his tee time. (AP/Wide World Photos)

took pictures. And Seve smiled and waved and closed the door and we drove off. But it took him quite a while to admit that maybe it was his fault about the tee time, and I kind of got blamed. . . . And it wasn't true. In fact, if it wasn't for me, he would never have got there at all."

That was not the opinion of a sizable number of officials and members of the press, who felt that the whole affair might have been stage-managed by UMI. "More than one world-class American . . . felt very strongly that . . . Ballesteros had demeaned the U.S. Open in particular and golfers in general with his disgraceful performance at Baltusrol," wrote Ben Wright of *Golf World* (September 1980). "The players in question feel that the gulf between American and European golf . . . has been immeasurably widened by the talented Spaniard's inexplicable conduct, and it is difficult to disagree with them, although I had to point out to them that Ballesteros's two 'handlers,' who should have ensured his presence on Baltusrol's first tee at the appointed hour, are American."

Wright goes on to speculate whether anyone may have been responsible for Ballesteros's missing his starting time so that he would save face after a first-round 75 had left him twelve shots adrift of eventual winner Nicklaus and Weiskopf, and these include a high-ranking official of the USGA. Says Wright: "It is hard to understand Ballesteros's behavior, particularly since he was also accompanied by his brother. It was obviously very hurtful to us that the British Open and U.S. Masters Champion should behave in such an unprofessional manner. No one in a privileged position in American golf will be anxious to bend over backwards to help Ballesteros in the foreseeable future, at least until he has wiped the slate clean."

A week after the U.S. Open, Ballesteros was offered five thousand pounds to play in the Greater Manchester Open, but turned it down. His brother Manuel said in a statement: "Seve is still upset by what happened in America, but that has nothing to do with him turning down the offer."

Those were gloomy times for Ballesteros. Whether at home in Pedreña or out on Tour, all served to remind him of the trauma of Baltusrol. He had nightmares where he was blindfolded and facing a firing squad but woke up an instant before he was shot, and others where he was late to the first tee while playing in the World Cup with Piñero, and disqualified. "Many times I see people, at night," he said to Doust. "Not in dream, no, no, I tell you, *people*. I wake up and see somebody leaning over my bed—maybe a man, maybe a woman—but when I open up the light, nothing. It has gone away."

In press conferences he was even more self-deprecating than usual, constantly alluding to his pet themes of missed tee times and luck, but it was not until the Dutch Open at Hilversum that he actually confronted the specter of the U.S. Open head-on.

"It was my fault," he admitted. "I was stupid. But I felt like a dog which had been kicked."

Then he pulled himself together and swept to a four-stroke victory, much to the delight of the huge galleries that had turned out specially to see him. It was one of few bright sparks in what was a comparatively dull second half of the season. The editor of *Golf World* commented: "All of [Ballesteros's] wins were in the early part of 1980 and I am left wondering if there is any significance in this. For the rest of the year he was disappointing and his attitude and approach to the game that gives him his living left something to be desired. . . . The smiling face is not instantly there now—a few wrinkles have appeared—and he showed at the World Cup that he wants nothing to do with any golfing activity which does not guarantee him money on the table before he starts. As Peter Alliss says of him, 'I hope he does not get too tough and that he takes time to smell a few flowers on the way.' "

But Trevino, asked what he thought was the matter with his young friend, jumped to his defense. "The kid is going through the first slump of his life," he said abruptly. "People keep asking him what's wrong and it's bugging him. He can't go into a restaurant and enjoy dinner anymore. I really feel sorry for him because he really is a tremendous player and a good guy. He asked me how I handled my bad times and I told him: 'Seve, there will be days you can't do anything right. You have to stay with it and work your way out of it.' "

PRIDE AND PREJUDICE

"Winston Churchill always said, 'Adversity is what makes you a man.' "

Gary Player, Palm Springs, March 1992

In order to understand the events and far-reaching effects of 1981, it is first necessary to know that they had their roots in the evil of appearance money. One should also realize that appearance money did not always have the notoriety it does now, and that in 1971, when John Jacobs was handed the responsibility of trying to make a nonviable golf circuit into a marketable enterprise, he considered player inducements to be an essential ingredient in the tournament division's long-term success. Before the appointment of Jacobs the British Tour, such as it was, had been run by the PGA with the aid of a handful of freelance financial advisers. As a result, it had made little progress. An average season consisted of seven or eight events with a total prize fund of two hundred fifty thousand pounds, and individual purses of less than a tenth of that, in which the winner and four or five other players made money, eight or ten broke even, and 150 were out of pocket.

To Jacobs, a former Tour player, it was unacceptable that this situation should be allowed to continue. He set about contacting the existing Tour patrons and explained to them that in future a minimum prize fund would be imposed. As a consequence, several key sponsors withdrew their support. It quickly became obvious that if the British Tour was to survive, two things needed to happen: (1) It had to expand into the rest of Europe; and (2) Europe's top players had to be encouraged to support their own circuit rather than that of the U.S. With this in mind Jacobs created a rule which stated that any player who had won a major championship had the right to negotiate for appearance money. This idea was not as revolutionary as it sounds. It had been an open secret since the days of Henry Cotton, and possibly long before, that certain professionals received incentives to play. In 1971, however, Tony Jacklin was alone among the Europeans in meriting them. After he had won the U.S. and British Opens, he was paid in the region of two thousand pounds for events on this side of the Atlantic and ten thousand pounds for those in Japan. IMG, his representatives, made the most of their good fortune, Jacobs watched the Tour flourish, and everybody was happy. Until Ballesteros came along.

It is possible that UMI had asked, or been offered, appearance money for Ballesteros from the time he finished second to Miller at Birkdale, although officially he was not entitled to it until after he had won the money list at the end of that year. Certainly, Musgrove has a clear recollection of the Spaniard saying to him in September 1976, during the Sun-Alliance Match Play Championship, that he had been paid to show up. "They're giving me money to play," the Spaniard had remarked. By 1979, even before he had won the British Open, Ballesteros was able to command fees of more than five thousand dollars per tournament; in 1980 he was paid seven thousand pounds, with additional bonuses for winning; and in 1981 Ed Barner decided—inflation being what it was—that his client could ask for eleven thousand pounds, plus first-class airfares, expenses, and a bonus for winning.

That was the straw that broke the camel's back. Early in the previous season several sponsors had expressed outrage at the figures they were being expected to pay Ballesteros and had run crying to Ken Schofield, the executive director of the new European Tournament Players' Division (ETPD). The first stirrings of dissent were felt at Tour headquarters. A ban on appearance money was discussed. Word reached Ed Barner. In March, when the British press met for the launch of a major deal between Ballesteros and Slazenger (worth two hundred fifty thousand pounds over five years), he took the opportunity to inform them that unless sponsors paid the going rate, his client would not be playing in their tournaments.

He might just as well have tossed a match at a keg of dynamite. The resulting explosion was heard right around the golfing world and was the beginning of what Schofield bitterly describes as "that very, very public and very lamentable year."

It's strange how full of irony life is. One moment a rule is being created to allow Jacklin to reap the maximum benefit of his two major victories through appearance fees, and the next there is talk of that very same rule being abolished immediately because Ballesteros is making too much money from it. Of course, these incidents took place almost ten years apart, during which time the PGA and the Tour had gone their separate ways, Jacobs had resigned, the total prize fund for the season had risen from seven hundred thousand pounds in 1975 to a projected 1.8 million pounds in the 1981 season, and the appearance-money rule had been adapted so that the winner of the preceding season's Order of Merit was also entitled to receive it.

Joe Collet says that clandestine meetings between Schofield and those sponsors who wanted to cut the throat of the appearance-money monster had been held then, but that due to lack of support from other patrons their campaign had proved ineffectual and had ultimately resulted in surrender on the part of the Tour. "Then it all got out of hand again, and I don't know who was to blame, but the fees got bigger and bigger, and more and more tournaments realized they couldn't even get a field unless they paid Tom, Dick, and Harry. And there were probably more people who weren't at the top of the Order of Merit, who were asking for plane tickets and hotels and things, and so the sponsors went back to Ken again. The details have escaped me, but what I do remember was there came a point in time when Seve was going to be singled out as an example."

That point was in the autumn of 1980. The ETPD committee had rendezvoused at Wentworth to review the appearance-money situation. Once before when they had met, Jacobs had tried to convince them that the reason the rule had been instigated in the first place—to attempt to compensate top European players for earnings which they could otherwise make in prize money alone in the U.S.—was still justifiable. Ballesteros, for instance, was the winner of two major championships and three money lists. How could he now be expected to play on his own continent for peanuts when he could make ten times as much in Japan or America? "I'm very sorry," Jacobs had declared to the room at large, "but I think you're wrong. You're dealing with a very proud Spaniard and you're saying that he shouldn't have appearance money, but you're still allowing Lee Trevino and Tom Weiskopf to have it. Why?" This time there was nobody to argue Ballesteros's corner. The committee, led by chairman Neil Coles, ruled that with effect from the first tournament of the new season no ETPD member could request appearance money, although he would be allowed "expenses" of up to ten thousand dollars. Perversely, American players who commanded fees of up to forty thousand dollars for appearing in Europe were free to continue to do so. As if this policy was not farcical enough, there was also a loophole in the rule which meant that although a player or manager couldn't actually *ask* for appearance money, there was nothing to stop a sponsor from offering it to him.

Farcical or not, the rule was imposed. Before the 1981 season had begun, the die was cast, and the wheels of misfortune had begun to grind inexorably along the path toward destruction.

Wednesday, April 22, 1981, Madrid. Lightning, like the devil's pitchfork, split the dark sky above Puerto de Hierro, sending the small group of players who had ventured out to practice scrambling hastily for cover. Since dawn the rain had fallen with relentless efficiency. Play had been suspended when the golf course was reduced to a relief map of rivers and ravines and, with more rain forecast, the prospects for a four-round tournament were bleak. Inside the clubhouse the atmosphere was no less stormy. Brandy glasses clinked and cigarette smoke swirled thickly as the Madrid Open committee pondered a singular conundrum: the disappearance of Severiano Ballesteros. They had before them a letter of explanation. At least, if it didn't exactly *explain* why he had gone absent without leave, it did inform them of his whereabouts. Regretfully, Ballesteros would not be defending his Madrid Open title that week as he was under obligation to compete in a conflicting event on the Japanese Tour. Would the committee be so kind as to grant him a release?

A stunned silence greeted this announcement, followed by a cacophony of Spanish cries as members of the committee gave free rein to a wide spectrum of emotions. They were enraged; they were embarrassed; they were embittered. Ballesteros was Spain's finest player, not to mention the title holder of the Madrid Open and a major draw card in terms of ticket sales, and all promotional material had been prepared with this in mind. What on earth was to be done? And what of the manner in which the release had been requested? That, too, should be taken into consideration: (1) Ballesteros had flown to Japan on Monday of the Madrid Open; (2) The letter had allegedly been delivered on Tuesday; (3) Under the rules of the ETPD, any member who wishes to play in a tournament which clashes with an ETPD event must obtain a release from the ETPD.

"MY DRIVING IS LIKE MY GOLF," HE SAID MOCKINGLY WHEN QUESTIONED ABOUT THEM. "I AM NEVER ON THE FAIRWAY."

The Madrid Open committee debated these issues at length and it was late in the day before they decided that the Spaniard would be given a release.

"So what happens now?" Dobereiner asked the next morning. "Possibly a fine. Possibly a refusal to pay the fine. Possibly a resignation from the ETPD. Possibly no Ballesteros in the Ryder Cup team. At all events the most promising career in world golf will come under serious threat, and that is the greatest of pities because the new rule forbidding the asking of appearance money, which Ballesteros sees as an act of personal victimization, is no more than the expression of a pious hope. There are many ways in which a top golfer can be persuaded to include a tournament in his program and players take advantage of them, as is their due."

People like to say that bad things happen in threes. They don't really. They happen in twos or fours or even twenties. It all depends on when you start counting them and when you stop. If you began in June 1980, for example, you would say that the black dogs were barking when Ballesteros missed his tee-off time at the U.S. Open. But if New Year's Day in 1981 was your starting point, then you would probably include the two minor car crashes in which Ballesteros was involved. They were both his fault, and caused the wreckage of two different vehicles.

"My driving is like my golf," he said mockingly when questioned about them. "I am never on the fairway."

The next thing that occurred was the European Ferries' press conference in London on February 11, when Ballesteros signed a five-year contract as touring professional at La Manga in Spain. He informed the gathered media that he would be competing in only six or seven tournaments in Europe that season, most of which would be in Britain. Instead, he intended to play around seven events on the U.S. Tour and at least five on the lucrative Japanese Tour. "They want to see me in Japan," he explained. "They play for double our prize money and they are also offering me as much as thirty or forty thousand dollars a tournament." He made no bones about the fact that the decision to spurn the European Tour was a means of retaliation against the new rule. "Sponsors don't have to pay me appearance money, but also I don't have to play in their tournaments," he observed, knowing full well that he would continue to be offered money in suitcases. "I think it should be left to the sponsors to decide who they want and how much they want them. If they want all the publicity then they must pay for the good players."

But when Ballesteros arrived at Augusta in April to defend his Masters title, after a lackluster performance in the Greater Greensboro Open, he was considerably less blithe. Four days earlier London Weekend Television had released a documentary in which he was seen to say that, "Appearance money will never disappear," and to state categorically that he owed the game nothing. "Do you not know how much I give to golf? I start when I was nine and since then I live until I am now twenty-three. That all the way for golf. You think that is not enough? I think that is enough." According to Doust, he had also received a hostile letter from the executive director of the Tour. "One thing you should know straight from me," Schofield allegedly wrote, "is that no one player can, from this day forward, expect to clear two hundred fifty thousand dollars in appearance fees before teeing off on the European Tour."

These troubles were clearly weighing on Ballesteros's mind. He was sullen and taciturn during his interviews, and would give little away save that he had undertaken to playing Japan during the week of the Madrid Open. His game, too, was not what it should have been. After parring the first six holes in the opening round of the tournament, he proceeded to drop seven strokes in eight holes through Amen Corner and finally returned a card of 78. His outburst in the winter—"Every day, business and rain, business and rain. I have no time to think, I have no time to relax, to concentrate on practicing my game. I tell you, I have *never* been so poorly prepared for a season.

I will play no good at the Masters"—appeared to have been a prediction. The following day he scored 76 and missed the cut by six shots.

On May 6, having played truant for a fortnight in Japan, Ballesteros returned to Europe for the French Open at St. Germain. He refused to take on the mantle of the prodigal son, insisting instead that he was the "white sheep of a prodigal family." If the tournament committee fined him he would not pay it, whether it was five pounds or five thousand. "I have many other places to play apart from Europe. Maybe I will play the Japanese Tour." There was no doubt that he believed the Tour to be making a scapegoat of him and felt that the creation of the appearance-money rule had been inspired by the jealousy of lesser players. It plainly cut him to the quick that the ETPD failed to appreciate what he had done for European golf. At the same time, he regretted the chain of events that had brought him into conflict with the Tour. "It is very sad. I feel sorry for the people who want to see me playing Britain and I hope they understand my position."

When the tournament ended, with Ballesteros tied for third with Sandy Lyle, he returned to Santander with a heavy heart. He had a week to wait, and possibly longer, before he would know the inevitable consequences of his now irrevocable decision to resign from the European Tour.

May 14, 1981, London. The *Guardian*: "Severiano Ballesteros is no longer a European Tour player. His name has been removed from the Ryder Cup points list and from the official money list."

Throughout the years, the blame for the events of 1981 and their repercussions has always been laid squarely at the door of UMI. But the whole affair really began and ended with Ballesteros. He wasn't coerced into doing something he didn't want to do. He did it of his own free will. As Roddy Carr says, "Seve has never been one to take advice. He'll do exactly what he wants to do, anyway." Early on in his career Ballesteros had told Collet and Barner that they should be more aggressive when asking for appearance money on his behalf. He felt he was as good as any American player and should be paid accordingly. His managers agreed. There were now two options available to Ballesteros. He could defy his own nature and give in gracefully; content himself with playing for nothing but the love of the game each week while U.S. golfers committed daylight robbery before his very eyes. Or he could rebel. Characteristically, he took the line of most resistance.

"He was adamant that he should get appearance money," Collet recalls. "We told him that there were going to be sanctions imposed if he continued to be paid, and that the only way around that was to withdraw his membership, and then as a nonmember he could charge what he wanted and get paid. And since he felt that it was more important to continue to be able to be appreciated and be compensated based on his merits than it was to be a member of a second-rate tour—which it was at the time—he agreed with our strategy to withdraw his membership. And we did that on the promise he had with John Jacobs that it wouldn't affect his Ryder Cup standings."

With Ballesteros's permission, Collet sent a telex to Schofield. "On the basis of which way you decide on the ruling," he wrote, "I'm provisionally withdrawing Seve's membership from the Tour."

The theory behind this was simple. If Ballesteros had already resigned from the Tour, he could not have broken any rules by playing in the Far East during the Madrid and Italian Opens, and should not therefore be subjected to disciplinary action. The ball was in the court of the ETPD. All they had to do was accept this piece of logic as unassailable, put any notions of fining him or suspending him out of their heads, and Ballesteros would withdraw his resignation.

The ETPD accepted Ballesteros's resignation with effect from the date it was received, which meant that because he wasn't a member when he went to Japan—where he was understood to have been paid sixty thousand pounds' appearance money—he would not be punished. Officially, he was now restricted to playing in his own national open and a maximum of two other European events as a nonmember. In reality, he could accept invitations to play every event on the calendar. And he could rejoin the ETPD if he wished to by signing the standard players' declaration agreeing to abide by the rules. From that moment on he would be eligible to win points for Ryder Cup selection.

If only life were so simple.

With Ballesteros safely in Spain for a month of enforced rest, the battle between UMI and the ETPD began in earnest. "My only contact [with Seve] at that time, rightly or wrongly, was through Ed Barner," Schofield says. "He was prepared to take out virtual injunctions against me talking to his client. My recollection is that there was very little in the way of letters between us. Most of it was a public shouting match at various press conferences and meetings. I can certainly vividly remember leaving one meeting at the Inter Continental Hotel on an impasse to go back to Wentworth, and being told that Ed's been on the phone nice as nine-pins, as if nothing had happened. Yet an hour earlier we were going to have all the lawyers in the world dealing with us. So that was the nature of the debate at that time."

In June Ballesteros arrived for the U.S. Open. Off the course events had taken a new and rather bizarre twist. The ETPD had released a statement announcing the impending return of Ballesteros to the bosom of the European Tour, and claiming that the appearance-money dispute had been resolved. They were still saying the same thing a week later when Ballesteros teed up in the U.S. Open at Merion. Barner, on the other hand, was insisting in "increasingly extreme language" that it was more bitterly contested than ever. He called a press conference and informed the media with brutal frankness that the ETPD announcement was premature. Nothing could be gleaned from Ballesteros. He was secretly afraid that anyone he spoke to would remind him of his missed tee-off time at Baltusrol, so he avoided conversation altogether. His normally sunny demeanor had vanished, to be replaced by a surly, noncommittal facade, and he went about his business on the golf course with singular unenjoyment. This had no effect on his ability to manufacture miracles, but it did alter his response to them. On the fourth hole in the first round he visited three bunkers in an attempt to reach the green. When he came to play his fourth shot from the unfamiliar environment of the fairway, he found his ball had been cut and was smiling at him. He pitched up to the putting surface and there succeeded in holing a fifty-foot putt across a steep slope for par. Thunderous applause greeted this effort. For once, Ballesteros made no acknowledgment, but simply walked away as though weighed down by a burden too oppressive to bear.

The following Wednesday, having scored 73, 69, 72, 75 to finish forty-first at Merion, he issued a statement in which he said that he had decided not to accept membership of any tour organization for the rest of the year. He regretted that this would exclude him from the Ryder Cup, but could see no other choice. "Having been the object of apparently intentional efforts to portray me as disloyal and mercenary," he wrote, "and then further being discriminated against in specific ETPD regulations, and finally to be excluded from the ETPD Order of Merit while other nonmembers are included, I can only say that it has hurt my feelings very much. Where I once felt at home, recent actions by some have made me feel very uncomfortable."

In July Ballesteros made one of his rare appearances in Europe at the Scandinavian Enterprise Open, for a fee of almost twenty-five thousand dollars (the same amount he had been paid to play in the French Open). Whether for this, or for some other reason, he appeared to have had a change of heart. For one glorious week he was his old smiling, wryly self-deprecating self again. He marched the fairways as if he owned them, thrilling the galleries with his boldness and vigor.

"He was very intense," David Feherty says. "I don't think he was intentionally aloof, but he had that incredible burning ambition, that single-mindedness. A guy like Faldo is the same, although he's chosen to do it a different way. He's done it in a more clinical fashion. Ballesteros just followed his instinct. You know, there's the hole, let me get the ball into it in as few as possible."

On the seventeenth hole in the third round the Spaniard drove deep into a forest off the tee. Most golfers would have seen only one avenue of exit: a short chip onto the fairway. Ballesteros, thankfully, is not one of them. Having prowled about in the undergrowth for some minutes searching for options, he at last spotted a tiny fragment of sky through the surrounding foliage—an escape route only if you are one of those people who believe that threes are 90 percent air. Ballesteros is, and his seven-iron flew cleanly through the gap and landed ten feet from the pin for a birdie. Further manifestations of genius allowed him to record-closing rounds of 68, 66, for an eleven-under-par total of 273, to win his first tournament since the Dutch Open the previous summer.

The manner of victory prompted Louis T. Stanley to observe a few months later: "The young Spaniard has demonstrated how a cavalier style of play, a boldness of method, can dominate opponents and courses alike. He had immense talent but unfortunately a Latin temperament that quickly becomes depressed. In many ways he is his own greatest enemy. . . . Ballesteros must not put himself on a pedestal with an appearance-money price tag on it. Quite naturally he wants to make as much money as he can from his skills, but it is a mistake to use muscle in bargaining. . . . Rather than risk the label of being called greedy, the Spaniard would be better advised to listen to mature advice. He will make plenty of money out of golf in good time. In the end public opinion and private friendships are more valuable than an inflated check. He has a considerable following and it would be sad if they were disillusioned."

There is no telling why Ballesteros's fellow professionals first turned against him. It may, as he claimed, have been sparked by envy of his achievements and of the worth sponsors placed on him, or it may just have been a gradual erosion of the respect he had earned. It began when he broke with the time-honored tradition of returning to defend a title, was fueled by reports of his avarice, and then his resignation from the Tour fanned the flames. At any rate, his relationships with other players, even those who had once been close friends, started to deteriorate.

"Well, Seve in those years was going his own way," Piñero explains. "He thought he was right and he was doing things for himself, and a lot of people on the European Tour, we thought he wasn't 100 percent right. But from what I can remember, the European Tour felt he tried to put them in a situation where it was: You or me? Seve or the European Tour? In 1981 he was a fantastic player. He had won the Masters the year before. But he forced them to choose. And I think that a lot of players felt that no matter how big you are, the European Tour has to be bigger. We all accepted that he was brilliant. That's why there was such a great discussion, otherwise there wouldn't have been. But one of the problems with Seve a lot of the time, is he thinks he is right all the time. And he is a person. He's right *on* the course.

Only gentle Chino Fernandez spoke out in Ballesteros's defense, angry at what he felt was a "hypocritical" attitude on the part of many of the players. "When he was on top everybody wanted to play with him. Even on the putting green, they wanted to be nearby. When the appearance money came out in public, most of the same people that wanted to be beside him started talking against him. . . . I talked to some of those players and told them that I thought they were unfair. Because every week there were a bunch of players that wanted to play a practice round with him. And then suddenly he was by himself. I don't think it was anything to do with appearance money, the way people reacted. I mean, those players didn't realize that because he was playing we had sponsorship and more spectators coming to the gate. They could only be jealous because he was getting appearance money. I told them: 'Well, next time it could be you. Or somebody else.' And I said: 'Who's guaranteeing that the sponsor's going to put the money that they want to pay Seve in the prize money?' They *want* Seve to play. And it's been proved that 25 percent more people come through the gate when he's playing."

OUTCAST BY OFFICIALDOM AND FAIR-WEATHER FRIENDS, BALLESTEROS WHILED AWAY THE LONG, LONELY DAYS IN PEDREÑA, PRACTICING FOR HOURS AND HOURS BY HIMSELF.

Outcast by officialdom and fair-weather friends, Ballesteros whiled away the long, lonely days in Pedreña, practicing for hours and hours by himself, the way he had when he was a little boy. "I felt everybody was against me," he said later, "and I became scared of people. I felt like I was in a restaurant alone and people whom I didn't know were talking about me." At intervals he emerged to play in one of the few tournaments on his sparse schedule. He finished thirty-ninth in the Open at St. George's won by Bill Rogers, and was the only European to make the cut in the U.S. PGA Championship at Atlanta Athletic Club.

But by now it was becoming increasingly obvious that, one way or the other, the great appearance-money debate had to be resolved. How it actually was is another of those wonderful mirage-like stories, which looks all very realistic and convincing when contemplated from a distance, but has a tendency to fall to pieces under close surveillance. Ostensibly, Ballesteros was fast using up his exemptions in America, was tired of flying back and forth to Japan, and had finally accepted that the European tour would not be bending the rules on his account. On August 11 he formally reinstated himself into the ETPD. This was taken to mean that he had settled his differences with the tournament committee over appearance money. Barner then sent out a bland statement to the effect that, "The accomplishments of ETPD members in this year's British Open Championship indicate that the day is not far off when ETPD events may not need the extra drawing power of American professionals. This could signal the end of guarantees and a dramatic rise in the prize money on the European Tour." Ballesteros was then welcomed back into the fold with open arms and all was seen to be well.

Soon after this cease-fire Schofield came across the Spaniard in the transit lounge at Heathrow Airport, where he was awaiting a connecting flight. They exchanged careful greetings, then stood for a moment or two in awkward silence. "I just want to play golf," Ballesteros suddenly burst out.

"I just want you to play golf," Schofield said reassuringly. And they made a pact then and there that they would not be revisiting the "desolation" of that year with anyone—which they haven't. But they did endure an initially unpleasant period where the same journals that had reported that Ballesteros had been "stripped of his membership" and had "his hand slapped because he was asking for appearance money" after his resignation, insisted that he had been "forced to admit that he wasn't bigger than the game and, tail between his legs, had re-entered the ETPD." But then it all died down and these days hardly anyone ever mentions it.

As to who was responsible for the whole unfortunate business, no one can ever say. Collet admits that at that age he thought he was "a pretty tough, savvy manager. I probably just thought it was a pretty clever thing to do."

"I think he was badly represented, that's what I think," Jacklin says. "I went through that with IMG. When you're young, as I was and Seve was, you need the guidance of somebody who's older and wiser to tell you how to behave, and what you must do and what you mustn't do. And all you were to those managers—Ed Barner for Seve and Mark McCormack for me—was a money-making machine, and they never looked upon you as anything other than someone who was going to make it for them. Send you off to play these tournaments after the British Open. . . . When I won I went to Westchester and I said, 'You know, I'm not interested in playing here.' Understandably, I was exhausted. He said: 'A two-hundred-fifty-thousand-pound first prize [which was the biggest first prize in golf then] and you can't get interested!' I said, 'I'm not a machine, Mark.' "

"I regret 1981, of course I do," Schofield says feelingly. "If you were going to try and look for something good that came out of it, the only positive thing could be that it left such a deep impression on everybody, not least Severiano, who for a time in his life felt he might never play Ryder Cup golf again. . . . The pain and discomfort of 1981 may have given him an extra dimension to say to himself, 'I will now show the world how committed I am. If anybody ever doubted it, they must have been very mistaken.' So in a perverse way it may have done some good."

What wasn't so good, from Schofield's point of view, was the speed at which the specter of appearance money returned to haunt him. All things considered, Ballesteros never really stopped getting it. With the exception of the British Open Championship and events on the U.S. Tour, he was paid every time he teed up in 1981. And then gradually it became generally understood that if you had won a major championship or had finished in the top three on the Order of Merit, you were entitled to appearance money. A decade on, it had spread like a virus and become a massive problem again, with players like Ballesteros, Nick Faldo, and Ian Woosnam earning well in excess of sixty thousand pounds before they had struck a golf ball each week. So Schofield climbed up on his high horse and read the riot act about the principles—or lack of them—involved in appearance money and the whole thing started up all over again. Only this time, Ballesteros wasn't held up as an example.

"I don't think there's anything the matter with it," Collet argues. "It's business. The guys that gripe about it are the guys that don't have enough charisma to be able to command it. You should talk to Lionel Provost who runs PromoGolf in France. This whole thing of appearance money created stars, and stars created spectacles, and now France is a major golfing power in Europe. If they hadn't brought over stars and paid them fees, where would golf in France be? They still have no French golfers that are worth two cents. And who does that affect? That affects the Chris Moodys of this world who benefit from having bigger purses and more tournaments to play in. I think there's a very sound argument to be made in favor of it."

In 1992, after a two-year investigation into appearance money by the tournament players' committee, with the cooperation of every sponsor, golf association, and federation, the European Tour finally came up with a set of guidelines on how a golfer may be officially encouraged to consider a particular tournament in his playing schedule. "Most people are adult enough to know that business is business," Schofield said frankly. "If Nick Faldo has signed a contract with the General Accident Assurance Corporation immediately after they've secured sponsorship of the European Open and, yes, part and parcel of that is that he will play in three of their tournaments, I don't think anybody regards that as appearance money. *I* certainly don't. The players don't. The sponsors don't. Mr. Barner's position was different. His was: 'Here is a gun. You send me a check for twenty-five thousand dollars and my man will play. No check, he will not play.' You know, that was it."

The interesting part about 1981 is that, according to Collet, the battle only ended when the European Tour "basically just gave up and said anybody could get appearance money. Ever since then, there's been no problem. Until 1991 when they started saying, 'Boys, now that the Tour's grown a lot, wouldn't it be better in an ideal world if we didn't have this?' And most of the golfers said, 'Well, if we can be sure that nobody's cheating and everybody's being treated the same, fine.' So then the PGA devised this bonus pool thing . . . and they also invented this Champion's Challenge format, where they coincidentally pay rather high fees for this other event which is the same week as the PGA Championship, but only the top guys are invited, and then they play the PGA Championship because it's such a *great* event. But they've tried to meet 'em halfway and I respect their creativity with what they're trying to do. I'm not going to say it's hypocrisy and double standards. I'm going to say, I think the Tour understands that this is a fiction of our times and it goes on. It's like, everybody smokes pot, so what are you going to do? Keep arresting people? Or, short of making it legal, you just place a little fine on it so that you can show that socially it's unacceptable behavior *but* we're not going to persecute people. That's kind of what they've done with appearance money."

At the end of that controversial season, Louis T. Stanley wrote an epitaph for the Spaniard in the *Pelham Golf Yearbook*: "The tragedy of 1981 has been the virtual eclipse of Severiano Ballesteros. The endless, tiresome hassle over appearance money left him isolated and a stranger to the European Tour. His visits to America were disastrous and best forgotten. Scandinavia produced a ray of hope, but one swallow does not compensate for the losses. The decision not to agree to his demands is right. In no way can the Spaniard justify special treatment. The hard and expensive lesson he has learnt from the sorry business is that the game can do without him. By now nobody comments on his absence. He belongs to yesterday and nothing is duller than old news."

9

NO EASY RYDER

"The curiously comical aspect of everyday events conceals from us the very real suffering caused by our passions."

Stendhal, *Scarlet and Black*

The Ryder Cup affair began innocently enough—like all of these things do—with a phone call and a promise. At that time Ballesteros was still considered the *bête noire* of professional golf, was still in the United States, and was still giving the ETPD a run for their money; but he was fast wearying of the struggle. He missed the amiable eccentricity of British and Continental Tour events and the easygoing camaraderie of Europe's players; he missed Spain and Spanish food and speaking Spanish; and he missed his home and family. And so it was that a month or six weeks before the B&H International at Fulford in York, the last event with points counting toward Ryder Cup selection, he was sitting in his hotel room, pondering the chances of a peaceable reconciliation with the hierarchy at Wentworth, when the telephone rang.

"Yes," Ballesteros snapped abruptly, for he has a passionate dislike of the instrument.

"Hallo? Hallo, good evening, sorry to trouble you. . . . Would it be possible to speak to Seve Balles—oh, Seve, it's John Jacobs here."

The conversation that ensued was one of notable ambiguity—notable because how else could it have retained its news value or capacity to wound or provoke anger for more than a decade? In essence, Jacobs, who was to captain the 1981 Ryder Cup team, was trying to persuade Ballesteros to return to Europe and attempt to play his way into the Ryder Cup, which he could do quite easily by improving his Order of Merit standing, since the top ten players on the money list would automatically be awarded places. The final two members of the team were to be elected in a meeting at Fulford, venue of the Benson and Hedges International, by the Ryder Cup committee—in this case, Jacobs, Neil Coles, and Bernhard Langer, the season's leading money winner. "If you don't qualify automatically," Jacobs allegedly told the Spaniard, "I can't promise you 100 percent that you will be in, but I promise you that you will have my vote."

"Which I believed meant I would be in," Ballesteros says, "because he was the captain and the captain is the one who chooses the players. If I was the captain, even though I might have consulted with Bernhard Langer and Neil Coles, ultimately it would be my decision. Anyway, those were the words Jacobs used."

Jacobs, however, insists that what he actually said was: "Seve, I can't guarantee you'll be on the team. I'm one of three. If you will come and play in the Irish Open and the B&H, that strengthens my position very much more."

"But that's not easy to explain to someone who doesn't speak English very well," Jacobs says, "and who probably didn't understand the actual voting situation. He said: 'Oh, I'm playing very badly.' And he was very down and he was cross and he was anti. And he didn't come and play, and therefore I had no leg to stand on. But Seve's reported as having said that I said that I could definitely get him on the team. And I couldn't."

Now, in 1981 the Ryder Cup was a subject already very near to Ballesteros's heart. No sooner was Jacobs off the line when he had repeated the exchange, verbatim, to Collet and Barner and, partly for the reasons previously listed, i.e. that the European Tour "basically just gave up and said anybody could get appearance money," etc., and partly because he believed Jacobs to have virtually pledged him a place on the team, he was reinstated as an ETPD member before many moons had passed and was looking forward with some pleasure to the matches at Walton Heath on September 18. There was only one snag. Because the negotiations between UMI and the Tour had taken several weeks to conclude, they had effectively put an end to any hopes that Ballesteros might have had of trying to earn his way back onto the Ryder Cup team. As a result, he (or his management company) decided that it was hardly worth him entering the few Tour events remaining that did officially count toward Ryder Cup selection—not even the B&H, which aroused an enormous amount of displeasure and almost certainly had a bearing on the final outcome of the situation—when he was bound to be one of the wild-card choices of the committee anyway.

Well, the day of the meeting at Fulford rolled round and Ballesteros was conspicuous by his absence. Jacobs, rather unhappily, set off in the afternoon to interview the existing team members on whether or not they thought the Spaniard should play at Walton Heath. Of the ten of them, excluding Langer, but including Faldo, Bernard Gallacher, Des Smyth, Jose Maria Canizares, Eamonn Darcy, Lyle, Sam Torrance, Howard Clark, and Piñero, only Gallacher felt that Ballesteros merited a Ryder Cup place. "You're the captain," he told Jacobs, "but if I were captain I would want Seve on the team."

"Everybody else said no," Jacobs recalls. "The Spanish boys, for instance, like Piñero, who are his friends, all thought that Seve was behaving very badly by arguing and not coming to play and so on. So when this meeting started, with the three of us, I said: 'Well, what do you think about Seve?' And both [Neil and Bernhard] said: '*No!*' I said: 'Well, that's the end of that then.' *I* wanted him in but . . . "

But Jacobs didn't say so—at least, not in so many words. He seemed to have taken it for granted that Coles and Langer were aware that that's what he would have liked to say, had the circumstances been altered, and then accepted his position as hopeless without bothering to try to assert himself, which he had every right to do as captain.

"But everybody *knew* I wanted Seve," Jacobs insists. "Because I went and argued his case at the Tour headquarters in May and they were there then. Neil Coles knew, but Neil was adamant that he shouldn't be in. Neil would substantiate that he and Bernhard Langer said no." He clicks his tongue in exasperation. "When people say, '*John Jacobs* voted against Seve . . .' I was a committee of three. Now, in 1979 Seve was on that committee. *He* was the leader of the Order of Merit. And we sat down at the Irish Open at Royal Dublin, Seve, Neil Coles, and myself, to choose the next two [wild-card players]. And on that occasion Neil Coles said, 'John, you're the captain, tell us who you want.' I didn't get that in 1981, because if I had I would have said Seve straight away. But then Neil knew I would have said that."

To Ballesteros, the news that he had been cast aside by the committee was a bolt from the blue—utterly unforeseen and unexpected. It struck him forcibly, like a body blow. He felt fury, he felt pain and sheer bewilderment, but, more than anything, he felt the deep sting of betrayal. "Piñero and Canizares had both said I should not be on the team," he recalled later. "That was a pity. I was very disappointed at that because I always felt that I helped them and that they were good friends. I don't know if it was jealousy or whatever but it was the one time they could help me and the one time they could hurt me, and they chose the second option."

"I do remember John Jacobs asking me how I felt," Piñero says defensively, "but in the end it wasn't our decision. It was the decision of three persons. And today, because of what happened to the Ryder Cup and because of what happened with Seve's career, those three persons are still trying to find an excuse for what happened. But if we hadn't won the Ryder Cup in '85, and if Seve wasn't as good as he's been, nobody would have any discussion at all. Nobody. You have to make the decision that seems right at the time [because you haven't got the benefit of hindsight]. I don't remember very well, but I think I said to John, 'Seve's good enough to be on the team, but he's not doing the right thing to be on the team.' But if you put me in the same situation again, I'd probably do the same thing. I did what I did and I stand by it. I will not try to excuse myself."

HE FELT FURY, HE FELT PAIN AND SHEER BEWILDERMENT, BUT, MORE THAN ANYTHING, HE FELT THE DEEP STING OF BETRAYAL.

Piñero's role in the drama, however, along with that of every other team member, ended when he gave his opinion to his captain. Thereafter, the responsibility for what was, ultimately, a masterpiece of tragicomedy, became the sole property of Messrs. Jacobs, Coles, and Langer. They started their meeting by establishing, collectively or individually, that Ballesteros was not going to be on the Ryder Cup team, and they turned their attention to selecting the players who were. There were three contenders: James and Jacklin, who occupied the eleventh and twelfth positions on the Order of Merit, and Oosterhuis, who played the U.S. Tour more or less full time, but who had never lost a Ryder Cup singles match, and who had also just won the Canadian Open. "We all agreed on Peter Oosterhuis," Jacobs says, taking up the story. "No question. He was the obvious next one. And, of course, it would have been Peter Oosterhuis and Seve. That's who it *should* have been. *Not* Tony Jacklin. Tony was at the end of his career. Tony couldn't knock a putt in to save his life . . . [although] he was still a very good player. . . . But it always hurt me that Tony should be that upset because we chose someone who was ahead of him in the averages. Tony and Vivienne [Jacklin] were tremendously supportive of me in 1979. But I had to dismiss all these things in lending my voice, and the three of us were absolutely at one about Peter Oosterhuis. And we had a lot of discussion about Tony or Mark James, and in the end the three of us came down to Mark James. But I stupidly said, 'Well, we didn't pick Tony because we think he was probably too old.' "

Jacobs was correct about Jacklin's reaction. He was upset. Very, very upset. But the battalion of emotions that marched through his brain when he found out that he wasn't on the team were mere cadets when compared to the detachment of crack troops that went on the warpath when he found whom he had been replaced by. In theory, the Spaniard's Ryder Cup place had been given away to Oosterhuis, while Jacklin's had been handed to James. In practice, it made not an iota of difference. The facts, whether you dress them up as sheep in wolves' clothing or wolves in sheep's clothing, are always the facts. Ballesteros, one of the greatest players ever to strike a golf ball; and Jacklin, who was still a good golfer by anyone's definition, even at the ripe old age of *thirty-seven*, and who played well enough at that stage in the season to hoist himself into twelfth place on the money list, had been passed over in favor of one of the players who had wantonly disrupted the 1979 Ryder Cup.

"The thing that surprised me," Ballesteros says, "although I have great respect for him and we are now good friends, was that Mark James was picked and I wasn't. In 1979 James was fined for bad behavior during the Ryder Cup. It was a joke that they went for Mark James instead of me in 1981."

The Ryder Cup owes its existence and its name to Samuel Ryder, an English seed-merchant who had been advised to take up golf for the good of his health (physical, that is). After a time he came to prize the professional game above all else and because of this did two exceptionally generous things: (1) He engaged Abe Mitchell, one of the finest postwar British players, as his personal teacher, so that Mitchell would not be burdened with the duties of a club professional and would be able to devote his energies wholly to practice and to tournaments; and (2) he donated a trophy to the PGA in 1926 for use in an international match, the purpose of which would be to foster goodwill between the golfers of the USA and those of Great Britain and Ireland. The former was a noble gesture and worth a good deal to Mitchell and to golf generally, but it is the latter for which Ryder will always be remembered. He invented a tournament which might, ultimately, come to symbolize an entire game.

THE EARLY RYDER CUP MATCHES WERE DOUBTLESS ENTERTAINING AND FULL OF INCIDENT, BUT BY 1977 THEY HAD BECOME SO PREDICTABLE AND DULL THEY WERE IN DANGER OF EXTINCTION.

The early Ryder Cup matches were doubtless entertaining and full of incident, but by 1977 they had become so predictable and dull they were in danger of extinction. Only three times since their inception had the British carried home the trophy: Every time the Americans teed up they won. This had its thrills initially but these quickly wore off, and the day came when Tom Weiskopf, having earned himself a place on the team, elected to go elk hunting rather than participate in the matches. Nicklaus then wrote to Lord Derby, the president of the British PGA, saying he feared for the future of the Ryder Cup unless something was done to revive interest in it. Knowing that, at twenty, Ballesteros was the best golfer in Europe, he suggested that Continental players be included on the British and Irish team.

Thus, when the 1979 Ryder Cup team went to the Greenbrier at White Sulphur Springs in West Virginia, two of its members were Spanish. That was the match that five men and a dog went to see, for it was held in the South and Lee Elder, the first black Ryder Cup player, was on the American side. It was also the week when Sam Snead, who had once been pro at the Greenbrier but who had fallen out with the club, sneaked onto the premises to see Ballesteros, whom he had long looked forward to meeting. And it was the week where the Spaniard sacked his caddie, a local boy, after only one day. Jacobs, who was captain that year, considered Ballesteros and Antonio Garrido to be the most outstanding of Europe's twelve players, and sent them out first in the fourballs on the opening day. That was all well and to the good, but they came up against Lanny Wadkins and Larry Nelson. Wadkins is a formidable opponent under any circumstances, but Nelson was in the peak of form and playing electrifying golf. When the pair of them reached the turn, they had a better-ball score of 28, which led inexorably to a win of 2 & 1. "Garrido and I played against Larry Nelson and Lanny Wadkins three times and they beat us three times," Ballesteros says admiringly. "They played brilliantly. Nobody could have beaten them. They were unbelievable.

"We played against Fuzzy Zoeller and Hubert Green in the first day foursomes and there was a bit of an incident on the sixteenth green, where we won the match. Antonio conceded a putt to Hubert and then threw the ball back to him with his putter. I guess Hubert was upset because he was losing. Whatever, he started to say something in English and Antonio got upset, and it was a very difficult situation there. I remember I had to stand in between them. They both got very cross and I nearly had to act as referee. At that moment I could see that the Ryder Cup was important. Even though we didn't play for money, we played for pride."

Pride or no, when the fat lady sang it was the American anthem that played: The U.S. team had strolled to yet another victory, with a score of sixteen to ten and two matches halved. At least, that is what the record books say. What they don't say is that behind the scenes the Europeans had been handicapped by the tomfoolery of James and Ken Brown.

"They behaved unbelievably stupidly," says Jacobs, still capable of experiencing incredulity at what occurred after all these years, "and I'm blowed if I know why. Right from the word go, when they appeared at the airport dressed as though they were going on a camping holiday . . . they just set out to be as disruptive as possible. The other ten performed wonderfully. You must appreciate, we were going into the singles one point behind and I hadn't had the services of those two, and Seve and Garrido had only won one point. . . . What did they do? Well, the opening ceremony is a flag-raising thing and it's televised, and those two guys didn't show up. . . . Finally, they did show . . . but they wouldn't stand to attention and just chatted away. At the dinner the night before the Ryder Cup started, when people were taking pictures, they covered their faces. Wouldn't have their pictures taken with the team. I mean, incredible things. . . . James pulled a muscle on the first morning playing with Ken Brown, so I had to play Brown in the afternoon with Des Smyth. And, of course, he hit a couple of bad shots early on and then just didn't talk to anybody. Just hit it and walked up the fairway. And I had to apologize to Des Smyth in front of the whole team."

Ballesteros, who Jacobs describes as "a superb member of the team," was so horrified at how demoralized the other ten players became that he immediately went, cap in hand, to Angel Gallardo, his captain at the Hennessy Cup in 1978, and apologized profusely for his own behavior then, which had also been less than exemplary.

The amazing thing about the Ryder Cup saga is that, if you met those two delinquents now, you would refuse to believe that the complete episode was not a figment of the overactive imagination of the media and one or two officials. Brown is as quiet as a mouse, and has nice manners and a sweet smile, and James has a wonderfully dry sense of humor, and is one of the most popular and admired players on the circuit. Both of them have played in several Ryder Cups since 1979 and have been models of decorum and contributed greatly to the overall success of the matches. The contrast is so striking, in fact, that when I interviewed Jacklin I put it to him that they might have been unfairly criticized.

He looked at me as if I had suddenly grown horns. A spasm of pure white rage crossed his face. He made an almost visible effort to control himself, then burst out vehemently: "*Unfairly criticized!* I would have sent them home. They didn't turn up for meetings, treated everything as a joke, didn't stand to attention for the Queen when the flag was raised; Mark James ordered six hamburgers—there was only him there!—and just signed the bill and left it. I mean, pranks that my children would have never ever played. It wasn't just childishness, it was sheer effort to disrupt everything. They folded their arms when the flag was going up and the anthem was being played . . . and just general behavior that was totally unacceptable. I remember my wife then, Vivienne, and Lesley Gallacher, taking them outside during dinner one night, and just saying, 'What do you think you're playing at?' They were just like . . . like yobs. But the effect that their behavior had on the team was devastating, because there was no team unity there at all. It was ten [good] guys and those two. But you can't play and win matches like that. And so what I could never understand was why Jacobs condoned it. But I said, 'The guy [Jacobs] deserves another chance. He had those two on the team.' And then he goes and picks one of them again! Now, I don't understand that kind of mentality. If somebody treats me badly and lets me down, I'm not saying they don't deserve a second chance, but I'd certainly find a different way to give them a chance. I wouldn't give them the chance to screw up again."

Brown had no excuses. "In those days it was less of a team effort," he says simply. "We were a team but there wasn't really team spirit, which is what Jacko and Seve brought in '83. It was just a catalog of minor incidents that would have ended if the captain had stood up and said: 'Come on, lads, this is a team effort.' But that wasn't Jacobs's way. But I'm not blaming the captain at all. If we'd been doing things properly [in other words, if they had not had plastic shoes, poor quality bags, and bargain-basement team uniforms), we wouldn't have been doing these things at all. Did I regret it afterwards? Well, I'd have loved someone to say something at the time. At the actual time of the event I didn't really think we had done a terrible amount wrong, but when you add it all up . . ."

However, this sorry chronicle does explain why Ballesteros and Jacklin were so outraged by the actions of the Ryder Cup committee in 1981. To begin with, an attempt *was* made to salve the feelings of the Englishman, by inviting him to Walton Heath in an official capacity. "I told them to stick it in their ear," Jacklin said candidly. "I was so disgusted with the way that it was dealt with. And I didn't want anything else to do with the Ryder Cup. . . . And if I was mad Seve was twice as mad, because he was that much younger than I was and his Spanish blood was boiling, as you can well imagine."

Indeed, it was. The week after the decision was made, Ballesteros told the press that he did not deserve to be on the team and that it did not bother him one way or the other. That is typical of him. The more hurt or angry he is about something the more he will try to turn it around and either use it against himself or pretend it couldn't matter less. He usually accompanies this with a brave and extra-bright smile. But years on, when he was asked by *Golf World* whether he thought he would have been selected if he had played in the B&H International, Ballesteros replied, "We are talking about revenge here. It's like Nick Faldo not playing the German Open . . . and the captain saying: 'If he doesn't play the German Open I'm not going to choose him.' It's like revenge—it's a personal feeling between two [people] against the team and against European golf. That's not the way to do it. If I were the captain I would pick the best players as wild cards, even if I didn't like them personally, because that is the best way for the team and for European golf. It's a tremendous mistake to let personal feelings interfere with that decision."

In thinking this, he was not alone. A number of journalists, supported by the public and a proportion of the players, took Jacobs and his cohorts "to court" on these and other charges, and returned a verdict of guilty. Bill Longmuir considered Ballesteros's omission from the team to be "the most ridiculous decision that has ever been made." He unconsciously echoed Jacklin, who had called it "the single most ridiculous thing that's ever happened in the Ryder Cup." [Seve] had not really played enough golf in Europe to establish himself in the numbers situation," Longmuir says. "He was having a war with the European Tour . . . and he was playing a fair amount in America. But he was in no-man's-land, really. He was an unhappy man, there was no question about that. But the bottom line, in my mind, was that at that time he was still our best player. He was our greatest strength. Somebody voted against him, I don't know who it was, but it was the wrong decision. Seve is such a force to be reckoned with that you cannot afford to leave him out of the Ryder Cup team. I know, he's done the wrong things at times and said the wrong things but, you know, he's a golf pro, he's not a politician."

"I think most people were of the opinion that if Seve had wanted to play in the Ryder Cup, all he had to do was tee up in the last tournament and win something like one thousand pounds," James says. "And since he's obviously capable of that, most of us wondered why he didn't do that. And also, he treated the Tour with such contempt that year that I don't think anyone had any sympathy for him, and I think he would not have enhanced the team spirit at all. I think he was very unpopular with most players around that time. He was milking the Tour and players simply didn't like it."

Langer agrees: "All he had to do was play one more tournament and he would have been on the team anyway. And he decided not to do that. Just to prove the point. He didn't want to be a member of the Tour. And [he did] all sorts of things which weren't very good for the image of the Tour. And then in return he expected the committee to vote him on the team. We probably should have done on his playing ability, but we felt he wouldn't have been a good man for the team."

"Seve felt that he had been betrayed," Collet recalls. "Putting aside the fact that he had played from a rather strong position and withdrawn his membership—that's all fair in love and war—but overtures were made, you know, 'Come back, everything will be all right and it won't affect the Ryder

Cup.' And then you do that and it's reneged on. . . . To this day, Seve does not know what happened. And we never will."

Ballesteros continues: "Two years later, at the 1983 match in Florida, Bernhard Langer approached me during the opening ceremony [Langer denies this] and said: 'Seve, I want to explain about the situation in 1981. I want to make sure that you understand that I wasn't the one who voted against you. Neil Coles and John Jacobs did.' I said: 'Thank you, Bernhard, nice to hear that from you. I appreciate it.' Nearly two more years later, Jacobs called me in to the office at the PGA European Tour and we had a chat. Ken Schofield was there. Jacobs said that he had read an article in which I said I didn't understand why Jacobs had voted against me. Jacobs said: 'No, that's not what happened. I asked Neil, and Neil said no, and I asked Bernhard, and Bernhard said no, and so I was in the position that I didn't have any other way to go. So we all went for no.' "

One morning in April 1983, nearly eighteen months after the deplorable sequence of events that culminated in the repudiation of two of Europe's best players by the Ryder Cup committee, Jacklin was practicing his putting stroke only minutes before going out to play a tournament, when Schofield walked up to him and calmly asked him to captain the 1983 Ryder Cup team.

Jacklin was dumbfounded. His immediate response was: "How the hell can they invite me to do this when what's gone on's gone on?" But since he didn't hold Schofield responsible for what had happened, he agreed to at least consider the proposal. "I was angry, angry as hell. But I kept saying, 'If I do it, I want to do it my way.' I said, 'I want Concorde; I want an unlimited amount of clothing; I want our guys to feel equal to the Americans when they stand on the tee.' And every demand I made, they accepted. Then I sort of said to myself: 'Now, hang on. Are you going to keep a vendetta going with this thing forever?' And it was clear that the Ryder Cup was going to survive much longer than me or anybody else. So I decided at that point to let bygones be bygones and to do it."

But the biggest hurdle was never going to be persuading Jacklin to captain the Ryder Cup team. It was going to be winning over Ballesteros, who, at that time in his life, could scarcely have been more disinclined to participate in the matches or less well disposed toward anybody who may have been guilty of complicity or duplicity in the 1981 affair. This is where Schofield was smart. He knew that Jacklin would be the ace in the pack. He realized that in Ballesteros's present frame of mind the only man who could hope to win him over was the player who had suffered the same fate he had and at the same hands. "Well, if I couldn't do it, nobody could," Jacklin agrees. "Lord Derby, who was president at the time, didn't want to talk to him. So I went to talk to him at the Prince of Wales Hotel in Southport. He listened and listened and listened and he started arguing. I said, 'There's no point arguing with me because I *know*. . . . But at the same time, Seve, you've had a bloody tough stretch. You've been on the carpet for appearance money and this, that, and the other, and I'm not sure your image is everything it should be in this country. You're a great player and you've got my total sympathy. I know what you're going through. You're Spanish, you're trying to play somewhere else, you're trying to do your best everywhere, you want everybody to love you, and it's getting mixed up. But trust me when I tell you, if you do this and let bygones be bygones and we can make this work, you will have an unbelievable following in this country because they'll adopt you as their own.' "

But the wounds were still too raw for Ballesteros to forgive and forget as easily as Jacklin might have wanted him to. All the hurt and anger he had been suppressing for so long came rushing out in a tide of invective as he told the Englishman, in a few choice phrases, exactly what he thought of those who had spurned him. When he ran out of steam he didn't exactly say yes, but he didn't say no either. "I thought he was going to do it," Jacklin admits. "I was able to say to him, 'We're going to go by Concorde, we're going to have the best golf bags, we're going to have the best cashmere blazers, we're going to have whatever *you* want. We'll do the thing together. You can be my sounding board on the golf course. Together we can make it happen.' And, of course, he came round."

In the second week of October 1983 the European team flew by Concorde to Florida. When they arrived at PGA National in Palm Beach Gardens, they found that the Americans, while less complacent than they had been in the past, were confident that victory was a foregone conclusion.

143

"The heat," explained Nicklaus, the U.S. captain, listing off the reasons why his team were unlikely to be beaten. "The Europeans won't be accustomed to it. There's the Bermuda grass. They won't know too much about that. Then there's the fact that we win most of the time. . . . If you *feel* you should win, then more often than not you do."

How prophetic his words almost were, but not in the way he intended them to be: After the first day's play Europe led the United States by 4½ points to 3½. One of those points—earned in the afternoon fourballs against Floyd and Curtis Strange—had been contributed by Ballesteros and Paul Way, who, to the amazement of all, the European captain had paired together.

"[Paul Way] needed help," Jacklin says frankly. "I know how I felt when I played my first Ryder Cup in 1967. You're as nervous as hell. You need the comfort of somebody looking after you. I mean, there's another view; you say, 'He's a cocky little bugger, he'll get by.' But that never works. The stress and the tension are so difficult to cope with."

Ballesteros accepted the pairing without a murmur, and it wasn't until lunchtime on the second day of play that Jacklin realized anything was amiss. Angel Gallardo approached him wearing a nervous frown. "You should talk to Seve," he told the Englishman.

"Why?" Jacklin said, alarmed.

"Well, he's not happy."

Jacklin needed no further bidding, and at once went looking for the Spaniard. He found him in the far corner of the locker room, brooding.

"Everything all right?" Jacklin said briskly. "Any problems?"

Ballesteros made no reply; he was wrestling with his conscience. He stood up abruptly. It was a sweltering day and the air was sticky and oppressive. His pink shirt clung to him wetly. He peeled it off and, flinging it down on the bench, blurted out: "This *boy*! This Paul Way! I can't believe it. I'm holding his hand all the time. Every shot, I'm trying to play my shot, I'm trying to play his shot. I feel like his father."

"Seve," Jacklin said quietly, "you are his father in here." He touched his temple. "That's why you're playing with him. Is that a problem?"

Ballesteros held a mental debate. He came to a decision. "For me," he said proudly, "it's no problem."

"And they [Ballesteros and Way] went out there in the afternoon and won again," Jacklin says. "And ironically, Paul Way won his singles match and Seve only got a half—which, because Seve is so hard on himself, he blamed himself for. 'If *I'd* won my match we would have done this, that and the other. . . . !' But, I mean, his contribution has not just been what he's personally achieved during the matches. It's the rub-off that other people have had because of his presence, as well."

"He's always been the absolute inspiration to the team," Ken Brown says, "and Tony got him 100 percent on his side. In 1983, a couple of matches he almost won single-handed."

"I thought he was God at the time and I thought: 'We cannot lose,' " Way recalls. "We only lost one game so I was nearly right. I found it easy playing with him because he encouraged me and wherever I put him, especially in the foursomes, he would make up for it. So it eased the pressure. I always remember he over-helped me. He was going, 'Do this, do that.' And I didn't really listen to him after a while. I did what I wanted. But he was very helpful."

It was in the singles matches at PGA National that Ballesteros hit one of the greatest golf shots in the history of the game. His opponent was Fuzzy Zoeller, the 1979 Masters champion and a strong, exceptionally talented player. The Spaniard had fallen behind at the second but had recovered with four consecutive birdies, whereupon the American promptly won four holes in a row. They were all square when they came to the last hole, a magnificent 578-yard par-five, with sand all down the left and water down the right. There, Ballesteros hit what he later described as "one of the worst drives of my life." It buried itself almost invisibly in the tangled Bermuda rough on a bank above the face of a bunker. He slashed at it with all his might with a wedge, but only succeeded in moving it twenty yards forward into another bunker, where it finished on an upslope, just beneath the lip. It was the stuff of nightmares. What could he do but play out sideways with a sand wedge?

Zoeller, meanwhile, was having problems of his own. After driving into the rough, he had played out sideways and now faced a two-iron shot to the green. He turned to watch the Spaniard, who was pacing up and down like a tiger, his face dark with fury and determination. There was a three-wood in his hand. He was going to try for the green. Zoeller stared at him in amazement. He watched as Ballesteros climbed into the bunker, aimed fifty yards left of the flagstick, wriggled his feet deep in the sand, and then lashed at the ball with every ounce of strength in his body. It shot out of the bunker

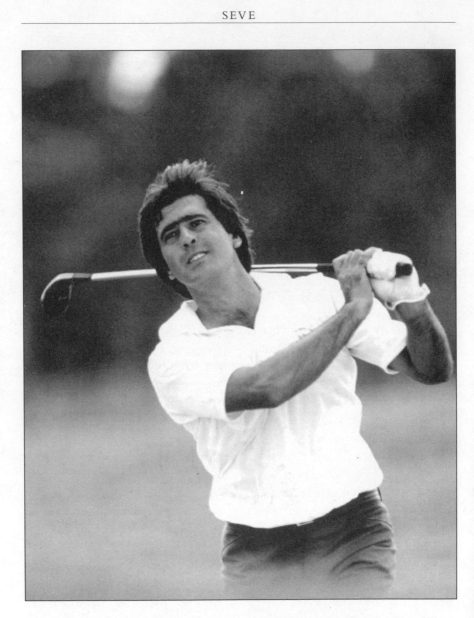

That's the look of a man who knows that the three-wood he has just blasted out of a fairway bunker in 1983 Ryder Cup play is looking pretty good as it heads toward the green 245 yards away. Seve's incredible "recovery" shot ended up on the fringe, from where he got up and down to halve his singles match with American Fuzzy Zoeller. (© Phil Sheldon)

like a rocket, flew an incredible 245 yards and finished on the fringe of the green, from where he got up and down for a half.

"That was one of the best shots of my life," Ballesteros said afterward, while an incredulous Nicklaus described it as "one of the greatest shots I have ever seen."

But Ballesteros's joy was blighted by Europe's loss by a single point (11–12) to the United States. "I think we were very unlucky," he says. "There were a lot of frustration because we thought we played well enough to tie at least. It was like losing in a play-off—it was very sad. Nearly the whole team cried on the eighteenth when we lost."

10

AMEN CORNER

"It's a work of art. It's like playing a Salvador Dali landscape. I expected a clock to fall out of the trees and hit me in the face."

David Feherty, Augusta National, April 1992

If you were someone who knew nothing and cared even less about men who hit golf balls with sticks and you drove unseeing past the interminable T-shirt and memorabilia stands that line the streets of Augusta in the second week of April, you could quite easily be through the town and out the other side without ever realizing that you had only been minutes from a show as finely choreographed as any on Broadway. There is nothing to suggest, in the grim facade of Burger Kings, malls, and drab hotels lit by neon signs with missing letters, that behind them lies a golf course as lovely as the Garden of Eden, where spring is eternal and the flowers are always in bloom.

Nowhere does life imitate art more closely than at Augusta National. Ever since 1930, when Clifford Roberts, a New York investment broker, persuaded Bobby Jones to partner him in the creation of "a retreat of such nature and such excellence that men of some means and devoted to the game of golf might find the club an extra luxury where they might visit and play with kindred spirits from other parts of the nation," it has thrived on elitism, perfectionism, tradition, and the careful maintenance of an illusion which, though beautiful, is an illusion nonetheless. At Augusta, one is invited to suspend disbelief. To consider the world a place free from poverty, discord, suffering, and sordid commercialism. To marvel at the glorious (artificial if nature has made them anything but) azaleas, rhododendrons, and dogwood, the divine blue of Rae's Creek (dye added), and the harmonious effect of a color-coding system so regulated that a man carrying a white polystyrene cup would not be allowed onto the premises until he had either disposed of it or exchanged it for one in the appropriate shade of sunshine yellow or bottle green. To wonder at the bravery of the golfers who, like latter-day Daniels, tread a wary path through the lions' den that is Augusta. And to be uplifted, as the tournament nears its dramatic conclusion, by the triumph of human spirit.

To keep reality in abeyance for a short time is no hardship; Augusta is an escapist's paradise. The arcane rules of the club make it even easier. Advertising of any kind is expressly forbidden. All references to money are considered obscene. Tickets for the main event cannot be begged, borrowed, or stolen, and the privileged few who already hold them have had them handed down like family heirlooms. But while some of the measures taken to preserve the sanctity of Augusta National have, over the years, seemed unnecessarily draconian, they have nevertheless combined to ensure that the Masters is not only the most unique event in the world but also the most aesthetically pleasing. The course itself is gorgeous. There is no sensation to compare with that of lying in the shade of a whispering pine on a warm spring day, drinking pink lemonade, breathing in jasmine, and watching the greatest golfers who ever lived pit their wits against an opponent as ravishing as Augusta.

"This place has no present tense," Thomas Boswell said in *Strokes of Genius*. "Cathedrals have a similar quality, and the mansions of state. But they don't command 365 acres, nor do they often create such ambiance. This is life, buffed and burnished."

When Bobby Jones first visited Augusta, he was struck by the sensation that the land before him, then a nursery, "had been lying here for years just waiting for someone to lay a golf course upon it. Indeed, it looked as though it were already a golf course, and I am sure that standing today where I stood on this first visit, on the terrace overlooking the practice putting green, one sees the property exactly as I did then. Year by year I myself have sat in the same chair on the same little balcony, upstairs, looking through the wisteria down at the same scene, while the same colored waiter comes out and says, 'You like the same as last year, sah? Beefeater on the rocks?' " Everything, indeed, is the same, and it is only by looking at the scoreboard that you can tell which year it is—a Palmer year or a Nicklaus year . . . "

Or even a Ballesteros year.

The Spaniard fell so deeply in love with Augusta that he named one of his companies Amen Corner. His performances at the Masters through the years, and the public's perception and reception of them, have been inextricably linked to subtle changes in his own personality and to the ebb and flow of his career. Collet describes his regard for the course as "almost a reverence." Ballesteros admits that it's true. "I love this course," he says fervently. "It is like Pedreña, where I learned to play as a child. I feel I am at home here. That is why I am happy. I treat it with respect, like an older person. Sometimes I take a few advantages, but always there is respect."

His affection for Augusta blossomed with his victory in 1980, fluctuated slightly when he missed the cut in 1981, and grew strong again when he finished third in 1982, one shot behind Craig Stadler who beat Dan Pohl in a playoff. On that occasion he was let down by his putting. The greens had been replanted with bent grass—the pace of which was so excessive that he felt it added a stroke per round to the difficulty of the course. Tom Watson observed that the putting surfaces were the fastest he had seen since Oakmont in 1962, and Billy Casper took a half-dozen putts on the second hole.

In 1983 the greens were quicker still. In practice Peter Jacobsen, trying to reenact Casper's six-putt, started the ball rolling about eighteen inches above the hole and watched it rim the cup, gather momentum on a slope as smooth as glass, and eventually come to a reluctant halt fifteen feet past. Later, a notice appeared in the clubhouse to the effect that the cut on the greens was one-eighth of an inch, on the tees one-quarter of an inch, and on the fairways seven-sixteenths of an inch.

Ballesteros was advantaged by the fact that, when he arrived in Augusta, his putting was "phenomenal," and he was in fine fettle generally. In the preceding weeks he had played in the Doral Open, where he had missed the cut, not being match-fit, in the Honda and Bay Hill Classics and in the Tournament Players Championship, and had done reasonably but not exceptionally. However, he was enjoying his golf again and, the hurts and recriminations of 1981 long behind him, was relaxed, approachable, and looking forward to the new season. More importantly, he was happy with his golf game. On practice days he strode jubilantly along the spacious fairways as if the worries of the world had suddenly leaped from his shoulders, with great crowds of people pouring after him. Bold approach shots were experimented with, daring chip shots holed, and velvet putting surfaces scrutinized endlessly.

"The greens are brilliantly designed," Ben Crenshaw agreed. "The fifth and the fourteenth greens are really supposed to resemble St. Andrews' greens and they do. I've always thought, too, that if you have a golf course that's entirely filled with trouble, then you're not allowed to think—you don't have room to think. But at Augusta you widen the scope and you actually have room to think because the danger's not imminent. Imminent danger is where you can see it directly before you in some form, but deferred danger is what you feel is lurking out there somewhere. . . . I think it's a higher art form that way."

Ballesteros was more succinct: "Every time you make a mental mistake you pay for it."

He made his first mistake at the first hole on the first day of play, when his opening drive hit a tree. It rebounded onto a sloping lie near a fairway bunker, from where he proceeded to play his recovery shot into a greenside bunker and take bogey. All the signs pointed to an indifferent start. But Ballesteros merely laughed in the face of adversity and went on to make six birdies—one of them at the 535-yard eighth, where he was the only man in the field to reach the green in two. Had his tee shot at the sixteenth not spun away so sharply that it caused him to three-putt from long-range, he would have completed round one in 67 strokes. As it was, he finished a shot behind the leaders Raymond Floyd, Jack Renner, and Gil Morgan at four under par, along with J. C. Snead, Charles Coody, Jim Hallett, and Arnold Palmer—whose day it really was. Fifty-three years old and in contention for the Masters! All Augusta resounded with the cheers of his army. Walking off the course, the Spaniard, who had plenty of his own supporters, was cornered by an American sportswriter, who asked him bluntly if he was playing better than he had when he won the Masters in 1980 and was "all over the place."

Even a man with a hide as thick as that must have quailed beneath the look Ballesteros gave him, and it was followed by a curt: "Why you only want to see bad shots? Why you not want to see my good ones? I hit only two bad shots that day and I was ten shots ahead with nine to play. I cannot be all that bad."

On Friday the heavens opened and the Great Flood descended. Streets became rivers, pretty blue streams evolved into muddy torrents, and the pressroom flooded to a depth of three inches. The powers that be, while ruing the potential cost of such a disaster and wishing that they could just touch a button and have a new backdrop of blue sky and fluffy white clouds wheeled in, congratulated themselves that they had built a dam in Rae's Creek and had thus prevented the eleventh, twelfth, and thirteenth holes from being washed away. But for the first time in ten years, play was abandoned.

Saturday was Ballesteros's birthday. He celebrated it with his beloved father, who had accompanied him to the Masters for the first time, and with a small circle of close friends, whose tickets he had provided; including Dr. Campuzano, his first sponsor, Jorge Ceballos, his new manager, and a Miami airport official whom he had befriended some years earlier when the man had helped him with some lost luggage. He was twenty-six, a year younger than Nicklaus had been when he won his sixth major, and within reach of his second victory at Augusta.

The Golden Bear's hopes of a sixth green blazer had been raised, too. But shortly before the second round his back muscles went into spasm and he had to withdraw. "Doctors have told me that I can change my swing, stop golf, or put up with the pain," Nicklaus commented. "I don't like those options so I'll just carry on."

Ballesteros, after repeated excursions to orthopedic specialists, physiotherapists, and acupuncturists, had adopted the same philosophy. After his victory at Lytham in 1979 he told journalists: "I have a troubled back since 1977 when I played the Masters. It was just after I came out of military service and I had been practicing at Augusta the day before the tournament. I felt very uncomfortable with my back, and through the year is coming worse. For the next year I don't really have pain, is just uncomfortable. I feel like my shoulders are heavy, like I'm carrying a weight, and it was very difficult for me at Lytham because, maybe you see before I hit the ball, I swing three or four times because I feel stiff. The cold is bad for me. However, is no pain, but everybody ask me about my back. All the time you ask and I say, 'It's good, it's good,' but still people say, 'Seve, how is your back?' Then it work in my mind and that put me very much off."

The state of his health was not a matter of pressing concern to Ballesteros prior to the second round. Far more trying was the weather: Heavy showers during the night had left the course saturated and the going slow and, despite the best efforts of thirty-five greenkeepers and their squeegees, morning drizzle compounded the problem. Shortly before noon play

152

commenced from two tees. Ballesteros put his patience hat on and went boldly into the gloom, seizing the opportunity to mount an offensive while Augusta's defenses were lowered. Darkness fell before his mission was completed, but he was still a stroke behind Morgan, who had two holes remaining, at six under par, standing on the eighteenth tee. Keith Fergus was the clubhouse leader with a score of 139, while Jodie Mudd and Faldo were a stroke further back. Ballesteros's final hole was completed before breakfast on Sunday. The sun sailed briefly across the sky as he putted for a 70, but soon vanished and the third round was delayed while rain fell and put an end to the proposed thirty-six holes.

Player waxed lyrical about Ballesteros's talent and his victory in 1980, observing with obvious pleasure that the Spaniard had been "very complimentary because he said I taught him to win the Masters." He beamed. "Wasn't that something? That's a very nice compliment from a wonderful golfer like that. I have so much respect for the man and the golfer because I understand what he feels like. He also came from a poor home, and he *had* to survive. It's all very well to sit on the side and criticize. People are always going to criticize people who do well. The highest tree gathers the most wind. And the highest tree must have the strongest limbs and branches to take that. He's a trier; he's a battler. You know, both of our careers are very similar, and we've been very similar in our attitudes towards the game—to try your best, to give everything you've got. And when you've finished a round, if it's 78, you gave it 78 of your best. I've shot 80 but it's been 80 of my *best*."

In the third round Ballesteros's finest efforts were foiled by his inability to convert the few chances he had on the unpredictable greens. Nevertheless, he came off the course with a one-over-par 73 and his confidence still intact. His aggregate of 211 had left him in second place, one stroke behind Floyd and Craig Stadler, the defending champion, and one ahead of Watson, Mudd, and Fergus at the end of the day's play. Before repairing calmly to the practice green to work on his stroke, he told the media that, though he had played well, "my putting is not what it should be." He was reticent about his chances of victory. "This course is not easy," he said firmly. "I'm just trying to stay cool. Winning any one of the Big Four is great, but I'm still young. I don't have to be in a hurry."

Lee Trevino used to say that a lot of American players would like to hear him admit that Ballesteros was wild off the tee and—as a consequence, I suppose—lucky. "You'll never hear the great players say he's lucky," he remarked in Doust's book in 1981. "They'll say he's great, though. How great? Every generation or so there emerges a golfer who is a little bit better than anybody else. I believe Ballesteros is one of them. It won't be long before he's the greatest international player of all time. I'd say even more successful than Gary Player who, right now, is the finest international player who ever held a golf club. And Roberto De Vicenzo was [also] fantastic. But Seve, before he retires, should be better than them all. On a golf course he's got everything— I mean *everything*: touch, power, know-how, courage, and charisma. By the time he finishes, in about twenty years, he may not be equal to Jack Nicklaus—nobody will ever be equal to Jack Nicklaus—but he'll be more than equal to the rest of us—myself, Watson, Byron Nelson, and even Ben Hogan. Seve Ballesteros, through the 1980s, will be the successor to Jack Nicklaus."

That Trevino was absolutely and indubitably right has long since been proven. But in 1983 other American players made constant allusions to the Spaniard's "parking-lot shot" and to his marvelous recoveries, as if he were being unfairly favored by a sort of golfing genie. This grated unbearably on Ballesteros's nerves. He regarded it as a gross insult to his ability.

"Oh, you know I am a very wild driver," he told sportswriters sarcastically. "This is the only course in the world that is wide enough for me. Every fairway is two hundred yards wide, so I can use my driver."

Gullible, they wrote it down, they drank it in. They perpetuated the myth. They could hardly have been more wrong.

Five days after they struck their first shot in earnest, Ballesteros and Watson stepped out onto the tee in the final round of the U.S. Masters. Before them, as vivid and panoramic as an expressionist painting, stretched the crisp fairways of Augusta, hemmed with towering pines and airbrushed two shades of green. The world's No. 1 player and the Young Pretender rehearsed their swings before the pleased gallery with graceful, economic movements.

When they were announced by the starter, they powered their drives down the fairway and walked briskly from the tee, each preoccupied with his own thoughts. After the first round Ballesteros had told the press that he thought an eight-under-par total would win the tournament. "I'd be happy to take it now and go home," he had said with a laugh. He still felt the same way now. But his confidence was running high, and when he reached his ball he took out an eight-iron, struck it smoothly to six feet, and was away with a birdie.

It was a perfect day for golf. The sun beamed down from a cobalt sky, and the gentlest of breezes ruffled the leaves and pulled at the hats of the delighted crowd as they crossed from green to the tee. The second hole at Augusta is a 555-yard par-five named Pink Dogwood, which makes it sound like a walk in the park. Actually, it's anything but. Ballesteros appealed to its better nature with a fine drive, a majestic four-wood to twelve feet, and a single-putt for eagle.

"Hell," grumbled Tom Kite, who later emerged form the pack to finish tied for runner-up with Crenshaw for the tournament, "I can't even stop a wedge that close to the hole on that green."

But the Spaniard had only just begun. He narrowly missed a birdie putt at the third and he did make one at the 205-yard fourth, hitting a towering two-iron shot to within a few inches of the flag, and establishing a three-shot lead that no player seemed capable of challenging. Watson was literally punch-drunk with incredulity. "I felt like a fighter getting knocked down twice in the first round," he said. "I was in a daze. . . . I still thought I could win, though. A lot of things can happen. Byron Nelson made up six shots in eleven holes at Augusta. It *can* happen. Especially on the back nine." But the nearest Watson came to presenting a threat was when he drew within two shots of the lead after eagling the eighth. Thereafter, he seemed to go into a decline. Ballesteros reasserted himself with a birdie at the ninth to turn in 31.

"I always knew that he had great touch, great feel," Watson said admiringly. "That's his strength, his ability to maneuver the ball with a club, especially with the shorter clubs. His weakness has obviously been a tendency to get wild and hit the ball sideways. I'm familiar with that because I do the same thing. But when he's on, he's certainly a very exciting person to watch and also to play with. He impresses me with the type of shots he can play. He works the ball left to right and right to left, which is essential for a great player to succeed and have a great career."

It wasn't a poor drive but an overambitious approach shot that caused him to take bogey on the tenth, and a wayward iron off the twelfth tee cost him another. Undaunted, he smashed a huge drive into the forest on the notorious thirteenth. All the imagination in the world was of no earthly use to him there; he could do no more than chip out onto the fairway. But he did have the courage to fire his three-iron approach straight at the pin, though it was positioned on the edge of the green at Rae's Creek, and very nearly made a birdie.

HE SIMPLY STEPPED UP TO HIS BALL AND, WITH THE CONFIDENCE AND DELICACY OF TOUCH THAT IS GOD-GIVEN, CHIPPED THE BALL INTO THE HOLE.

The rest of the field, in varying states of awe, astonishment, and dejection, had been left to eat dust.

"We just couldn't keep up," Crenshaw later admitted; while Kite exclaimed: "It's like he is driving a Ferrari and the rest of us are in Chevrolets."

The spectators at Augusta are among the most disciplined in the world. They do not stampede, catcall, or drop litter, and they regard the slim ropes which line the fairways as sacred and inviolable boundaries. It would be more than their lives were worth to think otherwise. Now, moving with that half-walk, half-scurry of children who have been forbidden to run in a school corridor, those of them who had not already done so joined the flood of people rushing toward the Ballesteros-Watson match, leaving the downcast and scowling Walrus and others like him to wallow in their own misery, and were vociferous in their support of the proud young Spaniard.

Throughout the round Ballesteros had worn an intent and unsmiling expression. It never altered even as he came to the final hole leading by four shots, and it remained unchanged when he flew the green with his approach shot and then began the long march up the hill toward the clubhouse and victory. His ball lay on an awkward downhill lie among the gallery. Ballesteros surveyed it impassively, hands on hips. His father watched anxiously from the crowd. Then he chipped and the startled gallery saw the ball bound forward a few paces and die on the bank of the green. But Ballesteros neither swore, looked heavenward for advice, nor cried "Why me?" in an anguished tone, all of which would have been perfectly natural and even appropriate

Truly a magician with a golf club, especially when it comes to recovery shots and chips, Seve watches his green-side chip at the seventy-second hole of the 1983 Masters Tournament fall, punctuating his second victory at Augusta National Golf Club. (© Phil Sheldon)

under the circumstances. He simply stepped up to his ball and, with the confidence and delicacy of touch that is God-given, chipped the ball into the hole. Then, finally, as the gallery burst into thunderous applause, a smile broke like sunshine across the young Spaniard's face.

If a man strives his whole life to achieve perfection, and if he measures that perfection by the attainment of his profession's highest honor, then the hour of his victory should be his alone to cherish, and should be sweet and untainted—not marred by the petty jealousies of others. For Ballesteros, that hour was over in moments. Watson had preceded him into the interview room and had remarked sourly that, if Ballesteros's chip shot at the eighteenth hadn't hit the flagstick and dropped into the hole, it would have run off the green.

"Sure," Ballesteros snapped when this was repeated to him. "And I suppose then I take ten putts and don't even finish in the top ten."

He was too filled with joy to allow himself to grow angry over something so trivial, but the implication—that he had been lucky rather than the best player in the field—was not lost on him, and he put it to the back of his mind to be reflected on another day.

"Would you say you are a better golfer than you were when you won in 1980?" queried a reporter.

"No," Ballesteros said, "just more experienced."

Another asked whether he was planning to quit Europe for the U.S. Tour.

The Spaniard shook his head. "I love to be an international golfer. I love to play in Japan and Europe and the U.S." He grinned. "Anyway, I love to travel because I meet different girls."

"Is it an ambition of yours to win the U.S. Open?"

"Yes," Ballesteros replied, tongue in cheek, "but I don't think I will. I'm not *straight* enough for those courses." His face was deadpan and the implication went over the heads of both the American journalist laboriously taking down his answer and his compatriots. "One day," he added, eyes twinkling mischievously, "I will come over and play the U.S. Tour full time and see how good I am."

April 21, 1983, Madrid. Ballesteros, the "lucky" champion, was in a car park once again—this time facing a two-hundred-yard shot of nightmarish difficulty to the green. He assessed the risks and weighed up his chances. They were less than even. Undeterred, he smashed the ball away. It climbed high into the blue yonder and disappeared behind the stands. The crowd, ten thousand strong, erupted. Ballesteros allowed a pleased smile to lift the corners of his mouth, rapped his club smartly against his shoe, and threaded his way back through the smiling spectators into the Bernabeu football stadium, home to Real Madrid, where he was demonstrating trick shots.

The Masters champion had arrived home from America to find himself a national celebrity, feted by ministers and kings. To begin with, he had tried to hide away in Pedreña but, having been forced into the limelight by the impending Madrid Open, where he was defending champion, he had resigned himself wearily to the attentions of public and press. The football stadium exhibition had been a platform for an announcement, by the Mayor of Madrid, Tierno Galpan, that two public courses were to be built in the city as a tribute to him.

"That is exactly what we need to give everybody a chance to play golf," a pleased Ballesteros said afterward. "It will make the game popular. I've waited for years for this to happen. . . . I am flattered that they want to name the first one after me. The Mayor sent me a cable congratulating me on winning again at Augusta and so did the King of Spain. The newspapers and TV gave very big coverage to the Masters, compared with almost nothing when I won the first time. Now they know about golf as well as football in Spain."

The curious thing was that, although two of his most cherished dreams—winning the Masters and helping to make golf in Spain accessible to the masses—had come true in the same month, Ballesteros seemed listless and dejected.

The reaction of the press to his Masters' win was equally downbeat— more critical than congratulatory. *Golf World* said that "It was undoubtedly an important victory for the Spaniard. Since winning his first green jacket in 1980, only nine months after capturing the British Open at Royal Lytham, he has won several tournaments around the world but has somehow failed to live up to everyone's expectations. . . . And Mitchell Platts, profiling Ballesteros, commented that, in the years since his first win in the Dutch Open in 1976, the Spaniard's career had seemed "punctuated by troubles. Seve has smiled. Seve has sulked. He has been labeled an enigma. Certainly, there are times when it is difficult to trace a reason for his sudden changes of [mood]. . . . Many of his problems have been attributed to a fanatical desire to succeed coupled with a reputation for being somewhat avaricious. . . . In his defense there is another side of Seve. [The] tales of meanness have some foundation but there are times when he shows a generosity . . . which few could emulate. In Madrid three years ago he was eating in a small tavern when he recognized several relatively unknown British golfers dining at a corner table. He immediately sent over a couple of bottles of wine. Then, while competing on the Puerto de Hierro course, he was disturbed . . . at the top of his backswing . . . by a couple of small boys eager to . . . get a glimpse of Spain's newest sporting hero. Such an intrusion into Seve's work routine would usually darken the skies; on this occasion he quietly and kindly gave the two youngsters a friendly [lesson] in etiquette."

On this note, the new season began. When he arrived at Royal St. George's in May for the European PGA Championship, he had already lost one playoff in Italy to Langer and had narrowly missed out on another at the French Open. At a comparative point in 1982 he had won four tournaments in a row and was, as Williams said, "almost in the Walter Hagen position of being able to ask: 'Who is going to be second?' " Nothing had changed in the intervening year. After a minor setback in the second round—when he lost his temper and broke his driver—he compiled closing rounds of 67 and 71 to edge out Brown and Lyle at Sandwich, the first golf course he had ever played in Britain and one he had once described as "Hell."

Two other things of interest happened before Ballesteros crossed the Atlantic for the Westchester Classic: (1) After finishing thirteenth in the Silk Cut Masters and winning fifteen hundred pounds, he was disqualified and given last place and two hundred because a spectator had spotted a discrepancy in his published first-round scores; and (2) He played nine holes of La Manga's South Course on his knees, accompanied by Manuel, Juan Mellado, the club pro, and Mike Bamber, the chairman of Brighton Football Club. Said Bamber: "It was an amazing performance. He only did it for a bit of fun but he played brilliantly. He went on his knees for every shot, even for two in bunkers, and only stood up to putt. He told me that that was the way he perfected his swing when he was learning to play golf. I've never seen anything like it in my life."

On Friday, June 17, following the first round of the U.S. Open, Johnny Miller declared that there were only two types of tournament golfers: Ballesteros and the rest.

Ballesteros, who had prompted this compliment by shooting 69 to share the lead with John Mahaffey, accepted it graciously enough but at the same time hinted that there was a deliberate campaign by the media to put him under pressure. It wasn't that he was feeling depressed or ill-tempered—quite the reverse; after winning the Westchester Classic, by hitting two shots of near-genius on the final hole for an eagle, he was positively bursting with high spirits. But he wanted to let them know that he hadn't forgotten past slights, nor the aspersions they had cast on his ability over the years.

How, a questioner wanted to know, had he managed to cope so well with Oakmont's grueling layout when the vast majority of the field had been crippled by it?

"Well," Ballesteros said, poker-faced, "I hit the driver three times and I expect to leave the fairway two times, but I get lucky and I hit it two times. I think I was very lucky today. I'm only twenty-six and I think I play the U.S. Open ten or fifteen times more. Maybe one day I will get lucky and win. That's the only way I can win this tournament—get lucky."

The American press were bemused. They looked to each other for help. Finally, one said: "How do the British journalists describe the way you play?"

"In the United States, I'm lucky. In Europe, I'm good," came the swift response.

Fernandez believes that the reason Ballesteros makes the comments he does about luck is "to make himself even stronger, to make himself work even harder. Because he knew inside himself that he could win majors. I mean, you can be lucky once, twice, three times, but not always. People who play golf know that you're not lucky every day. If you get good results it's because something else is in it."

The following day violent storms disrupted play and Ballesteros did well to shoot 74. Nevertheless, he was only three strokes off the lead and considerably more relaxed and at ease than he had been at the same stage in the 1982 U.S. Open, when he had scored 81, 79 to miss the cut. On that occasion, too, there had been rain delays and general mayhem as a result. By midnight on Thursday the tee times had still not been posted, so Collet resolved to get up early the next morning to find them out. When he did, it was to discover that Ballesteros was off in less than an hour.

"So here I was," Collet recalls, "a year after the U.S. Open incident and he's going to miss his tee time again. So we frantically got a car, and this time I went with him, and the car went along the edge of the road, honking, and we got there like fifteen minutes before. He was really upset about it. He said: 'How could this be?' I said, 'Well, we asked the right questions, talked to the right people, and they were just so disorganized they couldn't give us the answers, so what are we supposed to do?' "

No such disasters befell Ballesteros in 1983, and when thunderstorms brought the tournament to a halt in the final round he was lying third on the leaderboard behind Nelson and Watson with five holes still to play. Statistics show that on that day he went out in 38, while his two main rivals scored 33 and 31, respectively; that when he bogeyed the tenth and twelfth he was overtaken by Calvin Peete and Gil Morgan; and that when the curtain closed on the final drama Nelson was the winner and Peete and Ballesteros shared fourth place. What they don't explain is why the Spaniard finished fourth. They don't reveal that the Ballesteros that played Oakmont that week was of a species that had not previously been thought to exist. He was cautious, conservative, and concerned only with making pars. He was a metronome. He told the media, "You have to play here like a robot, by hitting one-irons straight down the fairway." And he did exactly that. In short, he played in a way that Faldo has since perfected.

The 1983 U.S. Open appears to be the first time in Ballesteros's career that there is any mention of him playing seventy-two holes in that restrained manner, so obviously alien to his nature. Subsequently, he has done it on numerous occasions and almost always to the detriment of his game. But he has remained convinced that he played the course the way it should have been played and that he should have won. In 1991 he told Guy Hodgson of the *Independent*: "I had a chance of winning going into the last round. But I think someone realized Severiano might be the champion, so they moved the tees back as far as they could. I'm not the most accurate driver. It made a big difference to me. I got 74, but if the tees had been further forward, as they had been for the rest of the tournament, I would have done much better. The U.S. Open is always tees and greens, very tight. There is very little opportunity to manufacture shots. You have to play like a robot, straight, straight, very mechanical. The [price] for [not] being accurate off the tee is too great. I've never been a robot. I'm famous for being in trouble. Then you can make shots, show your ability a bit more."

There is a hint of paranoia in this statement, just as there was in a comment he made to the tall Fijian, Vijay Singh, about his performance at the 1983 British Open at Birkdale. He had complained then that the punishing rough greatly reduced the chances of the flair players and made it "a mechanical game." He then proceeded to pussy-foot around the golf course for three rounds, only remembering midway through the final day that boldness, not wariness, had made him a champion, and he finished sixth.

"Lost ball at the second hole," the Spaniard told Singh. "Two thousand people watching! We shouted fore but we never found it."

The second half of the year passed without mishap. At the Irish Open, which he won, it was announced that the ball he had used in the Masters, a Titleist with 384 dimples on it, had been outlawed by the United States Golf Association (USGA). The approved ball had only 320.

"It's no problem for me," Ballesteros said cheerfully when told. "Why don't we all play with stones."

In September he dropped a lawsuit he had brought against the R. J. Reynolds Tobacco Company in the United States for using his likeness without permission to advertise their cigarettes, and drew nearer to winning the Order of Merit again. "Sure, I want to win the money list," he said at the Swiss Open in Crans-sur-Sierre. "But I only want it, Faldo *needs* it. He must be a little bit afraid of me to come here this week. I've won it three times already so now I want to be the number one in the world. Last year I was third behind Craig Stadler and Floyd, but this year I win nearly four hundred thousand dollars worldwide. In eight years I win two million dollars. That is not so bad, I think."

Compare Ballesteros's record with that of Palmer, whom he was to beat so spectacularly in the World Match Play in October. When Palmer was twenty-six he had just struggled through his first year on the U.S. Tour, he had won less than eight thousand dollars, and had finished thirty-second on the money list. Ballesteros, on the other hand, had won three majors and more than thirty championships worldwide and had earned more than twice as much money in 1983 alone as Palmer had in seven years. When the season drew to a close, he was runner-up to Faldo on the European Order of Merit and was almost universally acknowledged as the No. 2 player in the world. Only Watson was ahead of him.

II

HALLOWED GROUND

"I want to be the best again, of course. But right now I must be honest, and by looking at the results and the way I feel, I cannot lie to myself. I never lie to myself."

Severiano Ballesteros, Pedreña, June 1984

The eyes that peered out through the foliage were dark gold, liquid, and expressive. They vanished as their owner dropped to his knees and, crunching about among the fallen pine cones and twigs, tried to gain a clearer perspective of the distant flagstick, then reappeared with their black brows drawn together in a fierce frown of concentration as Ballesteros realized he would have to play the shot blind. The fifteenth green at Puerto de Hierro lay some 195 yards away, around a corner and screened by a small forest. On it, American Tom Sieckmann, his partner in the opening round of the Madrid Open, was practicing his putting stroke and wondering rather impatiently what had become of Ballesteros.

Ballesteros was deliberating his options. "I had two chances," he remembered later (most people would have said those were slim and none). "I could hit a low hook or I could hit a high fade." Having decided to pursue the latter course, he selected a five-iron, aimed fifty yards left of target, and smashed the ball into the air. It flew away in a curve as geometrically precise as the line-drawing of an architect, cleared the trees by inches, pitched ten feet from the pin, and trickled to a halt twenty feet away. Sieckmann looked skyward as if he expected manna to follow.

"Where on earth did that come from?" he said.

That Ballesteros was inspired by this single spark of brilliance in what had otherwise been an unexceptional day became obvious over the remaining holes. His pitch to nine inches at the last ensured a birdie and a score of 71—one of the few subpar rounds he had recorded all year. He followed it with a level-par 72 to make only his fourth cut in seven events, and his eventual second place was a fighting one, for he was struggling with a hook. Nevertheless, he had not yet grown desperate over the state of his game. "It is a little slump," he said, "but I am always like this," and his hands described giant peaks and troughs.

It was now the end of April and Ballesteros was in Spain for one of his infrequent appearances at the European Tour events. After almost six years of abortive attempts on the part of U.S. Tour commissioner Deane Beman to persuade him to switch his allegiance from Europe to the United States, Ballesteros had finally crossed the Atlantic and, since the beginning of the 1984 season when he had become a member of the U.S. Tour, thereby committing himself to fifteen events, had been based in America. The reason for this was not simply that a middle ground had been found between what Ballesteros wanted and what U.S. Tour regulations stipulated. Indeed, no compromise had been reached at all. It was because the Tournament Policy Board had, just like the poor ETPD committee before it in the case of the appearance-money dispute, been forced to see it Ballesteros's way. In 1978, when Beman had taken the unprecedented step of offering him his Tour card, the Spaniard had asked whether or not he would still be free to play in Europe as often as he wanted to. He was informed that although he would only be given three releases a year to play in overseas events, he could, as a foreigner, play wherever and whenever he wanted to on his home-country circuit. Ballesteros replied, quite reasonably, that Spain did not have a circuit and that the European Tour should be regarded as such. Beman wouldn't hear of it. He didn't see why the rules should be rewritten for a twenty-one-year-old who hadn't yet won a major. But as time went on and Ballesteros marched victorious from one British Open and two Masters, Beman became considerably less hard-line in his views. At length, he had given in altogether, and the Spaniard had won the right to treat Europe as his home circuit and had joined the U.S. Tour.

Like the hopeful voyagers before him, who, in good faith, set forth to discover the New World, Ballesteros quickly grasped that all would not be smooth sailing. In 1983 he had collected more than two hundred thousand dollars on the U.S. Tour in a limited number of appearances, in addition to the £113,864 he had made in official earnings in Europe. By the end of June 1984 he had played in twelve events, had had only two top-ten finishes, and was thirty-sixth on the money list. He had also failed to qualify for the final two rounds at Augusta after unwittingly taking two practice swings in a hazard on the thirteenth hole and incurring a two-stroke penalty.

BY THEN THE APPEAL OF THE GREAT AMERICAN DREAM HAD PLAINLY WORN THIN. HE WAS FED UP WITH HOT DOGS AND MEDIOCRITY.

"When I decide to play in the U.S. this year I knew there was a big risk involved," admitted Ballesteros. "I won two out of eight tournaments I entered last year, so this time people expect me to win six out of fifteen. But that's not possible. The standard is too good. Over there any one of fifty players is a possible winner, but here you're looking at maybe sixteen. Nothing has gone right for me. If I miss the green I always seem to finish up with a double bogey. When I'm going well, something always seems to happen and I lose a lot of confidence. There was a lot of publicity about me missing the cut in the Masters, but that really summed up my problems. I dropped shots because I grounded my club in a hazard which I didn't know was there and it cost me my place in the last two rounds. The cut was so close that I would have been only five shots behind the leader, and I would have still been in with a chance of winning."

His last tournament before returning to Europe was the U.S. Open at Winged Foot—"the toughest golf course I have ever played and the toughest of the championships to win." By then the appeal of the Great American Dream had plainly worn thin. He was fed up with hot dogs and mediocrity, and filled with a deep and insatiable longing for *paella* and the sweet hills of home. On practice days it seemed that his wish might be granted sooner rather than later. Winged Foot had been set up with traditional USGA severity; Ballesteros's erratic driving and indifferent putting did not augur well for his chances. But when the tournament commenced, he put away his driver, took out his one-iron, and, in the oppressive, ninety-degree-in-the-shade temperatures of New York that summer, exhibited a combination of magic and fire that thrilled the American crowds and earned him an opening 69. It turned out to be a flash in the pan. Having teed up in the second round a mere stroke behind the leaders Irwin and Jim Thorpe, he came crashing down with a 73, and was eleven shots adrift of Irwin going into the final day. At that point he announced, to the consternation of all, that he was abandoning his full-time commitment to the U.S. Tour. His next tournament would be the Lawrence Batley in England, three weeks hence, and in the interim he would be recovering in Pedreña. Of the remaining U.S. events, only the Buick and the PGA Championship had been penciled into his schedule. He had no plans, for the time being, at least, to play the obligatory fifteenth tournament.

So Ballesteros returned to his beloved Pedreña. Surrounded by the friends and family who adored him, he began, as he had a thousand times before, to heal the wounds that had been inflicted on his pride and self-confidence. This he did by lying on the beach, playing tennis and pelota, meeting old friends, and devouring liberal helpings of his mother's cooking. Vitamin tablets, too, were swallowed in large doses, for a blood test had revealed that a mineral deficiency may have been responsible for his tiredness and lack of vigor. Twice a day Ballesteros worked on his game, under the watchful eye of Manuel.

"Away from the course, everything is great," he assured Peter Higgs of the *Mail on Sunday*, when Higgs arrived in Pedreña a fortnight before the British Open to interview him. "But I am not happy with my game." Adopting the principle of all great players by following a negative thought with a positive one, he went on to explain that, although he had not been playing well when he went to Sun City in South Africa for the Million Dollar Challenge, he had won the tournament by five strokes. "That's the way in golf sometimes. I feel great, I expect to do well, and nothing happens. Other times . . . I'm unhappy about my swing and I win the tournament."

His victory in Bophuthatswana gave him considerable satisfaction because he had lost a nine-hole playoff there to Miller two years earlier in particularly galling circumstances. On the first extra hole Ballesteros had hit his tee shot to six inches. The American was six feet away but sank the putt with aplomb, and they went up sixteen, seventeen, and eighteen three times before Ballesteros missed a four-foot putt for bogey to hand the title to Miller.

"He couldn't come to the party afterward," recalls Brent Turley, who had accompanied the young Spaniard on behalf of UMI. "Manuel tried to get him to do it but he was back in his room, crying. It was a very emotional experience for him. It was just something he could not accept. Now, that is something that would be interpreted by many as being a human failing—which we all have. But it's also the guts of why he has been so successful."

Back in Pedreña, Ballesteros omitted to mention to Higgs that, on his return journey from Johannesburg to Spain, he had decided at the last possible second to take the night plane from Madrid to Santander instead of the one he was booked on the following morning. When he arrived home, he learned that the second flight had crashed in a runway accident and not a solitary passenger survived.

Destino had come to his rescue once more.

"You know, maybe why I don't feel too good is because 1983 was a tough year," Ballesteros mused. "It was a great year, the best. But I was under a lot of pressure and now I'm suffering a little reaction. That's why, maybe, I'm a little jumpy and nervous and my concentration has not been good.

"St. Andrews could be the place where it will come right. If I didn't think I could win, I would stay at home. . . . I have to be honest and say that my confidence and attitude aren't at their best. But I will be tough there, that's for sure."

Wednesday, July 11, 1984. When Ballesteros had first set out for a practice round on the eve of the British Open at St. Andrews, a genial sun had been shining, which had lent luster to great rolling greens and an ochre hue to the mounds and hollows. Seagulls had wheeled carelessly above the cornflower-blue bay and pilgrims had clattered joyfully through the streets of a "city given over soul and body to a tyrannizing game"—pausing only to gaze wistfully at the shops, restaurants, and museums which paid homage to that game—before spilling out onto the sacred links of St. Andrews.

Now, however, it was early evening. The sun was sliding down below the gothic spires and medieval rooftops of the famous gray town, and a mysterious half-light prevailed. At that hour of day, the Old Course was no longer a thing of beauty. Indeed, a dispassionate observer, standing in the shadow of the Royal and Ancient clubhouse and looking out across the flat, mousy links, would soon see her for what she really was: a sullen, ugly, frowzy old woman, riddled with ambiguities; as craterous and barren as the moon. Small wonder that when Sam Snead first came to St. Andrews in 1946, she struck him as being "an abandoned sort of place . . . so raggedy and beat up I was surprised to see what looked like fairway among the weeds. Down home we wouldn't plant cow beets on land like that."

Fuzzy Zoeller was equally unimpressed in 1984. "A guy could get lost out there," he said. "I stood on the second tee and started hunting for some sign of the course."

The sages nodded wisely. They had heard it all before. Each and every one of them had experienced the same sense of disappointment when they had first laid eyes on the Old Course, the conviction that whoever built it— whether God or man—had played a cruel joke upon golfers worldwide. The slow dawning of respect had come later, along with the thrill of discovering each of her many faces.

"St. Andrews is the course where you look down the register of champions and every one of them is a brilliant champion," enthuses Ben Crenshaw, a convert. "All through the ages it's probably been the most-loved and most-hated golf course. Most of them have learned to love it. There's a lot of learning to be done. There's a lifetime of learning on that golf course. For a mind like Bobby Jones's—and I think he's close to being the most cerebral player that ever lived—it fascinated him. He hated it at first. Didn't like it because he couldn't understand it. . . . Later on he became more tolerant of it, and the more he learned about it the more he loved it, because it was a puzzle. Later on, he said it was by far his favorite golf course."

Ballesteros had already been through the entire emotional spectrum with links courses in general, and had lately reached the stage where the intensity of his feeling for the home of golf could almost be described as worship. These and other thoughts were flitting through his mind as he rounded the turn at St. Andrews, flanked by his loyal friends, Chino Fernandez and the Brazilian Jaime Gonzalez. There was a rare smile on his face. Rare, because he had not often had cause to smile in 1984. Not only because he had been homesick and preoccupied with the state of his game, but also because he felt alienated by the Spanish golfers who had once encouraged him and protected him. For that, of course, he had no one to blame but himself. He had offended the nationalistic pride of many of them by demanding a large fee before he would consider participating in the 1978 Hennessy Cup, then

Ben Crenshaw certainly knew what he was talking about when he enthusiastically praised Seve's golf game: He often got to see the Spaniard up close and personal, as was the case during this match between the two at the 1984 World Match Play Championship. (© Phil Sheldon)

refusing to play in the World Cup a few months later; by resigning from the Tour in 1981 over the appearance-money issue, and then causing a rumpus when he found he hadn't been chosen for the Ryder Cup; and by deserting Europe for the fatal charms of the dollar.

Piñero had been quoted as saying that it was "very difficult now to understand Seve at times. . . . I don't think he changed himself, I think the people changed him. In the early days he was allowed to be himself. He had his close friends, the ones on whom you can always rely; but after he wins the big tournaments then everyone claims to be a friend of Seve and wants to be a friend of Seve. So I don't think the ways of Seve today are necessarily of his own doing. They have been shaped for him. I think Seve is introverted. Everyone gets to him and he cannot handle it. He doesn't like to be mobbed by people all the time. What he needs now, more than anything else, is a close friend and not the hangers-on. I spoke with Seve and I said that it was important for him to realize that away from his job he is still an ordinary person and that he must try to be his own person. I think Seve is a nice guy, but he has his problems. He has lost his way. What he needs now is more understanding."

No two players were more willing to provide Ballesteros with all the understanding he needed than Fernandez and Gonzalez. He had gone to them both during the Lawrence Batley tournament at the Belfry, one week before the British Open, and begged them to help him. "Well, he had played already for nearly six months and he didn't break 70 one round from January to July," Fernandez recalls. "He asked me if we could play a practice round together. I said yes, and one day we went to the practice range and I spotted what I thought was wrong. He was reverse-pivoting." Ballesteros had started to work on the fault almost immediately but, upon arrival at St. Andrews, was still not entirely convinced he had resolved it. Thus, he had come out onto the links with Chino and Jaime for one last attempt to search for the key that would turn his game around.

When twilight crept in purple robes across the quiet golf course, the three friends knew they had found it.

"They told me I was turning too much instead of just transferring my weight," Ballesteros says. "They both told me the same thing, so I did something about it. And it worked especially well for me."

Thursday, July 12, 1984. By the time Ballesteros teed off in the first round of the British Open, the white horses which had lain still for most of the morning were rearing energetically in the sparkling Bay of Firth. Such is the luck of the draw in this tournament. Some players encounter nothing but blue skies and sunshine, others have to cope with rain and gale-force winds. But today the weather was as perfect as could be expected at St. Andrews and it contributed greatly to Ballesteros's manifestly good humor. Several things were responsible for this sudden change of heart. One was the presence of his mother, now sixty-four, who had never been to the British Open before but who had come determined to see her son win; another was the overnight improvement of his golf swing and the subsequent lift of his confidence and spirits; and the third was the arrival of Carmen Botin, his girlfriend of two years, with whom he was staying at a nearby farmhouse.

The Ballesteros who strode so jauntily along the front nine of the Old Course bore little resemblance to the glum Spaniard of recent months. So cheerful was he, in fact, that it seemed at any moment as if he might break into a whistle. "It was as if he was at home at St. Andrews," recalled Nick de Paul, his American caddie, later. "He hardly put a foot wrong. If the others had realized just how totally in charge he was, I think they would have been very jittery."

Around the Loop flew Ballesteros and then along the holes called Bobby Jones, High, Heathery, Hole o' Cross, Long, Cartgate, and Corner of the Dyke, adhering all the while to his strategy of avoiding the Old Course's treacherous fairway bunkers. But just as it began to look as though he would hardly be able to help scoring 68 or better, he reached the seventeenth—the Road Hole. There he tried to cut his drive, hit a poor fade instead, and was compelled to take a four-iron from relatively thick grass. It ascended into the blue with all the enthusiasm of a snooker ball and fell back into the rough. Next, he attempted a wedge shot to the green but it, too, died and rolled in front of the bunker. He was now "looking at a six." Quelling his nerves, he putted bravely around the rim of the bunker. The ball ran down to about eight feet and he holed the putt for a "bogey that felt like a birdie."

"Today was one of the best rounds of the year for me," Ballesteros said after his round, beaming down at the world's press from the lofty heights of the interview platform. "Two more rounds like that and I will definitely be in contention on Sunday."

At the close of play he was lying third on the leaderboard with a 69, three under par, along with Faldo, Tom Kite, and Gonzalez. Ian Baker-Finch, the twenty-three-year-old Queenslander, was a stroke ahead of them, while the leaders, Greg Norman, Peter Jacobsen, and Longmuir—the same Longmuir who had conjured up a near-miraculous 65 to lead the British Open at Lytham in 1979 by one stroke—were at five under par.

Collet has always maintained that Ballesteros is not a superstitious man but only has a keen sense of traditionalism. Nevertheless, there are dozens of examples to support the theory that he is. He refuses to carry No. 3 balls, for example, never studies a putt from the left-hand side in case he misses it, and, since his first victory at Lytham, has always worn navy blue and white on the final day. He did the same throughout 1983, always putting them on for the last round of a tournament. During his champion's press conference at the Lancome Trophy, he indicated his clothes and said proudly, "Already five times champions this year." But the final proof is provided by Longmuir, whom he approached just prior to the British Open in 1985, offering to give him lessons to help him with his game. "If I see your name on the leaderboard, I'll know I'm going to win the gold tournament," Ballesteros said cheerfully.

"Yeah," Longmuir thought wryly, "but what about me?"

Longmuir has never led the British Open since, but to this day, if he runs into Ballesteros in the weeks preceding it, the Spaniard will say, "How are you playing? Are you hitting it all right? Have you qualified?"

It is, as Longmuir says, quite funny really.

Friday, July 13, 1984. On the second day of play Ballesteros was no less exuberant. "If I was worried a little about my game," he said later, "I thought of my friend Fuzzy Zoeller. All year he had not done much but then he went to the U.S. Open and won it. In this game you can never be sure."

But now the Old Course exerted her influence on the tournament. She was aided in this by the wind, which began by gusting teasingly but gradually grew more malevolent; by the sun, which had hardened the browning fairways and greens to the state of rare unpredictability; and by the two most notorious holes on the course, the fourteenth and seventeenth. "There's no other golf course in the world that changes so much with every little putt of wind," Crenshaw says. "There's an intricate set of problems on every hole. You're thinking about contours, little humps, and hollows. They all add up to what you can and can't do on a certain day. Things that you shouldn't do, things that you ought to do, things that you ought to have done."

Ballesteros did everything he ought to do, and did it magnificently, for sixteen holes. Then he came to the seventeenth—where he met his nemesis.

Peter Thomson, winner of five British Opens, one of them at St. Andrews, once remarked that, "as a planner and builder of golf holes worldwide," he had no hesitation in allowing that if one dared build a par-four such as the Road Hole today, one "would be sued for incompetence." James said he wasn't sure who had designed it, but that he'd heard he had escaped, while Crenshaw suggested that the reason the 460-yard seventeenth was the greatest par-four in the world was because it was a par-five. But Ballesteros,

THE WIND WAS SWIRLING NASTILY ABOVE THE HEADS OF THE GALLERY, AND IT SEIZED HIS SIX-IRON APPROACH AND PULLED IT INTO THE CAVERNOUS ROAD HOLE BUNKER.

who had been two shots clear of the field after thirty-four holes in 1978 when it put paid to his chances, simply described it as "the hardest hole I've ever played. The pin placings are so difficult. Maybe one day they decide not to put the hole on the green!"

Now, as he stood on the penultimate tee and surveyed the most infamous hole in golf, with its black railway sheds, its side-angled view of the monstrosity that is the Old Course Hotel, its scruffy grass and mottled heather, he resolved to improve upon his bogey of the previous day. But it was not to be. The wind was swirling nastily above the heads of the gallery, and it seized his six-iron approach and pulled it into the cavernous Road Hole bunker. Ballesteros needed two shots to get out and all of his skill to hit the second to four feet and hole it for a five. He was not alone. Of the 312 golfers who pitted their wits against the Road Hole in the opening rounds, 223 made bogey or worse.

That evening the young Spaniard who had, at the age of twenty-one, cheekily told a questioner that the way to play the seventeenth at St. Andrews was to hit a "good drive, good second shot, and one putt," laughed and promised: "Tomorrow I will par the Road Hole." On Saturday, after his third consecutive bogey, he amended his vow. "If I don't par it Sunday, I will come back and play it Monday until I par it." In victory, the first thing that crossed his mind was: "I keep my promise. I won't have to come back tomorrow."

At the end of the day Ballesteros was three strokes adrift of the leader, Baker-Finch, at 137, seven under par. Faldo and Trevino shared second place with him, while Longmuir was at 138. Watson, who had played in the worst of the weather, Fred Couples, and Wadkins were at 139.

Saturday, July 14, 1984. Soon after noon on the third day of play, when the air was mild and a brisk wind followed the field out to the Eden Estuary, Tom Watson, winner of five British Opens, found himself the grateful beneficiary of a slice of good fortune. His approach shot to the first green, having pitched millimeters short of the Swilcan Burn, bounded safely onto the green—thereby saving him a bogey or worse.

"Luck plays a great part in the game no matter where you play," said Watson, freckled and smiling, "but in links golf you have to depend on the bounce."

In 1984 Watson, the No. 1 player in the world (prior to the British Open Championship), was depending upon the luck of the bounce to help him make history by equaling Harry Vardon's record of six British Open titles. On Saturday it seemed he would not be disappointed. He had seven birdies and one bogey in a round of 66, and at the end of the day was sharing the lead with the indomitable Baker-Finch on 205, eleven under par. Ballesteros, who had had fourteen pars, three birdies, and a bogey, was two strokes behind with Langer, while Wadkins, Trevino, and Hugh Baiocchi were at 212.

Of Ballesteros, Watson said: "Seve's a very determined player, but I think superstition gets in his way. I believe sometimes he feels the golfing gods are against him and other times I think he feels that the golfing gods are with him. And I think sometimes that can be a hindrance."

Afterward, Jorge Ceballos, the Spaniard's manager, said that he had felt all along that it would come down to Ballesteros and Watson. "[Seve] told me he would claw his way through anything to win because he wanted it so badly. It did not matter about his golf and how he had been playing up till then. His form had nothing to do with it. He was going to get this one because he wanted it much more than anybody else."

Sunday, July 15, 1984. On the morning of the final round, when the loveliest water-color blue washed over the sky above St. Andrews and the air was filled with the mingled aroma of salt, crushed grass, and heather, Chino Fernandez drove slowly out of town. He had failed to qualify and felt duty-bound, therefore, to take his family back to London. "I left a message for Seve, but he never wants to read anything before he goes out. He doesn't like it. Maybe it's superstitious, but it's in case something he doesn't like upsets him before he goes out."

Nothing happened to disturb Ballesteros's equilibrium at all. Indeed, his composure, as he walked down the steps to the first tee, greeted Langer perfunctorily, and turned to gaze out over the Old Course, was remarkable. So was his appearance, for he was strikingly tall, broad-shouldered, and handsome, his face a deep rust color above his white polo shirt, his hair like a raven's wing. There was not an eye in the gallery that wasn't pinned on him. He set up over his ball, glanced at the ribbon of green and gold fairway which ran between the bright banks of spectators, and smashed his drive smoothly away.

The previous afternoon, following his round, Ballesteros had been interviewed about his antagonists, and had commented that Watson was a great player and "he's playing his best now and is confident and I think he is the man to beat." Later he was to say that his initial objective had been to try and beat Langer and then to concentrate on the others. He set about this task with a singular determination, hitting his approach shot to ten feet and keeping his nerve when Langer almost holed his from the fairway, knowing that golf is about how and not how many. But fury flitted across his face as his birdie putt stayed willfully above ground while Langer went to ten under par. "Pete Coleman was caddying for Bernhard," Nick de Paul recalls, "and Pete had caddied for Seve for a time, so he was thinking it was one-up on them. I thought: 'Things are going to be tight this afternoon.' And I know Seve was thinking the same."

Behind them Baker-Finch, who had proceeded blithely around the Old Course for three days with barely a scratch, had his first real experience of the darker side of her nature when he hit his approach shot into the Swilcan Burn. Watson moved swiftly and mercilessly to take advantage of his slip. But three putts at the second and fourth holes negated the advance he had made at the third, and when Ballesteros made his first birdie of the day at the fifth, holing from thirteen feet while Langer struggled to a bogey six, the American and he were tied.

At the sixth hole there was an incident which may have been more significant in the grand scheme of things if Ballesteros had been anything less than completely in control. He pulled his drive, scowled, and muttered, "It's in the bunker." Someone in the gallery cackled. Ballesteros spun around, eyes flashing. "You think that's funny?" he asked. There was complete silence. Only the fresh blustery wind and the dull roar of the sea could be heard. Eventually, the Spaniard moved off, and, when he found that his ball wasn't in the bunker at all, made par while Watson took three putts at the fifth and Baker-Finch took six at the sixth. Two holes later a five-iron to six feet gave him the outright lead of the British Open for the first time since he had walked off the final green at Lytham in 1979.

Now the weather began to change and gray clouds stole over the top of the flapping marquees. Ballesteros, tense, confident, and excited, marched resolutely through the gloom, hitting shot after immaculate shot. At the short eleventh, however, having just three-putted from seventy feet at the tenth, he misclubbed and his eight-iron tee shot rolled off the putting surface and came ominously close to the edge of the evil Strath Bunker. He took out his putter and tried to stroke the ball up the steep bank onto the green. It crawled reluctantly to the top of the hill and hung there. "One more roll and it would have gone right to the pin," Ballesteros says. As it was he made bogey while Watson birdied and resumed control of the tournament.

Thus did it continue—the delicate shifting of the balance of power. The huge crowds, high as kites on the melodramatics, whirled dizzyingly about them, their faces looming specter-like through the dust. At the twelfth hole Watson was over-ambitious and saw his drive vanish into the bushes in no-man's-land. But he birdied the next just as the Spaniard did the same at the fourteenth, and they were tied once again at eleven under par. On the fifteenth tee Ballesteros reached into his bag and, calmly and deliberately, pulled on the navy sweater he had worn to win at Lytham. His face was rigid with determination. When a putt which, had it dropped, would have given him a one-shot cushion going into the Road Hole stopped on the lip of the cup on the sixteenth, he simply squared his shoulders, set his jaw, and marched on with his head held high. "All the way round I felt good and clear and calm," he recalled later. "I held my game together through the

177

After holing the winning putt at St. Andrews in 1984, Seve explodes into a joyous celebration of his second British Open triumph, punching the air repeatedly while turning to salute the galleries. It was a moment he later described as "the pinnacle" of his career. (© Phil Sheldon)

excitement, particularly over the closing holes, and that is the key to my winning. I stood up to the pressure."

But now he heard the siren call of the Road Hole, who had lured so many men to their doom. He himself had suffered three of his five bogeys at her hands. Nevertheless, he believed the line he had taken all week to be the right one, so he drove out to the left. The ball homed unerringly in on the area of rough where it had finished on the previous two occasions. This time he had a good lie. He also had two hundred yards to the pin and an area of green no bigger than a postage stamp to work with. He chose a six-iron. Normally, he hits a six-iron no more than 165 yards, but knowing the adrenaline was pumping and knowing too that he might get a flyer out of the rough, he was confident it was the right club. Into the overcast sky it arched, then down onto the dangerous green. It was a stroke of genius. And no one but a champion could have played that shot, under that pressure, on that hole *and* almost make birdie from it.

Years later Ballesteros is still amazed by his own audacity. "The more I look at that shot," he says, laughing, "the more impressed I get myself. Because if you look at that shot, to put the ball where I did on the green, I guess, was very lucky."

"As we came off the seventeenth green, Seve said, 'There's going to be a playoff,' " de Paul recalls. "I said, 'If we birdie the last there won't be any need for a playoff.' I think it got him thinking positive."

When Ballesteros had hit his drive to the last hole, he turned and looked back at the seventeenth. There was Watson in prime position on the fairway. Well, Ballesteros thought to himself, "Watson is Watson. He is going to make a par and he can make a birdie at any time." And he struck his pitch shot carefully to fifteen feet to attempt to finish with a birdie.

Watson had rather less confidence in his ability to bring the Road Hole to its knees than Ballesteros gave him credit for. He was uncertain about the club he should take. First, he thought it might be a three-iron and then he thought it was a two. He selected the latter. Even before it had bounded off the back of the grass and onto the dreaded road, he thought that destiny was closing the door on history. And when he saw his ball pressed up against the wall, watched his chip race past the flagstick, and stood by helplessly as his par putt failed to fall, he knew it was.

In the vast amphitheater of the eighteenth green, Ballesteros played his final stroke—"the happiest of my life." Then, as the ball vanished into the hole and the crowd erupted, he exploded into a frenzy of ecstasy, punching the air over and over as he turned to salute the people who loved him.

More than two hundred miles away, Fernandez, driving through England, was listening to the drama unfold on his car stereo—which he wouldn't have done if he had been in Spain, for at the precise moment of Ballesteros's victory the Spanish broadcasting networks had switched over to a horse race. "When I heard that he won and in his speech he thanked his friends, it was fantastic," Fernandez says. "The only thing is, he still has to pay me whatever he owes me. He said, 'Well, 50 percent of this is for Vicente and Jaime who helped me.' I still have to get my 25 percent!" He bursts out laughing. "No, but it was very nice. . . . I was very happy and I thanked him for what he said. I told him, 'I would have been very disappointed if you hadn't said anything.' But he's not that kind of person."

"I can't tell you just what it means to me to win at St. Andrews," said Ballesteros, wreathed in smiles. "It has made my year without a doubt. When I won at Lytham in 1979, I win with the heart. But this time I won because I prepared myself so well. I had good preparation of the mind, good determination, and good thinking on the course. It meant so much to me to do it at St. Andrews and have the Spanish flag flying at the home of golf for a year. My first Open win was very special, but this proves that it was not a lucky fluke.

"Maybe it will make people think a little more of me."

Years on, sportscaster Tony Adamson went to Ballesteros to ask him to autograph a poster of his triumph at St. Andrews—that famous image of the Spaniard with his fist clenched and his face dark with emotion.

"That was some moment, that," said Adamson, who had been almost moved to tears by the wonder of it all.

"Yes," agreed Ballesteros, "the pinnacle."

12

THE DRY SEASON

"Action is transitory — a step, a blow
The motion of a muscle, this way or that —
'Tis done, and in the after-vacancy
We wonder at ourselves like men betrayed:
Suffering is permanent, obscure and dark,
And shares the nature of infinity."

William Wordsworth, *The Borderers*

John Brodie, an intelligent, good-humored Californian who was once a quarterback for the San Francisco 49ers and who went on to become a successful Senior PGA Tour player, likes to tell a story about a friend of his who went up to Dave Marr and said to him: "David, who's the best player in the world? The players know, don't they?"

"Well," Marr replied, "I suggest that you go out onto the practice tee and look around and whomever most of the guys are looking at is probably pretty good."

The man followed his advice and walked down to the range. When he arrived there he saw a group of about eleven players, including Norman, Strange, Woosnam, and Faldo, all standing about watching Ballesteros hit balls. He went straight back to find Marr. "Oh," he said, "I see what you mean."

By 1985, when Ballesteros flew into Georgia for the Masters, he was the No. 1 player in the world, both officially and by the consensus of Tour professionals across the globe, and had been accepted as such well before he became British Open champion for the second time, though his victories in 1984 had been spread thinly.

His principal rival during the season had been Bernhard Langer, the dedicated, athletically built German. Both men came from very similar backgrounds: Ballesteros was the son of a farmer, Langer a bricklayer; the former started playing at the age of seventeen, the latter at eighteen; both were caddies; both never had handicaps; both came from underdeveloped golfing nations; and both were gifted and extremely hard working. A strong element of competitiveness existed between them, possibly because they were so alike. In 1984 it was accentuated when Ballesteros beat the German at St. Andrews, lost to him in the Irish Open, beat him 2 & 1 at the World Match Play, and then finished fifth to him on the Order of Merit. At the Match Play it had bubbled over into open hostility.

> **"SEVE'S NOT EASY TO PLAY WITH. HE DOESN'T TALK AND HE NEVER SAYS 'GOOD SHOT'—OR VERY SELDOM. HE PRACTICES PUTTING WHEN YOU'RE OVER THE BALL."**

"Seve never speaks to me, so why should I be nice to him?" Langer told journalists on the eve of the final at Wentworth, thereby adding insult to the injury, for he had already been quoted as saying the Spaniard was "intimidating" on the golf course, which implied he was guilty of gamesmanship.

Ballesteros was hurt. He retaliated by declaring that he "would prefer to play Greg [Norman], he's more friendly," and the next day held a heated and very public exchange with Langer in the press center.

"I don't know how it started," Langer now says, of the discord between them at that stage of their careers. "We're very different. We never were very close friends. I think we respected each other, but we were big rivals for many years. . . . I said he was intimidating, but I really didn't know what intimidating meant, so I used the word in a different meaning and it all came out rather badly. The press made it even bigger. Seve's not easy to play with. He doesn't talk and he never says 'good shot'—or very seldom. He practices putting when you're over the ball and you can see him out of the corner of your eye. And he must know these things, and I don't think it's right. What I

Here's Seve in the mid-1980s performing at one of his trick-shot exhibitions, although such a shot could just as well have been the real thing in tournament play for the master of "geographically challenged" shots. (© Phil Sheldon)

meant was he was very difficult to play with, especially in match play. He read it in the papers or was just told by the press. He was kind of shocked. He didn't think we had a problem and he was very surprised. And we didn't really have a big problem. The only thing I was saying was that he's not very easy to play with."

A few days later they sat down together and talked over two things: Langer's comments to the press and the role he had played in the Ryder Cup controversy of 1981. "We cleared the air," Langer remembers. Langer listened while Ballesteros assured reporters that he bore the German no malice, and then the Spaniard stood at the back of the press center while Langer explained he had believed the word intimidating to be an innocuous one and had really intended it as a compliment to Ballesteros's powers of concentration.

Henceforth, an uneasy truce had existed between them, which was still in operation when Ballesteros came to Augusta in April 1985, brimming over with happiness and contentment. He had started the year well, by successfully defending his Million Dollar Challenge title and by winning the rain-shortened USF&G Classic in New Orleans by two strokes over Mahaffey, but then he had missed the cut at the Tournament Players' Championship (TPC) after shooting 76, 74. This setback did not dampen his spirits. He took a week's holiday at Doral in Florida, during which time he did not hit a single ball but just swam, lay on the beach, and fished, and then reappeared at the Masters on his birthday looking tanned and refreshed. Failing to qualify at Sawgrass did not seem to concern him in the slightest. "Last year I finished (tied for) third in the TPC, came to Augusta, and missed the cut," he said, smiling at the worried faces of the British journalists. "Perhaps my play this time in the TPC will be a better omen for the Masters."

To begin with, it seemed it would. In the opening round Ballesteros scrambled around the course and was fortunate to escape with a 72, but by the second day the work he had put in over the winter was beginning to pay off and he was playing with a fluid and beautiful rhythm. He scored 71 in that round and 71 in the next and, like the shadow of a black hawk, loomed large over the tournament when the final day dawned. Langer, whom fate had decreed should be drawn with the Spaniard, was not the only one afraid of him.

"I'd lost to him in the World Match Play three times," Langer recalls, "once in the final, once in the semifinal, and once in the second round, and in 1984 he won the British Open and I finished two behind. So it became more and more difficult for me because it seemed like the more we played head to head, the more I lost, even though there were several tournaments where I beat him. So at first I wasn't too exited about the pairing. But I said, "I'm not going to watch him today, I'm just going to play my own game. Whatever he does, it will not bother me." I told myself that the night before. I said, 'If he practices putting on the green, I will tell him to go away. If he does anything else, I will tell him what bothers me and I will not be upset if he doesn't say anything.' So I had a really clear picture of what I was going to do the next day. And I didn't have any problems."

On a gray, humid day in the south, Ballesteros teed off in the fourth round of the Masters, his brother Manuel at his side. Langer, golden-haired and fresh-faced but no less determined, came after them with an even, unhurried stride. Ballesteros drew first blood. His bunker shot at the second hole almost went in for an eagle, while Langer, from virtually the same place, took three to get down for a bogey six and was two behind the Spaniard before they had reached the third hole. But gradually it became obvious that Ballesteros had lost his touch on the greens. Putt after putt evaded the hole and denied him birdies, while Langer converted his chances with a three at the third and a two at the sixth. Ahead of them, Strange burned a fiery trail to the turn. Teeing up on the tenth hole, he was four under par for the day and four ahead of Ballesteros, Langer, and Gary Hallberg.

It was at that point that Langer glanced at the leaderboard for the first time. Realizing how much ground he had lost, he resolved simply to try his best, regardless, and to attempt to play the perfidious back nine in four under par. Ballesteros, meanwhile, had grown frustrated and his agitation was reflected in the color of his language (he rarely swears) and in his grimaces and heavy sighs. He looked on bleakly while Langer made successive birdies at the twelfth and thirteenth holes. Strange's flight to glory had already ended in tears. A three-putt on the tenth and a disastrous encounter with Rae's Creek at the thirteenth had brought him crashing down to earth. Ballesteros fought on gamely, making par after par but no birdies. It was not good enough. His last chance was a critical and brilliantly executed chip shot on the sixteenth, which would have brought him to within a stroke of the German with two holes to play had he holed it. But it narrowly avoided the cup, and the Spaniard threw himself to the ground in despair, for he knew that he had now left the way clear for Langer.

Walking off the seventeenth green Ballesteros put his arm around Langer's shoulders. "It's all yours," he said. "Well done. You've played some great shots."

Looking back at that tournament, through the brightly lit tunnel of time, it is possible to see it as the start of a dry season in Ballesteros's career—of a period when major championships seemed beyond his reach, when he lost his spontaneous smile and devil-may-care attitude, when he became increasingly discontented and preoccupied with holding his great swing in check. At the time, however, it was not noted as being particularly significant. Yes, Ballesteros had finished tied for second with Strange and Floyd at

185

284, two strokes behind his arch-enemy Langer, and yes, it had meant a lot to him to win, so it was obviously very painful for him to lose. But it didn't really matter, did it? Wasn't it still an achievement to be second?

And so it was that when Ballesteros teed up in the European PGA Championship at Wentworth in the last week of May (for a fee of thirty thousand pounds), he gave every appearance of having bounced back from his experience at Augusta without any aftereffects at all; indeed, he probably did, for it was only in the light of the events of the next two years that the 1985 Masters was of any consequence at all. Six weeks had elapsed since he left Augusta. In the interim, he had participated in a two-hundred-fifty-thousand-pound Skins game in Australia, along with Nicklaus, Watson, Faldo, Lyle, Langer, and Norman, where he had earned twenty-five thousand pounds for winning only one hole; had flown to Boston to visit his girlfriend, Carmen, who was at college near there; had finished tied for fifth in the Italian Open; and had acquired a racing bike. This last had become his new obsession. In the fortnight preceding the tournament, he claimed to have ridden twenty miles daily along the mountainous routes surrounding Santander, wearing five sweaters and two pairs of trousers to help him pedal away the pounds. He had also been using a hand-strengthening device given to him by Gary Player.

"All the top players have strong legs," Ballesteros insisted. "Look at Nicklaus and Watson. It's foolish to say you don't have to be fit to play golf. I want to be a better golfer, and the stronger you are, the more confident you are." He proved it by finishing tied for fourth.

In June, Ballesteros returned to America for the U.S. Open at Oakland Hills. In horrendous, blustery conditions he returned opening scores of 71, 72, and he was six strokes behind the leader, T. C. Chen, after two days of play. Then, when all eyes were on him after a third-round 69, he became obsessed with taking irons off the tee. He plotted his way carefully around the front nine of the brutal USGA layout like a man playing chess for his life, and it was not until he reached the turn and found that he had nothing to show for his attempts at self-preservation but a 37, that he lowered his guard and came home in 34. By then, of course, it was too late. Andy North had seized control of the tournament and Ballesteros was not even in the running.

Even Trevino expressed astonishment at the Spaniard's handling of the closing rounds. "Seve has unbelievable potential," he said, "and there is not a shot in golf that he can't hit, but he hasn't quite got down to managing his game yet." But the unnatural conservatism which had gripped Ballesteros's game in several major championships rarely did so in ordinary Tour events. When Trevino encountered the Spaniard in the Irish Open, he noted with awe: "I looked into his eyes and I could see the killer instinct coming out."

The victim on that particular occasion was not Trevino but the new Masters champion. Langer scored an incredible last-round 63 at Royal Dublin to catch Ballesteros, who had had a 66, and a force a playoff. But at the second extra hole, where they both had identical putts of twelve yards, the Spaniard sank his for a birdie three and victory. The following week Ballesteros won again. On the first day of the French Open at Strange Germain, he played golf of such flawless and exquisite quality that he scored 62, nine under par. It was the lowest round of his career on the European Tour. Twice before he had scored 61—once in a pro-am in Madrid and once in a tournament in Japan—but rarely had he played a round more solid or more perfect. He hit every single fairway off the tee and was putting for birdies or eagles on every one of eighteen holes, going out in 33 and coming back in 29. By the fourth round he had a seven-stroke lead and a 69 ensured him victory by two shots over Sandy Lyle. His prize money of £13,751 amounted to less than a third of what he had been paid in appearance fees.

THERE CAN BE LITTLE DOUBT THAT THE SPANIARD WAS ALMOST SINGLE-HANDEDLY RESPONSIBLE FOR THE METEORIC RISE OF EUROPEAN GOLF.

None of these things served to comfort him when he recorded a 75 in the rain-lashed first round of the British Open at St. George's. His momentum was interrupted when there was a lengthy delay in obtaining a ruling for him on the fourth hole, and he never seemed to recover it. He scored 74, 70, 73 in the remaining rounds and finished tied for thirty-eighth on 292, ten strokes behind the British Open champion, Sandy Lyle.

Lyle's victory was important for several reasons. In the first place, it meant he was the first British golfer in sixteen years to win the British Open. In the second, it drove home the point that the balance of power in world golf had shifted away from the United States to such an extent that three of the last six winners of the Masters and three of the last seven British Open champions had been Europeans. By the end of 1985 the Europeans had done the impossible and won the Ryder Cup, and the top three names on the world rankings were Ballesteros, Langer, and Lyle.

There can be little doubt that the Spaniard was almost single-handedly responsible for the meteoric rise of European golf then and for the glorious heights it has reached now. It was Ballesteros who first went to America; Ballesteros who became the first European to triumph there since Jacklin; Ballesteros who convinced the Europeans that the Americans were not invincible; and Ballesteros who gave them the courage to believe in themselves. As Ken Brown says, "After he won Greensboro we knew that if he could win in America, we could, because we knew how we compared with him and that we could beat him on any given day."

"Seeing Sandy and Nick win the British Open and watching Bernhard win the Masters, I gave a little credit to myself," Ballesteros was to say years later. "I think I was the one who proved we had this ability to win majors. I think I helped give confidence to the European players."

So the Europeans crossed the Atlantic one by one and by 1986, Brown, Faldo, Lyle, and Langer were all playing there regularly, and all except Brown had won tournaments there. Ballesteros, for his part, had encountered the same resentment of foreign participation from American Tour players that Jacklin did in the seventies. "You're only a nice guy here if you don't win," he said at Augusta in 1980. "They smile when I lose. But they don't say anything if I am winning. Except, maybe, that I am lucky."

When Langer won the Masters, Ballesteros told him, "I am happy that it was one of us Europeans that won and not one of them"—meaning the Americans.

Watson remembers Ballesteros being very unpopular with many U.S. Tour players in those years and thinks it had "a lot to do with his focus on the course, his desire to win. I think that manifested itself in some players' eyes as being cold or distant."

Jacklin sees it more as jealousy: "By 1985 he was right in his prime as a player. His abilities were recognized around the world. I mean, even the Americans, who are reluctant to admit that anybody's ever better than an American, couldn't help but believe that here was somebody that was special. He was *the* man of his time, as Hogan was, as Palmer was, as Nicklaus was,

in a given era that they dominated. And there was no question that Ballesteros dominated."

"I've *never* understood why," Crenshaw says of the prejudice of certain
American pros. "I was always for the foreign players. I wanted them to come.
Some were thinking, 'Well, he's coming over here and he's taking up my
spot.' I like to know where I stand, what you can learn from them. I've always felt we should welcome them. But our Tour can sometimes be con-
strued as taking care of its own."

"The guys on [the U.S.] Tour call it cherry-picking," explains Jay
Townsend, an American who plays on the European Tour. "They don't want
Bernhard and Seve and Jose and Sandy and Nick to go over there and play
when they want, make a bunch of money, like they do, and go home. They
look at how these guys are coming over and taking from them, they don't
see that they're going over to Europe and taking out. I think a lot of it's jealousy. It used to be that the Americans were the undisputed best players . . .
and now, in the last ten years, the [foreign] golfers have become stronger, and
the Americans don't like it. They don't want anybody coming over on their
Tour. It's their own deal."

In 1985 Ballesteros saw less of the American players than he ought to
have done for the simple reason that he spent most of his time in Europe,
despite being a member of the U.S. Tour. He finished tied for seventh behind
Langer in the European Open and then strolled comfortably to victory in
the Sanyo Open, the week after the Ryder Cup. Throughout this period he
was having problems at home, for his father was extremely ill. In a rare week
when he was well enough to travel, Ballesteros brought him over to the
World Match Play in Britain. Vicente came too and caddied for his brother,
and Ballesteros beat Langer for the second time in the final. When he returned home, he won the Spanish Open, prompting the secretary of state
for sport, Roman Cuyas, to offer seventy-five million pesetas (£326,000) for
golf-course construction after Ballesteros had gone on television to plead
for more spending on municipal courses. The government's offer meant that
six basic nine-hole courses could be laid out.

On Friday, November 1, while Ballesteros was at the Portuguese Open,
the following announcement appeared in the *Daily Telegraph*: "Severiano
Ballesteros's membership of the U.S. PGA Tour has been revoked by the Policy Board meeting in New York. He will not be allowed to play in Tour
cosponsored tournaments in the U.S. next year because he has played only

nine Tour events this year instead of the minimum fifteen. He remains eligible for the Masters, which he has won twice, for the U.S. Open, and the PGA Championship. Ballesteros can also play in the USF&G Classic in New Orleans in March as defending champion.''

To say that Ballesteros was shocked would be an understatement. Outraged is more accurate. Afraid of saying something he might regret, he refused to discuss the matter with anyone other than Ceballos, Schofield, and Beman. His only comment then was: "If the decision stands, it will be a terrible mistake. It's antisocial." Later he insisted, "The first thing I knew about a possible ban was when Mr. Beman wrote to me [in] August. I just thought I'd lose my membership, but still be able to play under the old sponsor's invitation rules."

"Seve has set himself on a course of confrontation with us," Beman retorted. "Now we have gone back to the old rules after his failure to comply with the new ones."

The irony of the situation was this: Not two years previously, Beman, in his desperation to bring the charismatic genius of Ballesteros to the American public, had created "special privileges" for the European players, allowing them to treat the whole of Europe as their home circuit. Now, he was not only punishing Ballesteros, he was also rescinding the privileges of every other European player in the top 125 on the U.S. money list. Non-U.S. Tour members would in the future be allowed to play no more than six tournaments a year.

Sports Illustrated dealt harshly with Beman, saying: "The PGA Tour has told the best golfer in the world to get lost and we agree with Ballesteros who says, 'It was a thoughtless decision that can only harm international golf.' "

Ceballos, who was almost as shaken as Ballesteros, pointed out that Ballesteros had fulfilled his fifteen-tournament commitment in 1984 but had felt that there was too much pressure on him and that it had led to a disappointing season. He also said that Ballesteros had already received twenty-six invitations to play in America in 1986. "What are those sponsors going to think?" he asked.

"When they started, you know, going at it," Collet recalls, "it was more like Seve criticizing Deane personally about the rules they had for the way the Tour worked, that they selfishly favored the Americans, that they were a little archaic and should be renewed. In fact, we wrote him a letter which suggested three alternatives: that they either reduced the number of tournaments one had to play in to retain one's membership, increased the number of exemptions that a player could have without being a member, or counted a couple of tournaments as those you could play on merit. And they said: "None of those are possible."

But while the question of whether or not Ballesteros deserved to be banned from the U.S. Tour was being hotly debated by the golfing press, a far crueler tragedy was being played out behind the scenes. Baldomero Ballesteros, Severiano's father and his best friend, was dying. His four sons rallied around him, but in March 1986 he passed away. Severiano, who had been closest to him, was devastated. It was the most traumatic event of his young life and the scars it left remain unhealed to this day.

"It was very hard on him," Fernandez says sympathetically, "because just when his father started to live the life Seve wanted him to live, he was gone."

It is Collet's belief that that, more than anything else, was the reason why Ballesteros failed to play in the required number of events.

"It's kind of an emotional subject," Collet says. "Seve's father was dying of terminal cancer. He had had one lung removed. Seve interrupted his schedule to be with him and to help make arrangements at the hospital, and he didn't convalesce well; he developed pneumonia in the remaining lung and expired. And it really shook him. He was very close to his father. And the fact that they were getting him checked up during the year—they went to Houston, I think, for the operation—made it very difficult for Seve to fulfill his commitments. . . . He's very proud and it's not easy for him to pick up the phone to anybody whether it's to his wife or to me . . . He just doesn't. A phone is some kind of an aggravation that's there. He only calls when he absolutely has to or when he's bored and there's nothing else. If he wants something, he calls; if he doesn't, he hopes you don't call him. And so what he should have done was call Deane Beman, and say: "Listen, Deane, I don't know if you know this, but my father's terminally ill. I know I've made some commitments to the Tour, but he's the most important thing in my life and I really need to be with him. It's so upsetting for me, my mind isn't on the game, and I just can't play all those weeks. I hope you understand."

"He probably didn't fully appreciate that it would be an issue, and then by saying nothing he created an issue," Collet explains. "It's very difficult for him to talk about his father. But, having sat back as a witness, I think that's what happened. I think had he called [Deane], that it would have been okay, because Norman had a similar problem one year . . . and they gave him a rain check. But that was because they were businesslike enough to address the problem proactively, whereas that's not Seve's nature. He's more reticent about doing things that a lot of people would do and he reaps the harvest. Because it's an emotional issue, he would sound to himself like he was making excuses if he talked about his father. So he just avoided the whole discussion and it looks like he was irresponsible."

The fifteenth hole at Augusta National has a reputation for changing lives and influencing destinies. It was to this par-five that Gene Sarazen came in the last round of the 1935 Masters, trailing Craig Wood by three strokes, and hit one of the greatest shots ever played—an albatross two—going on to win the green jacket and the playoff, and put the championship, then only in its second year, on the front pages. Fifty-one years later Sarazen, still wearing plus-fours and still sitting on his favorite balcony overlooking the golf course, was retelling the story for the umpteenth time. "My caddie tried to talk me into hitting a three-wood. But I took out my turf-rider [four-wood] instead. The moment I hit it, I felt something in my bones. Walter Hagen was playing with me and Jones was on the green. Twenty-one people were behind the green. The sun was going down. I wasn't sure it had gone in the hole until I saw all twenty-one people jumping up and down."

At virtually the same stage in 1986 Ballesteros was striding unknowingly along the fairway of a hole that would have a more-shattering effect on his career than any other single event. He seemed tense and, as one newspaperman put it, "too anxious to prove the ridiculousness of his situation, even if it was of his own doing." Already the U.S. Tour ban had cost him dearly. He had lost his job as touring professional for Doral Country Club and, apart from the USF&G Classic where he had missed the cut, and the Florida Cup Classic on the TPA minitour where he had finished twenty-second, had been denied competitive practice for the Masters. As a result, he was disinclined to talk to either journalists or officials. "Whatever happens now, this will be a bad year for me," he had predicted after the death of his father.

When he did speak it was to inform the media in no uncertain terms that when the tournament was over he would be the champion.

I will win this," he declared. "It will be mine by the time I get to the sixteenth on the last day."

On Sunday, April 13, 1986, Ballesteros came to the fifteenth hole of Augusta National in the final round of the Masters, leading by two strokes. All around him tidal waves of applause swelled and crashed, as the great gallery swung between the brilliant young Spaniard and the extraordinary spectacle of Nicklaus, age forty-six, rising like a phoenix from the ashes of an ailing career. The day was a fathomless, indigo blue. Sunlight and shadow flickered across Ballesteros's damp shirt and warmed his skin as he set over the ball on the five-hundred-yard par-five and prepared to drive. He knew as soon as he had struck it that it was a good shot. It boomed off the clubface into the clear sky and finished far down the fairway. Vicente, who was caddying for him, clapped him excitedly on the back. He scented victory. Two holes previously, when Ballesteros had hit a huge drive around the corner at the thirteenth hole, followed it with an approach shot to six feet, and holed the putt for his second eagle of the day, the brothers had shaken hands, as if in premature congratulation.

"I thought when I eagled the thirteenth I was the champion," Ballesteros said afterward.

Elsewhere on the course, that extreme pressure which only comes into play on the closing holes of a major was beginning to take its toll. Norman, the overnight leader, whom Ballesteros had caught by the turn, succumbed to it with a double bogey at the tenth and missed his putt to tie at the eighteenth. The Golden Bear's charge had been launched at the ninth. Playing with the fearless determination of a man who has nothing left to lose and everything in the world to gain, he made three successive birdies, and was only halted when he failed to get up and down on the twelfth. By the time he reached the sixteenth green, he was at seven under par and two strokes adrift of Ballesteros, having birdied the thirteenth and eagled the fifteenth. A birdie putt of one yard at the sixteenth would get him to eight under par.

Ballesteros and Watson were on the hole behind him, quietly waiting for the tumult to die down. The latter was on the green, facing a twenty-foot putt for eagle which would take him to seven under par. Reluctant to play until there was silence, he stood there motionless as the minutes ticked by. When he finally did putt, he missed. Ballesteros, meanwhile, was standing patiently on the fairway visualizing his approach shot and birdie putt. He had 210 yards to the flag. With a four-iron in his hand, Ballesteros lined up his shot. A sudden hush, unnatural after the clamor which had preceded it, had settled over the cool green fairway. A breeze lifted his hair.

One last glance at the pin . . . an intake of breath . . . a ragged, short, uneven, uncommitted golf swing . . . a gasp . . . a splash . . . a spreading ring of terrible ripples . . . calamity!

Nicklaus heard the roar as he walked to the penultimate tee. "It wasn't the sound of a cheer but it was the sound of a cheer," he recalled later. Ballesteros, cold with shock, holed out for a six; then three-putted the seventeenth. It was over.

"For a while we all felt that Seve, under the severest pressure, would always pull off the magical shot," John Jacobs says. "I think something of that left him when he dumped it in the water at Augusta. But I think he just stood waiting and waiting behind Nicklaus eagling and birdieing and holing putts, and everybody screaming and yelling. And obviously he took too much club. He was still leading by one or two at that stage, and he packed up on it—you could see he did. And I've talked to him since. He overclubbed because "the only way I could lose the Masters was if I put it in the water short." But he knew it was too much club and he stopped on it. And then, of course, Nicklaus birdied the seventeenth. And Seve had to stand there and watch this."

"You know, everybody says, 'Well, Seve hit that shot in the water,' " Crenshaw says vehemently. "Anybody, anybody can miss a shot like that. But it was so painful for him. And everybody said he was completely downcast for two years. Maybe he was. Who knows?"

"That shot, to me, looked like a fella who had not played a lot of golf that year, had not prepared," Nicklaus recalls. "And whether that was his fault or somebody else's fault, I don't know. But when he hit his second shot, he quit on the ball. It was not a good swing for him. It was a very defensive hope-the-ball-goes-on-the-green shot. It was not, 'I'm going to hit the ball and knock it on the green.' It was the kind of swing that I find myself making quite often early in the year, when I haven't been playing much golf. And I just sort of related to that. And that was obviously the shot that cost him the tournament, and it probably cost him a couple of years mentally."

"I don't want to take anything away from Jack," says Ballesteros, who eventually finished fourth after Nicklaus came home in 30 to win his sixth Masters. "He played fantastic golf. But I think for me not to win was almost a miracle under all the circumstances. Eight out of ten times I would have won. It was *destino*. It took a long time before I was confident with my four-iron again. You know, this is mental game. It really works on your mind. I lost my confidence, no question."

How deep were the wounds, or how lasting the scars, did not become obvious at once. The full extent of the damage to Ballesteros's psyche was only revealed gradually, over four or five years, until now it seems that of all the things that have shaped his character and governed his fate, none have had the impact on him that the 1986 Masters and the death of his father did—for the two are inextricably linked. But that April Ballesteros appeared to recover before the last putt was holed at Augusta. The very next week he was leading the Suze Open at Cannes-Mougins, jogging four miles daily with Vicente in preparation for the U.S. Open in June, and telling the press: "I was the only one in contention from start to finish at Augusta but no one even mentioned me on Monday morning. That hurt me. But I accept the challenge. I like it when the going is tough and I'll be going all out to win the Open."

The changes in him were subtle ones. They were noticeable in the 73 he scored in the last round to lose the Suze Open, in the slip he made to surrender the Madrid Open to Howard Clark after leading by two strokes going into the final nine, and in the bogeys he made in the fourth round of the Italian Open to finish tied for fourth.

He took two weeks off then and when he came back there was a harder, more resolute glint in his eye. A putting tip on the eve of the Dunhill Masters from his friend Jaime Gonzalez made an overnight improvement in his touch on the greens. He took only twenty-eight putts in the first round and was a stroke off the lead. For the first time since leaving Augusta, he began to smile. In the closing rounds he played glorious attacking golf that was a joy to witness and overcame his playing partner Robert Lee by two strokes with a score of 275, thirteen under par. Afterward, Nick de Paul described him as a new man. "You've no idea how much he wanted that Dunhill Masters victory," he said. "I have seldom seen Seve so nervous over the closing holes as he was then. All those narrow defeats this season were preying on his mind. He was desperate to win again."

Once Ballesteros had destroyed the mental barrier in front of him, he couldn't stop winning. To appreciate the sheer magnitude of his talent and the extent of his domination of European golf in the eighties, one need look no further than his playing record. In the decade between 1976 and 1986, he won more than fifty tournaments, was runner-up twenty times, third eighteen times, in the top ten thirty-nine other times, and, incredibly, missed only four cuts in Europe. In 1986 he followed his Dunhill Masters victory with successive wins in the Irish Open, the Monte Carlo Open, and the French Open, finished tied for sixth in the British Open before winning the Dutch Open (by a landslide margin of eight strokes), finishing tied first in the Lancome Trophy—following an unprecedented situation in which he and Langer called a referee after four holes of a playoff, having had to stop because night was falling, and asked if they could call it a draw and split the first and second prize of £33,313 and £21,505—tied for tenth in the German Open, and tied for fourth in the European Open. By mid-July he had already been paid an estimated £230,000 in appearance money (approximately £25,000 per event). When he won in Holland he achieved one of his greatest ambitions, to become the first player on the European Tour to amass more than a million pounds in tournament earnings. By the end of the season he was the No. 1 player on the Order of Merit for the fourth time, with £259,275, and his stroke average was 68.95. His playing statistics at the time of the Open were as follows: driving distance—277 yards; driving

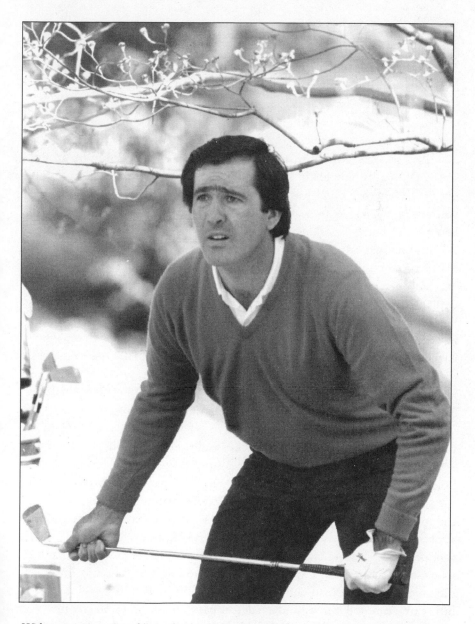

With great interest, Seve follows the shot he has just played out of the trees at Augusta's second hole during first-round play at the 1987 Masters. (AP/Wide World Photos)

accuracy—56 percent; greens in regulation—72 percent; sand saves—75 percent; putting average—29.25.

Two things put these statistics into perspective: (1) On the Tuesday after the British Open he sponsored a junior caddies' competition at Pedreña, the first event he ever won; and (2) During the same week he attended a ceremony to rename one of Pedreña's main thoroughfares *Calle Severiano Ballesteros*.

And so the season drew to a close and its hero returned to Spain in a blaze of glory. Its only blight had been the Masters. How much it was preying on Ballesteros's mind was shown at the World Match Play when, asked whether he would like to beat Nicklaus after what had happened at Augusta, he replied: "There is nothing to avenge. Jack Nicklaus is a great champion. I will take revenge from the golf course, especially from the fifteenth."

And so it was that, in the final round of the Masters in 1987, Ballesteros exacted retribution from the fifteenth hole and clawed his way back into contention with a birdie. Ahead of him, twenty-eight-year-old, Augusta-born Larry Mize, little known to anyone outside of his hometown, had hit his approach shot to four feet at the eighteenth and made three for an aggregate of 285. Desperate to catch him, Ballesteros struck boldly from the tee at the seventeenth. He was rewarded with a five-foot putt, which he holed for birdie. Norman followed him in from thirty-five feet. There were shades of 1986 at the eighteenth when the Spaniard bunkered his approach shot, but with marvelous composure he managed to get up and down and he, Norman, and Mize were tied for the Masters lead after regulation.

It was early evening when the three men teed off on the tenth, the first hole of a sudden-death playoff, and the tall pines cast long shadows across the jade fairway. Spectators were packed solidly from tee to green. Mize hit the longest drive, but each of them hit the putting surface in regulation strokes, and Ballesteros's ball finished twenty feet away. "I felt I hit my second shot perfectly," he said afterward. "Had the ball bounced one more yard, it would have run round to the hole instead of rolling straight on to finish off the green. With Norman and Mize both having birdie chances, I gave it a little extra, running it three and a half feet past. The sun was directly into my eyes on the return . . . I don't think I did anything wrong but I must have aimed left."

And missed.

Ballesteros reacts to a missed putt at Augusta's third hole in the final round of the 1987 Masters, although that same look pretty much expressed how he felt about five hours later after being eliminated in a playoff, with Larry Mize ultimately winning the tournament with his amazing chip-in at the second playoff hole. (AP/Wide World Photos)

"That was a harrowing moment for anyone that feels for a player," says Schofield, who went back to the clubhouse with the distraught Spaniard, "and I felt very bad for him at that particular moment. He was in tears. I said to him, 'Hey, come on, Gary Player would take the view that he hasn't lost the Masters. No one's beaten you over seventy-two holes.' And he went the next week and won in Cannes—such is the strength of the man—and by the time he got there that's the phrase he was using to the journalists. I think you have to give someone something to cling to. No one had beaten him over seventy-two holes. He lost in extra time. Small consolation, you might say, but at least it was something."

But during that long, tortuous walk along the tenth hole, away from the gay crowds and the duel for the Masters, Ballesteros was inconsolable. Head bowed and shoulders slumped, he wept for everything he had ever loved and lost—especially for his father, whom he had promised before he died that he would win the Masters at Augusta.

For that one moment in time, there was no sadder, more lonely man in all the world than Severiano Ballesteros.

13

A MEASURE OF GREATNESS

"I have found my heart again."

Rudyard Kipling, *Kim*

Ballesteros, in a mood of wistful contemplation, once remarked to Doust: "Bad luck sticks in my mind more than good luck. Sometimes I remember bad things that have happened to me."

Nothing was imprinted on his mind with such nightmarish detail as the Masters he felt he had let slip. He could remember as if it were yesterday flinging himself to the ground in an agony of despair on the sixteenth hole in 1985, when the chip which might have won him the tournament failed to go in the hole; he could not forget the winking pond on the fifteenth in 1986, nor the jarring feeling in his hands as the ball left the clubhead, nor the deathly hush, nor the snaking ripples, nor the blood turning to ice in his veins; and he still shuddered at the memory of that interminable walk back from the first playoff hole while Mize and Norman battled for the prize that should have been his.

Four years had gone by since Ballesteros had last won a major. During that time he had lost or been beaten in three Masters, two U.S. Opens, and two U.S. PGA Championships, and every one of them haunted him and gnawed at his psyche.

"It was wrong to settle major championships by sudden-death," he had said vehemently after the 1987 Masters. "I didn't want to say anything at the Masters because it might have seemed like sour grapes, but they must go back to the eighteen-hole playoffs. Even five holes, as in the British Open, is fairer. I don't want to take anything away from Larry Mize who chipped in

201

to win at the second hole, but I think it is more likely that the real champion will win in an eighteen-hole playoff. It's very disappointing to miss out for three years in a row. I feel I could have had four or five green jackets instead of two. But I was much more disappointed [in 1986] after being two ahead with four to play and going in the lake. I feel as much the Masters champion as Larry Mize because I tied after seventy-two holes."

No one was convinced—least of all Ballesteros. Later he admitted: "I lost faith in my putting when I missed that short one in the playoff. I started missing a lot of short putts after that; especially the crucial ones."

Gradually, as the seasons passed and the majors, golf's only real measure of greatness and the criterion by which Ballesteros measures himself, continued to elude him, that aura of invincibility which had surrounded him became eroded. He lost the Palmeresque audacity he had always had, the conviction that if it could be imagined it could be birdied or eagled, and along with it went some of the intrepidity which had been a feature of his game. He lost his nerve on the greens and his ability to win through willpower alone, regardless of form or good fortune. He lost, in short, like so many great players before him, that youthful belief in his own immortality.

Human nature being what it is, it wasn't long before people began to voice the unthinkable: Could it be that Ballesteros's genius, so dependent on inspiration, had left him? Could the pressure-cooker atmosphere of the last nine holes of the majors be causing him to collapse? "Nobody," insists Robert Green, "actually called it choking, but some people were wondering . . ."

Or could it be possible that the most gifted player of the modern era was washed up?

"Perish the thought that we have seen the best of Ballesteros," said Michael Williams, "but as time [goes by] . . . one does begin to speculate."

Michael McDonnell agreed: "The question used to be when would Ballesteros win another big title. But as he has not done it since 1984, some critics now want to know whether he will ever win again."

The reasons offered for Ballesteros's decline were many and various. Some suggested it was because the course of true love had not run smoothly for him and Carmen Botin; they had been talking of marriage for four years and nothing had happened. Others said that it might be due to his preoccupation with money, or even his ailing back, while there were those who were certain it was because he had tempered his golf swing to such an extent that he had taken the fire out of his game. "What's happened to Seve is rather like what happened to Arnold Palmer," Jacobs told Doust. "They were both wild hitters and fantastic putters, but once they learned to play, which in Seve's case came [around 1985 or 1986], their putting left them." His brothers, of course, were another problem. He had never won a major with any of them caddying for him. Fingers were pointed at the handshake between him and Vincente on the thirteenth hole of the 1986 Masters shortly before disaster struck, and at the animated conversations that the normally taciturn Ballesteros had with his siblings on the golf course. Then there was the matter of the row he had had with Vicente when he was sharing the lead in the final round of the 1987 U.S. PGA Championship. Moments later, at the 533-yard par-five third, a hole he had birdied for three consecutive rounds, he drove into the right rough, chipped out sideways, returned to the rough with his approach shot, went into a bunker, then into the water, and finally sank a ten-foot putt for a triple-bogey eight. He finished with a 78, an aggregate of 292, and a share of tenth place. "I thought I had a chance," Ballesteros, who had finished third in the U.S. Open at Olympic earlier in the season, said miserably. "But nothing happened. That's really what has been happening all year. It's my *destino* this year."

Whatever the cause of Ballesteros's inner conflict on the golf course, there was no escaping the fact that it had a radical effect on him outwardly. His face, always an accurate barometer of his moods, now mirrored his emotions exactly and the feelings it reflected were not happy ones. Gone was the impudent grin and the ready wit; he became distant, surly, and morose. "I can remember doing an interview with him," Jacobs says, "and saying, 'Seve, smile like you used to smile,' because he was always scowling and looking miserable."

"Every week everyone wants me to do 61," Ballesteros protested at the Lancome Trophy in 1987. "There is too much pressure on and off the golf course. Everyone wants just one minute from me and it turns out to be two weeks. If I am not careful I can get burned out and I do not want that. I want to keep playing for years." But at the U.S. PGA Championship he confessed: "People tell me I have to be more relaxed, that I put too much pressure on myself. I'm trying to convince myself that I'm a happy man."

No other player in golf has the power to move an audience, whether it be a gallery at a tournament or the public at large, the way Ballesteros does. No one has his ability to make them suffer with him, pull for him, laugh with him, or even weep for him, because no one fights as bravely or as well.

The matador: Ballesteros, his "cape" whipped back by wind and rain, turns warily to face the competition. (© Chris Smith)

On March 13, 1988, almost eleven months after his victory in the Suze Open at Cannes Mougins, his last win anywhere in the world, he put the smile back on his face when he took the Mallorcan Open by six strokes over Jose Maria Olazábal. A single swallow does not make a summer, but at least it is a start—one step taken along the slippery slope to recovery.

But by April, Ballesteros had stumbled once again. He had failed to qualify at the TPC, and had been left to rue the chances he had missed when he scored 73, 72, 70, 73 at Augusta to finish seven strokes behind the winner, Sandy Lyle. Worst of all, he had shot 76, 78 in the Cannes Open, to miss his first cut since the Silk Cut Masters in 1983 where he had been disqualified for signing a wrongly marked card. "Everything was bad," he said sadly. "I gave everything last week in the Masters and I gave everything I had left here as well. Nothing went right."

Precisely one month later, with no prior warning whatsoever, Ballesteros exploded gloriously into the limelight, when he beat Norman, Ken Green, and David Frost with a birdie at the first extra hole of a four-way play-off for the Buick Classic. It was his first victory in America in three years.

Wednesday, July 13, 1988, Open Championship, Royal Lytham.
Nothing in professional sport is as cruel, as tormenting, as hard a taskmaster as the ghost of past achievements. Ballesteros, who on Monday had played his first round of golf at Lytham since winning the British Open in 1979, knew it well and intended to use it to his advantage. Before coming to the tournament he had spent long hours looking at videos of his triumph in the hope that the magic would revisit him. "I think watching all those putts drop can encourage me to do well," he said earnestly. "I made a lot of putts on the last day. I think my putting is still as good. The only difference is that the ball doesn't go in the hole and I don't know why."

On that first day, in the biting crosswinds of Lytham, he had played with Lyle for the price of a sandwich. "I lost," Ballesteros admitted with a grin, "but it didn't matter because Sandy had to buy his own lunch. I didn't pay." The Spaniard and the huge, gentle Scot had been firm friends since

1985 when Lyle had won the British Open. Much to Lyle's surprise, Ballesteros had sent him a congratulatory telegram. "It was a nice gesture. I can't remember it word for word, but it was like, 'Congratulations, you deserve it.' The gist of the rest of it was: 'A word of advice. You can't please everybody. Just do your own thing.' I've always tried to take that bit of advice. You've just got to do what suits you and get on with it. . . . It's too easy to say, 'Yes, I'll do that for you,' and before you know it you've spent an hour at the course and you haven't hit a ball yet.

"I would say," Lyle observes, describing Ballesteros, "he's slightly on the shy side, although he's all right with his own little clique of Spanish friends. . . . I don't treat him any differently to how I treat my sisters or my father. I just talk to him and don't give him any bullshit, and if he's out of order, I tell him. And if he thinks I'm out of order on certain things, he'll tell me. If you try to be somebody you're not to him, then he'll see through you quite quickly. He's been to my house a few times. He's just part of the family, in a way. He watches videos, plays with the kids. He's down to earth, really. I think if you're a friend of Seve's, you're a friend forever. It's just a matter of breaking that barrier."

At Lytham, Lyle watched Ballesteros with slight incredulity as he retraced his steps over the last five holes of his victory. At the sixteenth, scene of the infamous car-park birdie, the Spaniard took a three-iron off the tee, a sand wedge off the fairway, and three-putted for bogey—the golfing gods having a fine sense of irony. "The way I won was a miracle," he said. "I had no game plan then. I just teed up and hit it. I haven't lost that old aggression, but now I try to tackle the courses the way they are meant to be played. Sometimes experience is an advantage, but it can also be a disadvantage. Until I won the Open, I just used to enjoy the game and do the best I could. Winning changed my life, but I feel fortunate to be where I am."

On practice days Ballesteros roamed the gray links in inclement weather and reminisced nostalgically about 1979. Trotting beside the Spaniard as he strode the fairways was his new caddie, Ian Wright, laboriously scribbling in his yardage book. At the Madrid Open in April, a week after he had missed the cut in Cannes, Ballesteros had approached the forty-year-old Yorkshireman and, on Chino Fernandez's recommendation, asked whether he would caddie for him. Wright, of course, was overwhelmed. Previously he had only worked for journeyman players like David Jones, Brian Marchbank, and Carl Mason, and his eyes lit up as he imagined basking in the reflected glory of a golfer as great as Ballesteros. He lost no time in agreeing. Terms were fixed and it was duly arranged that he should start at the European PGA Championship at Wentworth in May. When the big day arrived, Wright went down to the golf club, heaved the Spaniard's bag upon his shoulder, and waited at the tee. Ballesteros arrived for his practice round, drove off, and marched rapidly down the first fairway. Two hours and ten minutes later, he holed his last putt on the eighteenth. "I think," says Wright, "he was testing me."

One can't help but wonder why it is that Ballesteros decided to find a regular caddie barely a month before a major. Previously, he had felt so strongly about his brothers working for him that even when he was fined fifty pounds for employing a fellow professional (Vicente) to carry his bag, the old rule regarding caddies having been amended, he refused to comply. "It is a stupid rule," he announced. "I will definitely carry on using Vicente. . . . Maybe the PGA needs the money. It's no problem for me. Fines are tax deductible." The matter was something of an embarrassment because Ballesteros was on the committee, but an escape clause was found and from then on it was only fellow members of the European Tour who were not permitted to caddie. But now it seemed that his brothers were too busy with their families to waste their time toiling around golf courses. "Vicente has a wife and daughter and his job as a golf professional at La Manga," Ballesteros said firmly. "He needs to spend more time there."

Whether it was a chemistry, coincidence, or simply that a change is as good as a holiday, Wright's presence had an immediate and positive effect on Ballesteros. At the time of their meeting, the Spaniard was fourth in the world rankings behind Norman, Lyle, and Langer after a year with only one victory and one lost playoff. He had, however, had three seconds, six thirds, and five other top-ten finishes the previous season and had won more money per tournament in his restricted appearances than anyone else on the U.S. Tour. At Wentworth, with a different caddie by his side, he seemed overcome with optimism for the future. Standing on the first tee in the opening round, he smiled spontaneously and said to Wright: "This is the beginning of a new era."

And so it proved. At the PGA Championship, a week when he was more amiable than he had been in months, Ballesteros finished tied for runner-up with Mark James behind Ian Woosnam, in the French Open he was tied for fourteenth, and in Monte Carlo he was third. A fortnight later

207

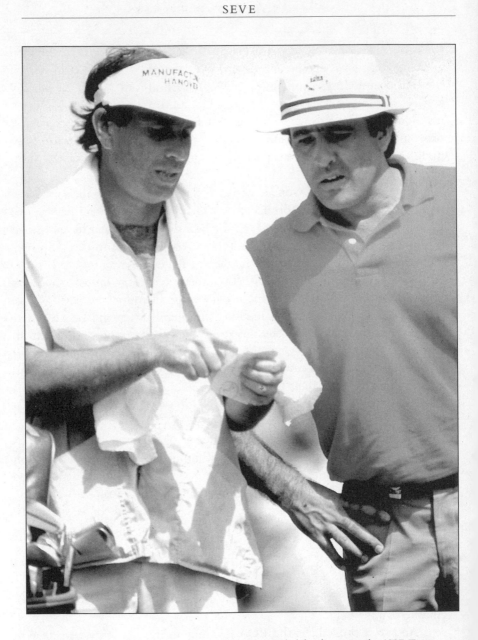

Seve and his caddie-brother, Vicente, discuss yardages and club selection at the 1987 European PGA Championship. (© Phil Sheldon)

when he left Pedreña, he was bound, with hope in his heart and a spring in his step, for the 117th Open Championship at Royal Lytham—the place where it all began.

Thursday, July 14, 1988. The greatest players who have ever lived have long been defined by their ability to raise their games to the big occasion. Thus, Jacklin, whose form was little better than indifferent when he came to Lytham in 1969, was able to reach inside himself and find courage enough to win the trophy; and Nicklaus, roused to fury by a newspaper article which declared him "done, washed up, and finished," was able to play the hardest back nine in golf in six under par and become the oldest winner of the Masters. Ballesteros, for his part, had been down on his luck and dispirited with his game before both of his British Open wins, but by concentrating his entire being on his goal each time, had achieved it, and his triumphs were triumphs of the spirit.

Now he sought to do the same thing again.

A malevolent sky hung low over the red brick houses as Ballesteros made his way to the tee for the first round of the British Open. His expression was absorbed but peculiarly eager. Earlier in the week he had described to Wright in minute detail his strategy for the tournament and now he intended to carry it out to the letter. A smooth swing, a careful putt, and he was away with a birdie two. He marched to the next tee, head held high. A second birdie followed, then another. A tense excitement began to take hold of him and it transmitted itself to the crowd. Their numbers swelled. Clinging to their candy-striped umbrellas, they struggled after their hero, blasted by the ferocious gale. Ballesteros was just hitting his stride. He swung boldly from the tee, and almost every drive found its target. His iron play was peerless, his short game magical, and his putting inspired. For a few moments, after gaining strokes at the sixth and seventh holes, he even found himself thinking in terms of a 29. But he missed from four feet for a three at the eighth and turned in 30.

By now Ballesteros was in full flight. Adrenaline surged through his veins. At the fourteenth hole he came unstuck. A slight hook off the tee was followed by a wicked pull over the heads of the gallery and deep into a thicket. It had unplayable written all over it before it left the clubface. "Instead of playing safe I got greedy," Ballesteros admitted afterward. "I tried to reach the green with a two-iron, but it was a bad shot." He dropped fifty yards away from the hole under penalty, played his "best shot of the day," a blind seven-iron to fifteen feet, and holed the putt for a bogey five. He marched on undaunted, leaning into the wild wind. His eventual score of 67, despite another unplayable lie, lifted him head and shoulders above the rest of the field. Only two other players had managed to break 70—Brad Faxon and Wayne Grady, both of whom were on 69.

"This is my best start in a major since the 1980 Masters," a delighted Ballesteros said. "Last year at Muirfield I had to wait twenty-eight holes before I got my first birdie. This time it took just one."

Friday, July 15, 1988. The week before Ballesteros came to Lytham he had spent a good deal of time out on his boat fishing. He caught fifty-two sea bass on one day, one on each of the next two days, and then fourteen on the last. "When I'm out there on the water [with his friends and his girl-friend] I can switch off, forget everything," he said. The therapeutic benefits of these activities were undeniable. Ballesteros was relaxed and approachable and looked to be enjoying himself again as he went about his business on and off the golf course.

On the second day the sun came out and touched the links with its fierce yellow glare. A keen wind blew, testing the ingenuity of the competitors, and on the third hole Ballesteros found a bunker, dropped a shot, and surrendered the lead. "I got a ticking off because the one thing we'd planned especially was to keep the ball out of the sand," recalls Wright, who rarely turned a hair during these admonitions, which increased in volume and intensity as the months went on. But the Spaniard recovered almost immediately and, with birdies at the sixth and seventh holes, resumed control of the tournament. The fourteenth broke through his defenses once again. He pulled his tee shot, hooked his second, and failed to reach the green. His eventual score of 71 left him a stroke behind Nick Price at 138, four under par. Stadler and Faldo were their closest challengers at 140, while Andy Bean was a stroke further back.

"The course is very difficult," Ballesteros explained. "Right now, I would settle for a couple of 71s over the last two rounds. I think four under par will be good enough to win."

Saturday, July 16, 1988. On Saturday, rain, opaque and unceasing, slanted across the links and pounded at the marquees with the thunderous roar of a waterfall. The ninth, tenth, and eleventh greens quickly became flooded, and at 12:20 P.M., play was abandoned. When fairways became lakes, the R&A decided, for the first time in British Open history, to extend the championship until Monday.

Sunday, July 17, 1988. On Sunday the atmosphere was strangely subdued. Ballesteros went out with Stadler and Price, swinging easily and concentrating hard. He and the Zimbabwean had known each other for years. When Ballesteros was playing regularly in America, they often met socially and went out for meals.

"Seve, I s'pose, doesn't really talk a whole lot on the course," Price says. "I play with a lot of guys who are a little more—not jovial—a little more talkative. But that didn't worry me because I just knuckled down and tried to do my own thing. But he was very, very courteous . . . Seve and I have always had a great friendship. But Seve is a difficult person to get close to. He doesn't open himself up to too many people. I don't think he trusts a lot of people. Everyone wants to be a friend of his, and I think some people really try to get close to Seve. Not me. I like him to be a friend, that's all. But, generally speaking, Seve's a very down-to-earth person."

HE WAS LEFT WITH NO SHOT. INVENTING ONE, HE REVERSED A SAND WEDGE AND TRIED TO STRIKE THE BALL WITH THE BACK OF THE CLUBFACE. IT MOVED SIX INCHES.

In the third round all three men seemed immersed in their own games, although the Walrus was plainly wishing he could be anywhere else in the kingdom. Ballesteros sailed along serenely until the 490-yard par-five sixth, at which point he had a run-in with a small tree. "I'm sure my driver hit something and kicked left into the bushes," Ballesteros said. "But you know me, I'm usually all over the place so maybe it was a normal position." He was left with no shot. Inventing one, he reversed a sand wedge and tried to strike the ball with the back of the clubface. It moved six inches. He persevered. This time it flew sixty yards. "One for practice, one to come out," joked Ballesteros, who then hit an eight-iron 195 yards to thirty feet and two-putted. He had only two birdies on that long gray day but stayed calm and good-humored until the end. At the close of play Price was leading by two strokes, at 206, over Ballesteros and Faldo.

In the interview room, the Spaniard was quietly confident. "It will be tough in the final round and the winner will be the man who can take the pressure. I have coped with it before, I don't see why I can't do it again. But you never know. . . ."

Monday, July 18, 1988. On the night of Ballesteros's return to Lytham, when images of his last victory came rushing sweet and vivid in his mind, he went up to his bedroom, sat down on the bed, and started to think. "I was back at Lytham. I was a winner here. I am a better player now than I was then—better swing and more experienced," he recalls. "I convinced myself I could win."

When he stepped onto the first tee in the final round of the British Open, that conviction was still with him, and his navy blue sweater and white shirt were the same he had worn to victory in 1979 and 1984. He nodded pleasantly to Price and Faldo, and they drove and set off down the fairway. The first objective of every man in the field was to win as many strokes back from par as they could before the turn, for it is only by laying the foundations of a good score on the front nine that a player has a prayer of surviving Lytham's inward half.

The Spaniard, tense and excited, pounced first, birdieing the sixth, and he and Faldo moved a stroke nearer Price on the leaderboard. A ripple of pleasure went through the crowd. They crossed to the next tee.

Then came a crucial development. On the seventh hole Ballesteros hit a beautiful second shot that pitched onto the front edge of the green, narrowly missed going into the hole, and ran out to fifteen feet. Price used the contours of the putting surface to bring his own in to six feet, but Faldo, whose approach was every bit as excellent as those of his playing partners, found his path to the flag blocked by a large mound and proceeded to three-putt. "I hit two great shots," he remembers. "I just couldn't putt the bloody thing because of that hump. But the way Seve was playing, he was like a bull in a china shop. He was unbelievable. He was very relaxed. I think that's one of the secrets in majors. You've got to be able to relax and, obviously, have all the strong stuff going on inside your stomach." Ballesteros, with infinite poise, stepped up to the ball and holed his putt for an eagle, sending deafening cheers reverberating around the course. Price then followed him in. From that moment they were out on their own, distant figures on the big yellow leaderboards. The race had begun in earnest.

"It became almost a match-play situation then," Price says, "although I tried to just stick to the game plan that had got me there and I'm sure he did too. But he has a wonderful ability, like all great players, to elevate his game one notch."

Ballesteros, racing to catch Price, lashed away from the tees with a fluid and powerful swing. One after the other, his drives found the fairway and his iron shots flew boldly for the heart of each green. Birdies were made at the eighth, tenth, and at the eleventh, where for the first time, the Spaniard took the lead. The atmosphere surrounding the leading match was electric. There were shades of Lytham in 1979—in the fresh wind, in the grin Ballesteros flashed after making a particularly audacious recovery, in the aggression of his driving, and in the wizardry of his short game. But the Ballesteros who won then had been little more than a boy, with a raw and elemental vitality about him. By 1988 that fierce, almost primitive quality of his genius had been tempered and polished, and what was left was a mature and self-assured man and a golfer at the peak of his game.

Later, Price was to say that he thought that Ballesteros "still had a lot of the [old] memories of Lytham fresh in his mind. I think the British Open in 1979 was so important to him that he felt he was unbeatable on that course. And I think he still feels to this day that he's unbeatable on that golf course. And he might be. Who knows?"

"I was surprised how good my nerves were," the Spaniard commented afterward. "I didn't expect to be so relaxed and calm, the most under control I have ever been in that sort of situation in a major."

"I don't know [whether you actually] 'know' you are going to win," Faldo says, trying to describe the sensation of being in contention for a major. "It's there for you to grab, that's almost the feeling. Knowing that you're doing everything right. It's just knowing you can cope with situations, I think that's the nice thing. You know, things might be going wrong at different times but you think, it's okay, everything's all right, I'm coping."

That, precisely, was Ballesteros's reaction to a dropped shot at the twelfth, which brought him level with Price once again at ten under par. At the following hole, when the Zimbabwean almost holed his second shot, Ballesteros sank an eighteen-foot putt for a matching three. In this manner they continued, thrust and counter-thrust, lunge and parry.

The sixteenth hole was the turning point. Both men took one-irons off the tee, Price hitting his 232 yards, Ballesteros 227 to the right edge of the fairway. The Spaniard deliberated over his 135-yard approach. "It's a nine-iron," Wright said. "Hit it nice and easy and you won't be far away."

"He hit a perfect nine-iron," recalls the Zimbabwean, who struck a sand wedge to seventeen feet and two-putted. "I mean, absolutely perfect. It wasn't a full one, it was just a nice, smooth nine-iron and he hit it up there to about three inches. I looked at it in the replay about three weeks later and I don't know how it didn't go in, because it actually came into the pin on the left and finished behind the hole on the right. So it must have lipped

Ballesteros long has been notorious for having his ups and downs with caddies. Here he is pictured in an obviously happier moment with caddie Ian Wright, during the 1988 British Open. (© Phil Sheldon)

the cup or something. It didn't put the trophy in his hands right then and there. He knew it, too. There was still two tough holes to go. But it sure helped his cause."

To the seventeenth they went, Ballesteros now leading by a shot. But Price still hung on doggedly, erasing the memories of how he had let slip the British Open in 1982, defying the men who had called him a choker. Even when his tee shot finished on a bare lie of caked mud, he didn't give up. He simply dropped clear without penalty, hit a brilliant one-iron into the green, and two-putted to equal the Spaniard's par.

On the right-hand side of the eighteenth fairway at Royal Lytham, some 260 yards from the tee, is a pot bunker craftily designed to trap the errant tee shot. Ballesteros drove first, launching the ball into the gray sky. Price followed its flight. It plummeted to earth and didn't bounce. "I think he's hit it in that little pot bunker," the Zimbabwean whispered to his caddie.

Ballesteros turned quickly to Wright with something akin to fear in his eyes. "Is it past the bunker?" he demanded urgently.

"I think it is," Wright said uncertainly.

"I knew then, when I stood on the tee, that if I hit a good tee shot I was going to have a very good chance to win," Price recalls, "because I thought the best he'd be able to do was make five out of there. And I hit absolutely the best tee shot I'd hit all day, about 290 yards [down the fairway] and into a perfect position."

The Spaniard began the long, nerve-wracking walk to his ball. All around him the towering stands of spectators were rejoicing at the return of the conquering hero, the roar rising to a crescendo.

"Are you sure it's past the bunker?" Ballesteros kept saying over and over again.

"Yes," replied Wright, his heart in his mouth. "I'm sure."

"When I got up there I was a little disappointed his ball had carried the bunker," Price admits. "Also, he had a pretty decent lie so he could get it on the green. I knew that I'd have to make three. He pulled his second shot. He hit a pretty good second shot but it went over the back edge. But I just never ever thought he'd make five . . . And I just tried a little too hard on that six-iron, I tried to get it too close to the hole. Instead of just playing it. . . . But, I mean, I was so fired up. I had visions of hitting that six-iron like this"—and he holds the palms of his hands about four feet apart.

In such circumstances are majors won and lost. Price hit his second shot thirty-five feet short of the pin, while the Spaniard's ball ended some fifty feet away in an awkward lie in the left rough. Silence, like a blanket, descended over the amphitheater of the eighteenth green. The only sounds were the muffled crunch of Ballesteros's spikes through the grass and the low murmur of his voice as he conferred with Wright and considered his shot. Then he played a feathery, delicate, chip, which popped up, skipped onto the green, then rolled and rolled until it came to a stop a bare three inches from the pin. It was over. Price tried gamely to hole his putt, rushed it too far past and missed the return, and so finished second with a score of 69. Ballesteros tapped in his own for a 65—which equaled the lowest final round in 117 British Opens and included an eagle and six birdies—an aggregate of 273, eleven under par, and a two-stroke victory over Price. Faldo was third at five under par, and Couples and Gary Koch were the best of the also-ran Americans at three under par.

"I had begun to think I was finished," an emotional Ballesteros said in the interview room afterward. "My confidence was down after I hit the ball into the water to lose the Masters in 1986. I was worried. But I decided all I could do was try and try and wait for my chance and momentum to come back. It was my turn to win this week . . . A round like that comes only every twenty-five or fifty years. It is the greatest round of my life . . . so far."

Nineteen eighty-eight was, arguably, Ballesteros's finest season. After the British Open he won the Scandinavian Enterprise Open, the German Open, and the Lancome Trophy in Europe, and the Taiheiyo Masters in Japan. He was the No. 1 player on the world rankings, the No. 1 player on the European Order of Merit for the fifth time with earnings of £451,559, the European Golfer of the Year, and was named Spain's Sportsman of the Year by Spanish sportswriters.

Officially and unofficially, his achievements were unparalleled—even the Americans acknowledged it.

"As we approach the 1990s, golf has home-grown heroes like Curtis Strange," Jerry Tarde wrote in *Golf Digest*. "We have international celebrities like Greg Norman. We have semiretired kings like Jack Nicklaus and kings who play like they're semiretired like Tom Watson. What we didn't have before July 18, 1988, the day he won at Lytham, was a living, breathing, practicing superstar.

"Now we have one. Severiano Ballesteros, the best golfer in the world.

"Long may he reign."

TO THE COURTROOM

"I badly want to win the tournament . . . but the money is not important. If I win, will I not eat the same breakfast on Monday morning?"

Severiano Ballesteros, European Open, 1984

The best golfer in the world was stretched out on the sofa in the front room of his rented house at Lytham, wearing jeans, a sweater, and a smile of pure happiness. He was thinking of Pedreña, where fireworks had lit up the sky a few hours earlier as villagers celebrated his third British Open victory.

"They've had those fireworks for four years waiting for me to win a big one again," Ballesteros said with a grin. "They were so old we weren't sure they would work."

He was calm, contented, and affable enough, but he also seemed curiously subdued. His answers to the questions of the journalists who surrounded him were quiet and from the heart. The key to his triumph, he told them, had been his putting. Vicente had suggested he move his hands closer together on the grip; he had tried it and it had worked wonders. "It's difficult to go out and play with confidence when you know your putting isn't good. It means you put pressure on your chipping because you know that you cannot hole the six-footers. There's no pleasure in that golf. Okay, it was called a slump, but even with poor putting I was always there . . . It is not possible to dominate all the time. I don't think it is possible for me to equal Jack Nicklaus's record of twenty [major] titles. I don't want to take anything away from Jack, but the gap between players is much closer than it was then."

At length, the interview drew to a close. The reporters closed their notebooks and gathered their belongings. They were just getting to their feet when the most extraordinary thing happened. For no reason at all, other than the fact he seemed desperate to get it off his chest, Ballesteros suddenly sat up and revealed to his astonished audience that, after years of anguish, he had finally bought out his contract with Ed Barner. "It was almost an afterthought," one of the journalists recalled later. "We were all ready to leave when he started talking about it. The whole thing was rather strange."

They settled down again to listen to his story.

In order to make sense of what happened next, one not only has to understand the circumstances that led to the breakup of Ballesteros's relationship with Barner, but also something of the personality of the latter and what motivated him. Edward Lee Barner was born in Arizona on May 10, 1940. The son of a motor mechanic, he graduated with a degree in communications and public relations, and, after spending two and a half years working as a Mormon missionary in West Berlin, set his sights on a career in television production. By the time he was twenty-five, he was a tour manager for a firm of Hollywood show-business agents, but in 1967, disillusioned with the entertainment industry, he left with the idea of moving into sports management. A year later he and Billy Casper formed Uni-Managers International.

That Barner had a unique gift for management was obvious from the outset. Joe Collet, who joined UMI in January 1977 as internal counsel shortly after leaving law school, remembers him as being one of the most talented men he had ever met for understanding what management meant, creating ideas, and solving problems. "He had a charming personality. He knew everybody he needed to know and if he didn't, he found out how to make them friends. Unfortunately, that didn't always last long-term, but he had this tremendous boldness and charming way of getting to decision-makers and celebrities. Even Princess Grace of Monaco considered him to be a dear friend and they used to write letters . . .

"But like a lot of people who have a tremendous amount of talent, they have an equally negative side if you get on the wrong side of them. And Ed, I think, had a bit of complex that people were not always straight with him at times, and that used to really grate on him. One of the problems that he had with clients is that he felt they would be willing to do little side deals and not include him, whereas he was offering total management services. It was like a marriage. You had to have complete trust in the partner. And as long as he found them big impressive deals . . . they were happy to pay the going rate. But when the deals were a little bit smaller . . . then they thought: "Why should I be paying a manager a fortune?" It was a philosophical difference. So what happened in practice is that a lot of them would find little cheap deals on their own and not tell him and then that element of trust became eroded. He'd tell them what he thought sometimes, which maybe diplomatically speaking wasn't the shrewdest thing to do, but it was very human of him to say: 'I'm upset, I'm hurt, I don't like it.' But he'd do it in such a way, with such finesse, that they would be really shocked. How could this amazing, personable person be so downright blunt and critical of their behavior, which they didn't think was so bad? And a lot of clients had their feelings hurt and pouted."

"He was a genius in some ways," observes Miller, whose own parting from Barner in 1978 resulted in a lawsuit. "He was very, very talented at marketing and managing. If there was a weakness in him it was that he was a little bit too possessive. . . . He would get you into things and then ask you if you wanted to do it and, of course, if you said no, he had already told them you were going to be there. That works okay when you're young and you need guidance and pushing along and directing, but when people get to the point where Seve was and where I was and where Billy Casper was . . . you don't want to be pushed, you just wanted to be helped. And Ed couldn't back off. That was his weakness and that's why he got into trouble with his clients."

Ballesteros had signed his first contract with UMI on October 17, 1975, on the day that he and Manuel had gone so warily to Barner's hotel room after Orville Moody's dire prophesies. It was a five-year agreement and stipulated that the Spaniard had to pay the company 25 percent of everything he earned, including winnings, appearance fees, and endorsements. In return, they would provide him with a complete management service. Collet, who is a talented linguist, was assigned as his account executive and was responsible for doing everything from arranging his schedule to negotiating geographically fragmented contracts. UMI had already conducted several endorsement deals for the young Spaniard, one of which had been a five-thousand-dollar-per-annum fee to play Mizuno clubs in Japan, acquired only weeks after Ballesteros had signed with the company. Barner had also discussed a new ball contract with Richard Brown of Dunlop Sports Company, Ltd. in 1976, the day before the British Open. Brown claimed: "The day after it he made totally new demands." But Barner was adamant that no agreement was made. But for the next three seasons the Spaniard did not play in the Dunlop Masters, and Doust maintains that it was Brown and Dunlop who led the sponsors' rebellion against appearance money in 1981. UMI, and principally Collet, negotiated more than two dozen contracts for Ballesteros in that first five-year period, including endorsements for everything from tomato juice to table-top games. Among the most lucrative were his Mizuno contract, worth around fifty thousand dollars per annum, and his Slazenger contract which, beginning in 1981, was to pay him in the region of two hundred fifty thousand pounds over five years. His income at that time was estimated at approximately one million dollars a season.

In 1981 Ballesteros's initial contract with UMI expired. When the renewal agreement came to be drawn up, there was a serious conflict of opinion between Ballesteros and Barner over what the former thought he should pay and the latter felt he should be paid. Finally, they compromised on 20 percent on specific deals and no percentage on winnings.

"Neither side was happy with it," Collet remembers. "We just lived with it and tolerated it and let it run its course."

"I think . . . the kind of things that bothered [Seve] are the ones that bothered other clients," says Brentnall Turley, who worked for UMI for four years as general counsel and also as a director. "Basically, there was not the veracity there on a lot of occasions. . . . And that was one of the things that concerned Seve. . . . Ed would get something done and do it very creatively and very effectively, but not be able to rein his temper and really obliterate all the good things that he had done. And if that's your manager, then other people say, 'Well, your manager is really a reflection of you.' And so you don't really want to be painted with that brush."

"It's too convenient to make Ed out to be the bad guy," Collet responds with some irritation. "Ed was a perfectionist and he was extremely good at doing what he did, but he was furious when somebody did not live up to his standards of integrity, which in turn caused him to react—not violently, but to be very obviously upset. And when somebody that you've only had pleasant words with and who has been a great moral support to you, like a psychologist almost, for two or three years, suddenly turns around and just chews you up one side and down the other, it just leaves you completely demoralized. And people couldn't live with themselves and that's why they left the company."

"Ed has called me everything that he possibly could," Turley says frankly, "and basically he's said that I'm a very dishonest person, which is really a reflection of what has been said about him. I left UMI in 1976 and went and opened up my own law practice. Johnny came to me a couple of years later and said: 'I want to leave UMI, would you be interested?' I said: 'Yes, I would be.' But Ed's position is that every client that left him was because of me. I didn't actively do anything. When Seve left UMI, [he] came to me because [he] knew that I'd lived through the Johnny Miller extrication."

THE PROBLEM WAS THAT THE SPANIARD COULDN'T JUST WALK AWAY FROM UMI WITHOUT A BACKWARD GLANCE.

In March 1983, on the day that Ballesteros's second contract expired, Collet resigned. He had known for two years that Ballesteros wasn't happy with UMI and wasn't going to renew his contract. "I tried to salvage it, and Ed, occasionally, would try to compromise. But it was just better that they parted at that point in time because they didn't see eye to eye. I just was kind of getting burned out at that point. Seve was what made my job interesting for me."

The problem was that the Spaniard couldn't just walk away from UMI without a backward glance. In the seven years he had been with the company, it had "obtained scores of endorsement contracts for him which paid him several millions of dollars in revenue." These deals were all covered by a clause in the initial contract he had signed which stated that if a client left UMI, the company would continue to receive its commission in perpetuity, for as long as the client had a relationship with the manufacturer or sponsor concerned.

Ballesteros, who by then had put his affairs into the hands of Turley, a Los Angeles attorney named Jerry Phillips, and Ceballos, objected to this clause and a bitter dispute arose as to how much Barner and UMI were entitled to receive from the proceeds of ongoing contracts they had negotiated on the Spaniard's behalf.

"[Seve] felt, on the advice of Brent Turley and other people, that he could beat that [clause] in court," Collet explains, "and that the court would probably rule that a reasonable commission period at the end of the separation was fair but not for ever and ever. And it was that point that provoked an arbitration. Otherwise what could have happened is that UMI would be considered to have invoiced the deals that it had administered and sent him his share and retained its, and he would have been [able] to find other companies and do other deals and not pay UMI anything. But instead Seve chose to try and cut it off *right now,* and Ed chose to try and keep it for ever and ever, neither one of which was quite right."

In 1984 UMI initiated arbitration against Ballesteros and Spangolf Enterprises, the corporation under which he conducts some of his U.S. business. The following year a hearing was held before an arbitrator, who issued an award favorable to Ballesteros, and more or less determined that all commissions as per the letter of the contract should be added up to a point some two years beyond the date on which the agreement between him and Barner and UMI ended. According to Collet, UMI then tried to retain money on the contracts that it had serviced "because Seve wasn't being fair with them on other things. And so they had to have an accounting to determine how much would be offset from what one had against what the other owed him.

Following the arbitrator's decision, Barner filed an action in federal court to "vacate" the award and, when it was dismissed, threatened to appeal. Settlement negotiations ensued, the dispute was resolved, and on December 19, 1986, while arbitration proceedings were still pending, both parties signed a written agreement titled "Settlement Agreement and Mutual Release." Legal records show that "the funds that Barner and UMI retained, even without considering the offsetting effect of the funds Ballesteros retained, amounted to substantially less than one million dollars."

Thus do we come to the incident at Royal Lytham in 1988, following the Spaniard's victory at the British Open. It should be borne in mind that, while all of these legal battles and recriminatory rows were going on, Ballesteros was trying to play golf, come to terms with his father's death, overcome the devastating psychological effects of losing several major championships in the circumstances that he lost them, and wage a transatlantic war with Beman.

As a close friend of his said at the time: "Anyone who knows Seve will realize he could never push this ferocious dispute out of his mind. All his professional life he has been inspired to great deeds by his craving to stick it to someone. Go through his record and you can match his triumphs to his mood. Here's when he stuck it to the European Tour because they wouldn't permit him to ask for appearance money. Here's when he stuck it to the American pros for calling him lucky. Here's when he stuck it to Deane Beman for not changing the qualification rules. But how could he stick it to Ed Barner when the process of sticking would only serve to enrich Barner even further. If he won a major, he would be slipping a six-figure check into the pocket of the man he wanted to rid himself of. You see his dilemma."

Nevertheless, when Ballesteros did win at Lytham he was so filled with joy and relief at having cast off the double burden of his slump and the legal difficulties under which he had labored for so long, that he momentarily dropped his guard. He forgot that the settlement agreement between himself, Barner, and UMI had contained a clause which provided that "[t]he existence and content of this Agreement are confidential," and therefore spoke sincerely to the journalists who surrounded him about how much he had suffered in recent years. It was widely reported and in no time at all Ballesteros found himself back in the courtroom. Barner and UMI filed an action against him for alleged slander and trade libel, and for breach of the confidentiality provision in the settlement agreement.

In July 1989, Barner and UMI alleged that, at Ballesteros's Open press conference, he had complained generally to reporters about the quality of the representation he had received over the years from Barner, citing as an example that in 1979 he had wanted to play in the U.S. PGA, but that Barner had told him to play in another event (the German Open) where he could earn five thousand pounds in appearance money. This, Ballesteros said, had led him to believe that "things were not quite right" with respect to his relationship with his manager. However, Barner insisted that he had, on the contrary, repeatedly urged Ballesteros to play in majors but that the Spaniard had preferred to go where the appearance money was.

Ballesteros then told journalists that he had been forced to pay "big money" to terminate his relationship with his manager. Asked whether that sum was more than one million dollars, he replied, "*Big money*," implying that it was in excess of one million dollars. He apparently added that Barner did not deserve so much money for the services he had provided, and alleged that he had personally gone to see Barner to discuss the settlement, saying: "I asked how much money he wanted. And I paid. I then said: 'Be happy but I do not want to see you again.' "

It was Barner's assertion that the above meeting had never taken place, and that Ballesteros did not pay Barner anywhere close to one million dollars. He maintained that since Ballesteros's statements were widely republished in everything from the *Sun* and *Golf Digest* to the *Bangkok Post*, both Barner and UMI had suffered specific damages, in that they had "lost certain business opportunities." The amount of these damages would be proved at trial but was believed to be over one hundred thousand dollars.

Ballesteros essentially denied every allegation that Barner and UMI made. But he did admit that the personal meeting he claimed to have had with Barner and indeed their alleged conversation had never taken place. He also acknowledged that he had paid Barner less than one million dollars.

"Seve was kind of feeling happy and he said too much and departed a bit from the fact situation," Collet says ruefully. "And the way that they wrote it up, it sounded very bad for Ed. And he got mad and slapped him with another lawsuit—ostensibly as a violation of the settlement agreement. That went on for a period. It ended up settling the arbitration and settling the other thing. I don't remember the figures of either one."

"Was it more than one million pounds?"

"Less."

"More than one million dollars?"

"Somewhere in that area. And then that was settled (April 25, 1990) and now everything's peaceful. That's where we'd like to leave it."

When Collet had resigned from UMI in the spring of 1983, Ballesteros had asked him if he would consider moving to Spain and handling his business. "I told him I couldn't," Collet recalls. "Legally and morally, I couldn't." A noncompete clause in the contract he had signed upon joining UMI prohibited him from taking any of the company's clients and starting a management organization of his own. But in November 1986, when that stipulation was no longer legally binding, chance brought the two men together again. "We were always good friends, you see," Collet explains. "When he came to California, he'd call and say hello. We'd go out to dinner. And after three years of this, one day I said: 'What's going on? How are things going?' 'Well, not so good.' And I said: 'Well, maybe I'd be interested in doing something.' And he said: 'We never closed that door.' "

In the years between leaving UMI and rehiring Collet, Ballesteros had put his affairs in the hands of his friend Ceballos. Previously an executive of the Spanish airline Iberia, and also a former executive director of the Spanish PGA until he could no longer tolerate the accusations of favoritism in the case of Ballesteros, Ceballos had become director of the Spaniard's company, Fairway SA, in 1981. Fairway had been formed while Ballesteros was still under contract to UMI, to develop and manage his Spanish business, which at that time included Seve Tours—an Iberia promotion to bring tourists to Spain on golf holidays, and a soft-drink line. It was, however, completely autonomous and independent of UMI. The Ballesteros brothers were the sole shareholders: Severiano owned 85 percent of the shares, while Baldomero, Vicente, and Manuel had 5 percent each.

Today there are three main companies: Fairway, Amen Corner, and Trajectory. Fairway is Ballesteros's personal management company. Headed by Collet, who has managed the Spaniard since 1986, it negotiates all his endorsement contracts and administers everything from fan mail to instruction videos. In 1981, as well as his equipment contracts, Ballesteros was paid to wear Rolex watches, drive a Range Rover (in partial exchange for giving three Leyland exhibitions a year), lend his name to Seve Tours, and hold five golf clinics per season at fifteen thousand dollars a time. Five years later, when Collet moved to Spain, there were twenty days a year when Ballesteros was obliged to be available for clinics, outings, photographic sessions, videotaping sessions, press conferences, etc. Apart from his obligations at an actual golf tournament, he spends just one and a half days a season on extraneous activities and makes four times the amount of money. His principal endorsement contracts are: Sunderland Rainwear; Dunlop Slazenger International, Ltd.; Sumitomo Rubber Company, Ltd., Japan; Hugo Boss; and Rolex.

"Endorsements today are probably of secondary importance to another whole area for these guys, and that's golf course design," Collet explains.

"Endorsements don't pay that much. . . . The company's objective is to get as much time and exposure as they can, and the manager's objective is to get as much money for as little time. . . . You don't need a shoe endorsement that pays you twenty-five thousand pounds a year if you have to do a day's worth of [video] taping every year, or half a day's worth of photography, or you have to sign autographs at a stand at the British Open. (IMG), in order to generate the fantastic sums that they publish—I don't believe that they're accurate—in order to justify the credibility they're trying to project, have got to give a lot of time to the companies . . . Have you seen *Golf Illustrated Weekly*? They have a picture of Nick Faldo in there, like a side of beef. You know how much the visor's worth and how much the shoes are worth. And it's all complete rubbish. All those figures you see in magazines about what the guys earn is complete rubbish. I know, because that's my business. . . . What IMG does, is they talk to you in terms of numbers. . . . And what they're usually quoting you is the total value of the contract when you sum all the years together, including projections of win bonuses and royalties that could come in, and lead you to believe that's what they get in a single year in pounds when it's what they get over the length of the entire contract in dollars and it counts everything. So that's how the figures get distorted and they're four or five times what they are in actuality. If Nick Faldo got the sums of money that are attributed to him in *Golf Illustrated*, he'd own half the companies that he's working for. People love to believe those things. They say, 'This is fantastic! It's so glamorous!' I disagree with the philosophy of using the media to print false figures which will generate more income by persuading sponsors that that is what other sponsors pay. I think it's in bad taste, really."

Amen Corner began as a joint venture between Fairway and Roddy Carr's company, Camcorp. Carr had continued to play pro golf himself until December 16, 1979, at which point he missed a four-foot putt in a tournament and quit the game. Thereafter, he had spent three years looking after women's golf in America for IMG, two years running IMG's office in Hong Kong, and three years helping to set up Nicklaus's golf design operation in Europe. In 1986 he approached Ballesteros with the concept of taking over the rights to the Spanish Open and helping to promote golf and raise the level of the tournament in Spain. Ballesteros agreed immediately. They nearly doubled the prize money, from eighty thousand to one hundred fifty thousand pounds, and sold it three years later to Peugeot.

In 1987 the Open de Baleares contract came up and it was decided to form a company that specifically and exclusively promoted European Tour events in Spain. Ballesteros became the new president of Amen Corner, as the company was named, and Carr took a share of it and became its chief executive along with Baldomero, the group chief executive of all the companies. At present Amen Corner promotes three European Tour events: the Spanish Open, the Open de Baleares, (or Mallorcan Open) and the Turespana Masters. The aim of the company is to make those three tournaments the best on the continent.

"The most impressive thing about [Seve] is he's highly intelligent," Carr says. "He understands the fundamentals of business. He would help me maybe twice a year when I need it, and he is always there at the right time with the right person to do the job in exactly the right way. . . . He will achieve more in an hour than I would in two months."

"He's very capable of sustaining a certain rhythm without a lot of interaction," agrees Collet. "We program him and he says, 'I want to do this, that and the other thing,' and then we'll work out the details and then say, 'Okay, here it is.' He does it and then we come back and give him another dose. We sort of do it in three-week dips."

This, of course, is when Ballesteros is in Spain, which, for a time, he was rarely, because his actual residence was in Monaco, where he "moved" in 1987. Needless to say, the Spaniard insisted that he wasn't a tax exile. "[T]hat's not the reason why [I moved here]," he told *Hello*. "After all, I have in Spain all my organizers and my golf course firm, as well as three other businesses that I pay my taxes on. The low tax rates in Monaco are obviously very pleasant, but the reasons I moved here are to maintain anonymity, which is provided here, and the weather, which means I can constantly train."

Collet adds two more reasons: (1) Proximity to an international airport; and (2) Intensive police surveillance and low crime rate. As he says, the Ballesteroses' sons are "invaluable" and at risk from kidnappers.

Ballesteros's third company is Trajectory, which essentially designs golf courses in Spain. His first three projects were done in cooperation with Dave Thomas, codesigner of the Belfry, after which he decided that if he formed his own company he would be able to "express" himself better. He has since completed courses in Japan, France (Pont Royal Country Club de Provence), England (with Thomas) and Spain, while others are either under construction or awaiting permits for construction or something of the kind. All of them are very natural and reflect the influences of courses like Augusta National. "I insist on incorporating the existing landscape," he said. "When people visit a Ballesteros course they should have the feeling that they are in a naturally designed field."

More and more of his time away from the golf course is taken up with course design, and he has confided to Carr that when his career comes to an end, it is to this he will turn. "Designing golf courses is one thing that I like very much. I think it's fantastic to go to one place and to see a piece of land that is nothing, and in one year you see a golf course. And to play there and to enjoy it and to give the chance to other people to have so much fun in the future, is something very special and I enjoy it very much. It's a pity that I cannot put as much time into it as I would like because I still like more the competition, but it's fantastic."

"DESIGNING GOLF COURSES . . . IT'S FANTASTIC TO GO TO ONE PLACE AND TO SEE A PIECE OF LAND THAT IS NOTHING, AND IN ONE YEAR YOU SEE A GOLF COURSE."

Meanwhile, after all these years, IMG is still trying to recruit Ballesteros. "We're trying," IMG's John Simpson admits. "You know, he's got his whole team around him at the moment. He knows what we can do and I think he's very complimentary about us, but it's all down to what he wants and what he perceives he wants. All I can say is that we could have done a helluva job for him."

Whether or not Ballesteros has made the right decision in steering clear of IMG, he has not suffered unduly. His annual off-course income, including endorsements, golf design, and returns from his clothing, cosmetics, and luggage lines (distributed mainly in the Far East), has at times been estimated at around seven million dollars.

15

HOME FIRES

"Half to forget the wandering and the pain,
Half to remember days that have gone by,
And dream and dream that I am home again!"

James Elroy Flecker, 1884–1915

The moment that Ballesteros stepped out of obscurity and into history at Royal Birkdale, shattering the sedate, gentlemanly, and colorless world of professional golf with his Latin looks, swashbuckling style of play, and captivating smile, it was obvious that sport had found itself a hero worthy of romantic fiction. Other players tended to be bland by comparison, both in personality and appearance, and were inclined, like Watson and Kite, to wear clothes in muted shades of beige or brown. Ballesteros, on the other side, was not only tall, dark, and handsome, he was also arrogant enough, charming enough, dashing enough, and unpredictable enough to have stepped straight from the pages of a Harlequin romance. Ed Barner, with his keen eye for star quality, recognized this in an instant. So, too, did the media, whose curiosity about his life off course grew in proportion to the spread of his fame. What did he do when he wasn't playing golf? "Did he," they wondered, "have a sweetheart waiting faithfully for his return in Pedreña?"

Ballesteros would always just laugh and reply, "Many, many, many girlfriends."

When they persisted, their efforts came to naught. No player is more adept than the Spaniard at sidestepping questions, personal or otherwise, with a grin and a self-deprecating quip. Nevertheless, his appeal to women was undeniable. "Wherever he goes, girls flock around him," McDonnell wrote in the *Daily Mail*, the week after he won the British Open in 1979. "He enjoys their company but can also be slightly callous sometimes. There is no steady girlfriend. After his romantic interludes, he's impatient to get back with the gang."

"He was very shy of women," explains Doust, who knew something of the man and not the myth. Once Ballesteros had snapped at him: "Trevino and you and everybody have suggestions for me. I don't know if I should have a holiday. I don't know if I should have girlfriend."

"After he won the Masters for the first time and he went to California for the Tournament of Champions, Williams and I had dinner with him," Doust remembers. "We were talking about women—he was very successful with women, actually. We said: 'What do you really think of women?' He said: 'The trouble with women is they're very sticky.' And Williams and I didn't know what the hell he was talking about, whether they clung to you, or whether their skins were actually sticky! I think that he meant the second. I think he meant they're a bit sticky! Maybe they sweated when they saw him or something, I don't know. Oh, and then he had that awful stuff in *El País* when he was very young, and he said women were second-class citizens."

In the course of that particular polemic, which appeared in the Madrid newspaper in 1980, Ballesteros remarked to the Spanish journalist conducting the interview: "You women want equality but you'll never get it because women are inferior to men in all sorts of ways—physically, intellectually, and morally. There are exceptions, but on the whole women are inferior to men." He himself was still socially immature at that age and more starkly black and white in his thinking than he has become, but his attitude was typical of his background.

Ballesteros's "romantic interludes," as McDonnell called them, were indeed fleeting. So much so that he can only recall having one steady relationship in his youth. "I was sixteen and dating one of the local girls in the village. I went to play in a tournament, where, I remember, I thought of her most of the time, but when I came home she left me for no reason. After that, there was no one until Carmen because I was absorbed by the game."

Some time before the unhappy day when young Severiano was dropped by the village girl, *destino* had occasioned his father be hired as a periodic caretaker of the house of the Botins, one of Spain's richest families. When the Botins were out of town, it was the duty of Ballesteros Sr. to ensure that vandals did not ransack their Pedreña home before they returned.

As the months passed and the families became better acquainted, Severiano, who by then was fifteen years old and on the Spanish Under-15 team, began giving lessons to Emilio Botin Jr., son of the man whose house his father cared for, as well as his children. One of these children—the sister of Carmen, his future wife—had what is described by Collet as "not a romance but a close friendship of the sort" with Ballesteros. Carmen was still only a child.

"Carmen received her first golf lessons from me," Ballesteros recalls proudly. "Then she went to study in Switzerland and later in England, where I met her in 1981 when I won my first World Match Play Championship at Wentworth. That is when we fell in love, and we've been together since."

Carmen is the quiet, dark-haired, dark-eyed daughter of Emilio Botin Jr., president of the Bank of Santander and one of the wealthiest men in Spain. According to *Forbes* magazine in America (quoted by *Golf Digest* in October 1988), Banco Santander "is the only major Spanish bank still controlled by a single family. The Botins' visible stake is only some 5 percent. But knowledgeable sources say affiliated Botin entities bring the total to 25 percent, worth around $1.5 billion." Money not being an obstacle, Botin Jr. decided that his daughter should have a classical English and American education. Thus, she was sent to Saint Mary's in Ascot, Berkshire, the same convent attended by Princess Caroline of Monaco, and to Brown University in Rhode Island, where she graduated in 1987 with a bachelor's degree in organizational behavior.

Carmen and Ballesteros began seeing one another intermittently, and by 1983 they were dating as regularly as they could hope to, given that he spent half his season in Europe and she spent a good deal of time in the United States. The next summer there were rumors of their impending marriage, but at the Open Ballesteros joked, "She won't have me," and hinted that it was because Carmen herself felt she was not old enough. There is, after all, a nine-year age difference between them. However, it was generally believed—and still is—that her father was reluctant to allow them to marry because of the humble circumstances of Ballesteros's birth, and for that reason it pleased the tabloids greatly to cast him as the villain of the piece in a Romeo-and-Juliet-type romance—the autocratic father who would stop at nothing to prevent his precious daughter from marrying the son of a peasant farmer. This saga went on for years and much innocent pleasure was derived from it, as the following piece by Dobereiner (*Golf World*, April 1988) shows:

> In our popular press, whose salacious obsession with secrets of the boudoir totally eclipses any notional interest in sport, Ballesteros is presented as the victim of unrequited love. Romeo Ballesteros, son of a poor dirt farmer from the wrong side of the tracks, sighs beneath the balcony of Juliet (Carmen Botin, actually, daughter of the high-born and wealthy president of the Bank of Santander, near Seve's hometown of Pedreña).
>
> See how she leans her cheek upon her hand: O! that I were a glove upon that hand, that I might touch that cheek.
>
> Juliet demonstrates that her expensive education at St. Mary's and Brown University in Rhode Island has not been wasted by responding: "O, Romeo, Romeo! wherefore art thou Romeo?"
>
> The plot now thickens. In his office at the bank, father Botin studies the statement of Romeo's account. Each figure is followed by a seemingly endless row of zeroes, like the wheels of freight trains rolling across La Mancha bearing treasures to his vaults. An eminently suitable son-in-law, he concludes.
>
> But mother Botin, the blue blood of the Capulets rising in her gorge, has a proper scorn for money, especially new money. You can, she asserts with vigor, take the boy out of the caddie shack, but you can't take the caddie shack out of the boy. I will never permit the most fragrant flower of the Capulets to be united with a Montague.

The speculation increased as the years passed and the promised wedding failed to materialize, despite the fact that Ballesteros, Carmen, and Botin Jr. were frequently to be seen together and in the friendliest of circumstances. In May 1987, for example, Ballesteros shot a record-breaking eight-under-par 64 at the Spanish Open at Las Brisas, delighting his prospective father-in-law, with whom he was playing in the pro-am. Nevertheless, the repeated postponement of the marriage began to be held up more and more as one of the major causes of the Spaniard's lack of inspiration on the course. At the British Open in 1988 Carmen told the press: "Seve's private life is private. His golf is separate." But she added, "We will be getting married pretty soon, but not just yet."

On Friday, November 25, 1988, Severiano Ballesteros and Carmen Botin were at last married. Only their immediate families were invited. "Otherwise," Collet explains, "there would have been literally hundreds of people there." They were married in Santander but they led everyone to believe it would be at Carmen's grandfather's other house, out in another village. They let it out and they said, "This is a big secret, don't tell anybody," knowing full well that it would get around and it would seem like an authentic secret and so everybody would be flocking out there on that day. And that's precisely what happened. They also planned it for three days after Seve came back from Japan, and the honeymoon was going to be in the Caribbean. Nobody in their wildest dreams would believe that after coming all that way he would then get married and go on another trip, because it's just so unlike Seve it's unbelievable. They told his mother the day before the wedding.

"IT WAS JUST A COMPLETE DISASTER," COLLET RECALLS, PITYING BALLESTEROS, WHOSE EFFORTS TO KEEP HIS WEDDING DAY SACRED AND AWAY FROM THE PRYING EYES OF PRESS AND PUBLIC HAD ALL BEEN IN VAIN.

"I found out the morning of the wedding it was happening," Collet continues. "One of our secretaries went downstairs to buy a newspaper and heard over the radio: 'Seve Ballesteros has just been seen coming out of a church in his wedding attire and they're driving off now. . . . ' His brother Baldomero hadn't come to work and Manuel was still at La Manga Club at that time, so he wasn't there. I thought, 'Well, it wouldn't surprise me if it's true.' And sure enough, minutes later it was all confirmed."

In this way, Ballesteros and Carmen had the private wedding they wished for. No photographers were allowed, and the only pictures that resulted from it were informal ones taken by a member of the family with a small camera. Sadly, the couple took the roll of film with them to the Caribbean and had it processed there, whereupon an unscrupulous person in the photo-lab made extra copies and dispatched them to a news agency, which duly had them published around the world. The photographs were unflattering and of a poor quality and, to make matters worse, the news agency captioned them incorrectly so that the names of the people who appeared in them were wrong.

"It was just a complete disaster," Collet recalls, pitying Ballesteros, whose efforts to keep his wedding day sacred and away from the prying eyes of press and public had all been in vain. "It caused a big scandal."

Ballesteros has always been an intensely private man. Ever since those first lonely and difficult days on Tour in 1974, after which Manuel had advised him to go home until he recovered his spirits and his game, Pedreña has been his refuge, the place where he goes to heal himself when the pressures of fame get too much for him.

"When I go home and when I stay in Pedreña, my village, it's probably the only place that I feel a normal person," he says. "My friends, they see me as a normal person, they don't see me as a superstar. They respect me, I respect them, and I feel very happy and very comfortable. I can do a lot of things and the people are not on my shoulder, which sometimes happens when I'm on the Tour—which is part of success but it's tough. And I feel extremely happy there."

Years ago, when he was still very conscious that he had to be seen to be a resident of Monaco, he told *Hello* magazine that he derived as much pleasure from being there as he did from being in Spain. "There are only two places in the world where I feel at home. One is my home in Monte Carlo, where I can walk around the streets without anybody talking to me. Anywhere else, what always happens is someone comes up to you and says: 'Hey, Seve, I saw you on television. Why did you miss the fifteenth hole?' and so on. That doesn't happen in Monte Carlo. Carmen and I spent all yesterday afternoon shopping and didn't get disturbed once. The second place is Pe-dreña. There I find the same peace and quiet as in Monte Carlo. To me, the people in Pedreña haven't changed since my youth. They accept me for what I am. Even though I now live in Monte Carlo. I still belong to this village. When I'm home we play cards together, go clay [pigeon] shooting, or just sit in the bar and watch a football game on television, like the old times, and that makes me really happy. Anywhere else, you're looked at through differ-ent eyes when you achieve fame or have a lot of money in your account."

As soon as all four Ballesteros brothers were professionals, and were ei-ther attached to golf clubs or on Tour, their parents retired, drew on their state pensions, and were taken care of by their sons. Severiano then built a luxurious villa only an iron shot away from Real Club de Golf de Pedreña, complete with swimming pool, gymnasium, tennis courts, practice bunker, and putting green. There, in the winter months and during his midseason weeks off, when most players are resting, drinking beer, and growing idle, Ballesteros puts himself through a rigorous training schedule. Beginning at eight o'clock in the morning, he spends an hour doing calisthenics-type ex-ercises, lifting weights, stretching, and working out on special machines de-signed to ease his back problems; eats breakfast; goes down to the golf club and either plays eighteen holes or hits two or three hundred balls; practices chipping, putting, and bunker shots for a couple of hours; goes home for lunch; and returns to the golf club and either plays or practices for the re-mainder of the afternoon.

"I practice every day," Ballesteros says, "including Saturday. On Sunday I play only in the morning until one o'clock, because on Sundays at the golf clubs there are many people and it's difficult."

In between the Spaniard somehow finds time to run, play tennis, swim, sail, fish, and cycle. He has become more health conscious over the years. He never smokes, rarely drinks even decaffeinated coffee, has shandy instead of beer, and seldom imbibes wine. His diet is watched with equal care. Where once he tucked into high-cholesterol foods with gay abandon, now he eats more carbohydrates, such as pasta, which give him energy. And when he is preparing for a major, he adheres strictly to a carefully calculated regime of nutrition, exercise, practice, and rest.

"His strengths," Carr says, "are his desire to work and his passion. Peo-ple have no idea how much he works, no concept of the amount of hours he puts in. And he does it every day, rain, hail, or storm. He'll be up at

Santander, it'll be pissing out of the heavens, and he'll be there with his wet suit on hitting balls. All the time. He might get up and ride a bike after that and go and do his weights and his training. He never stops. A Tour event—that's not his work schedule. His work time is at home. So when people say, he's at home resting, he's at home grinding himself out."

When Ballesteros does want to relax, he watches videos, plays cards with his friends, or goes out on his boat. When he feels so utterly overwhelmed by the pressures of success that he just has to escape, he goes hiking in the mountains with his sports psychologist, a man by the name of Caycedo, who is based in Andorra. Dr. Caycedo was introduced to Ballesteros by a television presenter in Barcelona whom he dated for a brief period at the start of 1980. He is an expert on *suffrolgia*, a form of positive thinking, and he interviews the Spaniard and prepares cassette tapes for him to listen to on his Walkman.

"I don't know exactly what goes into them," says Collet, who often roomed with Ballesteros on Tour before Seve married Carmen, "but every once in a while I'll know he's locked in the room and he's got his headset on, and we don't disturb him during that period. Then he comes out and everything's fine and he has dinner and plays golf the next day. He doesn't like to talk about it, really."

"What the doctor says to me is private," Ballesteros told Doust. "But it helps me to relax and convinces me I am good."

"I'll tell you something about Seve," Collet says. "When he was a youngster he skipped school a lot, never really was very fond of academics, so anything that required him to do a lot of reading and analyzing or writing down figures and stuff he didn't have much of an affinity for, and anything that he could do just with his hands or talking came more naturally to him. One of his friends in the U.S. suggested he play chess. He said, 'Oh no, that's for those intellectuals. I don't want to do that.' But the guy kept on so he tried it and he said, 'I don't like this,' and he quit. But his friend just kept on and, I think, let him win once or something and it gave him a little confidence. Finally, he took an interest in it and he started playing. He was a very amateur player. When he started getting better he asked me if I knew how to play, and I played him and soundly thrashed him the first few games. But he was more determined than ever that he was going to beat me because that would prove something, so he kept working on it and I'll be doggone if the last three times we've played he hasn't beat me. He's got pretty good. He's a very aggressive chess player. I can see how that might be a factor in his golf game because it's just attack, attack, attack all the time."

Like all great competitors Ballesteros loves to watch sport. He is a cycling aficionado and follows the progress of the top riders with an enthusiasm matched only by his love of football. Trajectory, his golf design company, sponsors a third-division football club in Santander, which he goes to watch most Sundays when he is in Pedreña. "They can really play," Ballesteros says with pride. Such is his competitiveness that he even wants his own football team and the teams he supports to be winners. Santander, a second-division club, is another of his favorites, "but the real one is Barcelona football club. They have been my team since I was very young. I think they are the best in Europe."

The price of Ballesteros's athleticism has been the agony he has suffered with his back, although the origin of his problems is unclear. Doust suggests that it might have been caused by an injury he suffered while boxing as a child. He lost his footing, fell backward onto his coccyx, and limped for a fortnight. On another occasion he strained his back while lifting rocks on his father's farm. But Ballesteros himself feels that it may have been initiated by excessive practice in 1974, the day before the first round of the Under-25's tournament at Pedreña. He hit seven hundred balls in the cold and rain, and woke the next morning with shooting pains in his back. Desperate to play, he had a series of painkilling injections, which almost certainly

A DISCAL HERNIA WAS DIAGNOSED. THE SURGEON ADVISED HIM TO UNDERGO AN OPERATION TO FUSE THE WEAKENED VERTEBRAE. BUT BALLESTEROS, TERRIFIED OF GOING UNDER THE KNIFE, REFUSED.

compounded whatever damage he might already have inflicted upon himself, in the same way that professional riders who administer lame horses with cortisone ruin them for life for the sake of a single event.

In 1977, on the advice of Cabellas, Ballesteros went to see an eminent orthopedic surgeon in Madrid. Dr. Carbajosa x-rayed him and discovered a minor injury in the lower back, notably in the fifth vertebrae. He suggested that Ballesteros take a six-month break from the game and sleep on a hard mattress with a board underneath. The mattress was easy enough to arrange; the rest was out of the question. Later that year he paid a visit to the Spanish surgeon who had worked miracles with Trevino's back after he was struck by lightning. A discal hernia was diagnosed. The surgeon advised him to undergo an operation to fuse the weakened vertebrae. But Ballesteros, terrified of going under the knife, refused, convinced that, if nothing else, it would affect his swing.

It was around that time he began his worldwide search for a cure-all in earnest. First, he tried acupuncture and spent several years wearing tiny needles behind his right knee and in his right shoulder. He visited eye specialists after deciding his vision was failing. An ear, nose, and throat specialist examined him and suggested surgery for the nasal congestion which caused his persistent cough. He was operated on for the first time in 1980 and has been in and out of hospital for the same reason on several occasions over the last sixteen years.

Initially, the Spaniard used to pour his heart out about these trials and tribulations, telling them of his fears that one day his ailing back might stop him playing. At the British Open in 1979, for instance, he confessed that he had spent months sleeping on the floor to ease his suffering. Thomas Boswell quotes him confiding to David Graham: "Only I will ever know how bad my back has ever been."

Then, quite suddenly, having been assured by a Californian orthopedic surgeon that his condition was not career-threatening, he arrived at the conclusion that speaking of his injuries gave others a psychological advantage over him. From that moment on he avoided the issue. "My back is fine. No problem." Only his close friends knew of the scores of specialists and alternative healers he continued to visit.

"He's tried everything," Collet says wryly. "I don't think it's been as painful as you'd like to believe but it's been constant and uncomfortable. He has no problem in the medical sense. I've been with him through every conceivable discipline that claims to have knowledge about the back that there is. We've been to podiatrists who say that maybe his arch is off or the shoes that he wears bother him, because they say there's a relationship between the stance that you take, your posture, and how your spine lines up. We've been to dentists who say that it works from the top to the bottom—if his bite is wrong, theoretically that could cause stress in the neck muscles, the neck would affect the spine, and so forth. He's been for therapy. He's had experts on exercise talk to him . . . about doing things that are supposed to keep the alignment nice and straight and reduce stress and strengthen muscles. We've been to a guy down in Stratford-upon-Avon, Dr. Hugo Kitchen, a homeopathic physician. His machine indicated that Seve's left side was stronger than his right, which means that he actually pulls the club through rather than pushes it and the braking muscles—as the doctor put it—are possibly weaker than the power muscles. He's given him a series of exercises to do to strengthen the other side so that it's symmetrical."

Collet sighs heavily: "I've been to regular orthopedic surgeons with him and they've examined and x-rayed him. There's nothing out of line; he has no slipped disc; he has no herniated disc. I think the problem is one of tension, not a physical disability or a congenital shortcoming. I think he's a perfectly fine specimen. What he does is he puts a lot of stress on himself and, of course, his back's going to ache. I don't know of a golfer in the world who doesn't have a backache once in a while. A golf swing is completely unnatural."

On August 20, 1990, Ballesteros's first son was born. A robust, healthy child with huge black eyes, his parents named him Baldomero Javier after Severiano's father. His arrival into the world (though premature) gave rise to the joke: Why did Carmen take so long in labor? Because the baby was demanding appearance money!

Ballesteros has always had a deep affection for small children and animals. Throughout his career they have been drawn to him and he in his turn has been gentle and endlessly patient with them, for they don't invade his privacy or try to steal his soul. So comfortable does he feel with children that when he went to play an exhibition match in Argentina in 1992, it was the most natural thing in the world for him to ask Fernandez if one of his young sons, whom he had met four years previously, could caddie for him, even though he was being accompanied to South America by his cousin, who was perfectly willing and able to carry the bag.

241

Newfound family man Seve Ballesteros, with wife Carmen and firstborn son Baldomero, named after Seve's beloved dad. (Globe Photos Inc., 1997)

"They were like two boys together," Fernandez recalls, smiling. "Because my son treats him like somebody else like him, and he likes that. So I think he will be a more relaxed person from now on because of his son. He loves children. For such a long time he lived a life, maybe not by himself, but the people around him made him feel that he's the only one. But now (that) he has a son he will not be the only one."

"You don't know how much you love children until you have your own," Ballesteros says. "It is something very special. And it is difficult to leave them. You don't want to miss anything. It is wonderful how quickly they learn and how smart they are. Then they cry when you leave for the airport. It gets harder and harder to go."

One of the hardest battles that Ballesteros has had to fight in his life is loneliness. As he says, "It is not normal for the Spanish people to leave the place where you were born for long spells. The philosophy in Spain is to stay close to the family." The bond between him and his brothers is still very strong, and the long periods he endures away from home in vast, impersonal hotels only serve to accentuate it.

"He's close to each of them in their own way," Collet observes. "Manuel started the pro Tour before Seve and was his guide and helped him along in the early years. Manuel did a lot of nice things for him, which Seve appreciates, and he has a special place in his heart for him. . . . The oldest brother, Baldomero, is, if not the father figure of the family, the one everyone kind of looks to for advice. Seve's very close to him in an emotional way, wanting to have his older brother's approval. It's important to him to know his brother's opinion, and they don't always agree, but one usually convinces the other and then they're in harmony. He likes to have Baldomero involved in a lot of the decisions that he makes. The younger brother, Vicente, is the closest to Seve in age and, I think, is the one Seve feels the closest to socially. He kind of makes him laugh the most. Sometimes he caddies, and sometimes he goes to watch his swing. Vicente is a very gifted teacher."

On the European Tour, Ballesteros turns to a handful of close friends for support. He trusts few people because, as Fernandez says, "He doesn't have time to choose the right friends. . . . When you get to the position he is, you get more inside yourself because you know those people are talking to you because you're famous or because they want to make business with your money or whatever."

Nick Price agrees: "Character-wise, I'd say he's an introvert."

"When he is with a few people, then he is very friendly and he's a nice guy," says Jose Maria Olazábal, who, along with Fernandez, Piñero, Lyle, Eduardo Romero, Anders Forsbrand, and Vijay Singh, is one of Ballesteros's most faithful friends. They had first met when they played an exhibition match for charity in Santander in 1984 and, recognizing the same qualities of fire, intensity, and determination in each other, had formed a lasting friendship. "Obviously, for me it was very special," Olazábal says, "and since then I have a lot of respect for Seve and I reckon he's a good friend of mine. But I think that he doesn't like crowds or people in general. Then what he tries to do is just try to avoid all those people, and sometimes it feels like he's not very friendly or a very nice guy. But that's the only reason why he reacts like that. When there is only four or five people he can be very, very friendly."

"He's changed," Fernandez remarks. "He's changed for the better. I'm not saying Seve wasn't good before, but he has improved in his social relationships. I mean, he's started to understand how other people feel."

"He's always been a hero in my eyes," Forsbrand says. "He's a wonderful man, absolutely wonderful. A lot of things have been said about him, but I think he's one of the best guys out here. . . . He's a great golfer and a very warm guy. Very warm heart."

Marriage and the birth of his children have, to some extent, chased the loneliness bird from Ballesteros's door. He still longs for Pedreña, but now at least he has a choice: He doesn't have to be alone if he doesn't want to be. "It helps a lot when you've finished the day," Ballesteros says. "If you've had a good day, you go back to the hotel and feel very happy, of course. But if you've had a bad day and go into the hotel, you don't feel very well. But once I go into the hotel and I see my wife and I see my little boy, I just forget totally all those bogeys that I make and all the double bogeys and those things, and it's something that helps a lot."

But he admitted to *Hello* magazine that although, "My family, my wife Carmen, and our sons are a huge part of my life, the centerpoint was, and always will be, golf."

"If Carmen confronted you with a choice of golf or family, how would you decide?" the reporter asked.

"I would try to keep on playing," the Spaniard replied, "although my family are much more important to me than golf. But I know it wouldn't come to that. Carmen knows I love my job so I would never be confronted with this choice."

"It is my hope for one of my sons (Baldomero and Miguel) to be a professional golfer," Ballesteros says. "I can make sure they don't make the same mistakes I did. The biggest mistake I made was to start playing professional golf so early. I turned professional when I was only sixteen. I should have started three years later. It was my decision, mainly because I had nothing else to do. I thought I was ready to play and I was. But for me, I think it was a mistake. In one way it was good to have success so quickly, but in another way it meant I was facing things for which I wasn't really prepared. And it took a lot for me to face some of those things. In one way I regret it. I lost all my growing-up years. I haven't lived a normal life."

16

HARD DAY'S NIGHT

"The least thing upset him on the links. He missed short putts because of the uproar of butterflies in adjoining meadows."

P. G. Wodehouse, *The Clicking of Cuthbert*

Sunday, June 17, 1990, U.S. Open, Medinah. At first glance, nothing was amiss. The club flowed back as beautifully as ever, a sharp crack rang out, and then the crowd surged forward with one movement under the bright summer sky. Ballesteros, club in hand, eyes on the green, proceeded after them up the opening hole of one of America's toughest golf courses in the final round of the U.S. Open. His proud head was held high, his stride was determined. Even his name occupied its usual place on the leaderboard. It was not until he played his second shot and then his third that it became obvious that something was horribly, perhaps irremediably, wrong. It was there in the hesitancy of his club selection, in the tentativeness of his putting, in the uneasiness with which he examined each stage of his oft-repeated practice swings, in his deeply furrowed brow, in the agitated clearing of his throat, and in the hopeful but unmistakably desperate way in which he watched the fluctuations of scores. With Ballesteros, body language has always spoken more eloquently than words.

Three days earlier the Spaniard had commenced his bid for the title he has always longed for. When he made two birdies in the first three holes, an expression approaching cheerfulness had appeared on his face and he had momentarily cast off that air of despondency which had hung like a cloud over him all season. Almost as suddenly, however, he had lost control of his driver. From there on in he had hooked wildly from every tee, and it was only his ability as an escape artist that had allowed him to hit sixteen greens in regulation and score 73. The following day his attitude was one of defiance. But after nine holes, despair was getting the better of him. Goaded by the prospect of missing the cut, he launched himself into his tee shot at the par-five tenth and hooked it into a fairway bunker. His recovery shot clattered in amongst the trees. He had 130 yards to the green and no shot. Low-hanging branches blocked all escape routes. Finally, he selected a six-iron and, to the amazement of his audience, hit an exquisite punch shot which never rose above waist-height off the ground, pitched just short of the green; skipped between two bunkers, bounded onto the putting surface, and came to a stop eight inches from the pin.

Inspired, Ballesteros fairly flew home, scoring 32 for a total of 69. Two days later, he was four strokes behind the leaders, Billy Ray Brown and Mike Donald, and in contention for the U.S. Open title. Then he arrived at the par-three second. Standing on the tee with a club in his hand and Lake Kadijah yawning at his feet, he did something which he himself would have thought inconceivable in the days when he was young and intense: he lost concentration. Later he confessed, "My thoughts were everywhere but where they should have been."

"Ahhh!" moaned the crowd in sympathy as his ball curved out over the water, wrestled briefly with the wind, and then cleaved the oil green surface of the lake. They craned forward to gaze into its quivering depths. On the tee it was as if Ballesteros had been hit by a mortal blow. His shoulders sagged forward in utter dejection; the light went from his eyes. "After that, I just put myself down," he said miserably, having finished tied for thirty-third. "I was there to win and I hit it in the water. If things are going badly it becomes a kind of routine."

Ballesteros had been on the road to nowhere since the beginning of the new season. Some said that his journey may even have started sooner, for since 1989 there had been signs that all was not what it should be. His first finish of the season was a tie for fifty-fourth in the Open de Baleares and, although he had victories in the Madrid Open, the Epson Grand Prix, and the European Masters, they were interspersed with a twelfth-place tie, a seventy-sixth-place tie, a thirty-eighth-place tie, a twentieth-place tie, and two missed cuts. Nobody thought anything of it. Golf is too capricious a game and the golf swing too mysterious a movement for any player to be expected to perform year in and year out at a consistently high level, least of all a player as inspirational as Ballesteros. There are just too many intangibles involved. And at the outset of the 1990 season, everything seemed to be much the same as usual. He tied for third in Dubai, tied for fourteenth in the Mediterranean Open, and then won the Open de Baleares in a playoff. What could be more normal than that? Ballesteros himself agreed. "My game is back," he said cheerfully. "It was the best I've felt on a golf course in six or seven months."

The first indication of the nightmare that was to come occurred a fortnight later at the Nestle Invitational in Bay Hill in Florida; Ballesteros took nine at one hole and missed the cut. It was the second-worst score of his career. His worst had been the eleven he had notched up in the Spanish Open at La Manga in 1974 when he was seventeen years old. Nevertheless, he finished third the very next week in the Houston Open and all seemed to be well again. Which it was, if you looked no further than the record book. What the results didn't show was that while the Spaniard had had three birdies in the first eight holes and picked up another trio at the eleventh, thirteenth, and sixteenth to be tied for the lead going into the closing holes, he had also clipped the trees with his approach shot on the seventeenth to drop a shot and lose the tournament. Afterward, he claimed there had been mud on the ball.

At the Masters he seemed disgruntled and generally out of humor, but no one would have described his form as bad. He shot 74, 73 in the opening rounds and complained that he had been disadvantaged by his late starting time on the first day, since he was struggling with his putting and by the time he had teed off in the afternoon there were so many spike marks left by the rest of the field that they had only accentuated the problem. He three-putted both the sixteenth and eighteenth holes as a consequence. His fine scores of 68 and 71 on the last two days, which helped him to a tie for seventh place, were all that was needed to convince him that *destino* had, once again, withheld what was rightfully his. "Overall it was not too bad, but decidedly not what I was looking for."

247

Prior to the 1997 Masters Tournament, Seve had gone more than ten years without fulfilling a vow to his now-deceased father that he would win a third green jacket at Augusta. Here he is suffering through yet another of his Augusta heartbreaks, splashing a shot out of Rae's Creek at the thirteenth hole in the 1989 Masters Tournament, eventually won by rival Nick Faldo. (© Phil Sheldon)

The trouble was that each time Ballesteros returned to Augusta he was reminded of the promise he had made to his father, reminded too of the manner in which he had broken it and therefore confronted with proof that he was not invincible. When he won the British Open in 1988, he said confidently, "Now I can forget about hitting into the water at Augusta . . . and remember instead how I played today." But at that time he had no experience of how one shot, one split second of lost concentration, could cause years of devastation. He found he could no more shrug it off than Nicklaus had been able to after Watson chipped in to beat him at the penultimate hole of the 1982 U.S. Open at Pebble Beach; or Hubert Green had been able to after missing that three-foot putt for victory at Augusta in 1978; or, most remarkably of all, Jacklin had been able to after Trevino had chipped at the eleventh hour to snatch victory from him at Muirfield in the 1972 Open.

But, in a way, the knowledge that someone else had been responsible for his failures at Augusta might have alleviated Ballesteros's suffering. As it was, he had no one to blame but himself. He set off for the Madrid Open, tired and unrefreshed. It did him no good at all to learn that one of his companies had become embroiled in a storm of controversy. It transpired that Olazábal was refusing to play in the Spanish Open the following week because Amen Corner had rejected his demand for a twenty-four-thousand-pound appearance fee. Instead, he had been offered thirty-six thousand pounds to play in the Spanish Open in 1990 and 1991, as well as in the 1991 Open de Baleares. Nothing could have been more reasonable since only major champions and past winners of the Order of Merit are entitled to appearance money and Olazábal didn't meet either of the criteria. He didn't see it that way, though.

WHOLLY UNEDUCATED IN GOLF ETIQUETTE AND DEVOID OF THE COMMONEST FORMS OF COURTESY OR HUMAN DECENCY, THEY SWARMED OVER THE FAIRWAYS LIKE RATS.

Essentially, the dispute was between Carr and Sergio Gomez, Olazábal's manager. Ballesteros insisted that he had nothing to do with the negotiations, but was embarrassed nonetheless. He reiterated what he had said a hundred times during the appearance money war of 1981—namely, that no player should be allowed to ask for a fee, although they should be entitled to accept it if offered.

With that, he went out onto the course, where his problems started in earnest. The news had only just broken that Carmen was pregnant, and the Spanish paparazzi, guessing she would be following his match, had arrived at Puerto de Hierro en masse. Wholly uneducated in golf etiquette and devoid of the commonest forms of courtesy or human decency, they swarmed over the fairways like rats, creating havoc wherever they went. After two hours, Carmen couldn't stand it anymore and fled in tears. Ballesteros had just had to step away from the ball at the short seventeenth (his eighth) because of all the scuffling and clicking and he had fluffed his chip, chipped again, missed the putt, and taken a double-bogey five. When he reached the ninth hole he appeared to be in a towering rage. His drive hooked obstinately away and finished halfway up a bank on the left side of the fairway. He clambered up after it, balanced precariously on the steep face, smashed at the ball, and had to take hasty evasive action as it came back at him like a bullet off a pine tree and vanished under a small bush. This he destroyed with a furious lunge, sending his ball straight into another tree, which luckily deflected it onto a place from where it was possible to reach the green. Squealing tires announced his departure.

The next day, wrapped up as much against the prying eyes of the press as against the Arctic wind blowing off the snow-capped mountains of Madrid, the defending champion added a 70 to his 76 and missed the cut.

It was now that the idea that Ballesteros had fallen into a deep slump really began to take root in people's minds. Previously, it had just been considered a spell of bad form. After that, it was only a matter of time before the smallest gesture and most ordinary stroke was taken as evidence that he was no longer the player he had once been.

Ballesteros had more on his mind than the state of his game, the antics of the paparazzi, or his differences with Olazábal—which by now had been resolved. Olazábal had appeared at the tournament on the first practice day and said quietly: "We are good friends and I would do anything for him. When he asked me to play on Monday, I said yes straight way." Ballesteros's most pressing concern was the outcome of the campaign to bring the 1993 Ryder Cup to Madrid's Club de Campo, the Spanish Open venue. He regarded it as his own personal crusade and had devoted a considerable amount of time and energy to it—even going so far as to lead a Spanish delegation to the PGA in February. He had also dwelt long and hard on the opposition he was likely to encounter. Consequently, when he walked into the press center after the first round of the tournament, having shot 74 and taken nearly five hours to do it in, he had worked himself into a state of rare fanaticism.

He sat on the podium and glowered, his body rigid with temper. Shortly before his arrival, Faldo, immaculately groomed and on top of his game, had breezed into the press center and, on being asked which of the favored Ryder Cup courses—Club de Campo, Royal Birkdale, or Portmarnock in Dublin—he considered most suitable, had replied that he thought Birkdale would give the Europeans the best chance of victory.

When Ballesteros was informed of this he was beside himself with rage. "Why should we play in England, why?" he cried passionately, eyes blazing. "Why should we play in Ireland, why? Spanish players have done enough for

European golf. We must have the Ryder Cup in Spain. I'm not saying I won't play if it doesn't come here, but remember one thing: I would be disappointed. I would lose a little bit of my desire for the Ryder Cup."

Order took wing; chaos reigned. Spanish translations were hurled back and forth.

"People should remember that, without the European players, there probably would be no Ryder Cup," Ballesteros said coldly when peace had broken out. "The future of the European Tour is in Spain. . . . Golf here needs the push the Ryder Cup would provide. It would be the best thing for the game as a whole. It is what Samuel Ryder would have wanted if he were alive today. To wait until 1997 would be too late."

Then he added darkly, "I feel I have played a part in the success of the Ryder Cup. This is the first time I have asked for anything."

There is no question that Ballesteros's tactics were tantamount to emotional blackmail. But it's important to realize that there was nothing selfish about his motives. He wasn't doing it to glorify the name of Severiano Ballesteros. He was trying to achieve, sooner rather than later, the same dream he had been committed to ever since he became famous enough to make any impression at all on the powers that be—that of bringing golf to every village in Spain.

"I've been fighting for a long time to build more courses for the Spanish people," Ballesteros told *Today's Golfer*. "But the people with power do not understand how important golf is."

"You have a situation in Madrid where there's six and a half million people and a bus driver can't go and play golf," Carr explains. "There's only one place he can go and that's Club de Campo at twenty-five pounds a round. . . . And that's basically what he's saying: 'Let's build some golf courses.' Because for the man in the street, it's still in the classification of elitist. And that's not what he wants."

"Sadly, because golf is such an elitist game in Spain, I don't think Seve will find that his terrific world presence over the last fifteen years has had the impact on Spanish golf that it should have had," Jacklin observes. "Sad, because it's not a game for the people in Spain, it's a game for the hierarchy. I know how disappointed Seve was when he didn't get those municipal courses off the mark, and I think he had fallouts with the mayor up in his hometown. . . . It's very difficult. I think golf in Spain is run by such a small circle of people that they're the only ones he's getting the recognition from."

"I have met many liars in politics," Ballesteros says bitterly. "I particularly remember one of the mayors at one of the villages where I built a course, who promised me he would build a driving range for the village and two years later he forgot what he had told me and repeated the same promise. These people are unbelievable. I would not like to be in politics. Politicians are only interested in their own positions. For them, it is much easier to build a football stadium. They get more votes. Golf to them has the image of being a very elitist sport."

In May Ballesteros came to Britain for the B&H International. He had narrowly escaped missing the cut at the Spanish Open and, though he eventually finished tied for sixth, was becoming increasingly anxious about the state of his game. His performance at St. Mellion gave him good cause for alarm. He scored 68, 77, 73, 76, and finished forty-first. Olazábal won. The only bright spot in the week was the statement by Ryder Cup captain Bernard Gallacher, to the effect that the Tour had recommended that the event be held at Club de Campo in 1993. "To play the match in Spain would be a particular tribute to Seve Ballesteros for all he has done in Europe, and we think that to leave it until 1997 would be too late since there is a possibility that by then Seve would no longer be an automatic choice."

On May 24, 1990, at the PGA Championship at Wentworth, it was confirmed that the Ryder Cup would not be going to Spain in 1993. It would be going back to the monstrously overhyped, overrated, pseudo-American Belfry. It was understood that Lord Derby, who eventually resigned over the matter, had had the casting vote. At home in Pedreña, Ballesteros was distraught. He issued a statement to say that he was "very disillusioned" with the decision and that his "motivation would not be the same."

This caused an immediate uproar. Relations between the European Tour and the PGA were already strained to a breaking point, and further animosity would result in a revolution.

"I was bitterly disappointed that the '93 match did not go to Spain," Schofield said. "There was no good reason for it not happening. Tony Jacklin was 100 percent correct. You can't go on taking—a third of the team was Spanish in 1985—and not giving. The 1997 match will go to Spain. If we did make an error, and it's always easier in hindsight, then it was tying the bid to one golf course. It wasn't just Spain, it was Club de Campo, and obviously a lot of people, including leading players, were not certain that Club de Campo was the right venue."

"There are two main reasons for playing the Ryder Cup," Ballesteros said months later. "One is the competition between the Americans and the Europeans. The other is to use the Ryder Cup for the benefit of the game—to make the game bigger all over the world. And the only way to do that is to take it to places that need help. Golf in Britain and Ireland is already developed. The next step is Spain, because Spain is playing a big role not only in the Ryder Cup but also on the European Tour. Also, I always felt that to take that Ryder Cup to Spain in 1993 would have been a reward for myself—*agradecimiento*, we say in Spain. I feel that it was an opportunity to say: 'Hey, we feel that Seve has done a lot for the European Tour, we feel Seve has done a lot for European golf. We feel golf in Spain needs a lift.' "

This rational statement only came later, however, and the whole incident was threatening to escalate out of control when it was diffused, suddenly and unexpectedly, by Olazábal. In response to Ballesteros's comments about the possibility of him losing his motivation and interest in the Ryder Cup, he simply said calmly and with a maturity far beyond his years: "Well, he had to say that, didn't he? When he gets on the golf course I know he will give 110 percent. He wants to kill everyone. He won't need any motivation."

Wednesday, July 18, 1990, British Open Championship, St. Andrews. Six years after the sun had set on one of the most glorious battles the game has ever seen, Ballesteros, its conquering hero, pulled up a chair on the interview platform and beamed at the world's press. He was the picture of health and happiness. Recent weeks spent fishing, practicing, cycling, and watching the Tour de France on television had relaxed him, and he looked more at peace with himself than he had at any other time during that strife-torn year.

"It's always nice to be back at the place where I have so many good memories," Ballesteros said, eyes sparkling with pleasure. The previous evening he had run round at the R&A dinner like a small boy, merrily collecting autographs from fifteen past champions. "I must say, to win the Open is something special, but to win at St. Andrews, that's something very few people have the chance to do, and I'm fortunate to be one of them. If I had to pick one of my three Open Championships, I would definitely say this is the one. It's very special."

"How is your game compared to how it was coming into the Open at Royal Lytham?"

"Well, it's much the same as it was in 1984, and the same as it was in 1988. It's true that it's not been very good, but there's still half a year to go and anything can happen."

"But what's the matter with your game?" a reporter demanded.

The smile left Ballesteros's face. "There's nothing the matter with my game," he said curtly. "There's nothing the matter with my swing. It's just a matter of confidence."

An American reporter waved his pen in the air. "Your swing change," he asked, "is it complete?"

Ballesteros's mood changed as suddenly as a shadow slides over the sun. "People keep talking about my swing change," he snapped. "Why should I change my swing when I've been the best player for ten years?"

WAS THIS THE SAME MAN WHO HAD SHOWN THEM CALLOUSED HANDS ONLY TWO MONTHS BEFORE, WHICH HE SAID WERE THE RESULT OF HITTING THREE THOUSAND BALLS AT PEDREÑA?

The European press cast covert glances at one another. Was this the same man who had shown them calloused hands only two months before, which he said were the result of hitting three thousand balls at Pedreña while he tried to implement the third swing change of his career? Was this the same Seve Ballesteros who had told them at the Italian Open: "I decided it was time to make big changes and I've spent hours with my brothers Vicente and Baldomero looking at videos and films of my major victories to see what I was doing. When I first started golf I swung the club too upright and kind of tilted at the ball. I made corrections and went too far and began swinging too flat. The result of that was hitting a very bad pull-hook under pressure, and that has been a killer for me."

And after admitting it was that shot that had cost him victory at the 1986 Masters as well as at the 1989 Ryder Cup, where he had hit his approach shot into the water at the eighteenth to lose his singles match against Paul Azinger, he added: "I've felt uncomfortable with my swing the last couple of years, and my brothers and I have been working on the way I pick up the club and take it back. They are major changes but I think they are necessary."

By the time he reached Monte Carlo in June he was no longer speaking of swing changes but was experimenting instead with different putters. The Ping that had won him more than sixty tournaments worldwide and had ensured he became, earlier in the season, the first European golfer to pass the two-million-pound mark in earnings, had been tossed aside like a broken umbrella. A few days later it was set to work again. The new putter had failed to bring about the miraculous recovery he was hoping for.

All of these things had, it seemed, slipped Ballesteros's mind. He also had amnesia where David Leadbetter was concerned. At the Western Open in the U.S. he had sought the advice of the man who had helped make Faldo great. Afterward, Leadbetter commented: "He needed someone to talk to about what he's working on. It was just a case of listening."

As the year went on and Ballesteros sank deeper and deeper into the mire, he began clutching at straws. Leadbetter was required to do more than just listen. "Seve has always had to guard against going left," he said. "Even when he won the Open at Lytham in 1979, you could see he was fighting to hold the club on line. When he won the Open there in 1988 he hadn't been playing well for some time, but once he won that he was off and winning again. With him, it may just come down to confidence, but I don't really think he's played really well for four years. Seve still has a young man's swing, and it's hard for his body to cope with the power it generates. He has a perfect grip, a perfect setup, and wonderful rhythm, but he does tend to hit the ball while off balance, leading towards a reverse-C position in his follow-through."

"Seve should just tee it up and let it fly," was Jacklin's opinion. "My advice to him is to ignore everyone. There's only one guy that made him great and that's him."

Faldo thought that Ballesteros's excessive leg action put strain on his back, causing him pain. "He still has a very good backswing but he loses it on the downswing. He needs to slow down his aggressive leg action. He's contorting himself. He should be trying to hit the ball with very little bending of the spine."

But, for now, Ballesteros wasn't having any of it. "I think my swing has been good to me so far," he said with a scowl. "It's just confidence." And he stalked off to practice.

In the second round of the British Open, on a cool, changeable day, Doust went out with Manuel and old Dr. Campuzano to watch Ballesteros play. They strolled across the links, buffeted by the fresh wind. After the first round the Spaniard had been full of smiles. He had scored a one-under-par 71, which could, he insisted, have been a 69, had it not been for the double bogey he took at the Road Hole. Now his face had taken on that familiar I'd-rather-be-wrestling-alligators expression he had worn all season. He grimaced, he sighed, he looked out to sea, he complained of his sufferings to Vicente.

His elder brother, with whom he had never won so much as an egg-cup, was temporarily taking the place of Wright; the Englishman and Ballesteros had parted company at the U.S. Open. Wright insisted that it was a mutual and completely amicable separation. So, indeed, did the Spaniard. The caddie grapevine had it that the Englishman secured car and clothing contracts on the strength of his position as caddie to Ballesteros, and that those, as far as his boss was concerned, were the final nails in the coffin of their relationship.

Out on the gloomy links, the Spaniard chalked up another bogey.

"*Que paso?*" the good doctor asked. What's wrong?

"His problem is in his head," Manuel replied. "He listens to too many people."

"Does he listen to you?" Doust wanted to know.

"No," Manuel said. "I don't tell him anything. He doesn't listen to me."

Manuel, like everybody else, had his own theory as to why his brother had come crashing down so ignominiously. "Men are like motor cars. They show signs of breaking down at one hundred thousand miles. Seve has gone farther. He's gone two hundred thousand."

Fernandez agrees: "I kept telling him for many years that he was playing too many tournaments and traveling too much." He feels that because
Ballesteros puts so much pressure on himself on the course he suffers far
more stress than most players do. "In one year he won on every continent.
And I told him: 'Sooner or later, you're going to pay for it.' And I think it
took longer than I expected. I think I thought it would affect him six or
seven years before."

"He's much older than his age in that he's been playing a long time,"
Miller told Hopkins. "He's got to learn to pace himself. He should wash this
season down the drain, go home, and set a new game plan. He should take
six months off because he's losing his freshness."

Inevitably, there was speculation about the effect on Ballesteros's game
of married life—fueled by his insistence that something was destroying his
concentration on the golf course and his refusal to say what it was. "We always used to say if they get married they're no good for a year," Musgrove
says sardonically. "That was one of our old caddie theories. Big change in
your outlook. Especially if you've got to be single-minded to be at the top
and all of a sudden you've got somebody else to think of."

But Carr was convinced that he was just finding fame and its accom-
panying pressures harder to deal with. "He gets unmercifully harassed—not
by the professional journalists on the Tour—but by everybody all the time.
He's unmercifully harassed *all* the time. Can't go to the toilet, can't go and
have a meal, can't go to the golf course, can't go and have an hour's practice.
That's the price he pays. I mean, if you listen to a question that an unquali-
fied Spanish writer would ask, it's pathetic. You know, sneaking into his private life and stuff like that. He's a very private person, Seve, and he wants it
that way and he's entitled to that. He's had horrific encounters that nobody
would ever know about with the press—following him and this and that.
That's all part of the harassment factor."

All of these things, together with his court battles with Barner and
UMI which did not actually come to an end until April 25, 1990, undoubtedly took their toll, but only Manuel, walking beside Doust and Dr. Campuzano at St. Andrews and watching his brother take a double-bogey seven
from a bunker at the fourteenth for an eventual 74 and another missed cut,
touched on what the real reason for Ballesteros's decline might be. "He's not
as keen on his golf as when he was a boy," he told his companions. "If it
snowed, I can tell you, he would no longer practice in the snow."

In March 1990, the day before winning the Open de Baleares, his only victory all season, Ballesteros observed that "some people want to become champions and when they become a champion—once they have that and all the tension and all the pressure that comes with it—they cannot take it any more. So they escape from it. That's why they come down."

By autumn it was beginning to seem as if he himself had fallen victim to that very syndrome. At the U.S. PGA Championship at Shoal Creek he had shot a second-round 83—his worst round in fifteen years of major championship competition and the highest score he had recorded since the opening day of the French Open in 1979—which included nine bogeys and one triple bogey. Added to his first-round 77, it left him nine strokes shy of the cut. It was the fourth time he had failed to qualify in eight appearances in America.

From Birmingham, Alabama, Ballesteros flew to Birmingham, England, where he sat behind a microphone in the press center at the English Open looking as persecuted as a man can look, out of chains. He refused to discuss the U.S. PGA, his golf game, his personal life, or anything related in any way at all to his career. Everything except the weather was taboo.

"Apart from the concentration problem, are you happy with the way you are playing?" asked a reporter once we had explored the outer limits of meteorological conversation.

"I say-a that I just don't want to talk about that," Ballesteros said miserably.

His unhappiness was remarked upon.

"*Unhappy?*" Ballesteros echoed, as though he were the most cheerful man in the universe. "I'm not unhappy. I'm just not happy with the way things are going for me in golfing matters."

"His intensity to win is like a drug, you know," Carr explains. "And when he's not winning, he's not happy. He was born to win. It's nothing to do with the fact that he's in a bad humor, or he's a bad guy, or he's angry, or whatever. He just hates losing, which is an ingredient of the great players in all sports. So that part of him was misunderstood when he was going through that period. He was just angry at not winning."

"The problem is that I don't have the same degree of concentration that I used to have on the course," Ballesteros confided to Robert Green. "I have trouble keeping it up for eighteen holes. I now get distracted very quickly and very easily; my mind wanders off on to other things—like a movie I've seen or what I'm doing for dinner—and that never used to happen before. Then I start to hit more bad shots, and then I can never get my concentration or confidence back. The longer the round goes on, the worse things seem to get."

At the Belfry things degenerated to the extent where, in the last five holes of the English Open, he missed a two-foot putt and took a bogey six to lose the lead and ultimately the tournament. The following week he demanded an appearance fee of approximately one hundred thousand dollars, plus travel and accommodation expenses, to play in the German Open. On being refused it, he stayed at home in Pedreña, where Carmen gave birth to their first child. A month later, he appeared at the Lancome Trophy looking completely rejuvenated. It transpired that the joys of fatherhood were only partially responsible for this change of heart; he had also just beaten Manuel in a small local event in Spain and won two hundred pounds.

"More important than that," the Spaniard said with a grin, "I scored 71 and 66."

When the tournament ended, the smile had gone from his face. A visit to the pond on the eighteenth had cost him a double bogey, and victory, once again, had been denied him.

These were among the darkest days of Ballesteros's life. At the World Match Play at Wentworth in October, an event which he had dominated between 1981 and 1985 with his fearlessness, genius, and flair, he was twice humiliated: not only did he suffer the indignity of being unseeded for the first time in fifteen consecutive starts, he was also beaten 8 & 6 by Irishman Ronan Rafferty.

Ballesteros was devastated. Later, when that traumatic period was over, he said, "I was very aware that the golf I played was not that of Severiano Ballesteros. I felt as if it was not me out there, as if there was a devil inside me."

Looking at Ballesteros in his match against Rafferty, fretting and frowning, agonizing over club selection, hunching his shoulders, and biting his nails, it was hard to doubt his words.

When the season ended Ballesteros was seventh in the World Rankings and eighteenth on the European Order of Merit with earnings of £167,674. In three seasons he had missed five cuts in Europe, one more than he had missed in the preceding twelve years.

"My advice to Seve is to disappear for two or three months, get the swing right, work everything out," Faldo commented. "He's got nothing to prove any more."

"He hasn't got the yips," Miller told Hopkins. "He hasn't lost his nerve. He still wants to play. Golf is a game of misses. Seve was the best at recovering from them."

One morning Ballesteros, dejected, apathetic, and a shadow of his former self, looked in the mirror and said to himself: "Well, Seve, you have to do something to come back and be like you're supposed to be."

"And the only thing I did was work harder," he remembers. "And this is the key."

17

AFTER THE STORM

"We can secure other people's approval, if we do right and try hard; but our own is worth a hundred of it, and no way has been found out of securing that."

Mark Twain, *Following the Equator*

Monday, May 27, 1991, European PGA Championship, Virginia Water. Excitement swept through the Wentworth gallery like fire through a cane field. They poured down the seventeenth like an army of butterflies, past the last of the carefully screened mansions of celebrities and royalty, past the towering trees that separate green from tee, and then out onto the final hole where they formed a ragged and lively line along the fairway. Ballesteros came behind them, tense and absorbed. All afternoon he had courted danger without a qualm, thrilling the crowd with his great drives, bold escapes, and ingenuity around the greens. But at the sixteenth his audacity had caught up with him. He drove into the gallery and took bogey there, then blocked his drive into a grove of trees on the seventeenth, took two to reach the green and three more to get down, missing from four feet.

Now he felt nervousness take a firm grip on his heart. He had gone to pieces too often in this situation over the past year not to approach it with some trepidation. A fortnight earlier, he had scored a course-record 63 to lead the Spanish Open by five strokes after the first round, but had followed it with rounds of 70, 67, and 75, which allowed Eduardo Romero to catch him and force a playoff. The smiling Argentinean had triumphed after seven grueling holes at Club de Campo. "I had joy and sorrow today," Romero said. "Joy, because I won an important tournament. And sorrow, because I've beaten my friend and hero."

Ballesteros looked along the graceful curve of Wentworth's eighteenth fairway and made a conscious effort to force the image of that particular loss out of his head. He needed a birdie to catch Colin Montgomerie at 271, seventeen under par. "Seve," he said to himself, "you can't lose all the time. Something good must happen to you."

A few moments later it had. His approach shot flirted with a greenside bunker, but it landed safely and he chipped to seven feet. "I think if I had missed the putt on the last hole, that would have damaged my confidence," he said later, "because until the last three holes the tournament was in my hands."

As evening began to cast long shadows across the West Course, the Spaniard and Montgomerie made their way to the 471-yard, par-four first hole for the playoff, the vibrant crowd rushing ahead of them. Ballesteros, breathing deeply to try to settle his nerves, smashed his drive from the tee. Then a minor miracle occurred. As the ball hooked away toward rough, trees, and possible disaster, it collided with a parked golf cart. Ballesteros watched it spring into the light rough and felt his heart lift. It was a long time since fortune had smiled upon him. When he reached his ball it was lying on a slight slope, some 220 yards from the pin. He took a five-iron from the bag and, summoning every ounce of willpower he possessed, struck it smoothly into the crosswind with an easy, rhythmic swing. It soared over the shallow valley that crosses the fairway, pitched onto the green, and finished three feet from the pin. It was an awe-inspiring stroke.

"Given the situation, it was one of the best shots I've ever hit," Ballesteros said afterward. Montgomerie had no reply to it. He did, nevertheless, fight valiantly to the bitter end, hitting an exquisite chip and run to within inches of the hole before watching the Spaniard sink the putt for his first European victory in more than fourteen months.

The king was back and in full possession of his gifts.

When the 1990 season had drawn to a close, Ballesteros had reached the stage where victory was hardly in his reckoning. He had fought so long and so hard for so little reward, that he had grown weary and pessimistic. Caught up in this "thunderstorm," as he described it, he had been swept along, hurled about, and finally dashed upon the rocks of an ailing career and left for dead. There he had lain for several months, shell-shocked and weak—no longer capable of struggling. After a while, he had hauled himself to his feet and done what was required of him. He had punished himself with grueling workouts and marathon bicycle rides and runs. He had worked himself to a standstill on the practice range. And he had cut a sorry figure on Spanish television in December, explaining to viewers with much clearing of his throat that he had not been sufficiently prepared for the season, that his schedule had been wrong, and that he had changed clubs and they hadn't worked.

In February 1991 he had won a Skins game in the Canary Islands, and his confidence had begun to seep slowly back. But in the first week of March, the terrible pattern of 1990 had repeated itself. On practice days at the Doral Ryder Open in Florida, at the club where he had once been touring pro, Ballesteros had been very wild, even hitting a spectator. Gambling establishments had put him at 50-1, last in their list of favorites to win the tournament. He had justified their estimate by shooting 75, 78, and crashing out of the event, failing to qualify for the weekend by ten strokes. Next, he had returned to Europe to play the Open de Baleares, where he was defending champion. He confessed that he was in "bad health, low in confidence, and fighting a hook," and proceeded to compile rounds of 73, 75, 78, 68 to finish tied for thirty-third. The following week, he fumbled a one-handed tap-in from six inches to miss the cut by a stroke at the Catalan Open.

By then the idea that the king had lost his crown—that he would never ever be as great as he had once been—had become well and truly entrenched in public opinion. The media reminisced nostalgically about his glory days, the players talked of him in the past tense, and across Europe people described the man who had once been the most charismatic and exciting player since Palmer, as "ordinary." There was no more damning a word.

Then in the first week of May 1991, while steeling himself for a playoff and the possibility of losing yet another tournament, Ballesteros did what no one—least of all himself—was expecting: he holed a twenty-five-foot birdie putt to win the 120-million-yen Chunichi Crowns tournament in Japan by a stroke from Australian Roger Mackay. It was his sixty-first victory, and his first for fourteen months; ultimately, it marked a turning point in his career. Four things may have been responsible for it. One was the intensive coaching sessions he had had with Leadbetter at the Dunlop Open the previous week, from which it emerged that he should be trying to restrict the hip turn on his backswing; another was the metal woods he had begun using for the first time in his life ("I call it mental, not metal, because everybody thinks they can win more using it"); the third was his new Maxfli Tad Moore putter, which he had changed to after using a Ping Anser nearly all his professional life; and the fourth was the appointment of Billy Foster, his new caddie.

After Wright and he had parted by mutual agreement in August 1990, Ballesteros had not hired a regular replacement immediately. Instead, he had played out the season with a succession of sundry bag-carriers, among whom were a twenty-one-year-old hotel receptionist named Miguel, who helped him tie for twenty-first at the European Masters in Crans-sur-Sierre, and a local boy named Jonathan at the Epson Grand Prix. This last was considered so extraordinary that it triggered a discussion on how important a role he thought his caddie played in his success.

"Well," Ballesteros said, "I can give you a good example. At the French Open four years ago, my cousin was caddying for me for the first time, and for the first time he was walking on the golf course. He didn't know anything about golf. And I won and I shot 62, the course record. It shows something there." He laughed, pleased to have made his point. "But it's good to have a regular caddie," he added graciously, "because it's always good to have someone where you have confidence, and especially to talk to on the golf course. But the caddie in my case doesn't help very much. Not really."

He was asked what he demanded from the men who carried his bag: "Basically what I want from a caddie is staying quiet, having the right yardage, being there on time, and keeping up with me on the course. Some of them, they walk way behind."

Oddly enough, it was at the German Masters the very next week that Ballesteros approached Gordon Brand Jr.'s twenty-four-year-old caddie, Billy Foster, about working for him. Foster is a lithe, athletic Yorkshireman with a pleasant, easygoing manner and a ready smile. He is also thoroughly reliable and professional and, at the time the Spaniard spoke to him, had spent three years working for South African Hugh Baiocchi and five years with Brand Jr.

His aim was to retire at the end of the 1990 season, "get a decent job at home and play a bit of golf myself [he is a four-handicapper]." To this end, he had already handed in his notice. Ballesteros told him he was too young to quit caddying, and offered him a job the following season.

"I was very, very nervous," Foster says, recalling their first tournament together, at Doral. "I sat by the locker room with Pete Coleman, and Pete says, 'Oh, you'll be all right,' and I'm sort of shitting myself, you know. And a few footsteps come behind me and Pete says, 'Oh, he's here,' and I'm sort of 'this is him, the Great Man!' Turned round and he had a big smile on his face, and he said: 'How are ya doin', mate?' And straight away I felt a bit more at ease. Went out to practice and had a real good talk with him and felt as though I got to know him a little bit."

Foster's impression of Ballesteros before he started working for him was that he was "a bit intimidating. He's sort of like one of the best players there's ever been, and to be out in his company, you feel a bit dwarfed. In golfing terms he's royalty, isn't he? So, I mean, you feel six inches tall. But once you get to know him, he's just another human being. He's a super bloke. I find him funny. . . . He's a kind bloke. I think we get on so well because I might be a bit different. I'm very much down to earth with him, you know. A bit abrupt really. He ain't used to that. I go up and say, 'Now then, kid, how ya doing?' I guess it's a bit different."

But whether the sea–change in Ballesteros's career was due to the unique, almost brotherly relationship he formed with Foster, Leadbetter's coaching, his new putter, or his metal woods, it manifested itself in Japan with that twenty-five-foot birdie putt.

"When you hole a putt like that your confidence comes back," Ballesteros said with relief. "I also had no three-putts throughout the tournament. That is very important. Winning broke the barrier that was in front of me."

Four days after winning the PGA Championship at Wentworth, Ballesteros came into the Dunhill Masters press tent at Woburn looking irrepressibly cheerful and wearing, for reasons known only to himself, two hats: a tweed cap was pulled down over his hair; a blue Paddington Bear hat was perched at a jaunty angle on top of it. To complete the effect, he had on a scarlet shirt and a maroon sweater. There had been great hopes for an improvement in his dress sense when he married, but thus far Carmen has failed to exert her influence (if indeed she has any).

"Where did that tweed hat come from?" the press officer asked.

"It came from Scotland," said Ballesteros, who had just had seven birdies in the second round for a second consecutive 66 and was leading the field by four strokes. "Scottish hat." He winked and tapped the top of the press officer's balding head. This one would cover you a little bit," he suggested teasingly.

"IT MIGHT LOOK THE OTHER WAY BUT I'M A VERY HUMBLE PERSON, AND YOU NEED TO BE LIKE THAT IN THIS GAME."

"Why do you think you're playing so well, Seve?"

"My attitude is very good on the golf course. I'm very positive. I'm playing very steady and I'm not making any mistakes out there. I think I've played the last month nearly as good as I can play. I feel that I have a lot of fun out there and the good thing about it is that when I wake up in the morning I'm looking forward to going out to play."

"During the time you felt bad about playing, did you stop practicing?"

"I promise you last year I was practicing more than ever," Ballesteros said sincerely. "I tell you what, this game is not easy. There's a lot of frustration when things aren't going your way. It's not as easy as some people may think. It might look the other way but I'm a very humble person, and you need to be like that in this game. Golf, sometimes it becomes very tough, so you've got to be humble and you've got to walk with both feet on the ground."

No doubt about it, Ballesteros was back. Gone was the morose and sulky Spaniard of 1990, the black moods, the great man at odds with the universal press conferences, the "Why me?" grimaces on the course. In their place were the old piratical grin and the gentle, rather wry sense of humor that makes him so human and so likable. On the golf course, too, he was a new man. Drama and lighthearted adventure surrounded every one of his rounds, as he lashed from the tee, prowled about wearing theatrical expressions of anguish in the bushes, and conjured up wonderful little chip shots and recoveries. It was no surprise that great crowds flocked to Woburn to relive the past—to see Ballesteros play golf again the way he had done when he first won their hearts. And to the casual observer, he really did. It was only when you looked closer that you could detect a hint of caution and a kind of frailty that had never been there when he was young and dauntless.

But these did not detract in any way from the shot-making skills that have always made watching him such joy, and that were shown to the fullest advantage in the closing stages of the Dunhill Masters. After three rounds of the tournament Ballesteros had had a seven-stroke advantage, and might have led by two more had not Eamonn Darcy eagled the eighteenth on the third day. These strokes he squandered on a bogey at the second in the final round, a double bogey at the third, and another bogey at the fourteenth. Nevertheless, he still had a four-shot lead when he stood on the fifteenth tee on that bleak and rainy afternoon. Then he proceeded to hook his drive deep into a forest, where it came to a halt only a whisker from out of bounds.

Foster followed him worriedly into the trees. "He had no shot," he recalls. "I'm thinking, Chip out up t' fairway. Then he said, 'Just pull the stakes out up there'—about a hundred yards up in the trees. So I've gone up and pulled them out and I've looked and thought: 'The only gap I can see over there is about two feet.' And he pulled a one-iron out the bag and sort of hit it left of this tree and slicing. I'm standing over on the other side of the fairway. And about a hundred yards up the fairway this ball's appeared, and it's somehow raced across the fairway and gone into the greenside trap. Up and down. Par. Yeah, nice one, Sev."

One bogey and two pars later, Ballesteros won his second tournament in seven days by three strokes.

When Foster had first picked up Ballesteros's bag at Doral he, like most other people, had had a very good idea of what the Spaniard was capable of. Yet after months of working for him, he had still not ceased to be astounded at the creativity and genius of his recoveries. "Some of the shots he played were just miraculous. Unbelievable. Not many other guys would come close to even attempting them, and he'd pull them off. The imagination and the feel of some of them was scary." One example was a shot Ballesteros had played at a par-five in Japan, after he had hooked his drive and then had a flyer out of the rough into a dark and impenetrable forest. From where he stood, the only chink of daylight was a three-foot gap about twenty yards ahead of him, which was practically blocked by a stanchion that held up one of the trees. The most realistic exit route was behind him.

"I'm thinking, 'Well, there's just no shot,' " Foster recalls. "Get out backwards and make six if we can. And he says, 'Have you got a yardage?' And I'm thinking, 'A yardage? What do you want a yardage for?' I sort of walked over there and got a couple of numbers and said, 'You've got 220 yards to the front of the green.' He said, 'Give me a two-iron.' I've given him a two-iron and I've walked a hundred yards to the other side of the fairway and I'm thinking, 'Oh, Jesus Christ! This is an eight or a nine, this. If it hits the tree, it's just staying in there all day.' At the time he was more or less leading the tournament. And he's hit this two-iron out of the trees and he's somehow managed to get out through this gap and he's come out, and then there's a fifty-foot tree in the middle of t' fairway—it goes over that and soaring onto the green. I'm on the other side of the fairway, just laughing. I couldn't believe it. He comes out of the trees, big grin on his face. I said to him, 'A magician couldn't have played that shot!' He just laughed. He made par there as well."

Just how extraordinary Ballesteros's gift is for envisaging shots which are, in theory, inconceivable, can be measured by the fact that other professionals go out in their hundreds to see him play.

"I don't watch golf," David Feherty insists. "I don't watch golf at all. The Ryder Cup is the first golf that I've actually gone out and watched in fifteen years. But I would go and watch him. He has the most incredible imagination for the game. You know, if you can visualize it, you can do it; and he has the power to visualize the most extraordinary things."

"I remember seeing two things that really just stunned me about Seve," says Tony Johnstone, a Zimbabwean. "One was at the Scandinavian Open in 1980. On the fourth hole he hooked his second shot with a three-wood and buried it under the lip of the bunker. But it had gone into the *earth*—not the sand—into the earth lip. The whole ball was in the ground. You could only see the ball from inside the bunker. And he stood there and we thought, 'Oh, well, that's an unplayable lie. He's got to take a drop.' Well, he went through

every club in his bag except the woods, and he eventually decided on a putter. He turned his Ping putter on its toe, took a swing at it, and took a piece
of ground out the size of a brick. I mean, it was just not the sort of shot you
could have ever practiced. It just came to him. An inspirational shot. With
the toe of his Ping, he just smashed at it; the ball came out at a hundred
miles an hour, ran up the face of the bunker, hopped out, rolled down to
about ten feet and he holed it for a birdie. I walked in. I couldn't handle it. I
thought, 'Well, that's it. What am I doing out here?'

"The second time was at Chepstow a few years ago," Johnstone continues. "It was late evening and he was down at the chipping green with
Manuel, his brother, and he was just hitting trick shots. He was hitting balls
with a seven-iron standing at right angles to the green with the face wide
open and just catching the ball on the toe. And they were almost going at
right angles to him, but high and soft and landing on the green and spinning
backward. It was unbelievable. At one stage he was aiming straight at the
restaurant. I mean, if he had made a mistake it was going to end up in some
guy's soup at four hundred miles an hour. . . . Then he started stamping the
ball into the ground and hitting shots. You know, it's against the bounds of
science, but he was hitting shots with a ball that was entirely, 100 percent
underground. He was hitting these shots and getting them to come out high
and soft and land, then run three or four feet. I mean, it can't be done. It can't
be done. But he was doing it."

Until Collet took over his management and virtually eliminated his
company outings and golf days, Ballesteros's clinics were legendary. No
player in the world could equal him as a trick-shot artist. The day after he
won the British Open in 1984, he was on his knees at the Old Course—after
only three hours' sleep—hitting two-hundred-yard drives before fifty open-
mouthed businessmen. Later, he was taken by helicopter to the Belfry where,
having amusingly impersonated Trevino, Nicklaus, and Palmer, he put on a
breathtaking display of trick shots. The touch and ball skill he showed during such performances were as much proof of his greatness as anything he
did on the course.

"He has that Sam Snead talent," Crenshaw says enviously. "Sam Snead
just absolutely looks like: Here is the golfer. This is *the* way you're supposed
to look. This is the way you're supposed to play. And there's almost no weaknesses in their game. Bobby Jones had that kind of talent. Gifted is probably
a better word in Seve's case. He's got a wonderful physique. He has long arms

and he has wonderful hands. He's got his tremendous heart and the brains that go with it. He's also a player that's never been satisfied with what he's done. Ever."

Ballesteros had every reason to be proud of himself in 1991. In the fifteen events he played between the Dunlop International Open in April and the European Masters in September, he won three times and was only twice out of the top ten. His scoring average was 68.65. He was third in the Dunlop in Japan, second in the Spanish Open, tied for fifth in the Buick Open, tied for tenth in Monte Carlo, tied for eighth in the Scottish Open, tied for ninth in the British Open, second in the Scandinavian Masters, and tied for third place at the European Open and in Crans-sur-Sierre. He only had two disastrous tournaments—the U.S. Open in June and the U.S. PGA Championship in August.

His success could not be put down to any one particular factor. Rather, it was due to a dozen small things, all of which combined to make him more positive and confident on the course. Regular supervision from his coach, for instance, helped a great deal. Leadbetter felt he had "a couple of big flaws. I tightened up his swing. It was weak and sloppy; it had lost all its torque. He's still off line with some shots but before he was short, too. I also got him to open his stance a little when he was putting."

As the season went on and Ballesteros's form held and he continued to play with his old fire and enthusiasm, he became philosophical about past misfortunes and could explain more lucidly what had happened to him in 1990. "Everyone suffers a slump," he told *The Independent*. "Nicklaus did, Watson, everyone. Why should Ballesteros be the exception? Maybe it's a bit surprising it didn't happen sooner. I've had fifteen years of traveling, expectation, pressure. Also, I didn't play enough competitive golf. I'd be in one or two tournaments and then have a week off. It was stupid. I was trying to stay fresh but all I did was leave myself without time to find rhythm, to get sharp. I've learned the lesson. There are so many good players in Europe and America that you can't afford to stay away from tournament play too long. If you do, no matter how good you are or how big the reputation, you will suffer."

Altogether, Ballesteros was a far more amiable person throughout that season than he had been in years. Off the course he lowered his guard and became more approachable, and his willingness to help other players and to participate more in Tour life and in the good-natured banter of the practice range earned him new respect from his colleagues.

"I never really got to talk to him until a few years ago," Feherty says. "I mean, now we can sit and have a conversation. In those days, it was like talking to God. To be very, very good and to dominate in this game, you have to have an exceptionally high opinion of yourself. You know, that's a prerequisite. And that's often confused for arrogance or conceit. There were times when I might have thought he was that way, but having played with him in the Ryder Cup [1991], we saw the human side of him much more. He was a tremendous influence on all of the U.S. that week. You saw the vulnerable side of him. He was willing to open up and say, 'You are going to feel that way, we all feel that way. Don't let it worry you.'"

"He was pretty much like Nick Faldo for a long, long time," Mark James comments. "Very guarded, almost secretive. It's only the last probably two or three Ryder Cups that quite a lot of the players have got to know him at all. He's pretty much like Faldo. I'd say they're very similar personalities."

"Trevino, many years ago, lived like a hermit almost," Sandy Lyle remembers. "He'd give his all on the course and he'd give autographs, but when he was away from the course he got to the stage where he'd lock himself away in the room. Seve's a bit like that in some ways."

"I don't think he's the type of guy that you would ever get to know," Scotsman Stephen McAllister says. "I don't think he wants anybody to get to know him. I respect that."

"I don't really rate him—as a bloke," Australian Wayne (Radar) Riley says with a scowl. "I don't think he's got any time for any other people. I don't think he's got any time for our young players. I think he just walks straight by you in the locker room without even saying hello to you. I think he's rude. I think he's arrogant. That's probably what makes him so good."

"I never used to like him, but I do now," Malcolm Mackenzie says. "He never used to talk to anybody. But he does now. He talks to everybody now. He'll talk to rookies now, which he never used to. And if he sees a good swing on a rookie he'll go over and he'll say, 'You swing good, hey.' So he's helping youngsters, which is good."

When the season came to an end Ballesteros was, indisputably, the best. He had overcome Price in the final of the World Match Play to equal Player's record of five titles; he was the No. 1 player in Europe, and he had won the Vardon Trophy for a record sixth time with earnings of £744,236, and he was fourth in the World Rankings. "The key in golf is consistency," he said—"to make the putts and be good under pressure. And you've got to have a big heart. It is more important to have a big heart than a great swing."

One incident in particular illustrates how much Ballesteros was enjoying the game again. It took place on a summer's evening after the final round of the Scottish Open. The Tour caravan had already moved on to Birkdale for the Open Championship, and only a handful of players remained at Gleneagles. Mark Roe, who was one of them, took his sand wedge and putter and wandered out to the putting green beside the hotel. After a time, he looked up and saw a tall figure coming eagerly across the green toward him. It was the Spaniard.

"Do you want to have a game?" he asked Roe.

"With pleasure," the Englishman replied with a smile.

"Right," Ballesteros said, taking charge. "We'll play for one pound."

They played as twilight closed in, the Spaniard winning the first nine holes, Roe winning the next, and so on.

"That hour that I spent with him is something that I'll always treasure," Roe says. "It was wonderful. It was like being out there with a friend. And the banter was lovely. You know, he was trying to wind me up as much as I was trying to wind him up. He was at ease. And it's just a side of him that 99 percent of people would never get to see. It was almost like being out there with somebody who was sixteen years of age, you know, and you were kids and you were chipping around as juniors. It was a lovely side of him to see. We played until it went pitch black, then we had to finish because we couldn't see the flags. But even then, as we walked up the hill toward the hotel, he still dropped two balls down and turned round and said, 'Here, I'll show a little shot.' And I marveled at his enthusiasm, I really did. I think all that really matters to Seve, and all that has ever mattered, is the game of golf."

At the end of the evening, Ballesteros was up three pounds. He departed in the best of all possible moods, and Roe did not have the chance to play with him again until they were drawn together at the European Open at Sunningdale in September the following year. He walked onto the first tee, waited for the starter to announce the players' names, then turned to the Spaniard and wished him luck. Ballesteros returned the favor. "Shall we play for the three pounds that I won at Gleneagles?" he asked the astounded Roe.

A year and two months after the Scottish Open, when the "thunderstorm" had once again descended upon Ballesteros, the memory of that one perfect hour on the putting green provided a welcome light for him at the end of an increasingly hard day's night.

18

HEAD TO HEAD

"If you're a winner, you've got to be as hard as nails. The softest thing about you's got to be your teeth. And I learnt that playing in the States. I learnt very early on, that you've got to be single-minded and determined and tough. Very tough."

Tony Jacklin, *Jacklin Speaks*

The loyalties of the gallery were clearly divided. They looked from the old maestro to the young master and back again with growing consternation; but in the end it was Arnold Palmer, for he was the certain victor, to whom they accorded a hero's welcome as he walked down Wentworth's eighteenth fairway.

He acknowledged them with a wave of one great paw, his nut-brown face wreathed in smiles. At nearly fifty-four, it was almost more than he could have hoped for—to cross swords with this Spanish magician in the first round of the 1983 World Match Play and come out on top. "I'm looking forward to it," he had told the press on the eve of the tournament. I don't have many more matches like this coming up, matches which have this kind of value or distinction. Heck, I'm a grandfather. I've got a daughter older than he is."

Thus far it had been an excellent match. Apart from a brief spell at the fourth and fifth holes, where Ballesteros had birdied to go to one up, Palmer had been in control the entire way. The only slightly disconcerting thing was that he had missed putts to win holes on the thirteenth and fifteenth and had failed to match the Spaniard's birdie on the par-five seventeenth, which meant that he was one ahead when he teed off the last instead of two. He cast a glance at his opponent, who was prowling up and down, considering the lie of the land. Palmer turned away to prepare for his own shot. What did it matter, anyway? The match was won.

Ballesteros did not share Palmer's optimism. Having defied doctor's orders to play in the event in the first place (he had a virulent dose of flu), he now felt a kind of ruthless determination to be the victor at all costs. Victory, however, required an eagle and, after fading his drive, clipping the trees with his second shot to finish fifty yards short of the pin, it seemed an unlikely prospect. Still, he had everything to gain by trying. He addressed the ball and whipped it away with an easy, rhythmic swing. Up it went in a graceful arc and then down, down, down, a couple of bounces and into the hole.

"Oh, shit!" Palmer said distinctly and with feeling.

Ballesteros, his face alive with joy, just stood on the fairway and let the applause wash over him. The match went to extra holes and he won with a birdie at the twenty-first.

In years to come, when the finest players of this era have become the legends of the last, literature will show that while some have won more major championships than Ballesteros and others have earned more money, none apart from Gary Player have been his equal in head-to-head competition. That is because few men have been quite as obsessed with victory. No player revels more than he in the psychological warfare that is match play; no one is as adept at the freak shot, the unexpected twist, at the long climb back from the point of no return; and no one thrives more on the thrill of the chase, the bloody clash, and the moment of reckoning.

From the very first time that Ballesteros, aged eight, dropped a pebble on the ground and challenged all comers to strike it farther and more skillfully than he, he has been consumed by the desire to be the best. Throughout his career it has goaded him, gnawed away at him, and driven him to perform feats almost beyond comprehension. And it is this quality, more than anything else, that has made him the champion that he is. "Wherever he goes to play or whatever he's playing for, he wants to win and he tries to win," Fernandez says. "For example, in Argentina (exhibition tournament, March 1992), we played for nothing. He got appearance money, of course. He played for nothing but he wanted to win as much as if it were for a million dollars. And that's what makes him great. Because wherever he goes he wants to win and he works hard to win. Even in practice rounds, whenever we play for a coffee or a drink, he tries his heart out. When he's on the golf course, it's business. Which you don't see in other players."

THROUGHOUT HIS CAREER IT HAS GOADED HIM . . . AND DRIVEN HIM TO PERFORM FEATS ALMOST BEYOND COMPREHENSION.

"Great competitor, great competitor!" Trevino says with a laugh. "Oh my God, he hates to lose. I don't care if you're shooting marbles or playing pool or throwing darts, he wants to win. That's good. I don't have it in anything else. Seve has it in everything else, whether it's a foot race or what. If he's sitting with you in a room playing cards, he wants to win."

Dobereiner once said that in all his years he had never met another human being with Ballesteros's competitive drive: "Winning is his whole life and it does not matter whether it is on the golf course or playing shove half-penny, or arguing whether Maradona is the best footballer in Spain." In 1983 Dobereiner offered two examples. The first incident occurred during the Italian Open. He was sitting on the steps of his hotel, waiting for a courtesy car, and playing with a plastic toy in the form of a miniature racetrack. You wound it up, twiddled a knob, and attempted to steer a car safely through a series of chicanes. Each collision was recorded in a small window. If you completed the course without touching an obstacle, the symbol of a crown appeared in the window.

"Ballesteros," Dobereiner recalled, "strolled out and said: 'Let me try.' I would have said that it was impossible to get anywhere with the thing without resting it on a firm surface, but he held it in the palm of his left hand and started twiddling. "Shit!" He rewound and tried again. The car arrived. "Shit!" He sat in the back, absorbed by this new challenge. The twenty-minute journey through the hilly Tuscany countryside with an Italian at the wheel was not exactly tranquil. Ballesteros was totally absorbed by the toy.

His all-purpose expletive preceded each of about fifty rewindings. As we drew into the driveway of the Ugolino club he tossed the toy at me, along with a grin of satisfaction. The crown was in the window.

"Later in the year, at the Scandinavian Open, he was staying at the home of the sponsor and he was introduced to the game of pool. He was partnered with a good player, in opposition to two moderate ones. For his first few attempts he made a bridge for the cue with his left hand held about a foot off the surface of the table. They were playing for token bets and Ballesteros's side lost constantly, although he quickly picked up the rules and basic technique. 'We double the bets,' he announced. Ballesteros took charge of the team. He commanded his more experienced partner which ball to hit, which pocket to select, how hard to strike. He chided him for leaving the cue ball out of position. They played on and on, doubling the bets. Ballesteros ran out of small change. He went to his bedroom and returned with more money. Double up again. At last Ballesteros and his partner won a frame. Ballesteros picked up his winnings, representing a profit of a few pence on the evening, and announced: 'I have to play golf tomorrow. Good night.' "

In 1984, at the time the feud between Ballesteros and Langer was at its height, a friendly soccer match between the Spanish players and the Rest of the World was arranged after the Spanish Open at El Saler. The Spaniard captained his national team, and the German was at the helm of the foreigners. Stories of Ballesteros's aggression on the pitch that day, his monopolization of the ball, and his absolute determination to win, are part and parcel of Tour lore. The final score was 2-2, and postmatch celebrations included Ballesteros being thrown into the swimming pool.

It is this yearning for battle that has made Ballesteros one of the greatest match players of all time. His tenacity, fearlessness, and ability to haul himself back time and time again from the abyss of self-destruction have brought him five World Match Play titles—an achievement matched only by Player—and his exploits in them are legendary.

In 1982, for instance, the year after his first World Match Play victory, he met Lyle in the final at Wentworth. He was three up after eighteen holes and retained his advantage until the thirty-second, where Lyle won the hole with a birdie two. It was a wild and stormy day. Rain teemed down unpleasantly as they trudged home, but Lyle's valiant struggles earned him the fifteenth and sixteenth holes and the match was level after thirty-six holes.

They splashed to the first playoff hole in the dying afternoon. Lyle hit a booming drive up the center of the fairway; Ballesteros pulled his into the left rough. They marched purposefully from the tee. The Spaniard's recovery was remarkable, a three-wood smashed to thirty feet. Lyle had reached the back of the green with a one-iron and was less than half that distance from the pin. They waited while the green was squeegeed, for there were four or five puddles on Ballesteros's line. When the putting surface was almost clear, he replaced his ball, studied the borrow and, without further ado, sank the putt.

"That's just Seve," Lyle says admiringly. He missed his own putt to lose the match. "You can expect that."

"I've seen him pull off some of the darnedest shots I've ever seen in my life," says Crenshaw, whose weakness has always been his reverence for great players. He lost by a hole to Ballesteros in 1981 and then crashed to a 9 & 8 defeat in the semifinals in 1984. "In the '81 World Match Play final he hit two of the greatest shots I've ever seen. He hit it left in the trees on the twelfth—the par-five. I was on the right side of the fairway and I could see these people go in and watch him try to play the shot. There was a little lane. He was right up against the tree. He had no stance and he had to take the club and play it backward. I think he took a three- or four-iron. I saw him in there and he was taking these great big swings. And he hit this ball and it went off and hooked up the fairway and went forward about 170 yards. I was dumbfounded. So were the people watching. And then in the afternoon he hit a one-iron second shot on number three. He was just over the ball and almost ready to hit when the wind came up a lot harder. And he merely put the ball a little bit farther back in his stance and he hit this shot about four feet from the hole. His instinct is incredible.

"What's he like to play match play against? Oh, God! Oh, he's extremely formidable because, you know, he's never in trouble. You say, 'How the heck am I going to win a hole from this guy?' He's a very tough match player."

"Oh, in his day he was evil," Faldo says, laughing. "In a nice sense," he adds quickly. "It didn't matter where he hit it, he was always going to be in the hole. And if you gave him half a chance he'd be chipping in and he'd be holing ninety-footers and doing this and doing that. In the early days I did find him intimidating, yes. In the early days, you know, in match play, you'd think: How the hell am I going to beat this guy? Even when he's out of the hole he's in the hole. And it wasn't until '89 that I beat him [semifinals, 6 & 5]. I actually beat him on the fact that I knew his swing wasn't right. I thought, 'He's got a fault, keep the pressure on.' And it worked."

"I played against him in the World Match Play," Watson remembers with a wry smile. "He beat me pretty soundly there [5 & 4, second round, 1977]. In match play he's just like he is in medal play. He's very intense on the course. I think because of his intensity sometimes things bother him more than they should."

The *Oxford Dictionary* defines the word *gamesmanship* as "the art of winning contests by upsetting the confidence of one's opponent." When Langer described Ballesteros as "intimidating," it was this that he was taken to mean. Consequently, there was a great furor because golf is a game of honor and integrity, and gamesmanship is a cardinal sin. But how does one define gamesmanship more specifically? Is gamesmanship practicing your putting within your playing partner's field of vision when he is trying to concentrate on his own stroke?—which is what Langer accused Ballesteros of doing. Is it making contemptuous remarks about the inferior quality and flight of an opponent's ball on the first tee of a tournament? Or is it simply coughing when you shouldn't be coughing at all?

"I think a lot of the things that people say about him are uncalled for because I've never found him to be a bad sport or to have any other kind of gamesmanship or anything," says Price, who played against Ballesteros in the 1991 World Match Play final only a month after coughing, among other things, had caused a row at Kiawah Island. "I think he's the kind of person that if perhaps you do throw up the gloves he might throw them back at you. But I've never done that. And if he'd done that [practiced his putting], I would have told him. I don't think he ever does anything like that on purpose. I might be wrong."

The Spaniard and the amiable Zimbabwean met at Wentworth in the final, after the former had overcome Couples and Billy Andrade, and the latter Steven Richardson, Baker-Finch, and Faldo. Both men were at the top of their games; both were looking forward to the fight. "On the first tee, I said to Nick, 'Let's have another Lytham,' " Ballesteros recalls. "Then when he birdied three of the first four holes, I thought: 'Shit, he must be really mad at me.' "

But he managed to claw his way back and by the fifteenth he had squared the match. Two holes previously, however, at which point Price was still one up, a curious incident had taken place. Ballesteros had been standing on the fairway eating a piece of fruitcake while he waited for the Zimbab-wean to play his approach shot and, just as Price had initiated his backswing, a crumb had gone down the wrong way and he choked. Price's ball veered off into a bunker.

"First of all, to be totally honest with you, I don't think it affected my shot at all," admits Price, who eventually lost 3 & 2. "Because once I'm committed to hit the ball I go ahead and hit it. I looked around and . . . his eyes were glassy. So I knew he'd coughed. I knew that it wasn't a put-on. And I suppose with what I'd heard had been going on in the Ryder Cup—some of the American guys had been saying that Seve had this little cough that he put on—I had kind of looked for it the first five or six holes, but it never came out. I didn't know because match play is a little different sometimes. And he said to me then: 'Replay your shot.' [The referee informed him that that was impossible under the rules of the game.] I said, 'Oh, no, I can't do that.' And then when I walked up to the green, I hit it in the bunker. He was on the back of the green and he said: 'Let's take a half and go.' I sort of thought about it for a second and then I said, 'No, let's just play. It's fine.' And we played the hole out and halved it anyway. But I think that pretty much summed up how we felt about one another. It was like, the guy who played the best golf was going to win that day. And that's why I enjoyed it so much."

Says Mark McNulty, Price's compatriot: "Obviously, he wants to win. That's intimidating enough. Any great golfer, they can make themselves intimidating if they want to. Gary [Player] could be more intimidating than Seve ever was. But they're in the same mold, put it that way."

"I enjoy playing with him," says Australian Rodger Davis, one of the few men to have comprehensively beaten Ballesteros at match play. "I like watching some of the stuff he does—as a pro. I try not to let him get to me. And he's not trying to, you know. He's not doing it on purpose. It's just his natural way.

"He [used to] give off that aura that he was going to win and you had to try and stop that somehow in your mind. The way I did it when I played him in the World Match Play and I beat him 7 & 6 [second round, 1986]—admittedly, I had to play really well to do it—was by realizing that, if I watched him and watched his body language, I felt a little intimidated. So I didn't watch him. I just watched about ten yards in front of him, right, and when the ball took off through that ten yards I watched where it went—just in case he did hit one off line so I could help him find it, right. But that just stopped me looking at him. And he actually said to me after the match, he did notice that I wasn't looking at him.

"And maybe that got to him a little bit."

September 27, 1987, Muirfield Village, Columbus, Ohio. Red and blue stripes bobbed nautically on a sea of swirling color. Once or twice an arm had tried to wave a European flag, but it had fallen back helplessly when a roar went up and the tide of spectators moved on to the next fairway. The patriotism of the Americans went unrewarded. On the leaderboard the numbers changed: Europe 13½, U.S. 11½.

How different this Ryder Cup was from all those that had gone before it. How frenzied and how electric. Ballesteros, who through his commitment and presence, had done more than any other player to help generate this fervor, felt the difference, and was uplifted by it. He had known since the fifteenth hole, where he had holed an eight-foot putt to stay two up in his match against Strange, that the fate of Samuel Ryder's trophy was in his hands. Europe might have retained it, but they still needed a point to win it. He quickened his stride and hardened his resolve. Once he had said: "If you ever feel sorry for somebody on a golf course, you better go home. If you don't kill them, they'll kill you." Now, as they walked up the seventeenth fairway, there was a merciless glint in his eyes, and Strange would not have been human if he hadn't felt afraid when he saw it. The end, assuredly, was near.

In the Ryder Cup competition, all of the skills that made Ballesteros the world's greatest match player are heightened and sharpened to an astonishing degree. When he committed himself to the matches he committed

IN THE RYDER CUP COMPETITION, ALL OF THE SKILLS THAT MADE BALLESTEROS THE WORLD'S GREATEST MATCH PLAYER ARE HEIGHTENED AND SHARPENED TO AN ASTONISHING DEGREE.

281

himself absolutely; and it is his passion, his enthusiasm, and his achievements, combined with Jacklin's own talent and industry as captain and the sudden revival of American interest in the matches, that has made the Ryder Cup one of the extraordinary sporting spectacles on earth. He fought his heart out for a European victory in 1983. He cried when they drew. And when the European team convened at the Belfry in 1985, he and Jacklin whipped them into a state of rare euphoria, convincing them not only that they were no longer the underdogs in world golf, but that they, if anything, were the dominant players.

"We built on the experience of 1983 and we were sure that we were going to win in '85," Jacklin recalls. "I would never have said that before because you're always apprehensive and you put more pressure on yourself by saying it, but Seve and I were the backbone of the team, Langer and Faldo (we didn't get the performance out of Faldo in '85, he was going through a divorce), we made it happen, nevertheless. We were very sure and very confident, and that was a step to winning in '87 again. It all evolved very quickly, but it all evolved from applying ourselves positively to each area that needed attention."

"I think if [Seve] hadn't come along it would have been a different story," Ken Brown says positively. "He was the catalyst that made it all happen."

In 1985 Ballesteros, paired with Piñero after his original partner, Jose Rivero, "lost his driving" in practice, led the Europeans to battle in the first day's foursomes. Their opponents, Strange and Mark O'Meara, were four down after six holes but fought their way back to be two down after nine. Ballesteros then drove the green on the tenth for birdie to return to three up, and the Europeans won 2 & 1 on the seventeenth. In the afternoon the Spaniards won again, beating U.S. Open champion Andy North and Peter Jacobsen, 2 & 1, after Ballesteros had squared the match with a birdie on the fifth, a drive to eight feet at the tenth (almost holing the putt for an eagle two), and a pitch to three feet at the seventeenth. The rest of the European team had struggled in the foursomes, and when play was over the Americans led, 4½ to 3½.

When Sunday came, there had been a reversal of fortune. Europe led by two points. Ballesteros and Piñero had lost 3 & 2 in the second day's fourballs to O'Meara and Wadkins, but administered a crushing defeat to Stadler and Hal Sutton 5 & 4 in the foursomes. In the singles matches on the last day the Spaniard, resplendent in red, found himself three down with five to play against Kite. With a supreme effort, he sank a huge putt from the back of the fourteenth green to win a hole, followed it with wonderful birdies at the fifteenth and seventeenth, and was still furious with himself when his putt for a win slipped past the cup on the eighteenth and all he could manage was a half. It was incredible golf. The overall score at that point was: Europe 13½, U.S. 8½. Then North, tall, slim, and out of form, hit his drive to the last into the water. Sam Torrance, his rival, burst into tears of joy and, upon reaching the green amid scenes of great jubilation, sank the putt that won the Ryder Cup for Europe for the first time since 1957.

Ballesteros was almost overcome with emotion. "I feel like I won another British Open," he said. "It was fantastic. Tremendous."

There is no doubt that during the Ryder Cup Ballesteros reaches down very deep inside himself and produces something that is almost magical in its potency. "He's unbelievable," says Feherty, who witnessed his efforts with incredulity at the 1991 Ryder Cup. "It's almost like there's a force field around him. He gets this aura of invincibility."

"Well, he has a sort of tunnel vision," James agrees, "and at the Ryder Cup he channels that into the performance he can get out of the team as a whole, whereas someone like Faldo would tunnel it into his own personal performance. Seve is very much on top of everything that's happening on the team. Faldo isn't. And it does give the players a boost to know that Seve is there and there's every chance he'll perform very well because he does tend to play well in the Ryder Cup, specially with Olazábal."

"I think the change is that he is instilling in eleven others what's in him," Schofield says. "Manuel Piñero will tell you that in 1985 he felt that it would be totally unthinkable for him, playing with Seve, to lose a foursomes or a fourball. That was his feeling, that it would actually be impossible."

"I think Seve's always a fantastic player to play with," Piñero responds. "He's a great inspiration. The only problem with playing with Seve is, in a way, you need to have a very strong character. He's so brilliant and he puts everything into it, that if you don't have your confidence 100 percent, it can put you down. You can sort of get an inferiority complex. But he's the best partner in the world because he gives help and you can feel he is there. You feel he can beat anybody. Doesn't matter if he plays badly, he can still win the match. He's exceptional."

"I think that's probably right," Jacklin says. "I mean, I put Rivero with him one year and I changed and put Piñero with him. I think he's all right with Piñero and he's certainly all right with Olazábal. There's a camaraderie there and a mutual respect. I think other individuals find it difficult to marry up to Seve's standards. They feel inferior, you see. But he's no more difficult to partner than anybody else."

In Jose Maria Olazábal, Ballesteros found the perfect partner. To watch them at work in the Ryder Cup is to see teamwork at its most harmonious and the game of golf played as exquisitely as it ever can be. They are in perfect unison at all times.

"I really do enjoy playing with him in the Ryder Cup," Olazábal says, "and I think the reason why is maybe because of that first match we played when I was an amateur. I feel comfortable with him since then. I think that was a special thing for me. I always try hard when I play with him. We understand each other very, very well, that's the most important thing. He's not individualistic at all when it comes to team events and that, I think, is a point on his side. It's very difficult to get a great player who can be a great player and a great member in a team."

In 1987, Olazábal's Ryder Cup debut, they won three of their four matches together. They met the daunting partnership of Payne Stewart and Larry Nelson, who had played nine Ryder Cup matches over the years— and won every one of them—in the first day's foursomes and beat them by a hole. In the fourballs, against Strange and Kite, they put on one of the most amazing displays of golf in Ryder Cup history. Ballesteros began by chipping in from forty feet for a winning birdie at the first, and went on to make five more, including a forty-five-footer to win the tenth and a seventy-two-footer to win the seventeenth and end the match, 2 & 1.

"Did I watch Ballesteros?" a despondent Nicklaus, the American captain, said afterward. "Unfortunately, yes. He not only played his own ball, played Olazábal's ball as well. He played beautifully." The following day the Spaniards overcame Crenshaw and Kite by a hole in the second day's foursomes, but lost 2 & 1 to Sutton and Mize in the fourballs.

"It just seems like he goes into a different gear," Crenshaw says, recalling his match against Ballesteros and being unable to prevent a note of awe creeping into his tone. "He wants it so badly, and the spirit of the matches is so high, and I think he enjoys that arena. Certain players just relish it and somebody like Seve just elevates his game. It actually helps his game and it's

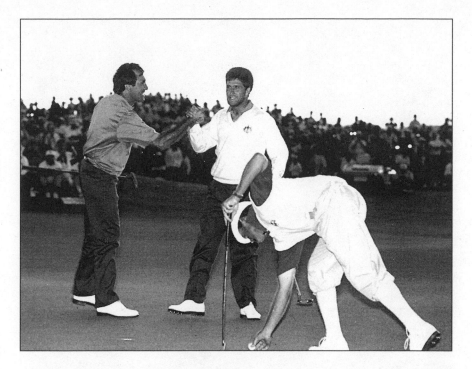

Seve Ballesteros and Jose Maria Olazábal (in the middle) are fellow Spaniards and a great match-play team, especially when it comes to Ryder Cup play against their American enemies. Here they congratulate each other after finishing off Payne Stewart and Fred Couples in a 1991 match. (AP/Wide World Photos)

wonderful. Some people, it frightens them and they have to go into the week and hope they're playing well. But, I think, no matter how Seve's playing, it charges him up to the point where he will be playing well. And I think he knows that."

Ballesteros, marching down the seventeenth hole at Muirfield Village, flanked by that roaring ocean of red, white, and blue, certainly did know it. His tee shot had been fluid and strong, while Strange's had been poor and his approach had run through the green. Ballesteros's second shot flew straight for the heart of the green. He strode after it, head held high, the cheers of the European supporters ringing in his ears. Then he sank the putt to halve the hole and win the match, and thus had the honor of guaranteeing the first European victory on American soil.

Their conquest complete, European team captain Tony Jacklin and Ballesteros celebrate the Europeans' victory in the 1987 Ryder Cup. (© Phil Sheldon)

A more fitting end could not have been scripted in literature.

"I played well today," he said. "This was my day."

"One of the things that I do remember," Jacklin says, "is that, after all the ceremonies and our victory dinner, I got all the players—they were all exhausted—to make this three-mile trip to take the trophy to where our supporters were. And I'll never forget walking into that hotel. It was frightening. I mean, the noise and the cheers and the sheer joy of everybody. I said, 'Just give two minutes of your lives to these people.' And when it came to it, I was the only one who stayed two minutes because I just had to get out. I had to get straight in my mind what had happened that day. And I went to Seve and I said, 'You know, you can go now.' He said, 'I'm very happy here. I'm very comfortable.' And I was the one that just scooted off and had a quiet whisky and contemplated the week."

By 1989 the Ryder Cup was a phenomenon, though nothing compared to what it became two years later and what it will become in the future. The chemistry between brothers-in-arms Ballesteros and Jacklin, bound by circumstances and a mutual desire to destroy the smug complacency of the Americans and prove once again that the Europeans reigned supreme, was almost tangible.

"They want to win at all costs," Brown comments, "within the rules of the game."

Thus do we return to the finest line of all, that which divides competitiveness at its most extreme from gamesmanship. In 1989 Ballesteros played Paul Azinger, one of America's most powerful and determined players, in the singles matches. Europe led 9-7 going into the last day, and they were the first pair out. "That's a tremendous responsibility," says Ballesteros, who had volunteered to play in the lead match after Ian Woosnam told Jacklin that he didn't want to.

The pressure both players were under manifested itself at the second hole. "I hit the ball a little thin and the grooves on my sand wedge cut it badly," Ballesteros recalls. "I asked [Paul] if I could take it out of play and he said: 'Seve, I don't think this ball is in bad shape.' It was a ridiculous thing to argue about. So I called the referee, and he said he thought the ball was still playable. So I putted—no big deal. But if it was the other way around, I would say change the ball if you want to. I mean, what advantage is that?"

But Musgrove insists, somewhat cynically, that Azinger had "already been told that Seve might do something like that," which is why he suggested calling a referee. "And [the referee] says the same," Musgrove continues." " 'You can't change your ball, it isn't cut.' Which Seve knows anyway. So with that he turns to Azinger and he says: 'Okay, if that's the way you want it, it's all right with me.' He can be all indignant then, you see, because he's made it look to the crowd as if Azinger's getting at him."

When they reached the fifteenth hole, the match was level. While Ballesteros hit a fine drive and second shot, Azinger drove into the trees, was short of the green in two, over the back fringe for three, and chipped in for a winning birdie. They halved the sixteenth and Ballesteros holed from eight feet at the next to keep the match alive.

GREAT ROARS RANG THROUGH THE AIR AS THE FATE OF EUROPE HUNG IN THE BALANCE, AND EVERYWHERE PEOPLE RUSHED, SWERVING, RUNNING, AND LEAPING DOWN THE FAIRWAYS.

By now most of the twenty-thousand-strong crowd at the Belfry was out of control and excitement was at a fever pitch. Great roars rang through the air as the fate of Europe hung in the balance, and everywhere people rushed, swerving, running, and leaping down the fairways. Jacklin weaved his way among them, crouched low in his buggy like a military commander, his dark glasses flashing. The atmosphere at the Belfry was thick and intoxicating: It went to your head like strong wine and made you almost dizzy with exhilaration. We watched the Spaniard and the American tee off, and Azinger's ball plummet like a stone into the water. We stifled our joy as Ballesteros strode up to his own ball, which was just through the fairway, not far from where we sat. Across the water, partially obscured by trees and bushes, we could see Azinger and the referee walking up and down and gesticulating. Then the most extraordinary thing happened. The spectators were cleared, the rules official stood back, and Azinger hit a huge third shot, which carried the water easily and finished in a bunker beside the green.

Ballesteros's expression never altered but it was clear that he was shaken. It was unlikely Azinger would make anything worse than a five, which meant that the Spaniard needed a four to halve the match. He handed his four-iron to Wright and took out a three. Then he clipped the ball thinly from its tight lie, and watched thunderstruck as the ball described a low curve into the water. It was Augusta revisited. The gallery was stunned; Ballesteros was enraged. "It didn't come out the way I thought," he said.

"I didn't pay too much attention to what Paul Azinger was doing," Ballesteros recalled afterward. "He was trying to drop his ball and I was concentrating on my shot, but looking back I have a feeling that something was wrong." (The referee saw it differently, however, and when Ballesteros and Azinger, far removed from the passions and heated patriotism of battle, talked it over at the World Championship in Jamaica a few months later, they agreed to let bygones be bygones.) At the time Ballesteros just stormed to the water's edge, peered angrily into its depths, and muttered under his breath in Spanish. Then he pulled himself together, selected a club, and played his pitch shot. It finished nearly twenty feet away from the pin, on the top tier of the green. Ballesteros lost his temper. Wright had given him the wrong yardage. For several seconds he heaped a torrent of awful abuse on the luckless caddie's head. Then he gathered himself once again, carefully studied the line of his putt, and holed it. Azinger splashed out the sand to five feet, holed out, and won the match.

At the end of the day both teams had fourteen points. Europe had retained the Ryder Cup but not won it.

Trevino is of the opinion that, day in and day out, Paul Azinger is the only American player who is a match for Ballesteros. It was fortuitous, therefore, that Azinger and Chip Beck confronted Ballesteros and Olazábal in the first day's foursomes and fourballs at the 1991 Ryder Cup at Kiawah Island. And it is interesting to note that, by strange coincidence, both of the Americans had had almost identical experiences with Ballesteros in majors prior to the event. In the case of Azinger, it took place in June 1988 in the final round of the U.S. Open—the one where the Spaniard finished third and might have won if it hadn't been for a 75 in the second round and bad luck in the last.

"Seve hit his drive out of bounds on the first hole and got off to a bad start," the American recalled. "I was playing great, five under on the front nine, right in contention. Instead of being quiet and disgusted with his own game, Seve was very encouraging to me when he didn't have to be. He kept rooting me on. On the fifteenth hole, he said, 'Make one more birdie and you will win.' I did birdie sixteen, but then there was a long wait at seventeen, and I bogeyed there. He said to me on the eighteenth tee, 'That was very unlucky for you to wait that long, but you can still do it. Birdie this hole. Think birdie, birdie, birdie, birdie.' He wanted to drill it into my head. I didn't win, but I'll never forget the way he treated me. When I'm forty years old and playing with some rookie kid in contention, I hope I treat him the same way.

"He's the world's best," Azinger added. "Nobody's close. Absolutely the best."

Beck—who has gone down in history for commenting mournfully, after he had been brutally thrashed by Ballesteros in the 1989 World Match Play (9 & 8, second round), "Every good man is tested in the crucible of humiliation"—had a similar thing happen to him at Shinnecock Hills in the 1986 U.S. Open. There, too, the Spaniard had had an opportunity for victory but had been unusually slow in pursuing it.

"My first true experience of Seve was when I played with him on the Sunday of the U.S. Open when Raymond Floyd won," Beck remembers. "I finished second. I was playing very slowly that day and yet I felt really wonderful and I was playing well and things were falling into place for me. But I remember on the last hole, he said, 'Come on, Chip. If you can birdie the last hole, you'll be the Open champion.' It was extraordinary. And I really admired him for that. It takes a great champion to do that. I hit it very close and I almost birdied the last hole."

Now, however, they were all at the Ryder Cup—the so-called War by the Shore—and relations were no longer so amicable. Azinger and Beck were three up on Ballesteros and Olazábal after nine holes in the foursomes when two things happened. To begin with, when Beck teed off on the seventh hole, Ballesteros noticed that the American had changed from a one-hundred-compression ball to a ninety-compression ball, thereby contravening the one-ball rule which had been specifically agreed at the teams' rules meeting, and in any case is in daily operation on the U.S. and European Tours. Ballesteros did not call the referee immediately. He and Olazábal debated what to do and, having discussed the matter with their caddies, agreed on the way to the tenth tee that if they were going to win, they should win fairly and on ability alone rather than because the Americans had been penalized.

They say that the road to hell is paved with good intentions. Bernard Gallacher, the European captain, was summoned to the tenth tee, where he spoke at length to officials. An unpleasant row ensued. Ballesteros had walked over and looked at Beck's ball on the ninth hole, but had said nothing to either of the Americans before sending for Gallacher.

"That was their mistake," Beck says. "I think they were afraid of upsetting us by declaring something that wasn't right." He confesses to changing his ball on the seventh tee but says that that was the only time it had happened. "I was just thinking of Paul [who had to play the approach shot]. I said, 'Paul, I don't think you can get there. I might as well play your ball.' Not thinking, you know. I don't think there's that big a difference [between the two balls], personally, but mentally, I think there's as big a difference as anything. If you get more compression on the ball, you get more spin on it. But that's part of human nature, making mistakes. And that's what it was. And, obviously, anything in match play that's not declared at the time, on completion of the hole or before the hole is completed and the score is marked down, is over and done with. So I was very happy about that. Because I felt we got away with something there. I thought: 'Hey, that's great. We made a mistake and got away with it. We're lucky.'"

On the tenth tee, the Americans had admitted that the ball had been changed. "We made a mistake," Azinger sullenly said, "but we certainly weren't cheating."

"We don't say that, Paul," Ballesteros told him. "It has nothing to do with cheating. Cheating and breaking the rules are two different things."

After about fifteen minutes they continued their match and the Spaniards won 2 & 1 and then beat them with the same score in the afternoon fourballs.

Meanwhile, the Americans had grown increasingly irritated by Ballesteros's persistent cough. "Well, it was very disappointing for me," says Beck, who was disturbed by it during the morning foursomes, "because it seemed like all the coughing and everything was catching me. I told Paul, 'It's bothering me. I just want you to watch it and if it continues, we'll say something.' But I didn't really want them to know it was bothering me. So I just mentioned it to the official after the ninth hole to make sure everything was on the up and up. And he was the one that reported it and did all the other things that made all the commotion. Paul Azinger and I never said a word. I just politely asked [the official], 'Joe, just check [whether or not they were coughing] and let me know if I'm just imagining things.' Because I didn't want to be that way. And after the round he came up to me and said, 'Yes, they were.' And I reported to Bernard Gallacher that the coughing was going on. When you have a cold, it's difficult to control it, but it's the nature of the game to control it. You either have to control it or just move away. Stay out of the game. That's the way I play, anyway."

At the end of the day Azinger caused still greater controversy by declaring Ballesteros to be "the king of gamesmanship."

It was not until the Volvo Masters, in the last week of October, that the subject came up again (Europe had lost the Ryder Cup, 13½–14½, despite the fact that the two Spaniards had contributed eight points on their own). Ballesteros, responding to Dave Stockton's comments to the British press a few days earlier, to the effect that he had tried to keep Azinger and Ballesteros apart during the matches "because Seve coughs and splutters a lot," brought it up and said vehemently, "Azinger said it happened once [the change of ball], but we know it happened three times. At first he denied it completely, then he changed his statement. I don't think for a minute he and Chip Beck were trying to cheat. They just didn't know the rule. Azinger is a great player, but he hasn't won a major tournament and I think he was trying to be a hero for his team. The American team were eleven nice guys and Paul Azinger."

Ballesteros denied that he had tried to put the Americans off by coughing. "I did nothing like that at Kiawah Island." But Olazábal conceded that the Spaniard did cough on the course. "I was coughing, too. We were not very well that week. But he was coughing when nobody was hitting shots. The fact is, they changed balls and they admitted it. Then they lost the match and now they're complaining about Seve coughing. That's rubbish. Azinger should not be saying anything when it is he and Beck who broke the rules. He should keep his mouth shut."

But as Ballesteros himself admits, "Above all, these things show how much everyone wants to win." Many things are said in the heat of the battle, few of them are meant. There is no question that Ballesteros lives for victory on the golf course whether he is playing in a pro-am in Tokyo or in the Ryder Cup at Kiawah Island. But that is what makes him great, and it is the positive effects of his desire, his genius, and his charisma that have helped make the game and, more especially, the Ryder Cup, what it is today. In five Ryder Cups he has won or halved twenty-one of his twenty-five matches.

"Oh, he plays with such passion and conviction," Jacklin agrees. "I mean, he's been fantastic. He's made things happen out there in Ryder Cup confrontation in individual matches that couldn't happen—just because of his commitment. He just *believes*. . . . I've seen it all through my life with individuals like Seve. I've seen it with Gary Player. I've done it myself on occasion. You can turn things around for yourself. There's a determination in some people that won't go away, and other people recognize it and they stand aside when they see it. Seve's done it on numerous occasions. I mean, in Ryder Cup conflict he's turned matches around, he's chipped in; he's done things in tournaments—against Arnold Palmer in the World Match Play, he chipped in at the last hole. He hit a shot out of the bunker on the eighteenth in 1983 against Fuzzy Zoeller that you couldn't hit. It was an impossible shot, but he did it. And he hit through the green on the eighteenth in two when nobody else got within sixty yards of it at West Palm Beach in the '83 matches. Superhuman things, you know. When you get rolling and the adrenaline gets going and you're excited, you get carried away with your own determination. It's a peculiar thing, but really great players all do it at certain times. They're concentrated yet totally relaxed about making it happen, and then it's almost like they have a premonition that they can do it. And it's a wonderful thing to see."

19

THE ROAD LESS TRAVELED

"To be a champion you have to live for what you do. For golf or football or any sport, you have to think and you have to live all the time for that, otherwise it's impossible to be a champion. And you must like it."

Severiano Ballesteros, Spain, March 1990

Eighteen years after his first harrowing days as a tournament professional, Ballesteros strode out onto the sun-speckled range at the Emirates Golf Club in Dubai, on his way to practice. It was still early but already the sky was a deep sapphire blue, and the air was close and warm. Caddies strolled about swinging practice-ball baskets, players gossiped, warmed up, or conferred with their coaches, and a small bottleneck of admirers gathered behind the Spaniard. He acknowledged them with a smile and a genial remark. Once it would have been a folly equivalent to entering a cage of hungry lions to approach Ballesteros while he was working on his golf game, but the inexorable march of time has mellowed him, just as it does everyone else, and now it seems as if he sometimes welcomes distractions, for they take him out of himself.

The years have wrought many changes in the man who, for nearly a decade, was the best player in the world. No longer does he glory so much in his own strength and ability, the way he did at Royal Birkdale in 1976; no longer does he hit the ball with such back-wrenching force that he is almost carried after it and has to balance himself with a sort of high twirling follow-through; no longer does he have an unruly mop of jet-black hair, cheap golf shoes, or Johnny Miller flares; and no longer do his dark eyes shine with laughter and with fire. Instead, he wears the finest designer clothing, has neat, carefully cropped hair, and strikes the ball with a stylish, elegant swing, perfectly on plane. Indeed, his whole aspect reflects the rites of passage he has undergone as faithfully as a mirror. Once he was wild, carefree, arrogant, colorful, and filled with *joie de vivre*; now he has learned patience through suffering and humility through insecurity.

Ballesteros waited while Billy Foster tipped practice balls onto the emerald grass, and then hit them crisply out toward the palm trees on the horizon. He was preparing for the Desert Classic, the second event of the season. The Emirates Club, where it is held, is literally an oasis in the desert, complete with flamingoes, fountains, flowers, and a great marble clubhouse in the style of a Bedouin tent.

"Still looking for Joe Collet?" he said inquiringly, when I walked over. He grinned. "Joe is in church. He's preparing for the next life."

"We should all be doing that," I remarked.

"Do you believe there is another life?" he asked.

"Yes. Do you?"

"I don't know, but it must be good because no one ever comes back from there!"

"Do you think there is, though?"

Ballesteros laughed, white teeth flashing in his dark face. "I will write you a letter from there and let you know."

He rapped his club smartly against his shoe and resumed practicing, propelling fifteen of the most perfect golf shots imaginable into the distance. Peter Smith, a talented Scottish player, but one who has never won a tournament in Europe, ventured closer, his face enraptured.

"There's something wrong," Ballesteros told him. "What do you think it is?"

Smith was taken aback. "I don't know," he said, embarrassed. "I haven't given a lesson in three years and I've never taught anyone at your level."

But the Spaniard insisted and so Smith found himself giving a lesson to a man who has one of the finest and most exquisitely natural swings in the game and who, until 1990, had been almost entirely self-taught. The next day somebody else was in Smith's shoes.

On the practice range Ballesteros's concerns about his swing seemed unfounded; on the golf course, less so. He had been working to perfect a right-to-left tee shot, which he felt was the key to conquering Augusta's par-fives, and he was caught somewhere between the two swings. Still, he was purposeful and confident and thus survived the consequences of his waywardness to score 66, 67 in the opening rounds and lead by a stroke over Anders Forsbrand. He had the advantage of being match-fit, as they say in professional sport. Where most players had taken a long winter layoff and were rusty and out of condition, Ballesteros had had a mere three weeks—one of the shortest breaks ever in his career—between the World Championship in Jamaica and the Asian Classic in Bangkok, during which time he had practiced and ridden his bike assiduously. It was all part of his decision, he said, to "play more golf in order to keep up with the competition. You've got to work harder to stay at the same level. Ten years ago there were about fifteen players capable of winning championships. Now there are between thirty-five and forty."

FOR THE FIRST TIME IN HIS LIFE, HE HAD ANNOUNCED HIS INTENTION OF BECOMING THE No. 1 PLAYER IN THE WORLD RANKINGS, A SYSTEM DEVISED AND OPERATED BY IMG.

For the first time in his life, he had announced his intention of becoming the No. 1 player in the World Rankings, a system devised and operated by IMG. Previously, he had not been enamored with it; besides which, he had always felt in his heart that, regardless of who was at the top of the rankings, he was the world's greatest player. Now he appeared to require proof of that.

Essentially, Ballesteros's schedule for the season has always been geared around the majors. He alters his preparation for the majors constantly. Some years his strategy has been to compete the week before; others he has deemed it better to rest.

"I firmly believe that he's taken too much time off in the winter in the past and therefore it's been difficult to get going in time," Collet said. "And we've had talks about this. His brother, Manuel, strongly feels that way and has been even more outspoken than I have. This year, he's trying an experiment. We convinced him to play in Jamaica just before Christmas, and also to start in Thailand. That cuts about four weeks out of this period that he normally sits around and gains weight and gets lazy and melancholy. I said to him, 'If you want to be a peak performer, you've got to make a sacrifice. The sacrifice has to be that you've got to maintain your skill level a little bit higher than you have in the past. . . . ' And the proof is in the pudding: he's leading the tournament."

On Sunday, February 9, Ballesteros won the Desert Classic, holing a ten-foot birdie putt on the second hole of a playoff to defeat Ronan Rafferty. It was eloquent testimony to his mental strength. In the third round of the tournament, after snap-hooking his tee shot to within four feet of going out of bounds, he had told Foster: "It's not working. We've got to rethink our ideas and play with what we've got." But his golf game was capricious and unreliable and, having arrived at the thirteenth to find himself two strokes behind, it had taken a supreme effort of will for him to single-putt each of the remaining holes to tie Rafferty at 272, sixteen under par. The Desert Classic was his fiftieth title in Europe and his eighty-seventh worldwide since that first triumph in the Spanish Under-25's tournament in 1974.

"Ballesteros has always been the best in the world," Rafferty conceded graciously.

"My determination is to go all the way to the end of the century," the Spaniard said. "One thing I'm very proud of is that I'm a great competitor. To win when you are playing great is easy, but to be confident when you are not (playing great) is something different and something great."

The following week he finished twenty-fifth at the Turespana Masters in Spain, after rounds of 78, 69, 73, 70, to become the first player to win more than three million pounds in prize money on the European Tour.

In March, Ballesteros teed up in the Open de Baleares. He had recently returned from an exhibition match in South America and seemed tired and uncommonly depressed. Only willpower drove him on. Asked what motivated him to keep practicing so hard and striving so resolutely to be the best season after season after season, he replied: "Discipline is the key in life for many things. You need discipline; you have to take care of yourself; you have to sleep eight hours every day; and you have to practice. I go to the driving range many times when I don't feel like it. I've just come from Argentina, and the way I feel at the moment the best thing for me would be to go to the hotel—my boy is there—and I would like to be there and play with my boy. But do you know what I'm going to do? I'm going to the driving range now because I know that tomorrow is a big day and I want to be ready. That's my profession."

After three rounds of the tournament, he was a stroke off the lead, but his mood remained unchanged. He insisted, with a halfhearted attempt at his old mocking humor, that he was "playing for second place." Then he admitted that he was struggling once again to keep focused on the course. "I really have a problem concentrating today. I'm playing quite well but there are a lot of players here this week and they're all against me. It's not very easy to win. I've played well for three rounds and I should be leading right now. But if the ball doesn't go in, you just have to be patient."

Patience proved an essential virtue since, with four holes to play, Jesper Parnevik, the twenty-seven-year-old son of a Swedish television personality, was leading by three strokes and Ballesteros was out of the running. That's when pressure brought its influence to bear. Parnevik dropped three strokes in the remaining holes and found himself in confrontation with the Spaniard in a sudden-death playoff. Six times they toiled up Santa Ponsa's steep 460-yard par-four eighteenth, until eventually, an hour and a half after they had set off, Ballesteros sank a four-foot putt for victory. By then he was panic-stricken about his travel arrangements to Pedreña and, having signed his card, sprinted across the car park to a waiting courtesy car and was whisked away.

Later, the golf writers followed him along the same dangerous gray highway to the airport. When we arrived, Ballesteros was pacing up and down by the ticket counter, looking utterly crushed and dejected. Anyone less like the jubilant winner of a six-hole playoff would have been hard to imagine. Carmen was twenty or thirty yards away, standing rather lamely on the concourse. It transpired that, although she had left the course ahead of him and had reached the check-in desk a full fifteen minutes before the plane took off, the Spanish airline they were traveling to Santander with had refused to hold the flight.

"British Airways, they wait for me, Concorde, they wait for me, but *Iberia*?" Ballesteros said bitterly. "Iberia, they can't wait." And he cleared his throat miserably as he reflected on the cruel irony of it all. "We come here at 150 kilometers an hour, risking the life," he added, his hands describing the heart-stopping journey. He folded his arms and looked glumly over at Carmen.

We stood around and mulled this over. "But surely winning the tournament was worth missing your flight?" said one journalist, voicing what everyone else was thinking.

Silence. Ballesteros stared morosely at the floor.

"*Surely* you'd rather win the tournament and miss your flight?" There was a note of amazed disbelief in the journalist's voice.

"That is something else altogether," Ballesteros said cryptically, without meeting anybody's eyes.

Jack Nicklaus was walking down the fairway at Lytham during the 1988 British Open, when he was confronted by a large pool of rainwater, the result of Saturday's flooding. He skirted it carefully, causing David J. Russell to remark with a smile, "I thought you could walk on water."

"That was a long time ago," Nicklaus replied wryly.

Ballesteros had reached the same stage. Gone were the days when he would march boldly over or through any hazard that golf or life presented him with. Now, like those men in insurance advertisements, he always carried an umbrella even when the sun was shining. And he always walked around puddles.

Little more than a year had gone by since he had emerged from his last slump and already he was in the doldrums again. It was hard to know why. Even he was at a loss to explain these great depressions on the graph of his career and only repeated the refrain of 1990, with one or two variations. His principal difficulties then had been confidence and concentration. "I had lots of negative thoughts," he said. "I knew I would win again. It was not a question of if but when—but I was not certain that I would be as good as I had been before." Now he began to talk of a lack of desire, although essentially they are all the same thing. "The desire is still there but perhaps not as much as before," he confessed. "When the desire and enthusiasm goes down, the concentration becomes more difficult. I still like to win but maybe not as much as when I first started. But that's natural; it happens to everyone as they get older."

The enormity of the cloud Ballesteros was under was illustrated at Augusta, where he opened with a 75 and followed it with an unbelievable 81 in the final round. Before the event he had been in tears as he vowed: "In 1992 I want to win the Masters for [my father]." The agony he went through after it was terrible. For months he had rehearsed for Augusta, changed his swing for Augusta, dreamed of Augusta, and convinced himself that he could win at Augusta for his father, and all he had succeeded in doing was wrenching once more at the knife buried in his heart.

Jacobs was unsympathetic. 'He's hugely gifted," he said, "but, you see, one of the lessons of golf is that you must never pack it in. I can't believe that he took 81 without thinking, 'Oh, to hell with this.' The score doesn't half mount up quickly if you ever think, 'Well, bugger it.' I can't believe that he didn't get a bit disgruntled."

Heartsore and travel weary, and at as low an ebb as he had been in the worst moments of his first season on Tour or during 1981 or 1990, Ballesteros trailed along to the European PGA Championship in May, where he was defending champion. The previous week he had been further demoralized by a thirty-fourth-place tie in the Spanish Open, but the sight of Wentworth's Burma Road course—which he loves because he feels it is similar in style and character to his home course in Pedreña—and an evening spent watching his beloved Barcelona win the European Cup from the second row of the Royal Box at Wembley, temporarily revived his enthusiasm. "If I am going to get my game back then this is the place to do it," he said hopefully, adding that he had won seven times in twenty-eight starts at Wentworth. "If I score well in the first round then I will pick up confidence and anything can happen. I always feel good when I play here."

But when the subject of his poor form arose, he lapsed back into his somber state and mumbled that his confidence wasn't very high. "Mentally, I feel very tired. Why, I don't know. I don't have much desire to play. It could be that I have played too much in the last year. I kept going, playing thirty-two tournaments in 1991, compared to my normal average of twenty-seven over the last ten years, but I am looking at taking at least three months off this winter."

Two days later he failed to qualify. Lyle, who had been paired with him in the first two rounds, described him as subdued. "I've never seen him so down. He could have been somewhere on Mars. He wasn't with it. He wasn't there at all."

Lyle's explanation for Ballesteros's fall from grace was that he had dominated European golf for so long that he had had his nose pushed out of joint when Faldo replaced him at the pinnacle. Faldo, who had spent the early part of his career "hoping there was going to be some competitive rivalry" between himself and the Spaniard, "but he was so good then," felt that Lyle was probably right. "It's the difference between your tail up and your tail down, isn't it? When your tail's up in this game you're blitzing it and trying to blast through everybody, and right now my tail's up and his tail's down."

There was no doubting the truth of that statement. Faldo, even before he won the British Open at Muirfield in July and then finished tied for second in the U.S. PGA Championship, was the undisputed world No. 1, while Ballesteros had followed his Wentworth nightmare with a tie for seventeenth place, a tie for twenty-seventh place, a tie for forty-second place, and two more missed cuts, to be lying twenty-first on the Order of Merit by August. None of this caused him as much pain as his performances in the majors, the only standards by which he had ever measured himself. He shot 79 in the last round of the U.S. Open at Pebble Beach to finish out of the top twenty; he missed the cut in the Open; and, most damningly of all, he withdrew from the U.S. PGA Championship, despite the fact that he had previously been very critical when other Europeans had done the same. In a faxed letter to the PGA of America, Manuel wrote on his behalf: "Please withdraw my brother, Seve Ballesteros, from this year's PGA Championship, the reason being that Seve is having some back trouble and he feels he won't be able to play up to his usual standard."

The strange thing was that, although Ballesteros looked increasingly tormented on the course, he didn't walk around like a bear with a sore head off it. If anything, he became a kinder, more compassionate person in inverse proportion to the decline of his game. Technically, he clutched with ever more desperation at the tiniest straws. He asked advice indiscriminately from almost any player he laid eyes on; rookies, journeymen, or coaches—they were all the same to him. In Monte Carlo, having spent two hours working with Forsbrand on the practice range, he walked into the palace courtyard in his dinner jacket, tapped the tall Swede on the shoulder, and there, before the startled eyes of Prince Rainier and his guests, proceeded to demonstrate the advance he had made with his swing since Forsbrand had last inspected it.

Forsbrand didn't mind in the least. "I enjoy spending time with him. He wants to listen and hear my view of everything, and I think it's in every player's interests to listen to different people."

"He asks different people, but he doesn't listen too much," Piñero insisted. "He goes his own way."

Eduardo Romero found the whole thing slightly alarming. He, like Player, felt that the Spaniard should be spending more time working out problems for himself and less time compounding them by overanalysis. "I play many practice rounds before the tournament with him," he explained, "and when he hit the ball perfect he say, 'Well, I want to hit it with a fade now.' I say, 'Seve, why? It's a perfect shot.' 'No, but I want to try it with fade.' And then he miss and miss and miss."

Ballesteros was honest enough to admit it was true. "Sometimes you try to change things for the better and your game ends up getting worse. Then you go back to your own style and that doesn't work either. You lose both ways."

Jacobs didn't believe that Ballesteros's sudden propensity to change his swing on a whim was anything new. "Seve's a bit like Nicklaus. Seve walks onto a practice ground and decides how he's going to play that day. . . . He's hugely gifted—a touch player to a degree. In other words, he can play extraordinary shots but in terms of repeat, repeat, repeat. . . . But those are the balances, aren't they? He's more gifted, in my view, than anybody who's going to become a mechanical player."

Ballesteros's answer to the confidence crisis he was suffering was the same as it always had been: He escaped to Pedreña and the warm bosom of his family. But now he had the added joy of seeing his tiny son, whom he had presented with a plastic club and who could already wield it so well that he managed, before the eyes of several astonished Tour players, to loft the ball from a tee eight consecutive times without once missing. His wife and child and his precious dogs gave him a great deal of pleasure. He had adjusted to married life and it had helped to fill a small corner of the void which has always existed in him when he is not playing golf. Once Trevino told him: "If you don't take up a hobby pretty soon, you're going to drive yourself crazy." But no matter how many interests Ballesteros took up, no matter how passionately he pursued his cycling, his fishing, or his football, the emptiness remained.

"One thing that was always hard for Seve . . . was that his life revolved around golf," Miller says. "I always knew that my children were much more important than my golf, where a lot of golfers are not that way. So when I played bad, it was like, 'Oh, what the heck, I've still got a good wife and kids, that's more important.' That was my fallback. And I had a lot of hobbies. I was passionate about fishing and racing cars and working on my ranch, and Seve basically didn't have any hobbies. His passion lies in golf."

Miller was aided considerably by his faith, whereas Ballesteros is a non-practicing Catholic. "Seve's basic philosophy is: Christian approach to life, don't do anything that you wouldn't like done to you, be honest in your dealings," Collet says. "He went to the baptism of his son. He goes to weddings and funerals and things like that, but it's difficult for him because he's very involved in his professional career." Nevertheless, he feels strongly that the Spaniard "needs to have some sort of personal philosophy, and that includes a hobby something more than winning golf tournaments, than fulfilling obligations, than being a good father. He needs something in his socio-religious background. I think there could have been times when he was down where, if he had something else to look to that would pick him up, that would help. Like doing something for somebody else who was even more down than he was. And lately he's understood some of that. He's been more active with charity work and doing exhibitions and things that have a charitable purpose. He seems more attracted to those than he is to some that just pay him a lot of money . . . because it makes him happy to see how much things mean to people. It makes him feel good."

The extent to which Ballesteros has come to realize the vacuum there is in his life apart from golf, was shown when he spent nearly two hours in 1992 talking to born-again Christian Bernhard Langer about religion. "He doesn't believe, but he doesn't not believe," Langer says. "He's searching."

But for the moment Ballesteros was far too preoccupied with the deterioration of his game to spend time dwelling on anything aside from swing theory. His appearances on the European Tour were few and far between and distinctly uninspired when they came. "I have no feeling for the game," he confessed in August, after spending several weeks in Pedreña watching the Olympic Games on television. "I don't know what is wrong. When I lose confidence I begin to change things . . . and I create a lot of confusion in my mind and every round is a mystery. When you get into that state you need a catalyst. Once you start making putts, for example, your confidence comes back and that affects the rest of your game. That's exactly what happened to me last year."

"Physically, he's got problems," Faldo said. "Obviously, he's suffering with his back right now and I know he has for a long time. It's tough on top players when you've been good and you go backward, because you know that all the work that you're doing is just to get back to where you were. That's the hardest thing for us. You don't want to go down."

But the bottom line was that Ballesteros had no desire to play, and nothing and nobody could arouse it in him. Nicklaus understood the feeling well. "I have a hard time getting inspired," he admitted. "I just don't have the belief in myself that I had. And Seve is saying the same thing. He says he doesn't get inspired, but maybe you use that as a pacifying thing to yourself. You say, 'Well, if I don't try real hard, then I can't be a failure.' You know what I mean? He wants to, but can't. I went through that stage in the early eighties where I really had the desire but I didn't have the desire, and I didn't want to work at it, yet I wanted to work at it, and I always had a built-in excuse for myself. Not that I wanted to use it, but I always had it. That's mentally what it does to you."

NICKLAUS UNDERSTOOD THE FEELING WELL. "I HAVE A HARD TIME GETTING INSPIRED," HE ADMITTED. "I JUST DON'T HAVE THE BELIEF IN MYSELF THAT I HAD. AND SEVE IS SAYING THE SAME THING."

After missing the cut in the British Open and the Scandinavian Masters, the Spaniard took a month off to recoup. Even an offer in the region of forty thousand pounds to play in the English Open failed to rouse his enthusiasm. Then he played in the European Masters in Switzerland the week his wife gave birth to a second baby boy (8:15 P.M. on September 3), named Miguel and weighing eight and a half pounds. Asked if he intended to withdraw from the tournament and fly home, he simply said: "I'm here to play golf." He finished tied for thirtieth, went straight to England for the European Open, and, if he had not failed to qualify, would not have seen his new son until ten days after he was born.

Manuel was under no illusions about his brother's decline. "Seve's problem is in his mind," he said frankly. "The more he thinks, the worse he gets."

"I used to think he was the best player in the world," says Romero, who has hero-worshipped the Spaniard for as long as he can remember. "But not now. Now, he's not confident. I don't know why. Golf is a very strange game, you know. And Seve lose the concentration. He told me, 'I can't hit the ball.

304

When I hit it I don't know where it will go—go right, go left.' It's unbeliev-able. He say, 'My head is not for golf now.' I think if Seve wants come back, he can. But he has to want to, that's the problem."

"I'm a great subscriber to the belief that people have a finite amount of bottle," Doust observes. "And I think that he's run out of his bottle. If he's in the forefront of a challenge now he'll back off. I don't think he likes pressure anymore. And he put himself under so much pressure always, year in and year out, round in and round out. There's a reservoir of that kind of strength that everyone has . . . and I think that he's exhausted his. You saw him last year in the Open, coming down the last fairway—I've never seen him behave this way—sort of waving to the crowd in a way that he was relieved that it was over. When he missed that short putt on the third green and that really was the end of his charge, you could see—or we Ballesteros watchers thought we could see, and he may have not recognized it himself—he was glad. You can't go into the kitchen always, and you can't keep going into the kitchen."

As the season wore on and nothing halted the Spaniard's downward slide, Doust's theory began to seem like a realistic probability. After brief ap-pearances at the Piaget Open and the German Masters, where he played his way shakily to ties for third and twelfth, followed by an even shorter visit to the World Match Play, where he lost by two holes to Jeff Sluman, he quit for the year, whereupon a statement was issued to the effect that he had devel-oped an allergy to house dust and was having to undergo treatment for it. When the season ended he was tenth in the World Rankings and twenty-eighth on the Order of Merit—his worst placing since 1974, the year he turned professional. Then, however, he had not had two victories to disguise the depths he had plumbed.

So ordinary did Ballesteros appear as he bowed out of the World Match Play at Wentworth, that for a moment it crossed our minds that we might have been mistaken about him all along, that the flame which burned so brightly in him had not been an eternal one, but a flickering candle which had been snuffed out by one too many gales. Herbert Warren Wind was con-vinced that this was the case. In May 1980 he had written in the *New Yorker:* "He is something else, this young Spaniard, and all things being equal he has an excellent chance of becoming one of the most authentically great golfers of all time." But at the Masters in 1991 he said disparagingly: "I think we may have overrated Seve. He wasn't a great player, finally."

Sometimes a man's life can seem like a river, shaped by outside influences from its source to the sea. Here's where it was a powerful stream, rushing gloriously and relentlessly over anything in its path; here's where it became a raging torrent, headstrong and irrational; here's where it was diverted from the straight and narrow by heavy storms; and here's where the years of drought reduced it to a trickle.

It was Severiano Ballesteros's *destino* to be born a farmer's son in a small village in northern Spain, to have three older brothers who were golfers, and to be spoiled, adored, and endlessly encouraged as he learned the game, yet at the same time be forbidden to play at the course he loved because of his social status, and thus be denied the perfect happiness which might have tempered his desire. It was his destiny, too, to be influenced by the presence of his huge indomitable father, who taught him how to be tough, independent, and resolute, and how to triumph in the face of all adversity.

When he left home at sixteen to become a tournament professional, he was confident, fiery, and willful, but also emotional, kindhearted, and passionately in love with the game. Protected by Manuel and by his loyal friends, Piñero and Chino Fernandez, he survived the trials and tribulations of those early days and began to live up to his incredible promise. In July 1976 he exploded onto the world stage at Royal Birkdale and experienced, for the first time, fame and adulation and that 'sweet, sweet' high that accompanies attainment of lifelong dreams. Three years later, when he won the British Open at Royal Lytham, he knew what it was to have everything—to be handsome, wealthy, and gifted beyond his wildest dreams; to have women, journalists, officials, and sponsors falling at his feet; and to have the power to say that black is white and be believed. In 1980 he soared to even greater heights with his triumph in the Masters and he dominated the European Tour and anywhere else he played. He began to find that not everyone appreciated his talent. The Americans called him "lucky," and Peter Thomson, president of the Australian PGA, described him as "a prima donna with an inflated ego and exaggerated opinion of his own importance."

The criticism and fury engendered by his missed tee time at the U.S. Open in 1980 was like a dash of cold water in his face. He grew rebellious, and the desire to vanquish his opponents on and off the course burned so fiercely in his heart that it threatened to consume him. Money and victory became his twin obsessions. Misguided by Barner and confused by his own instinctive hatred of being controlled by people in positions of power, he withdrew his membership of the European Tour, and learned what it is to be an outcast. The appearance-money battle won, he returned proudly to Europe, only to discover that he had been spurned by the Ryder Cup committee. Nevertheless, he resumed his position at the pinnacle of European golf, and once more was worshipped and fêted by ministers and royalty. By the end of 1983 he was the best player in the world. He was struggling to win Carmen's hand, to have the rules rewritten to accommodate him on the U.S. Tour, and to persuade his government to build golf courses for the people. He was moody and volatile as often as he was sunny and good-humored. Warren Wind commentated: "There seems to be a streak of capriciousness in Ballesteros. Almost as though he had risen to stardom too suddenly and had trouble adjusting to the realities of the world."

If Ballesteros were anyone other than who he is, if he wasn't the most-gifted, most-inspired, most-loved player of the modern era, we might doubt that he could ever be as great as he has been. If he wasn't so fiery, so charming, so kind, so generous, and so utterly human, we might forget who he is and how much he has done for the game, and how many times he has brought tears to our eyes with his genius and his heart. There is no player in European golf to whom he has not been a hero; there are few members of any gallery at any tournament anywhere in the world who wouldn't prefer to watch Ballesteros on a bad day than all the other great stars combined on their best, and there are few people in tournament golf whom he has not touched with some small gesture or word. All of his career has been a series of great peaks and troughs—genius does not manifest itself to order—and from every depression he has emerged to scale still greater heights. Among the top players, there are few who do not believe that Ballesteros will rise again and be greater even than before.

"I've always thought that Seve is the most gifted player that has ever been born," Tony Johnstone enthused several years ago. "Definitely. I don't think there's anything more awe-inspiring than Seve when he's in full flight. I'd like about 2 percent of his talent. . . . He's going to win plenty more majors. Plenty more."

"He has to be extremely proud of what he's accomplished," Crenshaw says. "I know that he knows he can achieve a lot more . . . and I'm sure that's frustrating to him at times because everyone knows that he's always had more ability than five or six people the game's ever seen. His talent is that unique. There are not many people that come along like Seve. They just don't. He's very special."

"I think he would be my greatest player of all time, because I didn't get the opportunity to see Nicklaus, and I didn't get the opportunity to see Hogan," Feherty says. "We might have seen the best of him, but he'll certainly be that good again. He's got too monumental a talent not to be. Getting married and having children and having a wife and all this sort of thing, that's an immense change. He'll win majors again, that's for sure."

"He's got such a terrific inherent talent and he's got a desire to succeed above all else that has sustained him for sixteen years," Jacklin says. "You know, one wonders how much longer he can go on. I would suspect he's had the best part of his career. I think he will always play golf. I think he will play seniors' golf, probably, but I think other priorities will come into his life that mean he won't be going just as hard at it as he's had to in the past. He's got a family now and all of a sudden he'll wake up one day and say, 'Hell, is life all about just going round on airplanes, playing tournament golf, or am I going to enjoy some other aspects of it?'

"But he's certainly in the top five of all-time greats. The others are all debatable. They go from Vardon to Nicklaus to Jones to Hogan to Snead to Nelson. All a player can do is try to be the best of his time. Seve was certainly that."

For his own part, Ballesteros has dreams of winning another five majors or a Grand Slam of titles, and of winning the U.S. Masters for his father. His love for the game he has graced with his brilliance and humanity is unquenched to this day, and the spirit of golf still lives in him.

"My ambition is to play as much as I can and to keep that passion for the game and that passion for competition. Because, of course, when I play bad I get a lot of frustration on the golf course, like everybody, but when I play good I have so much fun and so much pleasure that there's no money in the world that can buy that. And this is what I want. I want to keep that for as long as I can."

20

CONFLICTS AND INTERESTS

"When a tree falls down a lot of people want to take a cut out of it. My feeling is that this is what's happening. I have only one way to go and that's to reach the top again. Then I'll have my power back."

Seve Ballesteros on his trials, 1994

It was a measure of Ballesteros's continuing influence and his fiendish ability to stage-manage a situation that, minutes after entering the press center to discuss the 66 with which he had finished eighth in the Spanish Open, he had reduced the listening journalists to a shocked, scandalized silence. A small smile, somewhere between sympathy and satisfaction, tugged at the corner of his mouth. "Excuse me?" one was tempted to burst out. "Say that again."

It was May 1994, one week after the Spaniard's triumphant return to the winner's rostrum at the B&H International at St. Mellion in Cornwall, and Ballesteros had just alleged—with a breathtaking degree of casualness and calculated intent—that he had been offered a million-dollar bribe to help ensure that the 1997 Ryder Cup went to Valderrama in Spain.

"The offer did not actually specify that figure, but that was what it amounted to," he reported. "I have a letter at home which tells me I would get a percentage of the green fees and the sales of the building plots. It has nothing to do with the work I did in redesigning the seventeenth hole there, because I did that for nothing." He glowered at the room. "I don't like to be bought," he said proudly. "I have my principles."

310

The Spanish press contingent came noisily to life. Who, precisely, was he accusing? they demanded. When and where did he receive the letter? But Ballesteros was coy. He would say only that although he knew for a fact that the technical commission had advised the Ryder Cup committee that Jaime Ortiz-Patino's exclusive Sotogrande club did not have the minimum necessary facilities to host such a big infrastructure, Bernard Gallacher had told him that the committee was strongly in favor of taking the match there.

He paused for effect. "So one has to ask if those gentlemen on the Ryder Cup committee have received similar offers to one I received," he said piously.

For Severiano Ballesteros, struggling to retain some dignity, the journey from purgatory to top form had been a rougher ride than even his worst fears might have led him to suppose. He had begun the 1993 season with a brief, promising burst of form, finishing tied for third in Dubai. The following week, he missed the cut in the Asian Classic and entered free fall, producing a set of statistics that would have been hard to believe in his rookie year on Tour, let alone his sixteenth: five missed cuts, two top-tens, and a serious of embarrassing finishes, including a tie for thirty-fourth in Morocco, thirty-seventh in the Spanish Open, fiftieth in the Scottish Open, twenty-seventh in the British Open, seventieth in the Scandinavian Masters, and twenty-first in the German Open.

None of these results had any discernible effect on Gallacher, the European Ryder Cup captain. On the contrary; in July, he took pressure off the Spaniard by informing him that he was guaranteed a wild card. Less than a month later, he presented one to Olazábal. "Seve and Olazábal have formed the most outstanding partnership in the history of the Ryder Cup," he said. "I don't believe there is a partnership in the world which looks forward to stepping on the tee with them."

It was a contentious decision. On the one hand, there was no denying that Ballesteros was playing some of the worst golf of his career, but on the other, his psychological impact on the team was crucial. Among both players and public, there was an almost superstitious faith in the ability of Ballesteros and Olazábal—a kind of blind confidence in the power of chemistry over form—to combine to devastating effect in match play. Besides which, a Ryder Cup without Ballesteros's passion and fury was unthinkable.

On Friday, September 26, Sam Torrance launched the Ryder Cup's opening drive at the Belfry, and almost immediately things began to go wrong. In the process of hitting his shot, the Scotsman wrenched at an already painful ingrown toenail, and by the ninth hole he could hardly walk. On the mist-wreathed fairways, he and Mark James soon surrendered to the formidable partnership of Lanny Wadkins and Corey Pavin, and the Spaniards were dispatched 2 & 1 by Tom Kite and Davis Love III.

In the afternoon fourballs, where the U.S. team is traditionally stronger, the Europeans edged ahead by a point, largely due to the inspired debut of Peter Baker and the resurgence of Ballesteros and Olazábal. Gallacher's hopes rose. Torrance had been sidelined, effectively reducing the Europeans to eleven men, but the backbone of the team was still working well. Further encouragement was provided by Faldo and Montgomerie, Langer and Woosnam, and Seve and Jose Maria in the foursomes matches on Saturday morning. Gallacher, the "consensus captain," was reviewing the situation with optimism when he received a radio summons from Ballesteros shortly before lunch.

Tension formed a hard knot in Gallacher's stomach. He speedily departed for the fourteenth, where he arrived to find the Spaniards two up on Kite and Love. Ballesteros had missed the green right and was standing beside his ball, his face shadowed and anxious. He hurried over to Gallacher. Swallowing his pride, he begged the European captain not to send him back out in the afternoon pairings. He felt that he had let Olazábal down.

Gallacher was astounded. Later, he recalled that Ballesteros had appealed to him to replace him with someone else in order to allow him the time to go and work on the practice tee: "And despite speaking to Seve for several minutes, trying to persuade him that that might be the wrong thing to do, I felt that Seve, who always likes to lead from the front, who's never shirked a battle, especially that week, who loves the Ryder Cup, knowing how important it is to Seve, I felt I owed it to him to agree to his request. As it turned out, he couldn't find his game. He started well at the beginning of the week, his game was quite good when he came, and it deteriorated as the week went on, and by the time the singles came he was quite distressed.

And I personally wouldn't put Seve on the course when he felt like that. In actual fact, I even put Seve well down the list in the pairings for the singles to try and keep him out of the spotlight, because I've got so much respect for Seve, and I've never heard Seve ever, ever say to anyone that he didn't want to play."

For the European team, it was a crippling blow, made worse by the absence of Torrance and the withdrawal of Langer with a sore back from the afternoon fourballs. As if that wasn't enough, on Friday night, Baker's baby daughter was rushed to the hospital with suspected meningitis. Europe led by a point going into singles but the momentum had gone. Even before Ballesteros began with four bogeys in his match against Jim Gallagher Jr., the Ryder Cup was slipping, painfully and irredeemably, from the Europeans' grasp. When Langer was beaten by Kite, James by Payne Stewart, and Barry Lane (who had been three up with five holes to play) lost to Chip Beck, the die was cast. The last remaining hope was Costantino Rocca, who was one up over Love with two holes to play. When he bogeyed both, crumbling under the terrible pressure, the U.S. team won the match, 15-13.

"Nobody can blame Costantino," said Ballesteros, who was sent by Gallacher to comfort the devastated Rocca in the locker room and ended up doing most of the crying himself. "I felt very sad for him and I feel bad about myself. You can blame me. I played very badly. I tried my best, but it was not to be. I'm sorry."

For all intents and purposes, Ballesteros's season was over. Bruised and lonely, he attempted to work out his frustrations on the practice ground, watched over by an ever-increasing procession of teachers and gurus. "He's a difficult pupil in the sense that he can be strong-willed, very, very proud, and makes you prove to him that what you're telling him is correct," commented Simon Holmes, a former David Leadbetter assistant, whose tousled, sleepy presence followed the world-weary philosophizing of Sam Torrance and the blunt contributions of Manuel Piñero. "What I've been telling him is that what he *feels* he does and what he *actually* does are not the same thing."

In the end, it only mattered what Ballesteros felt. Holmes went the way of all the other well-meaning advisers, and Ballesteros struggled on, finishing a career-worst forty-second on the money list. It was the first time he had ever failed to win a tournament in a season. For such a proud man, these statistics must have cut to the bone, but *destino* had not finished with him yet.

313

At the World Match Play, an event he had won five times, he suffered the ultimate humiliation when he was beaten 7 & 6 by David Frost in the first round.

Afterward, he sat in the interview room with his head in his hands and tears in his eyes. "I don't know what to do anymore," he mumbled helplessly. There was something in his demeanor, in his sad gray features, and in the slump of his shoulders that suggested that he had reached the end of the road. He refused to deny that he was thinking of giving up the game. "I don't know what's wrong," he said miserably. "I've tried everything. Nothing works."

And with that, he quit for the year, leaving us shocked and silent, our hearts aching.

A sharp breeze tugged at the green and gold grasses of the Montecastillo course and accompanied Ballesteros into the clubhouse. Heads turned, mouths dropped open. Necks craned to follow his progress down the corridor. It was an impressive entrance under any circumstances; against the backdrop of 1993, it made for compelling viewing. For the better part of two months, Ballesteros had been endeavoring to strengthen the muscles in his ailing back at the Desert Institute of Physical Therapy in Scottsdale, Arizona. He spent more than five hours a day there stretching, running, cycling, and pumping iron, and the result was a tanned, chiseled physique and a military haircut, set off to perfection by a red shirt and toothpaste smile. "I have had to rededicate myself," Ballesteros said. "I have a lot of pride and it's been damaged."

He was reluctant to admit that the World Match Play may have seen him at the lowest ebb of his career, although he conceded, "I was very low."

"You gave us the impression you were thinking of quitting the game."

"Quit! What? The *game*?" Ballesteros smiled widely. "No, no, I might have quit for the year, but not forever. I'm only thirty-six. I'm just a kid."

As far as he was concerned, his "physical problems"—namely, the degeneration in his spine—had been a decisive factor in his bad results the previous season. "Since 1977 my back has been an important handicap, and lately it has been worse," he said. "I have not been able to sleep for the pain. I have been to chiropractors and witches and they haven't helped me."

However, it transpired that his back was the least of his concerns. The dramatic improvement in his overall fitness, coupled with the steady rehabilitation of his game, had brought back his old fighting spirit, and had shifted his focus to larger issues and new battlefields. Asked about the terrible trials of the previous season, he told the Spanish newspaper *El País* that the past two years had done him good. "I have become stronger mentally and have confirmed what I already knew, that I have a few friends, many acquaintances, and very many enemies—many more than I thought I had."

There was little doubt to whom he referred. There was only one item on Ballesteros's agenda, and that was the 1997 Ryder Cup venue. He had made up his mind that the only truly suitable venue for the matches was Novo Sancti Petri, the course he himself had designed near Cadiz. It was a safe bet that anyone who opposed him was considered an archenemy. The Spanish Golf Federation topped the list.

"The federation has always been a cancer," Ballesteros said sourly, "although that sounds very harsh. Their job has been to maintain a social circle. It seems incredible to me that these people who have done nothing for golf are arm-wrestling with me when it is I who have brought the Ryder Cup here. When we got the Cup in Spain nobody called me, nobody congratulated me, and nobody asked me for my opinion. It is very possible that if I hadn't played in the 1983 match, the Ryder Cup would not be what it is now. It is possible that the event would have disappeared altogether. It is bad that I have to say so, but I have to because no one else does. The federation say they have to remain neutral, but the obvious thing would be to consult various people and present a united candidate. Now we are all in a fight to see who wins."

The following day, Jack Nicklaus, who, as the designer of Montecastillo, one of seven candidates bidding to host the matches, was leading that course's campaign, announced that he in his turn planned to do everything in his power to bring the Ryder Cup to Jerez.

In retrospect, it is not hard to see why Ballesteros, anticipating war and believing himself friendless, should, in the spring of 1994, find himself being shadowed around St. Mellion by a mop-headed figure in a white rain jacket, making copious notes on a dollar bill.

IF O'GRADY WAS PERCEIVED AS AN ECCENTRIC, IT WAS BECAUSE HE CULTIVATED THE IMAGE. "I'M NOT NEARLY SO BINGO-BANGO-BONGO AS PEOPLE THINK I AM."

At Christmas, "Mad" Mac O'Grady, a former tour player and long-standing friend of Ballesteros's, had telephoned him to say that he had just completed a ten-year scientific study of the golf swing. These researches had resulted in five 250-page volumes known as *MORAD* (*Mankind's Objective Research and Development*). Twenty pages alone had been devoted to the shot Ballesteros hit into the water at fifteen at Augusta in 1986, and O'Grady had called to ask for his old pal's input and to see how his game was going. One thing led to another, and before the Spaniard knew what hit him, he was driving out into the desert near Palm Springs, California, with a box of old Seve photographs, which he proceeded to bury while Mac said a prayer. Mac then told him to cleanse himself by cutting his hair and stood him in a bunker and made him hit three-irons.

"Mac is a very good player," Ballesteros said of the quirky American. "He probably strikes the ball better than anyone else. He has only one problem—he cannot focus on what he's doing. He's too friendly with people. He has a great heart but a lot of people misunderstand him."

If O'Grady was perceived as an eccentric, it was because he cultivated the image. "I'm not nearly so bingo-bango-bongo as people think I am," he would tell people. On another occasion, he said: "Right now, I'm going through a catatonic, neurosomatic disorder. I'm in a total emotional upheaval." In April, at Augusta, he held an impromptu press conference on the lawn in front of the clubhouse, informing reporters that he had adopted a

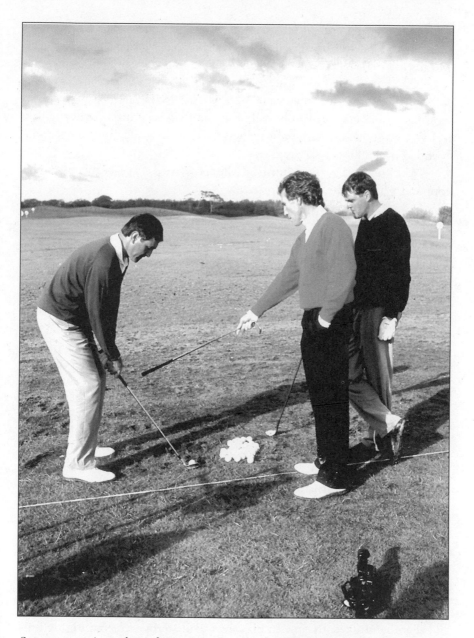

Seve gets a practice-tee lesson from swing guru and noted golf philosopher Mac O'Grady during the 1994 B&H International Open at St. Mellion. (© Phil Sheldon)

neuroscientific approach to Ballesteros's swing. The Spaniard had, he said, already incorporated thirty-eight of the forty changes he had recommended into his game. Ballesteros himself had declined to give details about their relationship, but O'Grady had no such scruples. He was in the midst of explaining that most teachers were "sycophants looking for a passport to legitimacy," and that Leadbetter had been charging Seve five hundred dollars an hour, while he, O'Grady, was helping him for free, when his pupil came storming over. He was plainly furious.

"Mac, where have you been?" Ballesteros cried. "I've been waiting an hour and a half on the practice ground."

He stomped off without waiting for a reply. O'Grady shuffled his feet in embarrassment. "Did you see the look of commitment and dedication in Seve's eyes?" he asked his startled audience.

Mentally, Ballesteros was still very fragile, but his confidence was returning by degrees. At The Players Championship, where he missed the cut by a shot, he sat in the locker room and talked about his achievements as a young prodigy and all they had meant to him. "I just feel that in life everything went okay for me, but everyone has to pay their dues and it looks like I'm paying them now. This is probably what's happening. Because I really feel that my game is there and it's coming along. So it's just a matter of being patient and waiting for my time. My time will come back, I'm sure of it."

In May, Ballesteros teed up at the B&H International at St. Mellion, still reeling from a double blow. The previous week, he had finished 138th in a field of 139 and now, to add insult to injury, the USGA had snubbed him by not inviting him to the U.S. Open.

"The tournament belongs to them, but my feeling is that I'm part of the history of that tournament and I think it's very unfair," Ballesteros complained. To his mind, his record and the fact that he had played in every U.S. Open since 1977 meant that he should have been given a place ahead of Arnold Palmer. He could attempt to qualify, but he hadn't had to pre-qualify for an event since the Portuguese and Spanish Opens in 1974, and he didn't see why he should do so now. "In Portugal I finished last in the qualifying because I shot 89. I took 56 on the back nine. My sponsor, Dr. Cesar Campuzano, told me: 'Don't worry, you're still the best in the world.' "

For the umpteenth time in his career, Ballesteros went out to play feeling persecuted, his most dangerous frame of mind. On the windswept, tightly contoured course, he shot 69, 70 to lead by a stroke at the halfway stage over Gary Orr and by two over Paul McGinley. He began the third round by rolling in a forty-footer at the first, a seven-footer at the second, and a thirty-footer at the third, eventually shooting 72 to lie a stroke behind Orr at the end of the day at 211. Afterward, he talked of how, just eight weeks earlier, his caddie Billy Foster had begged him to walk in on the twenty-seventh hole in Majorca, telling him, "I can't bear to see you suffer like this." Ballesteros had put a hand on his shoulder and said, "Billy, we are professionals. We must keep going. I never quit."

In the final round, an ecstatic, hopeful crowd watched Ballesteros grind out fifteen hard-won pars, and willed him on as he drove into unexplored territory at the sixteenth, chopped a seven-iron back onto the fairway, hit an indifferent wedge to fifteen feet, and holed the birdie putt. When he hit his approach at the seventeenth to three feet, the tournament was won, and the roar of acclaim that greeted Ballesteros's towering shot to the last, reverberated around the links as the crowd broke through the ropes and swamped their tearful hero and his police escort.

"It was difficult," admitted Ballesteros, whose victory by three strokes from Nick Faldo was his first in twenty-six months. He dedicated the tournament to Foster and O'Grady. "I have not been in a winning position for so long. I was nervous all the way; tense, tight. You know, there are nerves to compete, nerves to make the cut, nerves to finish in the top ten, and nerves to win. I know all of them."

As he had predicted, Ballesteros had restored his power. Now he used his newfound confidence to lend zest and determination to his twin objectives: to force the USGA to eat humble pie and offer him an invite, and to take the Ryder Cup to Novo Sancti Petri. His first move was to accuse Valderrama and the Ryder Cup committee of bribery and corruption at the Spanish Open, the week after his victory at St. Mellion.

David Huish, a member of the Ryder Cup committee, was outraged. "If Seve said that to my face I'd punch him on the nose," he said angrily. "I can't believe it. If he's suggesting that members of the committee have been offered inducements I'd take it all the way to the courts. It would be like winning the pools."

If there was one thing more intriguing than Ballesteros's insinuations and the splutterings of the Ryder Cup committee, then it was Jaime Patino's response to them—pure astonishment. In an interview with the *Guardian*, Valderrama's owner openly admitted that, in April 1993, one month before it

Seve shares the joy of finally breaking through to win the 1994 B&H International with caddie Billy Foster as the two approach the eighteenth green at St. Mellion.
(© Phil Sheldon)

was announced that Spain would host the 1997 event, he had decided to seek the support of Ballesteros, who, coincidentally, had redesigned the seventeenth hole while refusing to accept a fee. Patino had written to him offering him a percentage of Valderrama's green fees as compensation for the work on the seventeenth hole and "for your . . . agreement to support our candidacy for the Ryder Cup and in particular if you are prepared to publicly communicate your support to the press and the PGA executives at the Volvo PGA at Wentworth on May 28, 1993." The green fees alone were guaranteed to net Ballesteros at least £675,000. Nonetheless, Patino claims that he didn't consider the letter a bribe because the Spaniard had not yet been appointed a member of the Ryder Cup committee.

Said Patino: "I felt honestly that, knowing politics in Spain, it could become very nasty, as it did in the end, and that I could avoid all this nonsense. I knew that we had the best course and if we had Seve on my side there would be no opposition. You want Jack Nicklaus on your team, you give him two million dollars. There's nothing wrong with making someone a business proposal."

Initially, Ballesteros seemed to be of a similar mind. On June 22, 1993, he replied, thanking Patino for the "very kind offer to collaborate in your project," and asking for time to consider the offer. He signed the letter with *un fuerte abrazo*, a big hug. By the end of July, Patino had heard no more, and he wrote back to Ballesteros, explaining that he would withdraw the offer on September 30 if no further communication was forthcoming. On October 12, a letter arrived on Patino's desk, in which Ballesteros said that he had received similar offers from other Spanish clubs and was still unwilling to commit himself to any particular one. He concluded: "I thank you from the bottom of my heart for the interest you have always shown in me personally." Patino heard nothing more until the following year, when Ballesteros's bribery allegations appeared in the papers.

On May 26, Ballesteros went into the press center after a rain-soaked practice round at Wentworth, clutching a white scroll etched with pink handwriting. He had already dealt with the U.S. Open invite drama—"If I have to go and prequalify, I'll do that. I've filled in the form. You know me, I'm humble. I'll go there by boat, rowing, if I have to"—and now he was responding to the announcement that the Ryder Cup would, after all, be going to Valderrama. "There will be no questions, only answers," Ballesteros said with a sly grin, and unrolled his script. "My heartfelt best wishes are extended to Valderrama and Mr. Patino for winning the right to be the hosts in '97," he began. "Mr. Patino has worked long and hard to stage this prestigious event and I'm sure every one of the American team will enjoy Valderrama."

He extended his congratulations to the Ryder Cup committee and said that he had served golf for twenty years and would continue to do so. "I know that all the other clubs who were hoping to be selected are greatly disappointed. I wanted Novo Sancti Petri, but life sometimes is not so sweet. We do not always get what we want."

He added that he had written his statement the previous week. "I knew who was going to win so it was easy to write. I was 100 percent right."

As loser's speeches go, it was a masterpiece, a subtle interweaving of graciousness, diplomacy, and barbed comment. To cap it all, when Ballesteros walked out of the interview room the following day, Patino was standing in his path. Another man might have given his victorious opponent a curt nod or a cold handshake, but Ballesteros went rushing over to the little Bolivian and embraced him in a huge bearhug. To this day, Patino is still bemused by the whole saga. "When I saw him at Wentworth he grabbed me and gave me a big hug and said, 'You were too strong for me,' as if nothing had happened. He had a smile from ear to ear. I don't understand how he went off the deep end."

TO VALDERRAMA

"When a true genius appears in the world, you may know him by this sign, that the dunces are all in confederacy against him."

Jonathan Swift, *Thoughts on Various Subjects*

With hindsight, it is possible to trace the beginning of Ballesteros's decline as a major contender to the day after his victory in the 1988 British Open, when the energy and time he expended on conflicts began to grow in inverse proportion to the periods he played his best golf. By the midnineties, they dominated his life.

Once, comparing the personalities of Ballesteros and his brilliant Ryder Cup partner, Olazábal, Sergio Gomez, the latter's manager, described Seve as "naturally aggressive. In life, he tries to make room for himself with his elbows. That's what we say in Spain about someone who's always pushing ahead and trying to be one step further than the others . . . You will never see Jose pushing his arguments or pushing a situation to the boundaries. Seve's always on the edge of being impolite, and being so harsh with everyone that everyone is shocked. When Seve's not happy, he always threatens: 'I will lose interest in the Ryder Cup, I will play on the U.S. Tour, I will go to Japan where everybody loves me.'

"For instance, with the Ryder Cup course, Seve pushed the situation to the absolute limit: 'I won't be captain, I don't know if I will play again in Spain.' Jose, from the beginning, was favoring Valderrama. But not publicly, because he didn't want to be in that situation. He went to Ken Schofield and he went to George O'Grady and he said: 'Don't be stupid, the only place we can play is Valderrama.' He came to that decision because he said, 'Where can the Ryder Cup work? Valderrama. Why? Because Jaime Patino will make it work.' "

Ballesteros survived the Ryder Cup venue drama unscathed, going on to win the German Masters in a playoff with Ernie Els and Jose Olazábal later that season. He then began the '95 season with a victory in the Spanish Open in May, but by June his back problems had escalated and his game had gone into a tailspin. "If Seve has one defect, it is that he overweighs the short-term solution," said Joe Collet, with whom Ballesteros has now split (Roddy Carr has taken over his management). "He always wants a panacea, a quick fix. That has hurt him with building his game."

Significantly, he had parted with Billy Foster and fallen out with Mac O'Grady soon after the Masters. Then, within a week or two of the U.S. Open, he had engaged in a fresh struggle with Joey Jones, Foster's wholesome, efficient replacement.

Ballesteros had taken Jones, one of the most professional and reliable caddies on the Tour, for a trial outing at the B&H International. When that went well, he asked the young Liverpudlian to work for him full-time. Jones was reluctant. After years of caddying for players of the caliber of Ronan Rafferty, he had opened a highly successful hamburger business, Caddyshack Catering, on the European circuit, and, with a family to support and a mortgage to pay, he was not about to give it up. Ballesteros won him over. According to Jones, he guaranteed him a year's employment and agreed to pay him four hundred pounds a week plus 7 percent for a place or win (the average in Europe is three hundred fifty pounds a week with 5 percent for a place and 10 percent for a win).

The first sign that all would not be roses came the very next week, when Ballesteros won the Spanish Open and, out of the ninety-two-thousand-pound winner's check, presented Jones with just four thousand pounds. He had subtracted Spanish withholding tax, a PGA levy, and Spanish VAT. Most players pay for some or all of their caddie's hotel and travel expenses; Jones received nothing. Five weeks later Ballesteros phoned Jones at home and announced that he was dispensing with his services and taking on a Japanese professional who had worked with Mad Mac. "He wanted to kill two birds with one stone," said Jones, who issued Ballesteros with a fifteen-thousand-pound writ on the Friday of the 1996 B&H International at the Oxfordshire after receiving just four hundred pounds' redundancy pay. Added Jones: "Most players on Tour have a coach and a caddie, but Seve's so tight, it's unbelievable. He'd fallen out with Mac O'Grady over money because Mac billed him for a tournament, and this guy had worked for Mac so Seve thought it would help his game if he caddied for him. But where does that leave me? I've got a wife and two kids, and it took me five weeks to find another job. That's the reason I'm suing."

Ballesteros was furious. "I am a little disappointed," he said. "I was nice to him. I respect caddies and treat them well. I had no written contract and the matter has been passed to my solicitor. That's all I have to say."

Ballesteros attempted to have the case heard in Bilbao, Spain. Earlier in the season, Jones had confronted Ballesteros at a tournament in Spain, and claims that Ballesteros initially denied that he had promised to keep him on for the season "no matter what," but later admitted: "Well, maybe I did." Jones recalled: "He then said: 'Maybe I'll take you to Spain.' I wasn't sure whether he meant on holiday. I thought, 'I don't want a holiday, I want the money.' He knows what he said to me. He knows he let me down. And he knows I'm right."

Unfortunately for Jones, the case was thrown out of court. Foster remained as loyal as ever. "He's a hard man to caddie for, but he's great in the same breath," he said.

Then came the final day of the 1995 Ryder Cup at Oak Hill. When Ballesteros arrived in Rochester, New York, he was, to say the least, playing poorly. As Dobereiner pointed out: "O'Grady tried to flatten Seve's swing into a Hoganesque plane. At the Ryder Cup, Seve was in the transitional stage when his old swing was going out of commission and the Hogan model had not yet begun to bed down."

As a consequence, Ballesteros hit three fairways in three matches, and might have lost every match had he not partnered with David Gilford on the first day and coached him to victory. "David Gilford had the best caddie of all time," Foster said later. But even Gilford couldn't help him on the second day, and he and the Englishman lost their fourballs match against Jay Haas and Phil Mickelson because Seve could not see the woods for the trees.

In the singles, Ballesteros met Tom Lehman, the gifted midwesterner, whose calm, gracious manner belies his toughness as a competitor. The American was one up when he and the Spaniard reached the twelfth hole. Both men had birdie putts, and Lehman rolled his to within inches of the cup and then holed out without waiting for Ballesteros to give him permission to do so. Ballesteros promptly objected, provoking loud jeers from the partisan crowd. He informed Lehman that he had putted out of turn, and, citing Rule 10-1c, requested that he replace his ball and mark it.

It was an unpleasant moment. Everything Lehman had ever heard about Ballesteros's reputation for ruthlessness, gamesmanship, and ability to work miracles in match play came back to haunt him, and he summoned the official, J. R. Carpenter, and asked for his opinion. To the disbelief of the gallery, who greeted the news with hostile cries, Carpenter told him that Ballesteros was quite correct. Lehman replaced his ball and Ballesteros missed his birdie putt, at which point he magnanimously conceded Lehman's tap-in.

EVERYTHING LEHMAN HAD EVER HEARD ABOUT BALLESTEROS'S REPUTATION FOR RUTHLESSNESS, GAMESMANSHIP, AND ABILITY TO WORK MIRACLES IN MATCH PLAY CAME BACK TO HAUNT HIM.

In years to come, when history shines a light on Ballesteros's legend, that singles match—with all its hooks and slices, controversy, and impossible recoveries—will hold its own among the major victories and impressive feats, regardless of the fact he lost. No man ever fought with more courage, or played with more heart, with so few tools. Awestruck, Lehman said he felt privileged to have witnessed it, and Ballesteros's teammates, watching the board with incredulity, drew inspiration from it and achieved a miracle of their own: the Europeans, underdogs from the start, came from behind to win the Ryder Cup on U.S. soil.

"He has the best charisma in the world," Costantino Rocca, the Italian, said. "It's not important whether he plays good or not, it's his charisma and his effect on the team."

"It was the most amazing effort I've ever seen in my life," recalled Ken Brown, who commented on the match for Sky television. "Lehman was playing as well as you could possibly play, hitting the middle of every fairway and green. Seve was playing just as badly as you can play. He really didn't know where the ball was going. Yet after nine holes, Seve was just one down and you still had the feeling that if just one chink appeared in Lehman's armor Seve would have pounced and won the match."

In his 1995 Ryder Cup singles match against American Tom Lehman at Oak Hill, Ballesteros spent much of his round threading shots through trees and out of tall grass. Although Ballesteros eventually lost his lead-off match to Lehman, he inspired his teammates to victory by hanging in against Lehman much longer than his poor play suggested he would. (© Phil Sheldon)

Foster, who saw the match on television, could not get over Ballesteros's audacious escapes. "I'd go as far as to say that we wouldn't have won it if he hadn't been there," Foster said. "His inspiration pulled them through. Watching him playing Lehman, I was just laughing. I thought it was fantastic the way he just hung on and fought like a tiger. It gave the rest of the team confidence because they knew how badly he was playing and he was still fighting and it encouraged them to do the same."

"He's always incredible," Sam Torrance said admiringly. "He's probably the best team man who's ever lived. He's got so much heart and soul and he gives so much. The fact that he held Lehman for so long, even though he was hitting it off the golf course, had a filter-down effect that helped the rest of us."

In one of the most emotional moments of his great career, Seve popped open a bottle of champagne in joining his fellow Europeans in celebration of their upset victory over the Americans in the 1995 Ryder Cup competition at Oak Hill. (© Phil Sheldon)

"He's got so much pride," someone said.

Torrance laughed. "Pride or hate?" he asked.

When the Ryder Cup ended, Ballesteros announced that he would be taking a five-month sabbatical, an unprecedented interruption in the career of a great player. In spite of his contribution to the team's morale, the devastation of his game had left him saddened and dispirited. His fellow players thought more highly of him than ever. On Friday, December 15, they sent Ken Schofield, executive director of the European Tour, to meet him at Garfunkels restaurant in London's Heathrow airport and ask if he would captain the Ryder Cup team when the matches went to Spain in September 1997.

"I said to him: 'Do you want to do it on the committee's terms, because you might not want to.' " Schofield recalled. "We knew he wanted more than two wild cards, but there is a feeling that, although both teams want to win the Ryder Cup, there is something above that which is that every player should have the right to try and qualify."

One month later, Schofield went to see Ballesteros at his home in Santander, where he officially agreed to captain the European team. He stipulated that he wanted the right, should he qualify automatically, to drop himself if he didn't feel he was playing well enough Manuel Piñero would, in all probability, help him, but he didn't plan to nominate an official deputy until July, if at all.

"I remember asking him: 'Can you handle defeat?' " Schofield said. "And he replied: 'The fact that I am captain is no guarantee that we will win.' "

Five months after his abrupt, depressing departure, Ballesteros was back with a new set of Cobra clubs and the same erratic game. His first shot of the 1996 season was a blocked drive at the Moroccan Open, and his scores, 78 and 79, reflected more of the same. Bernhard Langer's suggestion, that he change swings if only to alleviate the pressure on his spine, fell on deaf ears, and Ballesteros withdrew from The Players Championship in March with a bad back and a familiar refrain.

"I have no confidence," Ballesteros repeated yet again. "Confidence is everything."

But there was more to it than that. Once Ballesteros was obsessed with nothing but the game, with the ultimate recovery, the most ingenious, floating chip or the most belief-beggaring birdie, but marriage and three children had changed all that. His golf had suffered as a consequence, but he had become a more complete person, a more compassionate person. "I'm scared of what is happening in our world," he told Derek Lawrenson of the *Sunday Telegraph*. "Maybe it is since having kids, I don't know. I used to drive a car fast and now I drive it slow. I look at the flowers on the trees at this course in January and I think, 'That never used to happen. Why are we having nuclear tests?' This is what happens when you get older. You see the world through more cautious eyes.

"It is the same with my golf. The first time I went in the trees I saw only the green and how I could put the ball on it. Now I see the branches and the roots and the trunk. Experience can be a marvelous asset, but it can also be bad, too."

When Lawrenson asked him how much his back had contributed to his results in recent times, he came close to losing his temper. "People don't realize how sensitive the mind is. The more I'm asked about my back, the more pain I feel. One of the things that is killing the superstars and why no player dominates any more is that there is pressure all the time. There is no release from it. I remember going to England when I first started and you could go into the lounge after a round and have a cup of tea. You can't do that anymore. Don't get me wrong, it's not a bad thing. It means the game is popular, which is good. But it does make it difficult—all the demands on your time, all the questions, the lack of space.

"People use my back as an excuse to say I'm finished. It's a very easy thing to say, isn't it? You can be a great champion for fifteen years, you have one bad year and that's it, you can't play anymore because of your back. It's the same as my cough; I wish there was a miracle cure but there isn't. Every morning I wake up with this itch at the back of my throat. Even changes of temperature cause me to cough. When I'm on the course I never stop coughing. Azinger thought I was trying to put him off all those years ago, but it wasn't the case at all."

But by the time Ballesteros arrived at the Masters in April, he was playing some of the most inconsistent golf of his life. "It's very painful when you have to talk all the time about these things," Ballesteros told Jaime Diaz of *Sports Illustrated*, when Diaz asked him what he felt was causing his problems: "It's not easy—why this, why that, and what are you going to do and why don't you do this. It drives you crazy. It's not good because the mind is very powerful, and everything is negative, negative, negative."

It didn't help that every player, coach, and caddie in Christendom had an opinion on the subject. "It's shocking to see how much Seve has deteriorated," David Leadbetter said. "At the top of his swing, Seve's clubface is shut. From that position, he cannot release the club properly and the inevitable result is that he either snaps the ball left or blocks it to the right."

Curtis Strange: "We all struggle at times but I have never seen a player of Seve's caliber hit the kind of shots he was hitting at the Ryder Cup."

"Even at his best I always thought Seve was living on the edge," said Lanny Wadkins, who captained the 1995 U.S. Ryder Cup team. "He erased a lot of mistakes with his short game. I equate Seve with Crenshaw, but Ben would have his straight-hitting periods. Trying to play from crooked drives can wear on you."

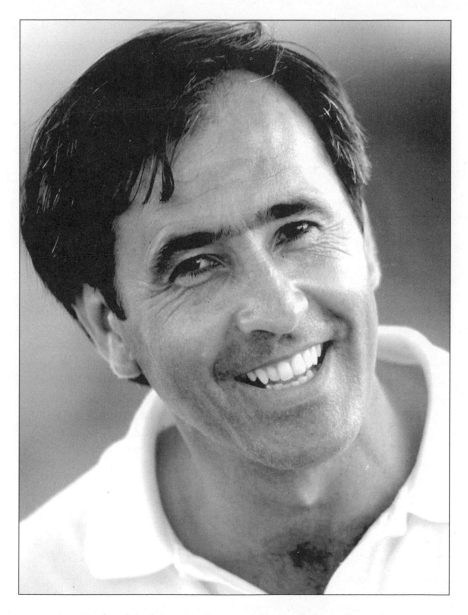

A year shy of his fortieth birthday and still in search of his good game, Seve still has the dazzling smile and dashing, dark good looks of a matinee idol. Here he is at the 1996 Dubai Desert Classic at Emirates. (© Phil Sheldon)

Even O'Grady gave his two cents' worth. "When it comes to competition, Seve burns like a nuclear reactor. But he became unhappy because he started letting winning majors mean everything. He got so disappointed that he stopped loving the game. He has to turn that reactor loose on the process of becoming a great golfer again. If he does, there's no doubt he can play as well as Norman. In fact, in a street fight, I'd take Seve."

On being informed of these observations, Ballesteros scowled. "My message to the teachers and everyone else who has been writing me letters is that I know a little bit about this game," he said darkly.

In June the U.S. Open rolled around again, and this time Ballesteros was not invited and did not, as he had in 1994, manage to play his way into the tournament. In Germany, he commented: "I have had two chances of winning the U.S. Open in the past, but I have never enjoyed that tournament. I won't miss going there this year. Sure, it's a major, but it's not a good tournament, because 80 percent of the game in the U.S. Open is about hitting the fairways. It takes away the skill factor. Everyone wants to compete in the U.S. Open, but then when they get there they all hope the week would finish quickly."

Asked whether there was a possibility of a last-minute invitation, Ballesteros responded: "No chance. The Americans only invite Americans. Everyone knows that."

A month later, the inspiration he had been hoping would revisit him during the British Open at Royal Lytham, the scene of his comeback victory in 1988, had vanished in a puff of smoke. "I've been lucky to win the Opens in such good style," he said before the event. "Nobody gave them to me, nobody threw them away." Then he confessed quietly: "But I don't mind if somebody gives it away in the next few years."

In October, Ballesteros returned to the milky columns, sun-dappled courtyard, and emerald fairways of the course he had fought so hard to better in the struggle for the 1997 Ryder Cup. In every respect, he had been as good as his word. In the two years since the match had been awarded to

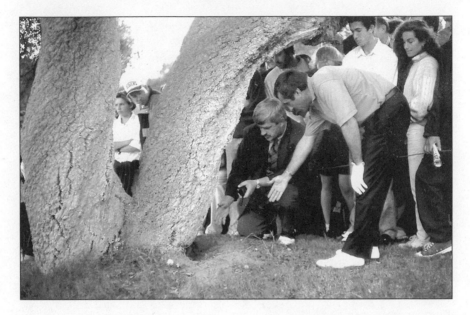

At the 1994 Volvo Masters, Ballesteros surveys the rather familiar sight of his ball in trouble. At least it's not out of bounds—this time. Anyone got an ax? (© Phil Sheldon)

Valderrama, he had done nothing but work positively toward ensuring that the event would be a success, and since being appointed captain, he had been personally involved in every decision from uniforms to locker rooms. In 1994 he had commented that it was impossible, in this day and age, to be both player and captain, but he seemed to have forgotten that, and Schofield, among others, encouraged him to believe that his biggest contribution could come on the course. "In the case of Seve, we are dealing with genius, and his best inspiration would be playing. He is, unquestionably, Europe's Arnold Palmer," Schofield said.

On the practice tee at the Volvo Masters, a group of caddies joked that Ballesteros's national pride meant that it would mean *more* than the European team's lives were worth to lose the Ryder Cup in Spain. "He'll bring back capital punishment," one laughed.

On the surface Ballesteros maintained a sardonic, confident facade, wittily responding to the news that Tom Kite, the American captain, with whom he had crossed swords in a Madrid tournament two weeks earlier, had visited

Valderrama. "I like to hear that he likes the course. At Oak Hill, the Americans liked the golf course very much and they lost. I'm happy he likes it."

He also exchanged words with Colin Montgomerie, who was the European Order of Merit winner for the fourth time running. Montgomerie had made the fatal mistake of criticizing Ballesteros's redesign of the pivotal seventeenth hole. "He's a great player but he's not a course designer," Montgomerie said.

ELEVEN MONTHS REMAINED BEFORE HE CAPTAINED EUROPE IN THE RYDER CUP, AND ALREADY THE PRESSURE WAS PROVING ALMOST UNBEARABLE.

George O'Grady, deputy executive director of the Tour, could not believe his ears. "We have a situation where the Ryder Cup captain, who designed the seventeenth hole, regards it as one of the best in the world, and Europe's No. 1 thinks it's one of the worst in the world. And they are diametrically opposed."

Ballesteros was unconcerned. "Monty never likes anything," he said with a grin. "The seventeenth is the most spectacular hole on the golf course. It's a tremendous hole—beautiful views, good for spectators, good for match play. When did you last see Monty happy?"

But he was only now beginning to realize what he had taken on. Eleven months remained before he captained Europe in the Ryder Cup, and already the pressure was proving almost unbearable. In a radio interview he said the job was becoming a "nightmare." Later, he insisted that he hadn't meant "nightmare" as such. "There is so much talk about the Ryder Cup that I am dreaming about it at night," he said after shooting a 76 for a thirteen-over-par total of 226 in the third round. "I can't talk about the Ryder Cup every five minutes. My job is to have a good team, but people are asking me when the road outside will be finished and how many people will be coming."

He reiterated what he said earlier in the season, which was that he would not be making an exception for players like Nick Faldo when it came to wild cards, particularly if they didn't make a concerted effort to qualify. Faldo had responded by drawing attention to Ballesteros's habit of changing his mind: "Throughout last year Seve was saying he should have four picks instead of two, and now he has done a 180-degree turn."

Opposing 1997 Ryder Cup captains Tom Kite of the United States and Seve Ballesteros of Europe make a playful grab for the Ryder Cup during a pre-Cup press conference. Seve was happy, too, because Ryder Cup play finally was headed to his homeland. (© Phil Sheldon)

"No one has a guarantee," Ballesteros said. "I will not be picking any wild cards before the last qualifying event." He had, he claimed, asked for his quota of wild cards to be increased from two to four and been rebuffed. "I still believe it's a mistake," he said.

Schofield insisted that two wild cards were sufficient. "If the European Tour can't keep enough of its players to compete in the Ryder Cup, there shouldn't be a Ryder Cup."

At the end of the day, the only thing that mattered was that Ballesteros, the bravest and most inspirational player in Ryder Cup history, retained his ability to thrill with his courage and his humanity and the diamond-bright shards of his game. "At his best, his explosively aggressive long game, combined with a touch as tender as a lover's caress, was a perfect expression of his personality," Dobereiner recalled, and Foster agreed.

"He's got more talent than anyone in the world, even now," Foster said. "That's why I've got so much respect for him. To me, his career is like that of

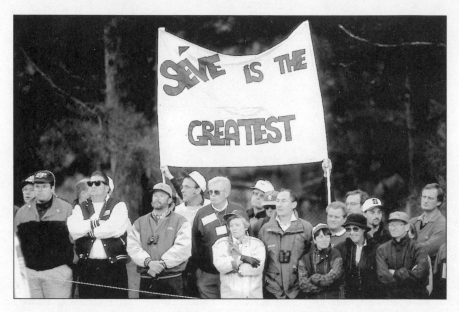

Fans at the 1995 Ryder Cup competition say it with their hearts. (© Phil Sheldon)

a world championship boxer. He's taken so many blows, so much punishment over the years, that it is getting harder and harder to pull himself up off the canvas. But there's no reason why he can't bounce back."

In *Golf Digest,* Jerry Tarde once estimated that there had been ten golfing geniuses since World War II: The first nine on his list were Snead, Nicklaus, Locke, Casper, Trevino, Crenshaw, Babe Zaharias, Mickey Wright, and Nancy Lopez. "Which brings us to the last golfing genius, the youngest of them all, and the one America never recognized—Seve Ballesteros. He, as much as any of the above, had the primal characteristic of genius: He could light his own fire."

In his heart, Ballesteros knew that nobody but he could light that fire again. "I was not wrong, was I, when I said that only once or twice does a man get to play so well?" he observed quietly. "I knew at the time I won the Open in 1988 that I had reached some sort of peak, that it was a round of golf that I would think fondly about for the rest of my life. I remember saying that I hoped there would be another as good, but there hasn't been. Now I think it will probably remain the best round I play. I hope to be proved wrong."

336

INDEX